LAW
ENFORCEMENT

LAW ENFORCEMENT

A Human Relations Approach

ALAN R. COFFEY

PRENTICE HALL, Englewood Cliffs, New Jersey 07632

Library of Congress Cataloging-in-Publication Data

Coffey, Alan.
   Law enforcement : a human relations approach / Alan R. Coffey.
     p.   c.m.
  ISBN 0-13-526161-9
   1. Law enforcement — Psychological aspects. 2. Interpersonal
relations. 3. Public relations — Police. 4. Law enforcement — United
States.   I. Title.
HV7921.C644   1990
363.2′01′9 — dc20   89–36259
                               CIP

Editorial/production supervision: *Raeia Maes*
Cover design: *Bruce Kenselaar*
Manufacturing buyer: *Laura Crossland*

 © 1990 by Prentice-Hall, Inc.
A Division of Simon & Schuster
Englewood Cliffs, New Jersey 07632

Printed in the United States of America

10 9 8 7 6 5 4 3 2 1

ISBN   0-13-526161-9

Prentice-Hall International (UK) Limited, *London*
Prentice-Hall of Australia Pty. Limited, *Sydney*
Prentice-Hall Canada Inc., *Toronto*
Prentice-Hall Hispanoamericana, S.A., *Mexico*
Prentice-Hall of India Private Limited, *New Delhi*
Prentice-Hall of Japan, Inc., *Tokyo*
Simon & Schuster Asia Pte. Ltd., *Singapore*
Editora Prentice-Hall do Brasil, Ltda., *Rio de Janeiro*

For Bev

Contents

Preface

This book — as its title suggests — is about more than the enforcement of law; it is about the human relations approach to enforcing law.

The *human relations* approach to law enforcement is the placement of emphasis on the many human interactions that go into enforcing law and keeping the peace. This approach underpins the main theme of this book — a theme that recognizes the community support of police as an absolute necessity for law enforcement to succeed.

The factors deemed most relevant in understanding the problems that impede such community support receive emphasis. Perspective is developed on these problems through the examination of the problem itself and its background — in one chapter examining the history of violence that mars American law enforcement. There is, throughout the volume, candid recognition of the limitations on police ability to solve many of the socioeconomic problems that so severely affect law enforcement. Such restrictions on police are presented as yet further evidence of the need for community support and the need to carefully evaluate the methods proposed in achieving such community support.

It is important to note that, while straightforward acknowledgment of problems is made, this book is intended to impart encouragement based on the author's firm belief that the field of law enforcement has proved itself exceptionally adaptive, particularly during the many years that have passed since the turbulent 1960s, and while at the same time taking the blame for the problems elsewhere in criminal justice and elsewhere in society.

TO THE INSTRUCTOR

The organization of this book includes fifteen chapters divided into four parts, plus appendixes for elaboration of specific chapter topics.

Part One is called *Alignment of Police and the Rationale for Enforcement* and has the main purpose of introducing the pressing need for community support. It consists of four chapters that acquaint the reader with the reasons for, the position of, and the restrictions on law enforcement. To emphasize the human relations approach, enforcement is discussed in terms of the limitations placed on police compared to the demands placed on police, without discussion of the methods and techniques of enforcement.

Part Two is called *Unrest from Social Change: Present, Past, and Future Impact.* The three chapters here provide the reader with some understanding of the phases and levels of community unrest, with distinctions between tension that is either controlled or dangerous. Violent community unrest is considered in the present, past, and future, again from the human relations perspective.

Law Enforcement and the Community is the title of Part Three, whose five chapters first examine a few theoretical causes of crime and then consider some of the police programs that help and some of the problems that hinder police and community efforts to deal with crime.

Part Four is called *Community Support Required for Police Success;* these three chapters build on the first twelve chapters toward an integration of the forces and influences necessary to gain and keep community support. Still emphasizing the human relations approach, Part Four examines police image problems, police–community cooperation, and police communication.

At the beginning of each of these four parts, a brief introduction to the chapters is presented. This introduction includes a statement regarding the relationship among chapters within that part, as well as the relationship of the part itself to the other three parts of the book.

ACKNOWLEDGMENTS

As always, the many police executives, judges, criminal justice colleagues, and fellow teachers will recognize their influence on my approach to this subject — and have my sincere gratitude. California State University, Los Angeles, Professor Dick Grace, with whom I was a co-author of *Principles of Law Enforcement* (first edition, 1968), and his friend Bob Vernon, Assistant Chief of Police, Los Angeles, both were most helpful in the building of resource materials needed for a subject of this scope. State University of New York Professor Ed Thibault was helpful beyond the many citations in this book from his masterpiece, *Proactive Police Management.* 1Integrity dictates that I acknowledge Chuck Anderson, who heads the Administration of Justice program at Cabrillo College, as the individual who, without knowing it, inspired me to stop all the researching and get on with the writing. Rick Over of the FBI, deserves my thanks.

The eighteen criminal justice books that I have authored and co-authored over the past quarter of a century brought me in contact with many excellent editorial staffs but none more competent and professional than this book's staff supervised by Raeia Maes.

A final word of acknowledgment that most (probably all) writers of college texts are sure to understand—my family—now including grandchildren Jenifer, Tyrone Alan, Stevie, Alan Joseph, still including daughters Alison, Annette, and Alana—but most of all, my everlasting gratitude to the ultratolerant and lovely Bev Coffey.

Alan R. Coffey

Law Enforcement Code of Ethics

AS A LAW ENFORCEMENT OFFICER, my fundamental duty is to serve mankind; to safeguard lives and property; to protect the innocent against deception, the weak against oppression or intimidation, and the peaceful against violence or disorder; and to respect the Constitutional rights of all men to liberty, equality and justice.

I WILL keep my private life unsullied as an example to all; maintain courageous calm in the face of danger, scorn, or ridicule; develop self-restraint; and be constantly mindful of the welfare of others. Honest in thought and deed in both my personal and official life, I will be exemplary in obeying the laws of the land and the regulations of my department. Whatever I see or hear of a confidential nature or that is confided to me in my official capacity will be kept ever secret unless revelation is necessary in the performance of my duty.

I WILL never act officiously or permit personal feelings, prejudices, and animosities, or friendships to influence my decisions. With no compromise for crime and with relentless prosecution of criminals, I will enforce the law courteously and appropriately without fear or favor, malice or ill will, never employing unnecessary force or violence and never accepting gratuities.

I RECOGNIZE the badge of my office as a symbol of public faith, and I accept it as a public trust to be held so long as I am true to the ethics of the police service. I will constantly strive to achieve these objectives and ideals, dedicating myself before God to my chosen profession . . . law enforcement.

THE AMERICAN POLICE OFFICER

August Vollmer, one of the truly great benefactors of professionalism in law enforcement, is often quoted as observing early in this century that the widely varied public expectations of police officers include wisdom, courage, strength, patience, leadership, kindness, strategical training, faith, diplomacy, tolerance, and an intimate knowledge of every branch of natural, biological, and social science.

Now, approaching the next century, the American police officer is further expected to somehow gain and keep the support of a community that remains mostly unaware of how close August Vollmer was in describing the ever increasing demands on law enforcement.

PART ONE

Alignment of Police
and Rationale for Enforcement

The general purpose of Part One is to acquaint the reader with reasons for, position of, and restrictions on law enforcement.

The problem of the general public at times conceiving of police as "most" of the criminal justice system will be discussed in terms of restrictions on police control over other justice functions. This restricted control over other justice functions will be related to the purpose of and necessity for enforcement of law in a free society. Contradictions and paradoxes will be noted.

The necessity of law enforcement will be related to further restrictions on the police posed by the constitutionally required due process of law. Finally, the further limitations on the police posed by the vast numbers of laws to be enforced and the limited number of police personnel available will be discussed as selective law enforcement.

1

Another purpose of Part One is to afford the reader a better understanding of the limitations on police as a background for reviewing the demands made on law enforcement, the subjects of Parts Two, Three, and Four. The demands on law enforcement contrasted with the limitations on law enforcement are intended to form a rationale for improved police–community relations, as presented in the chapters that follow Part One.

1

Law Enforcement: Component of Criminal Justice

Throughout history, police personnel have tended to think of their work in terms of either apprehending or in some other way dealing with criminals. The complexity of modern law, as we will note throughout this volume, has increased tremendously, but the tendency to conceive of law enforcement as "dealing with criminals" prevails. Certainly no valid criticism can be leveled at such a tendency. One main purpose of police is to *enforce* the law, which necessarily causes a focus on those who violate the law.

Law enforcement, however, has evolved to far more than the simple control of crime. The police role now includes keeping the peace, and numerous related responsibilities have evolved that in many instances make enforcing the law one of the most stressful occupations in America. The widely varied police responsibilities that exist beyond the control of crime are at least influenced by, if not controlled by, what will unfold as the concept of police–community relations. With successful police–community relations, the job of law enforcement, including its widely varied responsibilities, becomes much easier.

"Easier," it should be noted, is relative. Here we are observing that the extremely difficult job of enforcing law is easier *with* community support than without such support. Moreover, *effective* law enforcement, we will see, is impossible without community support. One of the many reasons for the need of community support is the ever-increasing complexity of police work for both the working police officer and the police chief as well:[1]

> Over the past 2 centuries, the United States has changed from a rural, economically concentric society to a nation characterized by diverse social, economic, and political units. Some of the institutions upon which society must depend for order and continuity have not been able to keep pace with the changes. The law enforcement system, in particular, is struggling to keep abreast of the present, while trying to determine what the needs of the future will be and how they can best be met.
>
> Law enforcement personnel agree that tomorrow's law enforcement administrator (LEA) will be operating in a highly charged, complex environment. Factors such as rising crime rates, increased population, social unrest, more sophisticated crimes, and accelerated administrative costs will challenge the LEA to reexamine traditional police methodologies and management techniques. . . .
>
> The law enforcement administrator will have to discard the role of "top cop" and become a true chief executive officer (CEO) with responsibilities paralleling those of top corporate management officials. Those responsibilities, however, will be added to a task not shared by business executives — the burden of maintaining order in the community.

"The burden of maintaining order in the community" is what police are *expected* to carry as a burden, regardless of how complex law enforcement is or becomes. This challenge, we will note, cannot be effectively met without successful police–community relations, the main theme of this book. Gaining the support of the community is essential for *effective* law enforcement.

Before considering community relations, we should examine the role played by police in criminal justice, we should consider the very nature of enforcement itself, and attention should be addressed to the effect of the constitutional Bill of Rights on enforcement. In this chapter, we will examine the role of law enforcement in the overall criminal justice system.

The role played by law enforcement in the criminal justice system, as well as in American society in general, is best understood in terms of the human relations involved. Virtually every aspect of law enforcement has to do with human relations: the interactions between individuals and groups and the interactions between those individuals and groups and law enforcement.

These interactions function in relation to principles of human behavior, the most crucial consideration in law enforcement.[2]

> There are certain human relations principles which govern the quality of police service. These principles must be mastered to achieve professional excellence.
>
> The human relations principles of attitude, verbal behavior, and non-verbal behavior are fundamental to police professionalism. On this foundation, the principles of

[1]James H. Earle, "Law Enforcement Administration: Yesterday . . . Today. . . . Tomorrow," *FBI Law Enforcement Bulletin,* Apr. 1988.

[2]*Human Relations in Police Service.* Los Angeles: Los Angeles Police Department 1988, p. 3

openness, objectivity, perspective, courtesy, and compassion must be learned and applied. The principles of stereotyping, cynicism, prejudice, arrogance, and provocation must, likewise, be clearly understood to avoid their negative effects.

Police professionals must master these principles just as a shipbuilder masters the principles which govern how a ship is built or a pianist masters the principles which govern how a piano is played.

The nature of police human relations must change with the times; the basic concepts remain the same but the context in which interactions occur are subject to change:[3]

> When there were no police radios, no cars, no computers, the earliest enforcer approached a citizen, smiled or frowned, gestured, spoke, and got compliance or conflict, cooperation or the fight of a lifetime. That was human relations then.

> Police officers help make their own screen image. Perhaps the best known example of this is actor Jack Webb's role as Sgt. Joe Friday on "Dragnet." . . . Over the years, the stern television image of Sgt. Joe Friday delivering paternal lectures to wide eyed white people ceased to fit the multi-cultural, multi-lingual, multi-national community. . . .

Human relations in law enforcement is *the* major consideration for effective police work and effective police–community relations. But human relations in law enforcement is an extremely broad area, with any number of topical areas from which to approach initial understanding.

An excellent approach to understanding law enforcement human relations is through the examination of the position and status that police occupy in criminal justice. The relationship between law enforcement and other components of criminal justice is important for reasons other than providing a foundation for considering human relations. One of the more important of these reasons has to do with police receiving the brunt of the problems when other segments of criminal justice fail; such problems as overcrowded prisons invariably wind up as some form of a police problem.

CONFUSING POLICE WITH OTHER JUSTICE FUNCTIONS

In an oversimplified approach, the justice system can be thought of as a sequence of activities known as law enforcement, the judicial, which includes prosecution, defense and the judiciary, and the correctional component, including probation, parole, prisons, and reformatories.

The typical citizenry of a typical community is unlikely to have a full understanding and definitely not a full appreciation of the numerous functions and activities of what we call criminal justice. Many, perhaps most, citizens tend to think of criminal justice only in terms of "the police." This tendency often creates totally

[3]*Ibid.,* Preface.

inaccurate public images of law enforcement. It is a major theme of this volume that police are in need of community support, and distorted and unfounded perceptions of the police function work against such support.

One problem is that police officials at times attach little importance to how accurately the community perceives law enforcement. This is unfortunate, because the perceptions of the public can damage the police image whether the perceptions are true or *not true*—perceptions can be damaging.

Unfortunately, this potential damage to police image is not always recognized, and a kind of acceptance of misconceptions takes place; the police feel that if they do not deserve blame it somehow just doesn't matter if they still get blamed.

Perhaps some of the problem has to do with criminal justice seeming too complex to understand; letting the police simply "represent" all of justice is a typical public reaction. Another part of the problem may be that police officials do not always agree on the existence of problems in general.

Many times community leaders *believe* that a problem exists when in reality a problem does not exist, at least insofar as the police perception of problems is concerned. Conversely, citizens may *not* believe a problem exists, when in the opinion of police a major problem does indeed exist. The human relations approach to law enforcement dictates that law enforcement recognize that community support is offered and withdrawn based on what is *believed,* whether true or not. Later we will observe that many avenues are available to the police in correcting misconceptions and misbeliefs. One of the first areas that police should address is the blame that frequently is directed toward law enforcement for problems that exist elsewhere in criminal justice. When the general community blames the police for problems created elsewhere in criminal justice, law enforcement must find ways to acquaint community leaders with the limitations on police control of justice.

So we will examine the relationship between criminal justice components not only because it provides a foundation for the human relations approach to law enforcement; we are also concerned with the limitations on police control and influence over other justice components. While it is true that the *rate* of arrest made by police sets the volume of criminal justice, it is also true that the disposition of those arrests is largely out of police hands. And, in the final analysis, the community support required for successful law enforcement may well depend on citizens coming to grips with how little control police have over other justice functions.

Not recognizing how little control police have over other justice functions is not the only impediment to public support of police. Even among citizens aware of the distinctions *between* justice components, there is often confusion over who is responsible for what *within* each justice function. For example, law enforcement may be recognized as a separate function, but confusion can still exist when it is considered how many varied *jurisdictions* exist within the function of law enforcement: city, county, state police, as well as many federal officials. A brief summary may be useful.

The public facing increased crime from failures in other programs, such as "community-based corrections," should note that the problem is *not* police respon-

```
ENFORCEMENT

POLICE, SHERIFFS, OTHERS

STATE TROOPERS, HIGHWAY PATROLS, OTHERS

FBI, MARSHALS, BORDER PATROLS, OTHERS

JUDICIAL

JUDGES: LOCAL, STATE, FEDERAL, APPEAL

PROSECUTORS: LOCAL, STATE, FEDERAL

PUBLIC DEFENDERS, DEFENSE ATTORNEYS

CORRECTIONS

PROBATION: LOCAL, STATE, FEDERAL

PAROLE: LOCAL, STATE, FEDERAL

PRISONS AND REFORMATORIES: LOCAL, STATE, FEDERAL

JAILS, HALFWAY HOUSES, OTHERS

JUVENILE

SAME FUNCTIONS AS CRIMINAL JUSTICE
```

sibility; another justice component, other than police, is accountable.[4] When offenders under correctional supervision are free to move about a community, any crimes they commit are subject to police response, and in many instances to public blame when the crimes continue. Distinctions between police officers and parole agents become somewhat blurred in the public's perception when crime rates are on the rise—again, confusion over the responsibilities of various justice functions.

In the context of potential confusion over differing responsibilities and functions, let's now consider criminal justice overall.

THE INTENDED SYSTEM OF CRIMINAL JUSTICE

Reference to *intended* is meant to call attention to the problems of the criminal justice system. Put another way, *intended* highlights that there is in most cases a significant difference between what the system is intended to do and what it actually does.

[4]See, as one of many examples, John H. Hylton, "Rhetoric and Reality: A Critical Appraisal of Community Correctional Programs," *Crime and Delinquency,* July 1982, pp. 341–373.

The system of criminal justice is an extremely complex series of activities that involves citizens, agencies, branches and levels of government, and the laws.[5] The various segments of this complicated operation at times operate independently of all the other segments, even independently of the problems of other segments.

Examples of this independence of the components of justice can be visualized in terms of police making arrests without regard for the requirements of prosecution, of prosecution arbitrarily refusing to accept cases in which police have substantiated the allegations, of judges prone to throw cases out on technicalities, and correctional personnel permitting convicted felons to operate more or less without supervision in the community. Some feel that the court, more than other justice components, tends toward operating to the exclusion of concerns for the problems of other justice components. But the truth is that the criminal justice system has been fragmented for many years and appears to be destined to continue to remain so.[6]

Fragmentation of justice has far more to do with the tremendous *overload* of the entire justice system than with the attitude of one component toward another; struggling to keep the system afloat has become the priority in many instances.

Setting aside for the moment concern for the fragmentation of justice, it is relatively simple to describe the *intended* system, intended to be simply a sequence of criminal justice activities that leads to successful societal control of crime. For example, consider the flow chart in Fig. 1–1.

Independent of whether or not the criminal justice system achieves what it is *intended* to achieve, it nevertheless can be thought of as a system having a *process* that in turn has input and output. The *input* to the criminal justice *process* is the crime problem. The *output,* or at least the *intended* output, is success in coping with crime. The process exists in terms of the activities of police, prosecution, judicial, and corrections; in the ideal, it is synchronized, harmonious, and effective in producing the desired output.

This intended system can be thought of as a linear system, a sequential system as depicted in Fig. 1–2. If the *input* is functioning adequately, then failure to achieve the desired *output* must be related to something wrong in the *process*. In particular, when police apprehend criminals and the criminal goes through the system only to continue being a criminal, then criminal justice didn't work, at least in this particular case. A closer look at the *process* of the justice components might be useful.

Process of Criminal Justice

The process of criminal justice is made up of the activities of police, prosecution, defense, judiciary, probation, corrections, and parole.

---

[5]See, for example, Report to The Nation on Crime and Justice, *An Overview of the Criminal Justice System,* Washington, DC: U.S. Department of Justice, Mar. 1988.

[6]Ibid. See also David W. Nebauer, *America's Courts and the Criminal Justice System,* 2nd ed. Monterey, CA: Brooks/Cole Publishing, 1984.

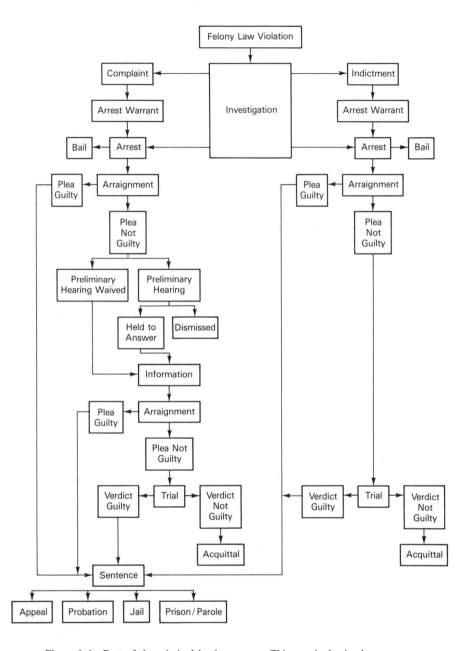

Figure 1-1 Part of the criminal justice process. This seemingly simple sequence of criminal justice "events" is complicated not only by the relationships between criminal justice components but also by constitutional restrictions. (Courtesy of West Valley College)

The Intended System of Criminal Justice

SYSTEM

Input		Process		Output
Selected		Police		Less
Law		Courts		Crime
Violation		Corrections		

Figure 1-2 Crime control as a sequence.

Prosecution. The individual official in small jurisdictions and the agency in large jurisdictions that hold responsibility for determining *if* a criminal matter is to be brought to court is the prosecution, the prosecutor or district attorney. Most states empower the state attorney general to proceed with prosecution of a case when the local prosecutor does not or cannot prosecute a matter considered appropriate for court. In federal court jurisdiction, it is the U.S. Attorney that makes the determination and prosecutes federal law violations. But the vast majority of criminal cases prosecuted in America are brought to court by the decision of the local district attorney. Local police are the primary source of cases brought to the D.A.'s attention, and local police usually shoulder the burden of gathering enough evidence for the prosecution's case, although most prosecutors have their own investigative staff as well.

Although the prosecutor is often the *legal adviser* of local *grand juries,* it is common practice for the D.A. to initiate prosecution through what is called a grand jury indictment, although other alternatives are available and sometimes utilized in bringing a criminal case to court.

Once the accused defender is brought to court, it is the responsibility of the prosecutor to convince the court and usually a jury of the guilt of the accused. Within extremely *strict* rules governing evidence, the D.A. questions witnesses chosen by the prosecution, and cross-examines witnesses chosen by the defense. Police officers are frequently witnesses for the prosecution in more serious matters (felonies), particularly homicide. Police officers also routinely assist in gathering physical evidence such as fingerprints, ballistics, and various other forensic forms of evidence. *See Appendix B for elaboration.*

Defense. The attorney for the defense holds the opposite responsibility from the prosecutor. In the adversary system, the defense attorney can be thought of as the prosecutor's opponent. This defense function is often performed by a *public defender,* an attorney operating as an employee of the jurisdiction rather than an employee of the accused.

Defense attorneys have, as officers of the court, identical responsibilities as the prosecutor insofar as witnesses and physical evidence are concerned, but for the opposite purpose of proving the innocence rather than the guilt of the accused. Defense attorneys are subject to the same stringent rules governing evidence. Physical evidence used by defense attorneys if often the result of private, rather than police, investigation. *Appendix B further elaborates on the concept.*

Judiciary. The judge presiding over a hearing or trial, as the case may be, enforces the rules of evidence governing the conduct of the district attorney and the

Police officer testifying in court. Police officers are often called on as witnesses as well as investigators in the court process. (Courtesy of Santa Cruz Police Department)

defense attorney. Various technical motions and objections by either of the two adversary attorneys are ruled on by the judge; such rulings subject to possible appeal to a higher court. The courts over which judges preside are generally referred to as either inferior or lower courts, or superior courts. The lower courts deal with criminal matters of less magnitude known as misdemeanors—whereas superior courts generally deal with the more serious matters known as felonies.

As we will note in Chapter 3, the accused has the right to waive a jury trial, thus making the judge not only responsible for conducting the trial, but for determining guilt or innocence as well—for evaluating, weighing, and judging the evidence of both sides. In the case of a finding of guilt, whether the finding is by jury or by the judge, the judge also has the responsibility to mete out the punishment—to sentence the offender who has been found guilty.

Probation. In most jurisdictions, probation officers supervise offenders who have been found guilty of an offense if the judge chooses to place the offender under probation supervision rather than in prison. Federal probation officers, as well as probation officers in some other jurisdictions, also supervise offenders after release from prison; such supervision technically is called *parole*.

In most jurisdictions, probation officers perform numerous investigative tasks for the court and are commonly the primary judicial resource in juvenile courts.

Corrections. The term corrections in most jurisdictions refers to the institutional programs in prisons, farms, reformatories, penitentiaries, and the like. A wide range of philosophies operates but generally within two broad categories of either *rehabilitation* or *punishment*. There is little consensus on what constitutes the most effective form of corrections, and this lack of consensus is compounded by the overcrowding in virtually all American prisons.

Parole. Similar to probation in concept, *parole* is an aftercare program intended to supervise offenders once released from prison, but *only* when there remains time on the offender's sentence. In this regard, it is noteworthy that there are specific length sentences and legal structures that enable some offenders to leave prison without parole supervision, having completed their sentence. The more common practice of sentencing has to do with a range, such as six to ten years. Such approaches are customarily interwoven with statutory authority for the prison administration to take into consideration *good behavior* as a formulated variable in determining the length of sentence. Many factors determine *if* an offender will be *on parole* after release, and for how long; the behavior of the offender in prison is a key variable. Another unfortunate variable is the overcrowded prison combined with the understaffed parole office.

Overcrowded prisons with understaffed parole offices are of particular concern to police. Pressures to release prisoners prematurely and without adequate parole supervision often increase the crime rate of a community, in some cases dramatically. Even among citizens of a community who claim to understand that the penal system is not the responsibility of the police, increased crime rates are often blamed on local law enforcement.

So the criminal justice system *process* is *intended* to reduce the crime rate, but in many cases it does not. Offenders who "go through the system" and keep on committing crimes are obviously not the fault of police who arrested them. Yet blame for the crimes committed by these repeat offenders often accrues to law enforcement; police often emerge as a kind of scapegoat.

Police as the Symbolic Scapegoat

If only one or two offenders were to be released from prison without being rehabilitated, it is unlikely that police would experience serious image trouble. But when the system doesn't work for sufficient numbers of offenders to cause major public concern, it is not unusual to eventually wind up blaming police for the problem. This is not difficult to understand when it is considered how *visible* police are compared to the rest of criminal justice. Police are the *most* visible symbol of American authority in any form, especially criminal justice authority (see Fig. 1–3). Police are readily available to symbolize and to be identified with anything known as a crime problem.

This is unfair in the context of the major *limitations* on police role in justice. Nevertheless, when an unsympathetic public fails to recognize the limitations on the police role in justice, this readily available symbol of justice frequently emerges as the scapegoat.

Scapegoating the police is not an intentional or deliberate effort on the part of any justice component, nor for that matter of the public. But while the *intended*

Officer responding to call; motor officer monitoring traffic; police cruiser at night. The overwhelming majority of criminal justice visibility for the public, as well as contact with criminal justice by the public, is police. (Courtesy of San Jose Police Department)

system of justice does not "intend" to scapegoat police, the *actual* practice of criminal justice frequently does just that and is likely to increase doing just that in the future, at least if current predictions prove correct that more and more people will come under criminal justice surveillance and control.[7] Law enforcement being scapegoated as a symbol for the failures of the court system and of corrections has more to do with the police image in terms of public concern. There are, however, other considerations—the *cost* of other correctional components.[8] The public funds poured into unsuccessful programs are *not* available to police budgets. This factor, too, can be removed from the *intended* design of criminal justice; nevertheless it is a factor that exists.

[7]See, for example, Marvin Zalman, "The Future of Criminal Justice Administration and Its Import on Civil Liberties," *Journal of Criminal Justice,* Spring, 1980, pp. 275–286.

[8]See, for example, Peter Haynes and Clark R. Larsen, "Financial Consequences of Incarceration and Alternatives: Burglary," *Crime and Delinquency,* Oct. 1984, pp. 529–550.

The Intended System of Criminal Justice

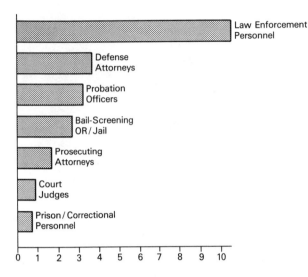

Figure 1-3 Public visibility of justice. Police are far more visible to the general public than any other segment of criminal justice. In most cases, police arrests begin the justice process. When offenders are released from court, from jail, or from prison and commit more crimes, the public expects police to control the problem.

Loss of Key Crime Deterrents through Failure to Achieve the Intended Purpose of Justice

Another, more devastating consequence of a breakdown in the *intended* outcome of criminal justice is the loss of a key deterrent to crime. The intended system would somehow provide the *certainty of punishment* for law violation and do so within constitutional guarantees and in a timely manner. Any veteran police officer, prosecutor, or (if candid) public defender readily attests to how *uncertain* punishment actually is in criminal justice, and how long it takes to achieve even when it does occur. The grim truth is that the courts are far too overcrowded to hope for significant relief in this regard.[9]

Not placing blame. It is important here to remind ourselves that we are not blaming any other segment of criminal justice for the increasing evidence that there are many failures; the overcrowding and underbudgeting problems of most correctional programs, as well as many courts, raise the question of how criminal justice components can do as well as they seem to be doing.

What we are attempting here is to lay a foundation for approaching the subject of human relations in law enforcement. This foundation of necessity must acknowledge that part of what impedes community support for law enforcement, and confusion over the precise role played by police in criminal justice certainly has the potential to be a major impediment to community support for police.

With that in mind, let's now examine what we have referred to as fragmentation.

[9]For further elaboration on the increasing success of criminal defense, see, for example, Alan M. Dershowitz, *The Best Defense*. New York: Random House, 1982. See also David A. Jones, *The Law of Criminal Procedure: An Analysis and Critique*. Boston: Little, Brown, 1981.

FRAGMENTATION

We have noted that each criminal justice component operating to the exclusion of concern for the problems of other components is related to the failures of the system. There are other ways to conceive of fragmentation of this kind, for example, a concept of criminal justice as a "system of systems."[10] But in the context of this introductory chapter, the fragmented process of criminal justice is the point of attention. Let's look closer at fragmentation in terms of how to know it's there and how to measure effectiveness.

Fragmentation and ineffectiveness can be measured simply in terms of crime rates that are not reduced and by law violators who continue to offend. In short, American society is not coping with crime when the criminal justice system is fragmented to the point that it is ineffective. The precise manner in which the criminal justice system suffers fragmentation can vary from one part of the United States to another or from one jurisdiction to another. Ineffective criminal justice that occurs through fragmentation, regardless of the local problem, is most often caused by a variety of economic and political factors, which in turn leads to each component operating to the exclusion of concern for other components. When police operate without regard to the prosecution or when the court shows indifference to corrections or police activities, the system is clearly not operating in an effective way—it is not operating in the *intended* way—and it is very unlikely to prove efficient.

This introduces or at least acknowledges the possibility that "an efficient operation" may not necessarily be effective. The point is that when any segment of a system functions in isolation from the rest of the system, the incurred fragmentation lends itself to reducing the system's *effectiveness* in coping with crime. Effectiveness in the case of society's effort to cope with crime is the primary responsibility of the criminal justice system.

Since *all* crime is never *completely* eliminated, success is a matter of degrees. In Chapter 4, emphasis will be placed on the reality that there are not sufficient numbers of police to enforce all law at all times, so attention is always directed to crime *rates* when discussing success or failure in dealing with crime. Put another way, since *all* cannot be *completely* eliminated, even in an ideal situation, increases and decreases in *rates* of crime determine success and failure.

In terms of fragmentation, let's consider an example of how criminal justice *could* work to reduce crime rates. Consider, for example, a chief of police and a county sheriff with bordering jurisdictional responsibilities. The chief prosecutor advises both law enforcement administrators that much physical evidence will be required for any conviction in local criminal courts. On examination of the actual reports, both administrators determine that either more resources (personnel and equipment) or fewer arrests are required. They further determine that this law enforcement problem is mutual and that sharing the cost of a mutual crime laboratory represents enough budget savings to increase the number of personnel to a desirable rather than a merely adequate level.

[10]R.J. Fisher, "Administration in Law Enforcement Viewed as a System of Systems," *The Police Chief,* IACP, Dec. 1981.

On still closer perusal, they agree that the court's insistence on more physical evidence relates solely to unwitnessed burglary. Statistically, it is determined that most of these burglaries occur in the sheriff's jurisdiction in the daytime and in the police chief's jurisdiction at night. With this awareness, each administrator directs the detective division of the police department to share with the sheriff all the information on daylight burglaries (heretofore thought insignificant) and the sheriff's detectives share with police all night burglary information (also heretofore thought insignificant).

This type of cooperation fortunately occurs, and it occurs often enough to confirm that the *intent* of the criminal justice administrators is generally good. On the broader scene of justice overall, such cooperation is not common; in the overloaded justice system, it is the exception rather than the rule.

The policies and routines of each component are frequently geared to their own particular *mission* and what they perceive as their mandate. And it is typical for most criminal justice agencies and departments to generate their own perception of their mission and mandate. All too often the policies and procedures flowing out of these perceived missions and mandates address only minimal concern to the problems of other concerns of criminal justice. More importantly, when the policies and routines are practiced consistently over a period of time, an ingrained resistance to change develops; the routines become the right way, and other justice agencies are doing it wrong.

System Consistency: Blessing and Curse

Before examining the problems associated with consistency, let's first consider the massive *advantages*. Consistency makes a police agency both predictable and therefore manageable, not to mention being organized. Training and performance are much easier when an agency is consistent and predictable. The personnel are likely to feel more secure. In spite of these significant advantages of consistency and predictability, *flexibility* in criminal justice operations is emerging as the most vital factor. Let's now take a closer look at the function of *flexibility* in a system that has acquired a rather permanent consistency.

If a home is equipped with an efficient furnace controlled by thermostat, it can be said that the heating *system* is available. This is a system because a consistent chain of causes and effects provides a desirable range of warmth on a predictable basis. In the case of this particular system, desirable results are produced on a self-adjusting basis. Complaints about excessive heat or cold are not required to get the furnace adjusted correctly; sensitivity to the problem for which the system is intended ensures consistent and proper adjustment to the system on an ongoing basis. The thermostat measures the temperature inside the house and then controls the furnace accordingly; this interaction of causes and effects produces the desirable result of healthy indoor climate.

Compare this heating system to one in which the occupant must run to the basement to make a manual adjustment every time a temperature change occurs. Also consider the overall system if any single part functions independently to the degree that it is not directly related to the overall *purpose* of the system, a thermostat, for example, wired to a light switch. Clearly, the system that adjusts itself to change not only produces better results and requires less effort; it necessarily becomes the *only* desirable system.

Relating this analogy more specifically to criminal justice, recall the example involving a police chief, sheriff, prosecutor, and court. Their individual functions are performed in a systematic manner to serve a common goal. Like the thermostat of the heating system, the prosecutor registered change and communicated this change to the police chief and sheriff. Had the thermostat been "connected wrong" the prosecutor may have communicated this information to the wrong functions, or to no functions at all.

Like the furnace, the police chief and sheriff responded with what was needed. Moreover, the systematic manner in which they interrelated made possible allowance for variations of many kinds. In other words, although the heating system responds to a single variable of temperature, the criminal justice system can and does respond to a great number of variables. Social, legal, and economic change, all involving many other changes, impinge directly on police, courts, prosecution –defense, and corrections through a number of "thermostats."

Change itself is the significant consideration in system flexibility. A brief glimpse at the significance of change (or, more particularly, *social* change) will illustrate the need for flexibility in a workable system of criminal justice. Tremendously oversimplified, changes during the history of the world might be thought of in terms of thousands of years that people have spent farming, compared to the couple hundred years of the blue-collar era (and the subsequent technical revolution that followed the Industrial Revolution). With this background of suddenly accelerate change, people now face an uncertain future with microtechnology, cybernation, and an explosion of knowledge having the effect of creating more information on a daily basis than was created during thousands of years prior to the twentieth century.

The ever-accelerating pace of social change, because it has directly affected the causes and effects within and without the justice system, requires incredible flexibility for the system to achieve its mission—to deal with American crime and keep the peace. The problem of inflexibility and indeed of fragmentation, in large measure, can be traced to the excessive consistency inherent in many of the components of criminal justice, a consistency that creates a virtual lack of flexibility.

Constant Change

As we will see in several later chapters, *change* is not optional. The constant contention between those seeking change and those who resist change is the very basis of our democratic government and will continue to be so.

The *consistency* of the justice system is therefore under constant pressure to change. Flexibility permits adjustments; rigid, inflexible consistency resists the pressure and generates greater tension. It almost seems that if something is operating well there is pressure to change it. Police are not alone in this perception. Many employers who fought hard to retain the practice of simply firing employees who sought improvements in working conditions are now negotiating labor contracts that include change and even define conditions for dismissal. Indeed, *police* personnel themselves now negotiate labor contracts, an unheard of concept on a broad scale only a few decades ago.[11]

Changes are inevitable, but particularly painful when they occur in opposition to consistencies in the system known as *tradition.*

Traditions: Some Great, Some Not So Great

Fragmentation between and within justice components can often be related to or even traced to traditions. Traditions are powerful; they are frequently the main core of an organization's *homeostasis,* its identity and equilibrium. It has been noted that police enter their careers frequently with sufficient talent to conceive of methods to improve their organization—improve on the problems of fragmentation, for example. Traditions, more often than not, either absorb such creativity or simply wear out the recruit's enthusiasm.[12] The philosophy of "the old ways are the best ways" frequently prevails at the cost of creative insight.

Being quasi-military in organizational style in most jurisdictions, the old ways of a police agency are particularly strong when set in policy by police administration. Put another way, when the "folkways and mores" of a police agency are buttressed with actual administrative policy, the tradition is exceedingly strong.

This is not to say that a police chief's support is required in order to have a tradition of resisting change. On the contrary, many far-sighted administrators have found, to their dismay, that innovative policies can be virtually subverted by traditionally oriented veteran line officers who are convinced that the old ways are better than the enlightened policy. In general, when traditional values are supported by the administration, however, the innovative spirit of talented new police careerists is not likely to survive. And many traditional police values, if changed, would seriously weaken law enforcement. For example, the traditional police values of *courage, honor, dedication,* and *honesty* are values that *must* survive other changes. But where the system stifles creativity and innovation that is needed to gain and keep community support for law enforcement, the values that cause the problem *must* be examined. This is necessary because police are and will remain the primary social control of a society that is geared to continual face-offs between those who want change and those who do not; police cannot afford outmoded traditions to impede the support of the community that is increasingly required for law enforcement success.[13] Let's look a little closer at the concept of police tradition.

[11]See, for example, Edward A. Thibault, Lawrence M. Lynch, and R. Bruce McBride, *Proactive Police Management.* Englewood Cliffs, NJ: Prentice-Hall, 1986, "History of Police Unionism," pp. 301–312. See also C. A. Salerno, *Police at the Bargaining Table,* Springfield, IL: Charles C Thomas 1981; Ed Cray, "The Politics of Blue Power," *Nations,* April 21, 1969, pp. 493–496; Hugh, O'Neil, "The Growth of Municipal Employee Unions," *Unionization of Municipal Employees: Proceedings of the Academy of Political Science,* Spring, 1970.

[12]See, for example, Louis A. Radelet, *The Police and the Community,* 4th ed. New York: Macmillan, 1986, pp. 90–92.

[13]See, for example, Pamela D. Mayhall, *Police–Community Relations and the Administration of Justice,* 3rd ed. New York: Wiley, 1985, pp. 133–134.

Ambiguity of Police Roles

Examining police traditions for the purpose of gaining community support can be aided by reflection on police roles that must take into account the reality that even basic police roles can be and are frequently ambiguous.

In the context of confusion and ambiguity of police roles, the definition of role is simply what the community expects police to do. Confusion comes from the ambiguity of such expectations; one segment of the community may expect police to do something entirely different than another segment may expect, and frequently with little or no clarification of what is expected until *after* police are forced to perform.

Making the problem even more difficult is the belief of the community that expectations are clear, when actually roles are ambiguous. The stress that this and other contradictory influences in law enforcement create is often compounded by the continuing demand to gain and hold the support of the community, and to do so in a professional manner. In this same context of stress related to ambiguity of role expectations, consider the simple factor of courtesy:[14]

> Courtesy must be practiced by department members in order to earn the respect and support of the community. In a free society, any government agency that fails to earn and maintain this support cannot attain its goals. . . .

Courtesy and all the other demands on professional law enforcement remain in place while confronting the stress of ambiguity in what is expected of police. These demands also remain in place during the *situational* role expectations placed on police, those roles that vary with the situation. Situational roles include what police are expected to do about traffic jams, even when an armed robbery is in progress. Perhaps even more stressful is the expectations of judges, prosecutors, defense attorneys, and juries for police to effectively apprehend the offender, but to do so without the slightest violation of the offender's rights, while at the same time confronting violence and great personal danger in such a professional manner as to thoroughly convince all concerned that excessive force was not used.

But even without these situational variations in what is expected of police, agreement about what the community expects is still a problem. For example, even if police and the general community were to agree that police simply arrest law violators, the role that would be accepted and agreed on would not fit the *reality* that police are expected to prevent or at least deter crime, as well as arrest those who are violators who are not deterred. Shifting to the other role emphasis point of keeping the peace, if police and the general community were to agree that keeping the peace was the law enforcement job, the problem would continue in that *reality* dictates police arrest law violators and enforce law in general, not merely keep the peace.

Role expectations regarding investigation, evidence gathering, and technical expertise combine with demands for legal sophistication, physical prowess, and

[14]Thomas J. Lange, "Cultivating the Practice of Courtesy," *Police Chief,* Arlington, VA: IACP, Jan. 1989, p. 35.

mental maturity to form an extremely complex set of roles and functions on top of the difference in emphasis on law enforcement or keeping the peace.

All this confusion about the police role exists in the context of the potential to use great force, even lethal force, in enforcing the law. Vague parameters regarding the use of force and the degree of force tend to obscure, rather than clarify, even the obvious role of law enforcement, the *enforcement* of law, the main subject of Chapter 2.

It should not then be surprising that strong police traditions emerge. The old ways are most likely to be "what worked" for the veteran officers who have confronted and suffered through the continuing frustration of ambiguity of what is expected.

Yet when these understandable traditions impede the acquisition and retention of the desperately needed community support for law enforcement, the question must be asked: Can police afford this particular tradition? This is a significant and vital question, regardless of the particular tradition and regardless of how strong the tradition may be. These questions *must* be addressed by police *if* the support of the community is to be gained.[15] Figure 1-4 illustrates the strategic importance of community support of police work. Police traditions that in any way impede such support raise questions that *must* be addressed.

There are many reasons for perceiving the *necessity* of posing these questions regarding traditions that impede the support of the community. In the chapters that follow, these factors will be considered. For our purposes in this discussion, it need only be noted that law enforcement and the equal administration of justice have become major national concerns in recent decades. The rapid growth of our cities, with the attendant problems in housing, education, employment, and social welfare services, has accentuated these concerns and has been highlighted by the increasing urban concentration of minority groups.

Crime rates have generally been higher in those areas where poverty, family disintegration, unemployment, lack of education, and minority group frustration and resentment in the face of social and economic discrimination (the ghetto syndrome) are manifest. Chapter 8 examines some of the theoretical causes of crime and delinquency independent of these factors, but it remains noteworthy that crime rates do associate with these socioeconomic factors.

The expectations, excitement, and additional frustration engendered by the civil rights movement of the past few decades have compounded the difficulties inherent in the entire process of law enforcement and the administration of justice. Police *cannot* function without the support of their community.

Foremost among the difficulties are the relationships between police and minority groups. Later chapters address many dimensions of this police–community relations challenge. The methods required to negotiate these problems are of little

[15]See, for example, H.H. Earle, *Police–Community Relations: Crisis in Our Times,* Springfield, IL: Charles C Thomas, 1980. For earlier perspectives, see A. Barres, "Alienation Factors in Police-Community Relations," *The Police Chief,* IACP, Apr. 1977; George B. Sunderland, "The Community: Partner in Crime Prevention," *FBI Law Enforcement Bulletin,* Oct. 1988.

	PATROL AND INVESTIGATION with COMMUNITY SUPPORT plus SUCCESSFUL CRIMINAL JUSTICE	PATROL AND INVESTIGATION with COMMUNITY SUPPORT without SUCCESS IN CRIMINAL JUSTICE	PATROL AND INVESTIGATION but lacking COMMUNITY SUPPORT without SUCCESS IN CRIMINAL JUSTICE
CRIME GETS REPORTED	Excellent	Good	Poor
KEEPING THE PEACE	Excellent	Good	Poor
DETER AND PREVENT CRIME	Excellent	Good	Poor

Figure 1-4 Community support when social custom is not enough. In the ideal situation, police would enjoy both the support of the community and the success of other criminal justice components. But even when other parts of criminal justice falter, good law enforcement is still possible as long as the community supports police. Without community support, enforcement cannot be successful.

value if the community in general does not support law enforcement. As a further indicator of the need to gain and maintain community support, it should be noted that many police officials decry the growing disrespect for law, the apathy of the public, what is perceived as mollycoddling of criminals by the courts, and political influence on the law enforcement process. As we will see in chapters that follow, the growing need for community support for law enforcement is not isolated to the urban areas in which the dramatic confrontations affecting law enforcement have occurred; even the smallest jurisdictions in America are encountering significant evidence that community support is an absolute requisite.

Gaining community support begins with acknowledging that the *nature* of enforcement is far different from other services provided by the government, primarily in terms of the individual's willingness to accept the service. Unlike many government services sought by the citizen, *enforcement* is frequently avoided.

In Chapter 2, the *nature* of enforcement will be examined for the purpose of providing a context for reaching cooperative relationships—a context for acquiring and retaining community support for law enforcement.

SUMMARY

This introductory chapter noted *human relations* as the appropriate avenue for approaching the subject of law enforcement. The ultimate need for the support of the community served by law enforcement was emphasized. It was noted that understanding the position and status of police in the overall justice system provides the best foundation for the human relations approach to law enforcement and ultimately the support of the community. The components of criminal justice were described broadly in terms of law enforcement, courts, prosecution-defense, and various correctional functions. The jurisdictional differences between different segments within each justice component were discussed.

A distinction was made between the criminal justice system that is *intended* and the actual justice system, which is plagued by fragmentation and ineffectiveness, mostly generated by tremendous overloading.

It was noted that police serve as the most visible symbol of criminal justice and are therefore blamed and scapegoated for justice failures. Consistency and tradition were presented as both blessing and curse within the criminal justice system in general and the police system in particular, consistency in tradition meaning a resistance to change that is often required for effective law enforcement.

The ambiguity and obscurity of the police role were discussed in terms of complex and varied expectations. The chapter concluded by noting the growing need for community support for law enforcement to succeed and the need for law enforcement to emphasize to communities the limitations on their influence in the overall justice system.

DISCUSSION TOPICS

1. Elaborate on the significance of crime rates as a measure of criminal justice effectiveness.
2. Discuss criminal justice fragmentation.
3. Contrast police function with any other criminal justice component.
4. State the relationship between change and system flexibility.
5. How do police become scapegoats through their status as symbols of criminal justice?
6. Discuss system consistency as both blessing and curse.
7. Elaborate on the ambiguity of the police role.
8. Relate community support for law enforcement to the fragmentation of the criminal justice system.

Relevant Problems for Discussion

A wide range of relevant problems impinge on the many variables discussed in this brief introductory chapter. The *range* of problems is itself the most relevant of the problems. By range is meant the varied problems that spread from the problem of fragmentation of the justice system through the ambiguity of the police role to the police often emerging as the symbol of justice as well as the scapegoat of justice problems.

Beyond the range of problems is the difficulty the public, and often the criminal justice personnel themselves, has in distinguishing between levels of responsibility in the justice *process*. Appendix D elaborates on some of the specifics having to do with the working relationship between prosecution and law enforcement. While there are other relevant problems in this regard, the working relationship between police and prosecutor serves as an example. The fact of the matter is that both police and prosecutors exercise an enormous degree of discretion in the justice process, and not always by the same standards. As will be noted in Chapter 4, law enforcement has no choice but to be selective in enforcing laws. All laws simply cannot be enforced at all times. But, as stated in Appendix D, prosecutors must also exercise a wide range of discretion, that is, exercise judgment in selecting cases.

The significance of this problem in the wide range of problems relevant to the position of the police and the justice system can be seen in terms of a fragmentation that is amplified by two different levels of discretion being exercised although often not completely aligned with the same goals, even though operating in the same system.

The ensuing difficulties related to this problem, as well as the other problems of the justice components, frequently are laid by the public at the doorstep of the symbol of justice — the police.

2

Nature and Background of Enforcement

The term *enforcement,* as used in law enforcement, usually calls up the image of crime, the deterrence of crime, the prevention of crime, and the apprehending of criminals. The nature of enforcement covers an even broader range of concepts than this, but deterrence and prevention may be useful as an introduction to the broader topic. Let's consider how prevention and deterrence are viewed in a large police agency:[1]

> Peace in a free society depends on voluntary compliance with the law. The primary responsibility for upholding the law therefore lies not with the police but with the people. Since crime is a social phenomenon, crime prevention is the concern of every person living in society. Society employs full-time professional police to prevent crime, to deter it, and when that fails, to apprehend those who violate the law. . . .
>
> While there are certain crimes that cannot be deterred, crimes committed against property and against innocent victims in public places are reduced by police patrol. Street crime is curbed by the potential criminal's fear of immediate apprehension or by the increased likelihood of detection . . . ."

[1]*Manual of the Los Angeles Police Department,* LAPD, Vol. 1, Nos. 130.10 and 130.20, 1988. See also Chapter 9.

The nature of enforcement includes in its description both the philosophy and police activities alluded to in this policy statement. But the nature of enforcement also includes the wide variation in how different communities go about implementing this philosophy and performing the necessary police activities.

Each American community is unique; it differs in many ways from any other community. Each community has its own geographical location, but, more importantly, it has its own population. The population, the result of differences in population size, composition (such things as age, sex, race, and ethnicity), and *wealth* creates its own unique philosophy and politics.

Police services *appear* similar in many ways because of the constraints of the Constitution, the Bill of Rights, and the laws that govern the police function; so also does the growing trend toward police professionalism make police services appear very similar. Yet the uniqueness of each community creates major differences in police services. It also creates differences in the approach needed for police to gain and hold the support of the community.

Support is an absolute requisite to successful law enforcement: "peace in a free society depends on voluntary compliance with the law . . . ."[2]

In addition to this *requirement* of public support to successfully enforce the law, communities have other needs for police services that cannot be provided without community support; consider, for example, the effort required by both community and police to make citizens feel as safe as possible.

There may be a community, or even communities, in the United States where citizens can walk the streets at *any* time of day and *any* time of night, without fear. The number of such communities is unknown; if they exist at all, they are very few. However, to the degree that such a claim could be valid in a community, to that same degree can both the citizens and the police of the community be less concerned with the increasing demand for better police–community relations. There are, sadly, a great number of American cities that may never achieve such a goal. But even in cities where the socioeconomic conditions forecast continued crime far into the future, good working relations between police and community groups will substantially reduce the crime problem; and reducing the crime problem is the primary incentive for communities to support their police, for the citizens of the community to get behind law enforcement efforts to control crime.

Community support for law enforcement is extremely valuable even in those unfortunate neighborhoods where a prudent pedestrian might fear walking at night. Good relations between law enforcement and the citizens of the community can prove to be an effective method of reducing the severest police problem, even if the problem cannot be totally solved.

The important question of *why* police must now and in the future be concerned with community relations has to do with the *nature* of enforcement itself, the subject of this chapter. Before examining the nature of enforcement, however, it may be useful to first look at one segment of police priorities.

[2]*Ibid.*

It should not be astounding that one priority of the police is training in the methods to gain a *positive public image*.[3] In spite of the high priorities placed on other demands for police sophistication and expertise in many additional areas, methods to obtain a positive public image are a police priority. The reason this should not be astounding is that the better the police image in the community, the greater the public support, an implicit recognition that community support is absolutely vital to successful law enforcement. What are the avenues to achieving and holding a positive public police image?

Police efforts in the area of community relations are by far the most promising approach to developing and holding a positive public image. More than gaining the sought after positive image, the development of good community relations has the potential for reducing some crimes, preventing others, and gaining public support for controlling the rest.

The significance of support from the community in dealing with crime can be evaluated from a number of perspectives, all of them positive. Consider for example what most would agree is, or should be, a *powerful* crime deterrent: speedy trial, with certainty of penalty if guilty, and a finality to the sentence.[4] Certainly everyone would agree that this sequence, if consistent, would indeed powerfully deter many from crime. But as all veteran police officers know, speedy trials are often delayed, sentences may or may not be the penalty for the crime committed (after plea bargaining), and the overwhelmed courts find little finality in the process following trial in a number of major cases. Without this powerful deterrent, police are in *urgent* need of community support.

There are those that might argue that police generally have a positive public image and there is no urgency to pursue improvements in this regard. This complacent point of view is generally based on the good image that was reflected for police in the last *comprehensive* research on this subject back in 1979.[5] But this favorable image was based on general questions and fell considerably when specific questions were asked.[6] Considering that police do in fact serve *all* the community and not just the majority, it has been noted, "It should not be comforting to be told by public opinion pollsters that most of the people approve of the police most of the time. . . ."[7] Police are visible and can be evaluated and rated, often without being

[3] Recent nationwide research by the FBI listed as sixth in the top 20 police training priorities the "Projection of a Positive Image. . . ." See Robert G. Phillips, Jr., "Training Priorities in State and Local Law Enforcement," *FBI Law Enforcement Bulletin* Aug. 1988, p. 12.

[4] See, for example, George Reed, and Dave Hunt, *Fear No Man*. Eugene, OR: Harvard Home Publishers, 1987.

[5] It was found that 81% felt police were "average" to "good," which was up from 79% in 1975. See National Crime Panel, *Criminal Victimization Surveys in 13 American Cities,* U.S. Department of Justice, LEAA, National Criminal Justice Information and Statistics Service, June 1979, and James Garolfolo, Criminal Justice Research Center, Albany, NY.

[6] See, for example, Melvin T. White and A. Menke, "A Critical Analysis of Surveys of Public Opinion Toward Police Agencies," *Journal of Police Science and Administration,* Spring, 1986, pp. 204–208, © IACP.

[7] Radelet, Louis A. *The Police and the Community,* 4th ed. New York: Macmillan, 1987, p. 110.

aware that this process is taking place.[8] Complacency or indifference regarding the support of the community is totally unjustified.

Fortunately, there are signs that police are gaining and to some degree maintaining community support. There has been a decline in such complaints as police brutality in the past decade. This is most fortunate because police now and increasingly in the future will need public support as the job of law enforcement becomes more and more complex. An integral part of gaining and keeping that public support is the positive image that we have already noted. But even more crucial is the inclusion of *human relations* concepts in the priorities established for enforcing law.

In one context, the human relations approach to enforcing law merely acknowledges the many human interactions involved in the dealings of police with the public. But as we will see in later chapters, the interactions are grossly influenced by attitudes, prejudices, biases, and experience.

With this in mind, let's now consider the nature of enforcement.

THE NATURE OF ENFORCEMENT

It would probably be helpful to establish what is meant by the term nature. To a large measure, the *nature* of enforcement as discussed in this chapter could also be called the rationale for enforcement. To fully understand enforcement's nature, it is necessary to understand *why* enforcement exists. Let's take a closer look at enforcement in this context.

Here we are considering neither the methods nor the techniques of enforcing law. Although enforcement methods and techniques are an integral part of ensuring compliance with law, we are *not* addressing the methods needed to, for instance, apprehend burglars or traffic violators. What we *are* addressing is the nature of the *need* to enforce law, a need that can be perceived either optimistically or pessimistically.

Pessimism versus Optimism

Unfortunately, the reality is that police work tends to encourage cynicism for many reasons that will be discussed in later chapters; cynicism is an all too frequent outcome of police careers. This is completely understandable with even a cursory consideration of the typical day in, day out encounters experienced by police officers. The literature has long reflected this pessimistic orientation.[9] While there is little basis for hoping that a career of enforcing law will ever encourage widespread optimism, it is nonetheless true that the nature of the *need* for enforcement is such

[8]See, for example, *How to Rate Your Local Police,* Washington, DC: Police Executive Research Forum, 1983.

[9]See, for example, Arthur Niederhoffer, *Behind the Shield,* Garden City, NY: Doubleday, 1969. See also B. Daviss, "Burnout," *Police Magazine,* April, 1982, pp. 9–18; B. Bennett, "Motivational Hangups of the Police Mystique," *The Police Chief,* Feb. 1979, pp. 36–37; Peter K. Manning and John Van Maanen, (eds.), *Policing: A View from the Street,* Santa Monica, CA: Goodyear Publishing, 1978.

that cynicism hurts and even cripples police effort to gain community support. Here it should be noted that the police philosophy actually functions in many cases at *two* levels: the administration and the line officer.[10] Put another way, the problems inherent in cynicism in enforcement are not always solved by positive approaches by police administrators, since the street philosophy of line officers may differ radically because of their continuing negative experiences.[11]

Police professionalism will be discussed in Chapter 3 to develop a body of enforcement knowledge on which to base professionalism, which will modify some of the countering influences of pessimism. For the purposes of this particular discussion, we are merely acknowledging that the nature of the *need* for enforcement is such that the more positive the approach, the more positive the results — confirmed views to the contrary notwithstanding.

From this brief aside, let us now return to the nature of enforcement, again noting that we are not addressing the methods nor techniques, but the basic *concept* of enforcing law. Perhaps the best starting point is the *concept of force* in enforcement — philosophically, how much force?[12]

Degree of Force

The amount of force it takes to effect a necessary arrest is on a scale ranging from none at all, through "come-along" holds, to weapons and firearms, to lethal force. Philosophically, an offender may be perceived as self-determined, making free choices to commit crime, fully responsible for his or her actions, and deserving of any punishment that comes his or her way. On the other hand, an offender might be perceived as controlled by external and powerful social forces, or a combination of both. When perceived in this manner, the offender at best is accountable rather than responsible for crimes and far less deserving of the punishment that may come his or her way.

The nature of enforcement is such that force may be required regardless of how the offender is perceived. If arrest is required and that arrest is resisted, sufficient force is *required,* but only to the degree necessary to effect the arrest.

So the answer as to *why* enforcement must exist must acknowledge that enforcement includes force, at least in many instances. From the human relations perspective, the emphasis here would be on using force only to the degree required. By required, we mean the specific degree of force necessary to ensure compliance with the law; we also refer to the requirement that someone have the authority and the power to exercise this force, the power and authority to regulate human behavior.

[10]See, for example, David H. Bayley, *Police and Society.* Beverly Hills, Sage, 1977. See also Michael K. Brown, *Working the Street: Police Discretion and the Dilemmas of Reform.* New York: Russel Sage Foundation, 1981.

[11]Ibid.

[12]Ibid.

Officer handcuffing suspect. (Courtesy
of Santa Cruz Police Department)

The Community's Need to Regulate Behavior

To our discussion of the police need for community support, we add the very real
need of the community for enforcement, a need created for many reasons, among
which are the following. When there is not enough of anything that is badly wanted
or needed, some will have more than an equal share of whatever that might be. If the
shortage is severe, only a small group will have these unequal shares. Barring the
hoarding process, the more that is available, the larger the group having an unequal
share. With unlimited availability of a commodity, presumably all shares could be
equal.

In America, money and the power that money provides more or less control
this process, but do so within the law. When the acquisition of scarce resources
includes robbery, burglary, or other theft modes, the specific victim is in urgent need
of someone to have the power and authority to regulate behavior. Collectively, the

entire community is also in such need. This need is compounded by the community's social ecology—the age, sex, color, density of population, and relative wealth of various segments of the population.[13] Put another way, there are many forces at work in the community that may cause competition for limited resources to spill over into those behaviors that are forbidden by law, behaviors that the community cannot or will not accept. Figure 2-1 illustrates the relationships between *demand, availability,* and *social controls.* Social controls are strained as demand increases and availability decreases.

In the broad societal context, this spilling over of competition for resources into crime relates in certain ways to the perceived strengths and weaknesses of individuals in the community. The armed robber perceives the robbery in terms of the strength used to intimidate the weaker victim. The violent street gang, when involved in robbery, still operates on the strength principle. Indeed it could be argued that the street mob, rioting and destroying limited resources, does so during a feeling of strength in large numbers.

Theoretically, were there sufficient resources for all needs and all demands, there might not be a need for designated enforcers of the law; in such a utopian fantasy, police would be superfluous. Of course, the question is moot. There are rarely sufficient resources for everyone's demands. There is continuing competition for limited resources. Moreover, there is an everpresent threat of violent crime within that competition, not to mention the crimes flowing out of the personal

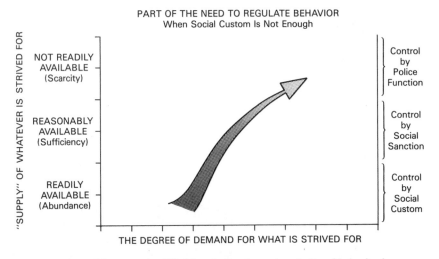

Figure 2-1 When oversimplified for clarity, the vast majority of behavior is regulated by accepted social customs and is strengthened by mild informal sanctions. Police must have this support in order to keep order. But just as police must have community support, the community must have enforcement for the violent crimes that are not controlled by the "law-of-supply-and-demand."

[13]See, for example, J.M. Byrne, and R.J. Sampson (eds.), *The Social Ecology of Crime.* New York: Springer-Verlag, 1986.

problems hidden in even the most affluent community. The community definitely *needs* designated enforcers of the law; human behavior must be regulated. Brief consideration should be given to how human beings evolved the need to regulate human behavior. In a sense, this evolution is also the history of police.

BACKGROUND OF REGULATING BEHAVIOR

Partial History of Police

We can speculate that in many ways the ancient and prehistoric groups of human beings had enforcement needs similar to those of modern-day communities. Archaeologists and anthropologists tend to be imprecise in relating the exact background of enforcement, but data continue to emerge that suggest that enforcement was one of the earliest concepts.

Prehistoric family groups merging into tribes for protection had more to worry about than wild animals and the hostile environment. Other tribes posed difficulties, as did members of the group who wouldn't conform to the group's norms.

Folkways and Mores as Rules

Not conforming to the tribal rule was probably a matter of breaking folkways and mores; a folkway is an expected consistency in some particular behavior, with a *mild* social rebuke or sanction for violation. Mores involve certain folkways that had a more serious penalty for violation. In any event, prehistoric tribes probably had rules for their members.

On a commonsense basis, it seems likely that tribes during the dawn of civilization followed leaders who were either able to personally enforce the rules or could draft or recruit individuals capable of such enforcement. Those who enforced the tribal rules internally were probably the same individuals who led the group during wars with other clans, combining the police and military functions and providing *protection* overall.

Historians tend to agree that Sumerian rulers evolved a judicial system. It is believed that the Sumerian king Ura-Ka-Gina, in approximately 2370 B.C., established the concept of injustice by curbing officials from unjustly oppressing the poor. Two centuries later, King Nammu codified the rules into laws that were implemented and supplemented by virtually all rulers of the first Amorite Dynasty of Babylon.

A major milestone in the evolving concept of regulating behavior was the Great Code of Hammurabi. King Hammurabi attempted to codify virtually all offenses and, equally significant, codify the penalties—extremely harsh penalties, but nevertheless codified.

A thousand years later, Mosaic Law was written and afforded yet another milestone in civilized effort to regulate human conduct. The rise and fall of the Roman Empire included many profound influences, among which was Emperor

Augustus's decision to remove military duties from certain elite legionnaires for the purpose of *police* work, meaning policing Caesar's personal safety and property security. Calling them *Praetorian guards,* Caesar Augustus established what has proved to be a continuous influence on police function.

In the context of early influence, Egyptian rulers established criminal justice procedures that resemble modern justice practices, particularly in the courts and in the context of an evolving civilization regulating human conduct.

The historical background of regulating behavior is somewhat obscured by the Dark Ages, particularly in Spain, France, and feudal England.

The background of constitutional government and individual rights is the subject of Chapter 3. In this brief discussion of regulating behavior, however, a major development occurred in England in 1829. At the urging of Sir Robert Peele, Parliament passed the *Metropolitan Police Act.* The significance of this event can be seen in that, prior to this development, England operated various approaches to the system that Alfred the Great had established using private citizens to make arrests for small rewards, beginning around the late 800s. Later, in the latter part of the 1200s, King Edward I established the first official police force, followed for hundreds of years by England's justice-constable and sheriff system.

The *Metropolitan Police Act* created a stable, consistent, efficient, military-type organization under government rule. This contrasted remarkably with the approach to criminal justice and the regulation of human conduct that had occurred in the past. Then, in 1856, the British Parliament passed the *Obligatory Act,* which obliged all jurisdictions in England to establish the Metropolitan Police Act approach to regulating behavior.

This background of regulating behavior will be further discussed in the chapter dealing with constitutional government. Noteworthy in the present discussion is that American developments in law enforcement were in a sense an extension of the English approach, including the justice of the peace, the watch and ward, and such police functions as the constable watch.

In our present discussion on regulating behavior, however, it is important that we now include consideration of the *purpose* of enforcement, the *reason* that enforcement is necessary. In effect, the purpose is descriptive of much of the nature of enforcement.

PURPOSE OF ENFORCEMENT:
PERSONAL SAFETY, PROPERTY SECURITY, AND GENERAL ORDER

As we will note in various contexts later in this volume, there are two separate views of law enforcement in American society. One view emphasizes the presumed deterrence against committing crimes that occurs when *enforcement* itself is emphasized. Police from this perspective are primarily enforcers of society's rules. The other view of police has to do with the general order presumed to result from police interacting with citizens who are thought to be somewhat at the mercy of social and economic conditions, sometimes even victims of their environment rather than criminals.

"Old-time" police roll call. (Courtesy of Santa Cruz Police Department)

Regulating behavior in a democratic society must, of necessity, employ some of each of these concepts. Considering the great personal freedom afforded by the American approach to democratic society, there is no other choice. This is why American law enforcement does indeed combine both of these views: deterrence through enforcement and general order through a wide range of police–citizen interactions.

General order, however, is more than simply police interacting with the community; it is one of the purposes of society having enforcement. Indeed, society *depends* on general order and, more importantly, the individual depends on society to provide protection, meaning general order, personal safety, and property security. See Fig. 2-2.

This dependence of the individual on society in this area has been consistent throughout the evolution of civilization. Some of the characteristics and salient features of *how* the individual depends on society have been modified in some ways by the explosion of technical knowledge in this century. But the underlying need is for society to regulate behavior enough to provide this protection: personal safety and property security.

Brief consideration of the alternative illustrates this compelling need. For example, how safe would anyone be without laws and designated enforcers of law? Wealth might be capable of some degree of protection, but certainly not on the order of a whole society committed to personal safety and property security. As for the property security itself, even *with* societal power on the side of the property owner, criminals continue to steal and rob. Imagine the results of withdrawing laws against property crime.

The history of enforcing law, which is in many ways the history of regulating human behavior, is a history of the individual and the group depending on society to provide personal safety and property security. As we will note later in discussing

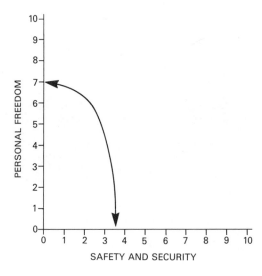

Figure 2-2 Safety and security: Trade-off with personal freedom. This graph oversimplifies and exaggerates the influence of personal freedom on the safety and security of the individual. Yet, there remains a definite reduction in safety and security as unlimited personal freedom is approached.

constitutional government restrictions, the individual in turn must submit to the rules in exchange for this protection.

In effect, the individual must relinquish a certain degree of personal freedom to gain society's protection. Those who do not respect this requirement are frequently the very individuals with whom police must deal in controlling crime.

Willingness to have one's behavior regulated, then, is a major consideration. Particularly in a democratic society that ensures great personal freedom, the willingness of citizens to be controlled is crucial. There are not enough police officers, nor could there ever be, to *force* acceptance of a free society's rules; citizens in a free society must be willing. But even though the citizens cannot be forced into willingness, it is also important to recognize that even in a democratic society enforcement *is* coercive.

In totalitarian forms of government, such coercion is usually backed by such awesome raw power that resistance is foolhardy. But what about citizens reacting to the coercive nature of enforcement in a democratic society?

Police K–9 detail. (Courtesy of San Jose Police Department)

ENFORCEMENT AS COERCION

In a discussion of the nature of enforcement, it is crucial that we acknowledge two simple realities: The first reality is that enforcement is of necessity coercive, and, second, many, if not most, people tend to resist coercion when they perceive it as unacceptable.

In this regard it is worth note that even voluntary conformity that occurs in the shadow of punishment for nonconformity must come to grips with the reality that coercion is a factor if enforcement is to be successful. Then, too, there are various levels of voluntary conformity. Many who conceive of their life-style as totally within the law violate speed laws as a matter of course. When the coercive influence of traffic citations is brought to bear on the lives of such individuals, their willingness to conform is likely to be at least in part accompanied by resentment. The less subtle the coercion, the more visible the resentment in most cases.

The not always subtle coercion of enforcement can account for the interest in public opinion polls regarding confidence of citizens in police practices. The very existence of public opinion polls suggests that there exist questions regarding the willingness of a community to accept enforcement. Perhaps the influence of coercive elements in law enforcement is better seen in the context of implied threat.

Implied Threat

In the broadest sense, the entire process of criminal justice is intended as a threat; it is intended to be a straightforward threat of unpleasant sanctions for any violation of criminal law. But, as we will see in Chapter 3, constitutionally guaranteed due process modifies this threat in many ways. And yet some degree of threat is intended by all criminal justice components, by the prosecution, the courts, corrections, and certainly the police, the additional responsibility of *protection of the public* notwithstanding.

Counterarguments note that criminal justice is only threatening to law violators, which is perhaps true. But even those who do not violate law are intentionally threatened by the intended consequences of criminal behavior. In the most professional format, this threat is *implied* more than overt, but nonetheless a threat. Consider, for example, the range of potential force a police officer brings to the *arrest* process, the threat of arrest being ever present in the context of possible law violations.

A fully cooperative offender should encounter little force during arrest, perhaps handcuffs in felony matters, but not a lot of force. As resistance to arrest increases, so does the force used to effect the arrest. Starting with body control holds and "come-alongs," force moves through intensity levels that include a range of disabling techniques from batons to firearms and lethal force.

The mere *potential* to use force in arrest, combined with the threat of arrest itself, may influence some, perhaps many, to forget the *nature* of enforcement, that both the community and the individual *must have* enforcement to ensure personal safety and property security.

Probably the most difficult of all *ongoing* career problems for law enforcement personnel is to reconcile these seemingly conflicting variables: to remain strong enough to enforce law against resistance, while staying professional enough to encourage the community to remember the *need* for enforcement. There are times when this cannot be done, and members of the community resist having their behavior controlled. When scrutinized carefully, such resistance usually relates to the reaction to perceived coercion, which in the extreme proves a total *unwillingness* to have behavior controlled. This unwillingness may relate to factors that will be elaborated in later chapters. But in the context of the coercive nature of enforcement, consider the following:

> a widespread belief that police are unjust or brutal results in loss of respect for, and cooperation with, any police officer. When people do not accept police authority . . . the police feel the need to assert personal authority by force. . . .[14]

Unwillingness to accept enforcement, then, can become the proverbial two-way street; the more unwilling people are to accept enforcement, the more *certain* police may respond in ways that create yet further unwillingness.

But the totally resistant person is not the only enforcement problem. There are many shades and degrees of resistance to having behavior controlled by coercion. In most cases, however, regardless of the degree of unwillingness, the resistance to enforcement has to do with not recognizing the exchange of conformity for personal safety. Put another way, when resistance to enforcement occurs, at least one probable factor has to do with people and police not having a clear understanding of the behavioral conformity necessary for police to provide the orderly environment. This then suggests further consideration of the *willingness* of members of the community to exchange their conformity for personal safety, property security, and freedom.

Willingness to Accept Enforcement

President Dwight David Eisenhower has been quoted by many as saying "There is no liberty worth anything which is not liberty under law. . . ." Even more relevant to the citizen's willingness to accept enforcement is president Theodore Roosevelt's often quoted comment: "No man is above the law and no man is below it; nor do we ask any man's permission when we require him to obey it."

In spite of these profoundly eloquent quotations, law enforcement personnel constantly encounter varying degrees of evidence that *full* acceptance of enforcement is far from a reality, at least full willingness to *support* law enforcement.

Such unwillingness of any segment of a community to support or even accept enforcement creates yet further police problems in dealing with hardened career criminals, the "real criminals" who appear (to some) to be beyond the help of social scientists.

> In the past man legitimatized his myths by cloaking them in a shroud of religion. But today we buttress our myths with pseudo-science, unnecessary technical jargon, and overintellectualized, often confusing theories. In the final analysis, we have duped ourselves into believing these criminalogic fictions. . . . After years of experience

[14]Eleanor Harlow, "Problems of Police–Community Relations: A Review of Literature," *Crime and Delinquency,* Feb. 1969, p. 4.

working with incarcerated offenders, the authors have come to realize that the source of crime involves choice, not genes, not drugs and alcohol [not] poverty. . . ."[15]

To whatever degree the hardened career criminal constitutes a separate challenge for police, any unwillingness on the part of other members of the community to support law enforcement compounds the problem and weakens law enforcement enough to justify serious effort to develop community support.

Fortunately, the majority of most communities willingly accept and even support law enforcement to some degree. Yet changes in our society bring ever increasing demands that police reach out to the smaller groups who do not support enforcement. Throughout this volume emphasis will be placed on the rewards to police, not just the minorities, when such efforts succeed.

In closing this discussion of the nature of enforcement, emphasis is placed on the reality that enforcement is an absolute necessity, is in no way optional, and is necessarily negative in the sense that it remains coercive. Furthermore, the nature of enforcement includes recognition that police have designated authority and are intended to have sufficient legitimate power to enforce the law, however complex the law becomes.

With regard to such complexity, Chapter 3 will address the confining characteristics of constitutional government on enforcing law.

SUMMARY

This chapter presented law enforcement as the common denominator among all American communities. It was pointed out that police need community support and community needs law enforcement. Also noted was the high priority that police should give to creating a positive public image, and this in turn was used as an emphasis point for arguing the need for community support of law enforcement.

The chapter introduced the nature of enforcement in terms of the rationale for enforcement rather than the methods and techniques of enforcement. Cited was the significance of limiting force to the level required combined with the authority and power to use force.

The chapter elaborated on the community's need for enforcement in terms of controlling competitive and survival behavior, adding the importance of personal safety, property security, and keeping the peace.

The chapter also briefly highlighted the background of evolving enforcement as a concept throughout history. Also elaborated on was the coercive element of enforcement in terms of the unwillingness of individuals to accept and support police practices.

[15]Glenn D. Walters, and Thomas W. White, "Crime, Popular Mythology, and Personal Responsibility," *Federal Probation,* Mar. 1988, pp. 24, 25. For a contrasting view in support of scientific analysis of criminal justice, see, for example, James R. Davis, *The Science of Criminal Justice,* Jefferson, NC: McFarland and Co., 1986.

The chapter noted the significance of the police's designated power and authority to regulate behavior as a background and a context for the discussion in Chapter 3 of the enforcement limitations posed by constitutional government.

DISCUSSION TOPICS

1. Elaborate on the reciprocal relationship of police and community in terms of police need for community support and community need for law enforcement.
2. Discuss what was noted in this chapter as the high priority police give to obtaining a positive public image.
3. Discuss this chapter's presentation of the *nature* of enforcement in terms of the rationale for enforcement rather than the methods and techniques of enforcement.
4. Discuss *coercion* in terms of the nature of law enforcement.
5. Relate the historical development of law enforcement to contemporary law enforcement problems.
6. Define the significance of society appointing police to exercise the authority and power necessary to enforce societal rules.

Relevant Problems for Discussion

Enforcement of society's rules was presented in this chapter as an absolute necessity in every community. Emphasis was placed on the police need for community support. The problem, or at least the potential problem may exist in police seeming to weaken their enforcement capability by courting and vying for the community support needed.

Put another way, *effective* enforcement suggests strength and power. Seeking support *may* run the risk of appearing to be some form of supplication or begging, or may create other images not commanding respect, or may appear weak and without power.

Obviously, police must retain the capability to provide the needed enforcement, so how to also gain community support becomes the question. The *theoretical* answer is to work from a position of authority and strength with community leaders in developing common police–community goals. But, as a *practical* matter, most communities have many different leaders whose goals are not the same or even similar, all of which creates pressure for compromise.

Compromise is not necessarily a negative factor in community relations unless the community's need for law enforcement is obscured. In this regard, usually a brief discussion with almost any group of *why* police should carry guns tends to establish the need for the community to have enforcement. Nevertheless, the paradox of police appearing so weak that they have to seek help from the community is a risk worth note in efforts to gain community support. This places emphasis on the style, strategies, and activities required to resolve the problem; intelligent and sophisticated approaches are needed. This in itself constitutes a strong argument in favor of professionalism in law enforcement.

3

Enforcement Limitations Within Constitutional Government: Argument for Professionalization

The fourth amendment to the United States Constitution reads "the right of the people to be secure in their persons, houses, papers and effects, against unreasonable searches and seizures, shall not be violated, and no warrant shall issue, but upon probable cause. . . . "[1] What do these and other guaranteed rights mean to police–community relations? The answer to that begins by examining what these rights and other rights have to do with enforcing law anywhere in America.

To get an initial feel for how the individual rights of American citizens affect police work, consider the following as one of many routine law enforcement situations:[2]

> Shortly after an armed bank robbery, a police officer approaches a man who matches a description of the robber. He orders the man, at gunpoint, against a wall, and pats down his clothing, discovering a handgun. Another officer encounters a well-dressed businessman collapsed on a downtown street. Searching the man's pockets, he locates

[1]See Appendix C and D. See also *Hale* v. *Henkle,* 201 U.S. 43 (1906) defining seizure, and *Brinegar* v. *U.S.,* 338 U.S. 160 (1949) defining probable cause, and *U.S.* vs. *Jacobsen,* 466 U.S. 109 (1984) defining search and seizure, and *Maryland* vs. *Macon,* 105 S. Ct. 2778 (1985) defining seizure.

[2]John G. Salus, "Emergency Searches of Persons," *FBI Law Enforcement Bulletin,* Jan. 1988, p. 24.

cocaine. A third officer interviewing a juvenile suspect in the investigation of a recent homicide, spots what appears to be blood on the shoes of the youth. Without arresting the youth, he seizes the shoes.

Each officer has made an on-the-spot decision to conduct a search, and each officer has seized what may be evidence of crime. The searches have been made without warrants, because the officers were confronted with circumstances that appeared to require immediate action. In the prosecutions that follow, the defendants will likely challenge the admissibility of the seized evidence, claiming it was obtained as a result of violations of their constitutional rights. Because the searches were performed without warrants, the burden of establishing their legality will rest upon the government.

The complexities for law enforcement emerge as soon as it is acknowledged that the citizens for whom these enforcement services are provided and the suspected law violators within the community have *exactly* the same rights.

Chapter 2 presented the nature of enforcement as having to do with the necessity to regulate human behavior; this necessity acknowledges both the police need for community support and the community need for police to enforce the law. While it is true that the nature of enforcement is indeed that straightforward, there are nevertheless numerous restrictions and limitations on the methods, techniques, and general approach to law enforcement. The purpose of this chapter is to examine some of these boundaries within which law enforcement must operate and to further present those restrictions as a rationale for further professionalization of the police.

To more fully understand the restrictions imposed by constitutional government on the enforcement of law, this chapter will examine some of the highlights of the history of criminal law and further discuss *due process* as defined in the Bill of Rights. Before doing so, however, a brief consideration of the significance of *rights* will probably be useful.

It is doubtful that anyone who has watched a few motion pictures with a law enforcement theme has not heard the *rights advisement* — "you have the right to remain silent — if you give up that right. . . ." Regardless of how "red handed" a police officer apprehends an offender, these rights not only must be communicated to the arrestee, but also these and other rights must be conscientiously observed. Beyond the guarantees of the Bill of Rights, the criminal law itself increasingly reflects this requirement, which is reason enough to examine the background of criminal law in greater depth.

The Constitution itself, and particularly the Bill of Rights, with the concept of the *consent of the governed* combine with the criminal law to form stringent guidelines for law enforcement in most cases and absolute mandates in the rest. These restrictions impinge on the entire process of law and justice, not just police.[3] Yet it is the police who must first come to grips with the confines of constitutional goverment — before the decision to arrest is made.

Let us now examine some of the salient characteristics of constitutional government restrictions on law enforcement.

[3]For elaboration of this subject, see, for example, Howard Abadinsky, *Law and Justice,* Chicago, IL: Nelson-Hall Publishers, 1988.

CONSTITUTIONAL GOVERNMENT: RESTRICTIONS[4]

The term *restrictions* is not intended to imply anything negative. The laudable Bill of Rights, the Constitution itself, and the Supreme Court's review responsibility to interpret due process are all part of the world's most advanced democratic process. Nevertheless, they and other restrictions in effect create limitation on enforcement of law, and this must be understood. Ultimately, these restrictions must lead to even higher levels of police expertise and competence. This, in turn, it will be argued later in this chapter, is a rationale for increasing the professionalization of police.

But in the sense that the Constitution and Bill of Rights clearly limit many areas of enforcement, they are confining and must be understood as restrictions. Within these confines, government in general and law enforcement in particular must ensure the orderly environment needed by the community, that is, must regulate human behavior, as discussed in Chapter 2.

Constitutionally formed democracies actually differ little from other cultures or societies in the sense that individuals have what amounts to a contract to *permit* their conduct to be regulated in return for personal safety and some degree of property security. Virtually all societies provide for personal safety and most for property security. The significant difference in a democratic constitutionally founded government is that the government operates only with the *consent of the governed*. Even so, the governed are still expected to conform to numerous regulations and laws inherent in the many statutes at the state, local, and federal level, in exchange for the personal safety and property security provided by most societies.

Another salient difference between law enforcement in a totalitarian government and a democratic constitutionally formed government is the right of *dissent,* the right of the governed to attempt to change the rules that police enforce. To many, this appears to be a paradox. Police attempting to maintain an orderly environment may in effect appear to be retarding the right of individuals to dissent. Conversely, if police fail to deal with many forms of dissent, they are not keeping their part of the bargain; they are not maintaining an orderly environment.

In seeking to promote the orderly environment through law enforcement, government restricts human behavior to provide personal safety and property security. Personal safety and property security, being the rights of those protected, then come into philosophical conflict with the right of those wishing to dissent to change the rules. As we will argue later in this chapter, an extremely professional approach to impartiality and objective enforcement is an absolute requisite to success within these constraints.

Yet another factor in constitutional government of more consequence than in other forms of government is the significance of the *will* of the individual. Much of what is called the wisdom of the ages deals with the relationship between the *will* of the individual and the rules of the society. Indeed, this relationship between individual will and society defines much of what is called social problems. For, in the final

[4]Some parts of this discussion were published earlier in A. Coffey, E. Eldefonso, and W. Hartinger, *Human Relations: Law Enforcement in a Changing Community,* 3rd ed., 1982. Passages from pages 56–63. Reprinted by permission of Prentice-Hall, Inc., Englewood Cliffs, NJ.

analysis, the power of the individual is equally potent whether in support of or in dissent from the society's system of providing personal safety and property security. When the *will* of the individual, particularly when masses of individuals are of the same mind, is opposed to the orderly environment for which police are responsible, major law enforcement difficulties are likely. When the number of individuals whose *will* opposes the orderly environment exceed police capability of coping, society is no longer able to assure personal safety nor property security. Any veteran police officer will surely agree that without general public support complete law enforcement is not possible; indeed, without public support, very little enforcement is possible. This adds yet another confining influence in constitutional government, the question whether the general population is for or against the orderly environment as maintained by police.

Consent of the Governed

For the most part, popular elections determine whether the general population supports or opposes the government. The presidential elections every four years, the senatorial and congressional elections at the federal level, and the various legislative structures in the 50 states afford the population a continuing method of condoning or rejecting whatever it is they perceive as government activities. Sometimes accelerating the pace at which changes in government occur through this process are such factors as economical recessions, depressions, or excessive inflation, along with wars and other major generators of unrest.

In this process the *will* of the majority prevails, presumably satisfying those involved with the orderly environment for which police are responsible. Consider, however, the *will* of those without sufficient votes to change politically that which they perceive is unjust, unfair, or inappropriate. Put another way, in the context of restrictions in constitutional government on law enforcement, those in opposition to the orderly environment as provided by law enforcement should be of great concern to police when they are frustrated through the political process. Minorities have various political remedies and other approaches to resolving perceived injustices, but when all else fails, violence also becomes an option, another form of the "consent of the governed."

The constitutional democratic approach to governing, when structured on the basis of elected representatives, does tend to cause those without a majority viewpoint to lose in the elective process. Although many alternatives are available within the law, other alternatives may emerge that are outside the law, a particularly important point inasmuch as police are *restrained* from intervening until law violation occurs.

Not surprisingly, many of those in law enforcement feel they are compressed between two restrictive alternatives, either to suppress change or to make change, neither of which is a workable alternative for enforcing law within the confines of a democratic constitutional government.

In reality, law enforcement has neither responsibility—neither to suppress change nor to make change. Also in reality, however, law enforcement responsibility begins immediately when the change process includes violation of law; the frustration emerges when it is clearly discernible that social change is bringing about the probability of such violation.

But even though police have no legitimate responsibility to either suppress or make changes, law enforcement nevertheless retains a crucial interest in government reaction to social problems, if for no other reason than to get early warning. Suppression of change may be appropriate in a totalitarian government, but it is totally unacceptable in constitutional government, however clearly certain forms of change warn of probable law violation. Until the law is violated, the police role is at best to observe. In effect, this restriction on the police function limits the police role in most cases to keeping abreast of precisely *what* changes are being sought and by *whom* and to attempting to remain detached from the appropriateness or inappropriateness of such change, and monitoring only the orderly environment necessary to continue government operation.

Emphasis should be placed on the complete lack of options for law enforcement in this matter. While police have no option but to observe ominous social changes until law violation occurs, it is possible to conceive of potential problems in a way that permits police to endeavor to *promote* an orderly environment.

The variables involved in understanding the police role in *promoting* the orderly environment can be seen in Fig. 3–1. These conflicting variables can be understood more clearly in terms of law violation. Indeed, the *law* is frequently the only tangible factor in many of the complex quasi-social situations that are so much a part of our democratic society. To get a clearer picture of the role of *law* in this quasi-social milieu that police often find themselves in, a quick summary of how the criminal law evolved as part of the orderly environment should help.

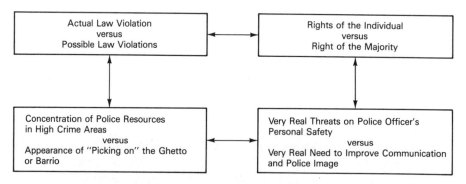

Figure 3–1 Orderly environment's conflicting variables—a few of many.

Background of Criminal Law[5]

This discussion of criminal law is not intended to deal with the technical aspects of jurisprudence. What is intended here is a generalized background of criminal law as

[5]This material was taken from E. Eldefonso, A. Coffey, and J. Sullivan, *Police and the Criminal Law,* Pacific Palisades, CA: Goodyear Publishing, 1972, pp. 5–12; with permission.

it relates to and underpins the police responsibility to enforce law and provide an orderly environment. The purpose of clarifying this crucial segment of restrictions on law enforcement is for the additional purpose of establishing the restrictions posed by the Bill of Rights, the Constitution, and particularly due process.

Common Law, Civil–Statutory Law, Criminal Law. For purposes of our discussion of due process of law, what we will call criminal law is actually a combination of early *common law* and Roman/French evolved civil–statutory law. Common law was derived from Germanic regions and later England, and has to do with developing law by using past court rulings as precedents. The civil–statutory law is written and legislated law. Common law remains "common" by using past court rulings on similar cases, and civil–statutory law uses specific, written, legislated law.

American criminal law incorporates both forms of law within the concept we will discuss as due process. For police, emphasis is on the civil–statutory law, or written penal codes that are legislated. In the judicial process, the past rulings of courts on similar cases are added to the penal code violation as an important consideration. In other words, due process combines both the common law concepts and civil–statutory law concepts.

Another important factor is the current use of the term civil law, in contrast with criminal law, in many police jurisdictions. Civil law no longer carries the original Roman/French meaning, but now is used to distinguish between criminal matters and noncriminal matters in court. Civil law by this definition has to do with torts and private lawsuits dealing with civil injury, and private wrongs.

Criminal law, by contrast, deals with specific violation of law that defines crime and seeks to prosecute those believed to have violated specific criminal laws.

Punishment for violating criminal law is intended to protect the public. Damages in civil matters are intended to correct a private wrong.

To avoid confusion with the two meanings for civil law, the term *statutory* law might be helpful. Figure 3–2 depicts the concepts involved in civil–statutory law, common law, criminal law, and due process.

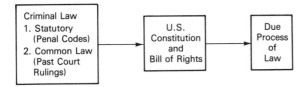

Figure 3–2 Criminal law, the U.S. Constitution, and due process.

In terms of examining the background of criminal law as part of the police responsibility for maintaining an orderly environment, an additional distinction may be useful. The common law is thought of as *accusatorial,* meaning just that, accusations. The civil law or statutory law is *inquisitional,* again meaning just that, an inquisition.[6] While these distinctions are useful for the purposes of understand-

[6]See, for example, A. Paulsen, and A. Kadish, *Criminal Law and Its Processes,* Boston: Little-Brown, 1962, pp. 993–1007.

ing the background of criminal law, they are not particularly significant in that American courts function under both. In this combination there is what some consider an excessive dependence on precedent; critics of judicial procedure at times complain of overemphasis on previous court rulings. This same body of criticism also cites what is perceived as excessive dependence on constitutionally dictated *due process,* a subject that we will discuss in more detail later in this chapter. Both precedent and due process relate more to common law than to what is referred to in this discussion as civil law or statutory law.

From a law enforcement perspective, however, the codified law, the legislative law, is far more relevant. Penal codes are statutory law even in jurisdictions where the statutes themselves cite the common law as a source of penal code violations, a jurisdictional matter that we will note later in this discussion.

The penal code of a jurisdiction is a codified statute known technically as *substantive* criminal law. Obviously, substantive criminal law is of particular concern to police because it is through this form of law that society prohibits homicide, rape, assault, robbery, and similar crimes against the personal safety, property, and security of individuals or other threats to the orderly environment. The two major categories of substantive criminal law violation that are best known are called *felonies* and *misdemeanors.* In most cases, the *penalty* for the particular offense determines the classification; felonies are punished more severely by prison, whereas misdemeanors are punished by jails and fines.[7]

In a discussion of the confines of constitutional government on law enforcement, it should be noted that the confusing concept of using punishment to determine whether a crime is a felony or a misdemeanor has more to do with the judicial process than with law enforcement. Law enforcement procedures must be adjusted in terms of the *severity* of the offense, but it is the judicial process that imposes the sanctions. Nevertheless, the concept of criminal liability, which also flows from the severity of the offense, holds not only the offender criminally liable, but also those who conspire with or abet the offender in the criminal act. It is not unusual for police investigation to include "accessories before or after the facts" that flow from this concept.[8]

In terms of restrictions on law enforcement, most jurisdictions codify specific limitations on police procedures insofar as a *misdemeanor* is concerned in contrast with a felony offense. In either case, the apprehension of the offender introduces police to the nature of criminal law and the confines of constitutional government.

In the case of misdemeanors (particularly traffic violators), the police's introduction to criminal law is often direct. Frequently, he or she not only arrests an alleged violator but directly participates in the court process. In the case of felons, his or her introduction to criminal law is frequently partial. By partial, we mean that the officer may or may not have further involvement in the criminal justice process. Following the arrest, the officer's direct involvement in the court process is in most cases up to the prosecution, and in certain rare instances up to the defense attorneys.

[7]49 *American Law Review,* 2nd 1223; 72 *American Law Review,* 2nd 434.
[8]86 *American Law Review,* 2nd 259; 95 *American Law Review,* 2nd 166.

But even in matters in which police are not directly involved following arrest, the court process remains a significant function insofar as police investigation is concerned; police investigations are quite frequently the total basis for prosecution.

And, as we will note later, the court's review of the accused's rights before, during, and after arrests make police activity extremely relevant to the prosecution. The *history* of the rights of offenders is most relevant in examining the confines of constitutional law on police.

The common law heritage of American criminal law is best understood through a review of the main sources of individual rights. Extremely significant legal immunities have evolved through the common law developed in medieval England. The right to *habeas corpus* is generally acknowledged as the primary source of individual rights and immunities.

Habeas corpus as a concept deals not with guilt or innocence, but rather the power of a judge to require that a prisoner be brought before the judge to determine the *legality* of the detention.[9] The right to habeas corpus was negotiated with English King John in A.D. 1215 and, though extremely important, many historians feel it is no more significant than the *Magna Carta rights* to jury trial.

Early English common law courts were presided over by judges doomsmen, who were, in general, neighbors of the participants in most court actions. During the Norman Conquest, William the Conqueror removed all ecclesiastical matters from the jurisdiction of the common law courts. This seemingly slight modification, however, resulted in an extremely elaborate system of ecclesiastical courts. These ecclesiastical courts, rather than adjudicate common law, dealt with *canon law*, at times obscuring the jurisdictional responsibilities of the common law courts. This dual court system functioning in medieval England brought into focus the *inquisitional* judicial procedure in contrast to the *accusational* judicial procedure, which is of extreme relevance to the enforcement of American law, which ultimately evolved to the *accusational* procedure.

The ecclesiastical courts of medieval England were modeled after similar courts in Spain during the infamous era of the Spanish Inquisition. The clergy of England performed their nonsecular judicial duties with the judge or judges acting as both prosecutor and jury. The inquisitional judicial procedure was more often than not conducted in secret. Someone who was accused or suspected was *compelled* to answer questions, although the physical force and tortures employed by medieval ecclesiastical courts in England were generally less severe than the brutal interrogation methods of the Spanish Inquisition.[10] Some of the characteristics of these inquisitional court procedures have survived to this day in modern America. Vestiges of the inquisitional system include the *grand jury,* the *coroner's inquest,* and certain secret legislative inquiries. The secret, inquisitional process in many respects retains the original characteristics of the *star chamber* on which the inquisitional process is modeled.

[9]19 *American Law Review,* 2nd 789.

[10]See, for example, A. Seagle, *The History of Law.* New York: Tudor Publishing Co., 1946, pp. 336–352.

Originally, the star chamber was a secret court held by the monarch in order to prosecute a person considered too powerful for an ordinary jury to remain unintimidated. Star chamber proceedings differed from the common law courts in that the star chamber was secretive. Other variations from the typical common law court were that a star chamber hearing was initiated by a "secret arrest," which could be made without indictment or charge and was frequently followed by confessions induced by torture. Other methods of dealing with the accused were the oath ex officio, a means of requiring a person to in effect accuse himself. So gross were the abuses of the star chamber with its *required* self-incrimination that the entire constitutional law structure of America explicitly forbids this approach. Eventually, what was termed the petition of light in 1618 provided that an accused person could not be required to incriminate himself.[11] This is extremely important in understanding the constitutional restrictions on American law enforcement.

With the passing of the inquisitionally oriented ecclesiastical courts of medieval England, jurisprudence returned to the *accusational,* or accusatorial, methods of the common law. But with the return of the predominantly common law came the problems of making the judicial process relevant in light of changes that had occurred decades or even centuries after the judicial precedence of the common law had been established. Put another way, part of the problem of returning to a law based on precedence was that the precedence was perceived as outmoded.

It is noteworthy that the statutes that would constitute the bulk of American criminal law customarily include common law in effect in England as of A.D. 1603, at least in a limited manner. In some jurisdictions, the common law has been recognized as the actual basis of criminal law. This permits a state to prosecute offenses that were considered crimes in England in 1603 even though there exists no statute defining such an offense to be a crime.[12]

The federal court system is an important exception to this liberal use of common law. In the federal court system, violation of a written statute or regulation is required for prosecution. Other interesting exceptions include Louisiana, Puerto Rico, and the Virgin Islands, where the judicial structure is completely independent of the common law tradition. Nevertheless, most jurisdictions derive their approach to criminal law and the restrictions on law enforcement from the common law heritage.

This common law heritage continues to be of significance to understanding the restrictions on enforcing law in constitutional government. The specific statutory criminal laws that make up the penal code evolved from common law in most cases. The body of laws that underpin police authority to ensure an orderly environment was shaped by the common law philosophies in most cases. More specifically, the definitions of crimes and their punishments flow from the influence common law had on most state legislatures. The most salient feature of the American criminal law system is the legislative decision to be guided by the common law itself, which, in effect, makes a kind of civil law out of the common law—a common law codified.

[11]Ibid., pp. 211–225.

[12]A. Plunkett, *A Concise History of Common Law,* 5th ed. Boston: Little, Brown, 1956, pp. 307–315.

In terms of the controls placed on the enforcement of law in America, it is noteworthy that from this very early inclusion of the concepts of rights and liberties from the Magna Carta an additional factor was integrated, the fierce independence of the early colonies. See Fig. 3-3.

In terms of this independence, the colonies prospered and grew steadily more self-reliant during the first century of their existence. It was absolutely necessary to become self-reliant because of the chaotic political condition that existed for nearly a hundred years following the establishment of a colonial economy in England; the mother country did not support, but rather drew from colonies.

This self-reliance proved to be a major influence in not only the adoption of both civil and common law, but in the forging into the Constitution and the Bill of Rights the Magna Carta philosophy with regard to individual rights and freedoms. In effect, this combination of variables, evolving through history, created what now must be recognized as the main restrictions on law enforcement posed by constitutional government.

One of the more significant of such restrictions is the concept of *presumption of innocence*. In effect, this philosophical position evolved to an absolute constitutional right—a presumption of innocence until proved guilty.

Presumption of Innocence[13]

Every student of criminal justice is familiar with the concept of constitutionally guaranteed due process, the extension of the common law just discussed. Due process is a path that *must* be followed until the accused person is *proved guilty,* within the strict confines of procedures governed by constitutionally guaranteed rights. The procedures do in fact make a presumption of innocence. Briefly, here's how these procedures (due process) work.

The person charged with a crime is in effect *protected* by the Constitution not only until proved guilty, but in many respects after proved guilty; convicted felons have protected rights.

The United States Constitution and the first ten amendments known as the Bill of Rights protect Americans from the federal government. The due process clause of the United States Constitution has evolved to a point that the Constitution also protects people from the state, evolving a little further each time the Supreme Court rules on a relevant case. Primarily, however, it is the constitution of the particular state that must be examined to determine the specific rights an individual has against his or her own state. Whether dealing with the federal or state criminal justice system, various code sections and evidence rules, often including common law rules, give the defendant every guarantee of what is known as a fair trial.

One of the many reasons police should be fairly conversant with these guaranteed rights is the significance of arrest procedures. When guaranteed rights are violated, an entire prosecution is at risk. But guaranteed rights are out of the sphere

[13]This material was taken from E. Eldefonso, and A. Coffey, *Criminal Law, History, Philosophy, Enforcement.* New York: Harper & Row, 1981, pp. 136–140; with permission.

of control of law enforcement. For example, due process includes the right to demand a jury to decide disputed facts in the case. The accused may waive the jury trial if he or she understands the nature of the waiver and the risks involved. Another guaranteed right of due process is that an accused person has the right not to be tried twice for the same crime by the same jurisdiction, as a right against double jeopardy. Double jeopardy means no one can be tried for the same crime more than once; a hung jury is not an acquittal and in this instance a retrial for the same offense is not double jeopardy. From a law enforcement point of view, a given criminal act may be an offense under two jurisdictions and thus the defendant may be tried in both. A good example is an auto theft in New York City in which the car is driven through numerous states to Nevada. In this case, there are at least two crimes: a state violation of the penal code section that covers automobile theft, and violation of federal statutes covering criminal activities across state lines and, possibly, unlawful flight to avoid prosecution. The accused may be charged and convicted of both crimes, without being subjected to double jeopardy.

Still outside the sphere of police control, but more relevant to police activities, is the due process right of bail prior to conviction—a right except in certain circumstances when the court, or statute, determines bail is not possible. This

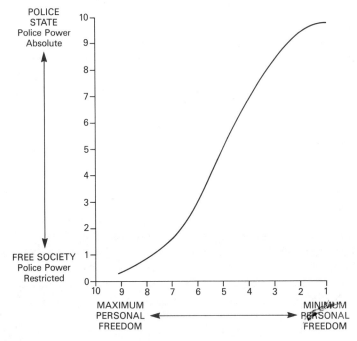

Figure 3-3 The impact of personal freedom on police power. The complexity of constitutional restrictions on criminal justice creates demands on police that can at times obscure the obvious inverse relationships between personal freedom and government power.

determination is customarily based on the severity of the offense and on the perceived likelihood of the accused fleeing the jurisdiction. Any offense punishable by death is a capital offense, and a good example of bail probably being denied.

Of particular significance in the ever increasing caseload of American courts is the due process right to a *speedy trial*. All accused have a right to a speedy trial. After arrest, he or she has the right to demand to be brought before a magistrate within a reasonable time, usually 48 hours. The defendant is also entitled to have his or her case adjudicated in an expedient manner. He or she may waive the right to open court. But unless the accused waives the right, the accused must be brought to trial within 60 days after the indictment of a grand jury or filing of information by the district attorney or prosecutor. If the defendant is not brought to trial, the case must be dismissed and further prosecution on the particular charge disallowed.

Recalling the discussion of police *symbolizing* the wrongs of the justice system, it is not uncommon for police to be blamed when individuals they have investigated and arrested are released. This is not to place blame on either the courts or the prosecution, but merely to acknowledge that the public perceives police more readily associated with a crime problem than other segments of justice.

A far more relevant factor in the guaranteed due process is the right to counsel at *every* stage of proceedings, including any police activity likely to culminate in arrest. The defendant has the right to counsel of his or her own choice at every stage of all proceedings in criminal justice in most states whether the defendant can afford counsel or not. Most states guarantee that if a defendant desires counsel and cannot pay the fee the court must appoint counsel for the defendant. The court should also inform the defendant of this right; Supreme Court rulings in the past have hinged on the failure of the court to inform the accused individuals of their rights. More significantly, a number of court decisions have hinged on a police officer's failure to inform the accused of this right.

The accused may waive the right to counsel. It is incumbent on an arresting officer to document as much as possible that this waiver is valid. In the court proceedings themselves, the court cannot force counsel on the defendant because another of the defendant's rights is the right to act as his or her own attorney. But whether it is a police officer or a judge, the weight of the Constitution so strongly underpins the right of counsel that every effort must be made to document the defendant's waiver; and in the case of the court, a waiver must be an intelligent decision as determined by the judge.

Of significance to police in terms of confessions, the fifth amendment guarantee of due process includes "no person . . . shall be compelled in a criminal case to be a witness against himself. . . ." This protection against self-incrimination is of particular significance to law enforcement charged with the responsibility of apprehending and gathering initial evidence, including confessions.

Noteworthy in the preparation of a case for prosecution is the fourteenth amendment's incorporation of this protection against self-incrimination for witnesses as well as the accused. In other words, the states are prohibited from forcing testimony from witnesses that may incriminate the witness. The court has an explicit duty to warn the accused of his or her right not to testify. The court must also accept

WAIVER OF RIGHTS AND WARNING
1. You have the right to remain silent and are not required to answer any questions.
2. Anything you say can and will be used against you in court.
3. You have the right to consult an attorney before you answer any questions, and an attorney may be present during the questioning.
4. If you have no funds to hire an attorney, the Public Defender will provide you with one to represent you at all stages of the proceedings.

Figure 3-4   Your rights constitutionally guaranteed.

the refusal of witnesses to testify based on self-incrimination — the famous "take the fifth" concept.

In terms of due process, police have little involvement in the determination of whether or not a defendant will testify. However, the prosecutor for whom the police gather evidence may be confronted with a restriction against commenting to a jury on a defendant's refusal to testify. Conceivably, the jury may be psychologically influenced by the defendant's refusal to take the stand and defend himself; but it would be what is called prejudicial error for the prosecutor to comment on this, an error that may lead to a successful appeal of any conviction. What is most important in this with regard to law enforcement is that the restriction against commenting on self-incrimination extends not only to the time of trial but also to the time of the defendant's arrest and anytime before or after when he or she claims the privilege against self-incrimination.[14] A police officer can unwittingly jeopardize the prosecution's case by failing to respect this constitutionally guaranteed privilege against self-incrimination.

In response to the turmoil and unrest that occurred in the 1960s (which will be discussed in Chapter 6) Congress passed the Omnibus Crime Control Act of 1968 and attempted to reverse what many perceived as the extremes, such as a *Miranda-type decision* forbidding the inclusion of evidence if some minor technicality in due process was bypassed. Specifically, there is an effort to provide for the admissibility of confessions on the basis of whether or not they are voluntary, even if the individuals rights were not known at the time. The doubtful question of voluntariness of a confession is left by such legislation to the determination of the court, thus having little *major* impact on the overall enforcement of law. It is noteworthy that a

[14]*Miranda* vs. *Arizona,* 384 U.S. 436 (1966).

prosecutor making an inappropriate comment on the defendant's failure to testify does not *necessarily* mean the reversal of a conviction.[15] If the appellate court finds that the prosecutor's comments about the accused's failure to testify were only harmless error, whatever that might mean in a particular jurisdiction, the appellate court is unlikely to reverse the conviction. Nevertheless, it is prudent for prosecutors to avoid the risk if the case is otherwise sound.

When the defendant opts to take the stand and testify, most jurisdictions allow the prosecutor some latitude in commenting on matters that the defendant fails to address, such as information the defendant probably had but failed to offer in testimony. Of little direct concern to police, but of considerable significance in terms of the prospects of conviction, is the defendants *waiver* of his or her right *not* to take the stand and testify. If the waiver is valid, the defendant can be asked questions about the nature of the alleged crime committed, as well as questions that might impeach the testimony and raise in the jury's mind the question of the defendant's credibility. A confusing debate among and within jurisdictions is the question as to whether or not the defendant must answer questions concerning other crimes previously committed. Some states hold that the defendant must answer all questions because he or she completely waived his or her right not to take the stand; other states narrow questions to those related to the specific crime to which the defendant is currently being tried. Yet another complexity is some jurisdictions allow impeachment of the defendant's testimony by showing collateral crimes. If a witness takes the stand in a trial for a previous offense, that testimony may, in some jurisdictions, be used against the defendant in the form of a confession or an admission.

Noteworthy with regard to the protection against self-incrimination is the concept of *failure to assert.* The concept means that where the accused person fails to assert the right against self-incrimination that right has been waived, assuming the person was advised of that right. From a police point of view, difficulties in this area lie in two areas: First, does the partial disclosure completely waive the person's privilege against self-incrimination. That is, does partially incriminating oneself necessarily waive the right against self-incrimination in other areas? Most states have held that if an individual makes a partial disclosure he or she may be questioned about all the facts concerning the alleged crime. The second and more difficult question is, What is meant by an incriminating question? Put another way, how do we define those questions in which the failure to assert could be thought of as a waiver of rights? Most courts hold that a question can be thought of as incriminating if the answer would bind the accused directly or indirectly to the commission of a crime or provide leads from which further arrests or criminal prosecution could result. Most courts hold that a question is incriminating only if it could result in *criminal prosecution.* If a crime is not directly or indirectly involved, the individual cannot claim the privilege against self-incrimination.

This is an extremely important distinction for police. Although the emphasis of this chapter is on the restrictions on law enforcement, it should also be pointed out that successful law enforcement *requires* diligent effort to investigate matters insofar as the due process restrictions allow, and due process restrictions do allow

[15]*Griffin* vs. *California,* 380 U.S., 609 (1965) and *Chapman* vs. *California,* 386 U.S., 18 (1967).

inquiry into matters where crime is not directly or indirectly involved. For example, if an individual might lose his or her job or disgrace his or her family or be subject to some civil liability, he or she cannot claim the privilege against self-incrimination. The court has held in *Gardner* vs. *Broderick*[16] that any public employee that refuses to answer questions directly related to his or her official duties can be discharged from the job. However, even though a public employee may be fired from the job, the incriminating answers *cannot* be used against him or her at a subsequent *criminal* prosecution if he or she was compelled to testify by superior officers. In *Garrity* vs. *New Jersey*[17] a police officer made a confession to a superior officer under threat of losing his job. The court held that his confession was involuntary and therefore inadmissible at a subsequent criminal prosecution. The threat of removal from office has been held by the court to be coercive and inconsistent with the voluntary waiver required in the due process privilege against self-incrimination.

A crucial factor in due process that is of extreme relevance to law enforcement is the right of an accused individual to confront the accuser. A defendant always has the right to have a witness testify in his or her presence, a particularly significant factor in many forms of police intelligence and undercover work. The defendant or the defendant's counsel has the right to cross-examine the witness against the defendant, to seek the truth, and to impeach the witness if counsel can show the witness is lying, mistaken, hostile, prejudiced, or whatever. The jury must weigh the credibility of the witness; but from a law enforcement perspective, the significant factor is that the accused has the constitutional right to confront the witness, often forcing very serious undercover considerations regarding future cases.

Specifically, this right has to do with the Sixth Amendment providing that "in all prosecutions, the accused shall enjoy the right . . . to be confronted with witnesses against him. . . ." This right of confrontation exists both in the federal courts and the state courts, because the due process clause of the Fourteenth Amendment includes the Sixth Amendment privilege. The right to confrontation exists "in all criminal prosecutions" (the key phrase) regardless of jurisdiction. This right has even been extended throughout juvenile court proceedings since a 1967 ruling.[18] Criminal prosecution does not include investigative proceedings such as legislative inquiries, coroner's inquiries, grand jury proceedings, or any proceeding that does not result in prosecution. It definitely does, however, refer to all prosecutions.

A related matter affecting law enforcement is the constitutionally guaranteed due process as it relates to informers. The United States Supreme Court has held that a police informer who testifies against a criminal defendant must reveal his or her name and address.[19] Regardless of the strain such a requirement may place on successful police intelligence efforts, this right is extremely strong. Defense counsel has the right to impeach the informer in much the same way as defense counsel has the right to cross-examine whoever is accusing the defendant. The attorney may attack the informer's credibility as a witness or other areas that might discredit the informer.

[16]329 U.S. 273 (1968).
[17]385 U.S. 493 (1967).
[18]*In re Gault,* 387 U.S. (1967).
[19]*Mith* vs. *Illinois,* 390 U.S. 129 (1968).

Police are not restricted to this constitutional guarantee in terms of obtaining search warrants or an arrest warrant; the courts often hold that the identity of police informers is not constitutionally required to be revealed to obtain such warrants. Nevertheless, this is an absolute requisite for prosecution.

This also relates to the concept of *probable cause.* In *McCray* vs. *Illinois*[20] the Supreme Court held that police did *not necessarily* have to reveal the informant's identity to establish *probable cause* for arrest and search. The court held, however, that it was necessary that the police testify to the informer's reliability to establish the validity of *probable cause.* In this reasoning, if the identity of the police informant is not *directly* material to the guilt or innocence of the defendant, his or her identity need not be revealed. The court emphasized some pertinent guidelines. The police officer, in open court, must describe in detail what the informer told him. The judge must be satisfied that the officer is telling the truth. When the judge makes this determination, the police officer's testimony can be admitted as evidence. Procedurally, there are many other significant factors having to do with due process. For purposes of this discussion, however, we have probably examined the due process sufficiently to establish the theme of this chapter—the confines of constitutional government on enforcing the law.

But the nature of due process is not the only restriction on law enforcement in constitutional government. Among other factors making the enforcement of law more restrictive is the very complexity of jurisdictional authority in American criminal justice.

COMPLEXITY OF JURISDICTIONAL AUTHORITY

As noted in Chapter 1, confusion, or at least potential confusion, exists in the variety of jurisdictional authorities inherent in each component of the criminal justice system. This complexity of jurisdiction is yet another limitation on the enforcement of law in constitutional government. Those appointed to enforce the law must have the *statutory authority,* with all the statutory restrictions, to enforce the law. These statutes are governed by the Constitution. But in the present context, the *complexity* of the wide variation in jurisdictional authority is yet another barrier.

Even the most conscientious, advanced students of law readily concede that no one person is aware of, let alone conversant with, *all* law, particularly when distinctions are made between federal, state, and local laws and ordinances. Even when divided into broad categories of law, relatively few claim complete expertise. Fortunately, this is not a serious problem because reference publications covering both case law and new legislation are available; the many sophisticated and timely summaries of recent court decisions and legislation can keep most criminal justice practitioners, including law enforcement personnel, reasonably well informed.[21]

But it is the public and the ordinary citizen that either complies with law or does not comply with law that should be of concern to law enforcement. It is

[20]386 U.S. 300 (1967).

[21]Abadinsky, op. cit.

unlikely that the typical citizen understands the vast array of law and ordinances intended to control his or her behavior or the wide variety of enforcement authorities empowered to ensure conformity. How then, in a constitutional form of government, can law enforcement expect law observance? From the ordinary citizen's point of view, this maze of sometimes conflicting law and seemingly disorganized jurisdictional overlap is so overwhelming that it is simply ignored. Even if the typical citizen attempts to understand certain laws, trying to grasp the comparative authority of various jurisdictions usually returns the matter to being ignored. Most individuals can see a clear distinction between the laws enforced by a traffic officer and the laws enforced by a border patrolman. But many would admit obscurity in attempting to distinguish between precisely what FBI agents do and what Secret Service Agents do—similar activities but different as well. Distinctions between lower court functions and higher court functions often are obscure at best, particularly when the complexity of the appeal court functions is included. It should not be surprising that many citizens conceive of probation and parole officers as more or less interchangeable in the state jurisdiction in much the same way that they are in reality in the federal correctional system.

A typical manner to resolve this confusion through ignoring it is to conceive of local police *as* criminal justice, as noted in Chapter 1. The problem with this symbolic role, however, is that the police cannot speak for other segments of the justice system, or for other segments of law enforcement for that matter. A combination of requirements of constitutional government sets up many jurisdictions. Add the due process restrictions to this complexity, plus the police rarely having the opportunity to explain the limitations on their responsibilities. The theme of this entire volume, the human relations approach to law enforcement, is that this very set of restrictions on law enforcement is the rationale for gaining community support for law enforcement. Gaining such support is by no means easy when the typical citizen is not conversant in the many limitations on law enforcement functions. Admittedly, this is patently unfair in that many of the problems we will discuss throughout this volume are totally beyond the ability of police to correct, and yet police must continue to strive for community support in coping with the consequences of those problems. Of necessity, coping with the challenge of gaining community support with so many inherent barriers in constitutional government requires the involvement of police management both in practice and in the trend toward police professionalization.

PROFESSIONALISM: RESPONSE TO COMPLEXITY[22]

Management Must Also Be Included

In acknowledging the significance of Sir Robert Peele's *Metropolitan Police Act of 1829,* Chapter 2 noted a turning point in the history of law enforcement—a turning

---

[22] A massive literature exists on police professionalism. An example of a very comprehensive approach can be found in Thomas J. Deakin, *Police Professionalism: The Renaissance of American Law Enforcement.* Springfield. Ill. Charles C Thomas, 1988.

toward professionalism in law enforcement. Since that time, many major contributions toward professionalizing police work have been made. In the opinion of the present writer, August Vollmer was one of the most significant of all the contributors to professionalized careers in law enforcement. Vollmer's writing and teachings have had great impact on all modern police training, information systems, and applied technologies.

The violence of the 1960s caused many to reconsider the strong comradery that underpinned professional law enforcement. A kind of community-oriented modification in some of the philosophical bases for police professionalism was made, and new leaders emerged, Patrick V. Murphy and Clarence Kelley to name two. Yet the commitment to meeting the challenge of increasing demand on law enforcement on a professional basis continues to be traced to Vollmer's writings and teachings.[23]

As the professionalization of law enforcement continues to evolve, the emphasis has tended toward preparing the working line officer to cope with the ever increasing complexities of police work. Certainly no one could argue against this trend as a need. But as the complexities of enforcing law within constitutionally guaranteed rights have increased for the working line officer, so also has the complexity of *managing* the police organization. Police management must increasingly be included as part of the growth of professionalism.

In the chapters that follow, a case will be made for police officials involving community leaders in policy setting, in the actual administration and management of the police function. The management skills and technologies involved in including community leaders, *while not abandoning the police mission,* are worthy of special attention and professionalization. The management techniques and methods required for success in this area are advanced and sophisticated. Put another way, the management of police agencies must involve those who represent the *will of the people* in designing services for those people, but must continue to accept the primary responsibility of maintaining an orderly environment and enforcing the law.

Beyond the need to integrate sophisticated and advanced police management techniques is the need to bring a *proactive* management attitude to the administration of law enforcement — proactive as opposed to reactive:

> Proactive leaders anticipate day-to-day events. They do not wait for events to reach them; they plan for events. They form a team that is flexible enough to seek a wide variety of solutions to the everyday problems of police management. This entails a deep commitment to contingency planning so that the eventual crises that do reach their desks do not overwhelm them. Crises, for the proactive police management team, are something to be dealt with and learned from, not simply reacted to.[24]

A proactive police official must, then, also be talented in the sense that the many abstractions and theoretical concepts impinging on police community relations do not obscure the law enforcement mission.

[23]Ibid.

[24]Edward A. Thibault, Lawrence M. Lynch, and R. Bruce McBride, *Proactive Police Management.* Englewood Cliffs, NJ: Prentice-Hall, 1985, p. 73. Reprinted by permission of Prentice-Hall, Inc., Englewood Cliffs, NJ.

A *talented* police leader is one who also has a high degree of intelligence. He or she must be able to understand theoretical concepts as they relate to the job and be able to create abstract plans and operationalize these plans. This involves a high degree of abstract manipulation of data and the ability to comprehend and make the most of the computer age.[25]

Later chapters will also make a case for simultaneously involving leaders of those minority groups who find themselves without sufficient political power to gain the votes it would take to be a part of the will of the people. Again this is a difficult management task for a police agency, requiring the most professional administration. But as we will see in later chapters, there is no real choice. Such involvement is necessary if for no other reason than the greatest potential problem for police exists among those very groups who are denied the political power inherent in the will of the people concept; the potential problem exists in the violent alternative available when political avenues are totally frustrated.

Sophisticated management technology required to approach these very difficult tasks also depends on training and education, as does all the professionalization of the police. It is therefore necessary to include management training in the professionalization curricula in all jurisdictions and, ideally, to approach it on a national level, bringing to bear the best thinking and the most promising management technology to police work.

In addition to the complexity of enforcing law within the confines of constitutional government, there are other arguments in favor of professionalizing the management of the police function:[26]

> The world's law enforcement executives and managers are today faced with making significant and difficult decisions regarding the acquisition of high technology. Some will silently allow central government engineers, programmers, and other specialists to make police technological acquisitions for them, with little or no law enforcement input.
>
> The various departments around the globe are at different levels of technological deployment. Yet, police agencies throughout the world are entering an era in which high technology is not only desirable but necessary in order to combat crime effectively.

If police administrators recognize that the constitutional confines on law enforcement are likely to increase rather than decrease, they can lead the way in professionalization, involving the most sophisticated approaches to management in the police organization. If however, police administrators do not involve themselves in professional growth, they are not providing a model of encouragement for the personnel who must confront the problems associated with due process, which are likely to increase in complexity. Personnel in such an unfortunate situation are unlikely to perceive education and training toward professionalization as an appro-

[25]Ibid., p. 25.

[26]Matt L. Rodriguez, "The Acquisition of High Technology Systems by Law Enforcement," *FBI Law Enforcement Bulletin,* Dec. 1988, p. 10.

priate goal. Such a situation will invariable punish police as the confines of constitutional government demand greater and greater skill levels merely to keep up with the fast paced changes.

Police officials can take heart in the increasing evidence that professionalization of the police in general is occurring, and to the benefit of law enforcement overall. Most dictionaries define profession as a occupation that demands advanced education and involves intellectual skills. It seems likely that there would be general agreement that these skills would include making judgments and using discretion in the area covered by the particular profession. This is extremely important in the context of recognizing the restrictions imposed on law enforcement by constitutional government.

Law enforcement within the confines of constitutional government requires professional skills in making the judgments and exercising the discretion necessary for police work, both at the line officer level and at the administrative level. In this context, the professional not only makes judgments and uses discretion but must of necessity hold the high qualifications necessary, for example, in the case of a physician, medical school internship and residency. While this medical model is often cited as comparable to police professionalization, there remains a difference in the level of development. In spite of this difference, in the field of law enforcement a great deal of the literature and many of the training courses on police subjects refer to *police professionalization* in a manner that almost suggests a clear comparison to medicine. In a sense, medicine continues to develop in terms of its body of knowledge; scientific research unfolds greater and greater understanding of disease and health problems. In this sense, a police profession is also in development.

The comparison of police and doctors on the basis of professional similarities may have begun to be taken seriously some two decades ago with a frequently reprinted, very widely read and appreciated analogy.[27] Shrewdly drawn comparisons of some reactions of police and doctors provoked substantial consideration. Even without the medical model, many states continue to expand and make specific certification of various minimum levels of police training. In some states, efforts continue to delineate training and experience in a manner that will justify issuing renewable licenses for certain categories of law enforcement. See Fig. 3-5.

While such certification and licensing are not intended to be at the same level as a license to practice medicine, the comparison of law enforcement and medicine continues as a kind of tone to written and spoken comments about police professionalism.

Not surprisingly, police administrators, managers, and line officers who are dedicated and serious about professionalization discuss the subject in the same manner — as though the precise body of knowledge for law enforcement exists *now*.

Perhaps the quickest way to examine the difference in the stages of the development of the police body of knowledge for the profession, compared to the medical body of knowledge for the profession, is to speculate on the basis of issuing a license to practice law enforcement.

---

[27]Victor G. Stretcher, "When Subcultures Meet; Police-Negro Relations," in Sheldon Yefsky (ed.), *Science and Technology in Law Enforcement*. Chicago: Thompson Publishing, 1967.

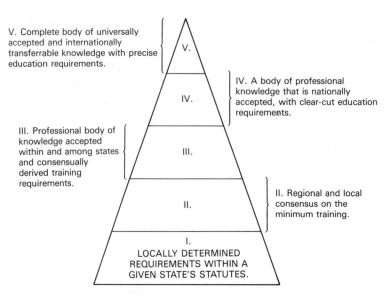

V. Complete body of universally accepted and internationally transferrable knowledge with precise education requirements.

IV. A body of professional knowledge that is nationally accepted, with clear-cut education requirements.

III. Professional body of knowledge accepted within and among states and consensually derived training requirements.

II. Regional and local consensus on the minimum training.

I. LOCALLY DETERMINED REQUIREMENTS WITHIN A GIVEN STATE'S STATUTES.

Figure 3-5 Levels of professional development. The professional standards for training, as well as education and experience, vary from state to state and from community to community. This variation, along with the complexity of constitutional limitations on law enforcement, impacts significantly on police professionalism.

Again, we are not contending that there is not a body of police knowledge. In some cases, the problem is more a matter of officers not receiving sufficient training in the body of knowledge that exists thus far:

> Police training is of paramount importance to both police supervisors and command personnel. Supervisors need to feel confident that their officers, at least, potentially know the fundamentals of the job. They also have to be concerned that their officers have a certain level of skill developed both in the technical aspects of patrol operation and defensive tactics as well as human relations skills.[28]

These human relations skills are probably the only skills still not fully developed into a transferable body of law enforcement knowledge. The technological methods of enforcing law are known and relatively easy to teach and relatively easy to transfer from jurisdiction to jurisdiction. The complexity of human relations skills in law enforcement begins with the reality that enforcement skill is a requisite part, but not the primary part. Furthermore, human relations skills demand sensitivity to the restrictions posed by constitutional government granting great individual freedom.

In this context, emphasis should be placed on the constitutional restraints on law enforcement, the body of knowledge that would place the professional police officer in the position to be licensed to practice constitutionally based enforcement.

[28]Thibault, op. cit., p. 253.

In any given jurisdiction, an argument could be developed that well-trained officers already exhibit the expertise necessary to hold such a license. But *unlike* the physician who can transfer her or his knowledge of anatomy, physiology, and pharmacology from state to state, police officers face an enormous difference between jurisdictions in the body of knowledge. An analogous common ground between a physician and a professional police officer would be what might be called "symptomology." A good physician, like a good police officer, will recognize symptoms related to their profession regardless of the jurisdiction—illness perceptible to the physician and criminal characteristics discernible by the professional police officer. Like medicine, there is a distinct difference in practicing law enforcement in a large urban area as opposed to a small rural area, and like the physician who finds major differences between practicing as a staff member in a large hospital and in small clinics, police officers find differences in the sizes of their organization.

Nevertheless, in the context of the confines of constitutional government, the *profession* of law enforcement is still in the developmental stage. A great deal of the body of knowledge necessary to build a profession already exists and continues to grow. Standardized agency accreditations and certifications have begun. Full professionalization may well be in the near future.

As full professionalization evolves, so also will we witness higher and higher standards of staff recruitment and training:[29]

> The training will become increasingly sophisticated. Law enforcement is attracting more and more college graduates. . . . Human relations skills including such topics as stress management will continue to grow . . . police training officials will attempt to fill in the technological gap with the use of the microprocessor revolution in communication. . . . Knowledge of communication has always been a significant need. . . . A curriculum providing basic human relations skills on an intense level. . . . A truly proactive department would synthesize planning and training in that both line officers and police supervisors would have a positive, "plan ahead" perspective. . . .

The human relations approach to law enforcement *is* a plan-ahead approach to law enforcement that recognizes the vast diversity of human conduct. Already a great deal is known about the human relations approach to law enforcement, certainly enough to establish minimum standards of police training in human relations. But the leadership, the *management* of police, appears to be *the* priority in police professionalization.

To continue to develop the body of knowledge necessary to have a *profession* that could conceivably lead to a license of necessity must prioritize management training. The management skill necessary to acquire the support of the community within the restrictions of constitutional controls on law enforcement is a high form of skill in itself. Beyond that, the leadership demonstrated by the administration seeking professional skills is a necessary influence on the continued growth of professionalizing line officers, a "practice what you preach" form of leadership.[30] It

[29]Thibault, op cit., p. 275.

[30]Good leadership enhances other factors as well. See, for example., R.G. Gilbert, R.O. Price, and C.W. Whiteside, "Characteristics of the Best Officers on the Force," *The Police Chief,* Sept. 1988.

cannot be overemphasized how important such leadership within law enforcement becomes as the complexity of constitutional government affects law enforcement.

Due Process and Constitutional Restraints
as a Reason for Police Professionalism

Through this chapter we have highlighted some, by no means all, of the complex restrictions on enforcing law. Police of the last century would probably be astounded at the never ending demand for new skills and new attributes in law enforcement. The professionalization of police no doubt is a reflection of the increasing constraints on enforcing law and the evidence that such constraints are likely to increase. Recognition of these constraints reached a peak in the 1960s and 1970s. In effect, in these two decades the restrictions of constitutional government formed an incentive to develop the professional skills needed to cope.

The vast literature on law enforcement and the generally demonstrated capability to cope with the most complex of social problems support the thesis that professionalization of police is occurring. Consider the certification of agencies.

The strides made in this direction include impressive gains in the sophisticated management technology that is being integrated into more progressive police organizations currently and promises to become more widespread in the future. In jurisdictions where advanced management concepts have been tried, police officials have demonstrated impressive results; they have demonstrated skill and talents necessary to integrate the widely divergent and hugely conflicting variables imposed by constitutional government during periods of rapid social change.

The significance of the police coming to grips with the confines of constitutional government is particularly crucial in terms of need for community support, the main theme of this entire volume. In terms of gaining such support from the community, Chapter 4 will examine the subject of selective law enforcement.

SUMMARY

This chapter cited the significance of the *consent of the governed* concept in terms of its impact on law enforcement and the status quo. Also presented were the restrictions on law enforcement posed by the social contract between the individual and the governed. The social contract obliges the individual to conform to law by a series of stringent constitutional guarantees.

Government was also presented as obliged to assure an orderly environment in return for the conformity of the consenting governed. A paradox was noted in the obligation of enforcement to support laws as laws change; what was once forbidden can become the behavior enforcement supports as laws change. It was noted that enforcement must deal equally and impartially with those who resist change and those who favor change.

Contradictory influences and requirements were noted in terms of law violation, individual and group rights, and the efficient use of police resources. Criminal law enforcement by police was highlighted in terms of its background.

The impact of guaranteed due process on law enforcement was examined. The complexity of jurisdictional authority was noted in the context of police being the most visible segment of justice.

The inclusion of organizational management in the turn toward professionalization was supported. It was noted that professionalizing police is increasingly necessary in terms of the complexity posed by modern American life and particularly the confines of constitutional government.

DISCUSSION TOPICS

1. Elaborate on the significance of *consent of the governed* in enforcing American Law.
2. Discuss what the chapter presented as a social contract between the individual and the government.
3. Elaborate on the government's obligations to provide an orderly environment in exchange for conformity by the consenting governed.
4. Discuss what the chapter presented as a paradox in terms of the obligation of enforcement to support laws as laws change and then to support the laws that replace such laws.
5. Elaborate the rationale for including *management* in the professionalization of law enforcement.

Relevant Problems for Discussion

The restrictions on American law enforcement that were presented in this chapter are further detailed in Appendixes B and C by noting selected sections of the U.S. Constitution and selected court decisions affecting law enforcement. In a democratic free society, these limitations on police cannot be defined as problems. However, the extraordinary effort needed to effectively enforce law within these restrictions can and does create problems.

The problem of violating the rights granted American citizens is a frequently cited matter. However, among the other problems created by the extraordinary effort to function within these restraints is the opposite problem, *excessive caution.* On the one hand, the Constitution, Bill of Rights, and continuing court decisions all rigidly uphold the rights of *anyone* accused of law violation. On the other hand, police reacting to such rights can conceivably become overcautious and may unwittingly reduce the deterrent effect that police are supposed to provide.

It is by no means a simple problem; trying to balance the rights of the accused against the safety of the public while striving to achieve the mission of the police is an ongoing process that depends on judgment and discretion rather than hard and fast rules.

Related to this problem is the added difficulty of *uncertainty* about the prosecution of the case and uncertainty about judicial dispositions of the case — uncertainties occurring at the very time police judgments and discretion are used.

From the law enforcement perspective, the balance of respect for the rights of the accused with the safety of the public and the mission of police is made more difficult by the often capricious outcomes of *any* police decision — a decision to arrest or a decision not to arrest.

Between these two extremes, not arresting those who should be arrested versus making arrests that violate constitutional rights, the goal is obviously to stay as much as possible geared toward public safety, but without violating the rights of the accused. In many cases, this does not allow for second guessing what the prosecutor or the court will do.

Philosophically, arguments can be made for and against arresting too few as opposed to arresting too many. The complex problem for police is to *not* become engulfed in either extreme while operating within the major restrictions of a democratic free society.

4

Selective Law Enforcement

Chapter 3 closed on the contention that the increasing complexity of law enforcement makes a good argument in favor of professionalism in police work.[1] Added to the growing complexities in law enforcement is the reality that we will repeat many times in many contexts: There are not enough police to enforce all law at all times and still keep the peace. The laws that can be enforced at any given time are in most cases *selective*. This chapter has that as the main theme — selective law enforcement.

We should acknowledge at the outset that all forms of selecting which laws to enforce carry some risk to the police image. Although we will establish the absolute necessity for police to be selective, it is obvious that small and large groups in every community *may* perceive selectivity in terms of excluding enforcement of those laws the groups favors.

The risks to the police image in selecting certain areas of enforcement for emphasis or de-emphasis also include the more serious risk of being perceived as being under the control of special interests — or, in the worse case, the risk of being subject to graft and corruption. There are exceptions, for example, the epidemic problem of drug abuse in this era.

[1] Complexity is by no means the only argument supporting the growth of professionalism in law enforcement. Many other equally significant arguments will be presented in later chapters.

DRUG TRAFFIC: EXCEPTION

In the present era, virtually every federal, state, and local legislature is coping with the public demand for stricter controls on drug trafficking and drug abuse. Most law enforcement jurisdictions are experiencing the same public pressure.

Public support, actually public demand for selective enforcement in the drug problem, can be viewed from this perspective:[2]

> Law enforcement has a responsibility to be involved in the prevention of all illegal or harmful activities. At this time in our nation's history, there is no crime problem or graver consequence than the drug problem. While law enforcement acts as a deterrent to drug abuse and drug trafficking, we know that the long-term answer to the drug problem goes beyond traditional law enforcement actions.
>
> The pervasive and complex nature of drug abuse in the United States requires an approach that incorporates both short- and long-range goals. The ultimate solution explicitly links effective drug enforcement with education for our youth, our parents, and our community leaders to prevent the demand for drugs in the first place.

As will be noted later in this chapter during a discussion of *public demand,* the police image is likely to suffer more from failure to respond to the demand to selectively emphasize drug enforcement than from treating drug traffic as just another crime problem.

But this is an exception in selective law enforcement, not the rule.

The reality of selective law enforcement is that police judgment and situational discretion determine *which* laws can be enforced with available personnel and resources and *when* such enforcement can take place.

Before pursuing this reality, let's review the conflicts in what is expected of police, conflicts that evolve from police role ambiguity.

On the one hand, police are expected to enforce law and, in doing so, deter criminal activity. On the other hand, police are expected to keep the peace, to provide the orderly environment discussed earlier.

If priority is given to enforcement in deterrence, it becomes clear the police would best be organized in a centralized manner, with emphasis on being highly specialized, with very strong command leadership, and with police *discretion* remaining mostly at the command or policy level. Ever increasing technology combined with the restrictions posed by constitutional government seems to favor this approach.

But when priority, or even mere consideration, is given to the task of simply keeping the peace (orderly environment), a more loosely organized police force is preferable; this force is decentralized and nonspecialized, working out of precincts or neighborhood offices, with discretion below policy-setting level.

Most would agree that police must integrate both of these factors if they are to

---

[2]Drug Enforcement Administration, *Law Enforcement's Other Role: Drug Demand Reduction,* Washington, DC: U.S. Department of Justice (Demand Reduction Section), July 1987, p. 1. For full elaboration of the material from which this pamphlet was taken, refer to Appendix F.

achieve an effective approach to dealing with modern crime. As a practical matter, it should be noted that no two jurisdictions in America deal with this organizational problem in *precisely* the same manner. Even when organizational structures appear identical, close examination reveals an extremely wide range of variation in the application of police *discretion*.

POLICE DISCRETION: ANOTHER ARGUMENT
FOR PROFESSIONALIZATION

We have already reviewed the complexity of constitutional government and its limitations on law enforcement as a rationale for the further development of police professionalization. The sometimes controversial subject of police discretion is yet another argument favoring professionalization.

Many of the controversies involving police practice either directly or indirectly relate to the discretion that police actually have, or are perceived to have, in choosing their mode of response to crime. This might be considered surprising in the context that most police activity is the type in which arrest and the discretion involved in arrest are not even relevant. Also, police discretion actually occurs at two or more levels, at the line officer working-the-street level and at various management levels. This raises the question in any discussion of discretion: Whose discretion?

Whose Discretion?

Controversy over police discretion and even the fear of such controversy probably account for the absence of a standardized administrative approach to this matter. Many police administrators approach the subject in terms of policy setting: the generation of guidelines and standard practices that substantially narrow the line officer's discretionary powers. In effect, this is an attempt to determine in advance what the pertinent discretion variables may be. Another substantial segment of police administration approaches the subject of discretion with a low profile by avoiding both policy statements and generalized guidelines, in favor of trusting subordinates to develop priorities that will prove appropriate when discretion is exercised.

The Low-profile Approach

When selective enforcement relates to such matters as parking citations in busy sections of the community, most police officials would agree that standardization and guidelines in such matters are appropriate. But when selective enforcement encompasses more serious matters, many police officials feel that a low profile is preferable, at least if wide publicity is not a significant need. In such a situation, guidelines and standards may or may not be issued insofar as discretion is concerned.

In defense of this approach, it must be noted that controversy often accompanies efforts to anticipate the many variables that may erupt into a demand for discretionary decisions. Indeed, eloquent arguments can be made for the position that, once all the known situations are named in guidelines, the sudden appearance of an unknown variable appears overwhelming.

The question of at what level the discretion *should* operate cannot be answered; the answer is a function of influences and forces that combine uniquely in each community. But, in general, it should be remembered that discretion operates to some degree at both the administrative level, with its various management levels, and at the line officer level.

The fear of controversies emerging over discretion utilized at any level may in part be the stimulus pressing the growth of police professionalism. As noted earlier, one of the most salient characteristics of any profession is the use of discretions based on known expertise. For our purposes here, the concept of discretion as to *which* laws to enforce and when to enforce them, and even how to enforce them, are the specific subject. But even in this context, the subject of police discretion continues to provide additional arguments favoring professionalization. But even with professionalization, there are simply not enough police to enforce all laws at all times and keep the peace at all times.

Put another way, coming to grips with the growing need to gain public support of law enforcement requires an understanding that there are not and never will be enough police to enforce all law at all times; discretion is not optional.

Examined out of context, choosing which laws to enforce can be potentially repulsive to the public. After all, laws are created to be enforced and usually with the belief that they will be enforced. But there are not enough police.

Need for Priorities

We by no means advocate ignoring law violation. It is instead advocated here that police prioritize the use of limited police resources as part of the effort to gain the support of the community for law enforcement. Specifically advocated here are clear guidelines for the working officer, as well as for supervisory and command personnel:[3]

> One of the critical elements that lead to the effective and efficient operation of any organization is written guidelines that establish the parameters for the behavior of its members. Organizational personnel cannot be expected to intuitively divine how an administrator expects them to behave, nor can they necessarily grasp the "big picture" within which the organization must function. Written guidelines can help to bridge the gap that often exists between how others expect officers to do their jobs and how they go about fulfilling the law enforcement function within a community without an understanding of those expectations. In preparing meaningful written guidelines for an organization, the law enforcement administrator should keep the following considerations in mind:

[3] James H. Auten, "Preparing Written Guidelines," *FBI Law Enforcement Bulletin,* May 1988, p. 7.

 Selective Law Enforcement   Chap. 4

1. Organizational goals and objectives must be developed.

2. Organizational goals and objectives must be examined to identify where the development of written guidelines will facilitate their attainment.

3. Prepare written guidelines after ensuring that the appropriate input is sought and considered.

4. Distribute written guidelines to all organizational personnel.

5. Conduct the training necessary to ensure that the intent of the written guidelines is understood and that the requisite skills and knowledge are acquired.

6. Evaluate and revise written guidelines regularly to ensure that they reflect the conditions current in the environment in which the law enforcement task must be carried out.

How Much Crime?

To appreciate the necessity of this prioritization, which we call here selective law enforcement, all police activities should be considered. This would be difficult to do in a quantitative manner, but *reported* crime may give some indication. The FBI annually reviews the national crime scene; an example of that review (Fig. 4-1) might afford an insight into the necessity to prioritize the community's enforcement efforts.[4]

What do these kinds of statistics suggest insofar as selective enforcement is concerned? First, such data confirm that there is a great deal of law violation. Equally significant for this discussion is the varying levels of severeness (some crimes are more severe than others), a subject presented later in this chapter. Another factor that can be drawn from such data is the obvious failure of deterrence; many offenders were not deterred. Furthermore, *a great deal of crime may have not been reported.*

Even if there are a lot more police officers, some offenses would not be deterred, but others would. Prioritizing certain selected laws for enforcement emphasis has the same effect as more police insofar as the laws that are selected are concerned.

With the numerous laws and ordinances on the books, these kinds of data are even more important in terms of prioritizing enforcement and for determining if success is achieved. But how, and perhaps when, do police need to choose the laws to be enforced with priority over other laws?

SELECTIVE LAW ENFORCEMENT[5]

Having noted that police discretion relates in many cases to controversy, further consideration of discretion is needed. In the context of community relations, the exercise of discretion always risks criticism, but, more significantly, it risks the appearance of *discrimination.* Recall the comments in the introduction to this chapter.

[4]Taken from "UCR Crime Statistics," *FBI Law Enforcement Bulletin,* Aug. 1988, pp. 7-9.

[5]See, for example, B. Reed, "Issues and Trends in Police Discretion," *The Police Chief,* IACP, Nov. 1980, pp. 54-59.

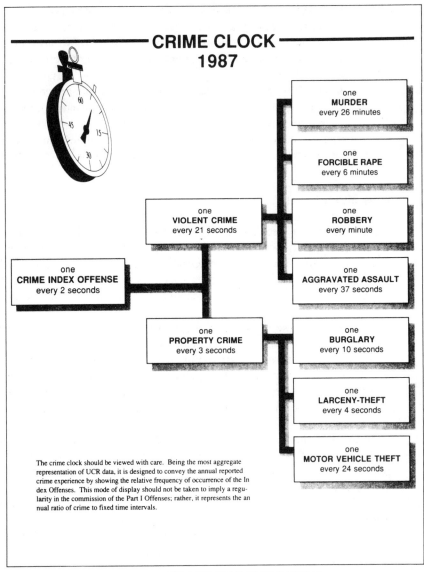

The crime clock should be viewed with care. Being the most aggregate representation of UCR data, it is designed to convey the annual reported crime experience by showing the relative frequency of occurrence of the Index Offenses. This mode of display should not be taken to imply a regularity in the commission of the Part I Offenses; rather, it represents the annual ratio of crime to fixed time intervals.

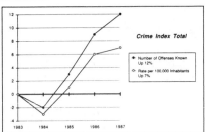

Figure 4–1 Crime clock "crime stats" supplement. (*FBI Law Enforcement Bulletin,* Vol. 57, No. 12, Dec., 1988, p. 9.)

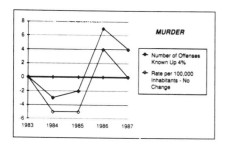

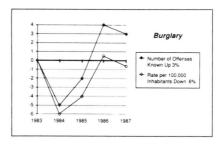

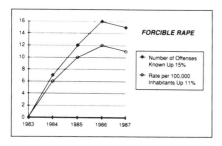

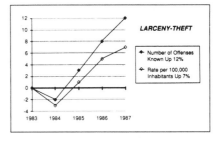

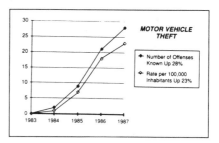

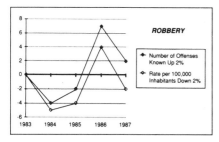

Crime Stats

January Through June 1988

Crime known to law enforcement agencies rose 1 percent in volume during the first half of 1988, as compared to the same period in 1987. The increase, recorded by the FBI's Uniform Crime Reporting Program, was measured by a Crime Index of selected offenses for which law enforcement agencies nationwide provided data.

Violent crime, as measured by the Index, increased 5 percent in volume. Among violent crimes, aggravated assult showed the largest increase, 7 percent. Forcible rape and robbery each increased 1 percent, while murder showed no change.

The property crime total increased 1 percent. In this category, reported motor vehicle thefts were up 8 percent, and larceny-thefts increased 1 percent. Burglaries declined 2 percent in volume, and the arson total remained stable.

Geographically, three of the four regions of the Nation showed increases in the Crime Index totals during the first 6 months of 1988 over the first half of 1987. The increases were 4 percent in the Northeast, 2 percent in the South, and 1 percent in the West. A decline of 2 percent was experienced in the Midwest.

The Crime Index total decreased 1 percent in the Nation's rural areas and in cities outside metropolitan areas. The suburban areas experienced no change, while cities with populations over 50,000 recorded a 3-percent rise.

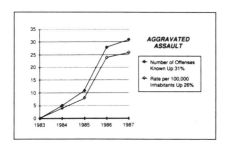

Figure 4-1 (Cont.)

Figure 4–2 illustrates the impact of factors that necessitate selectively enforcing law. Where these factors are overlooked or unknown to the public, the risks of appearing to discriminate tend to rise.

When police administrators anticipate this possibility, selective enforcement policy can be designed in a manner that reduces this risk. Line officers can also exercise discretion in a manner that reduces the risks of appearing discriminatory against a particular group or even a particular individual. The key is the involvement of community leaders in policy making or, at a minimum, the inclusion and *use* of input from community leaders.

Many believe that the failure of police to gain the support of the community in law enforcement has to do with the reluctance of police officials to incorporate community input in policy, a reluctance to allow the views of community groups to influence how policy controls police discretion.[6]

In the sense that selective law enforcement set by the administration in effect is intended to *curb* a line officer's discretion, some police officials tend to regard such policy as management that has nothing to do with community support for law enforcement.[7]

Obviously, the dictates of the laws themselves, the standards of prosecutors and court, and the statistics on serious crime are the major considerations, the primary concern of a police administrator in setting selective enforcement policy. But all these considerations are matters that can be explained to community leaders in the context of limited police resources. See Fig. 4–2.

The Laws Themselves

It is not uncommon for legislatures to include specific enforcement mandates that effectively eliminate discretion in specific crimes, particularly in certain violent crimes such as child abuse or "great bodily harm" in many jurisdictions.[8] Police officials who take the time to share this reality with community leaders have nothing to lose and stand to gain badly needed community support if law enforcement is to be successful.

The Standards of Prosecutors and Courts

The level of evidence required invariably translates into time and effort, usually by the police and usually at the expense of patrol or other police functions. This problem is so straightforward that community leaders rarely reject police providing information on this subject, at least if great care is taken to avoid the appearance of campaigning for more police officers.

[6]See, for example, Charles W. Thomas and John R. Hepburn, *Crime, Criminal Law and Criminology*. Dubuque, IA: William C. Brown, 1983, p. 357.

[7]Ibid. See also Report to the Nation on Crime and Justice, *Police Response to Crime*. Washington, DC: Bureau of Justice Statistics, U.S. Department of Justice, Mar. 1988.

[8]For elaboration on police discretion not under mandate, see, for example, M.R. Greerlee, "Discretionary Decision Making in the Field," *The Police Chief,* Feb. 1980.

The mere existence of police deters an unknown amount of crime. Police operations deters more. Yet there are not enough police to keep the peace at all times and enforce all law at all times. Selectively enforcing law is a necessity.

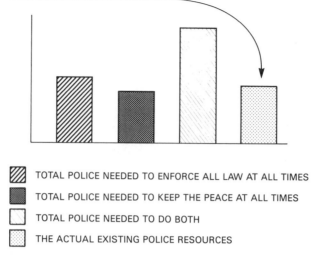

TOTAL POLICE NEEDED TO ENFORCE ALL LAW AT ALL TIMES

TOTAL POLICE NEEDED TO KEEP THE PEACE AT ALL TIMES

TOTAL POLICE NEEDED TO DO BOTH

THE ACTUAL EXISTING POLICE RESOURCES

Figure 4-2

Crime Statistics

Recalling the statistics presented earlier in this chapter, yet another avenue is open to police officials seeking to develop community support through involvement in selective enforcement policy. Statistics can be used to remove a great deal of potential controversy if *changes* in priorities must be made from time to time. The statistical increase of one particular type of severe crime is a readily understandable rationale for focus on that crime as opposed to continuing with a crime-specific program where the statistics show that crime is diminishing.

Put another way, when there is a consensus among community leaders on which crimes are the most serious, statistics reduce the arguments if enforcement priorities must change. Severity will be examined later in this chapter, but *statistics* quite frequently prove an excellent avenue of communication between community leaders and police officials.

Another matter of considerable importance in setting selective enforcement policy is the tax-conscious emphasis on avoiding the misuse of limited police resources (Fig. 4-3).

Efficient Use of Police Resources

Community leaders would probably be very interested in how wide the public demand for police services is; the typical citizen is likely to be astounded at the number of telephone requests for police services. Combine this astounding demand for police service with the walk-in request for services and in most jurisdictions,

Selective Law Enforcement

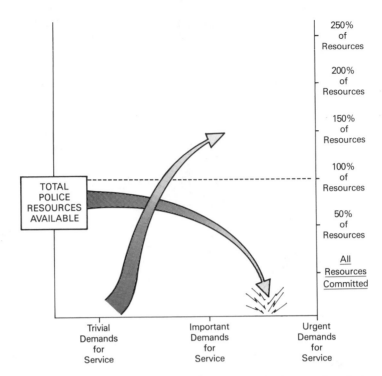

250%
of
Resources

200%
of
Resources

150%
of
Resources

100%
of
Resources

50%
of
Resources

All
Resources
Committed

TOTAL
POLICE
RESOURCES
AVAILABLE

Trivial
Demands
for
Service

Important
Demands
for
Service

Urgent
Demands
for
Service

Figure 4-3 Efficient use of police resources. Coping with the necessity of selectivily prioritizing enforcement practices is far more effective when community leaders understand at least part of the rationale dealing with a limit of police resources in relation to the demand for services.

whether big or small, an amazing variety of expectations from the public is apparent.

Then, too, the time of day calls come in, although somewhat patterned, never becomes predictable enough to distribute police resources accordingly; the real emergencies that erupt preclude such efficiency in planning.

Priorities for dealing with the demand for police service must then also include the concept of efficiency. But even though efficiency would be an ideal, the other priorities we have noted may or may not integrate *well* with efficiency; but limited resources require that the effort be made and that community leaders be informed.

Successful integration of efficient resource utilization into priorities requires more than analyses of available personnel. Establishing priorities has at least the potential for providing functional guidelines in selective law enforcement.

In its simplest format, the concept of priority can be seen by comparing *felonies* to *misdemeanors*. When a law violation that is a *felony* is in progress, a simultaneous *misdemeanor* would have a lower priority. Such a general abstraction allows the assumption that both command policy and line officer discretion would align with this *particular law enforcement.*

Police dispatcher. Personnel receiving calls from the public and dispatching police are an integral part of using police resources by predetermined priorities. (Courtesy of Santa Cruz Police Department)

Complex variables such as pursuit in progress may well justify certain modifications of this priority in certain circumstances. More tangibly, certain *misdemeanor* assaultive crimes against the person may well gain more legitimate police attention than a simultaneous property crime deemed in a particular state to be a *felony*. These kinds of considerations should encourage all groups in the community to perceive the police in a positive manner, an important factor if the support of law enforcement from the community is to be gained. But it is important to remind ourselves of the risks noted earlier in this chapter. The high risks of selective law enforcement appearing to persecute certain citizens is diminished by priorities on the efficient utilization of available personnel, which can be considered in the following context:

SEVERITY OF THE CRIME OR SITUATION

CRIME RATE IN A GIVEN AREA

PATTERN AND/OR TIME OF DAY

SPECIFIC CRIMES

CITIZEN DEMAND

From the perspective of police trying to gain community support for law enforcement, efficient personnel utilization is always the context in which any of these factors are considered. In this regard, CITIZEN DEMAND affords the greatest promise. But in reality the mandating nature of various penal codes in most jurisdictions forces first attention to *severity*.

SEVERITY

Felonies are more severe than misdemeanors and crimes against the person are more severe than property crimes. Riots in the street are more severe than most barroom fights, and armed robberies are more severe than most burglaries, exceptions in some penal codes notwithstanding.

Basic academy training generally acquaints the new police officer with this fundamental concept in prioritizing or selectively enforcing law. For this reason, it is not a significant training matter for police personnel.

What may be a significant educational matter for police to undertake has to do with communicating these factors to critics of the police—to acquaint the critics of law enforcement with the rationale for priorities relating to severity. Obvious though such distinctions between categories of crime may be to the professional practitioner, many community leaders are both appreciative and even surprised on learning the main considerations in such selective law enforcement.

Motor officer issuing citation. (Courtesy of Santa Cruz Police Department)

CRIME RATE IN A GIVEN AREA

Far more sensitive in terms of what was presented at the beginning of this chapter as risks for selective enforcement is selective enforcement by area—by neighborhood—a complex problem.

Efficient use of police resources may well be *the* rationale for setting a priority by area. But to both the citizens living or walking in the area and the citizens not in the area, selective law enforcement by this approach requires far greater clarity if it is to gain support or if it is at least to avoid severe criticism.

Challenging police efforts to clarify the reasons for selective enforcement by area is the frequent mixture of welcome from the victims of crime in the area and rejection by nonvictims of crime in the area. Another frustrating likelihood is that citizens elsewhere in the community may perceive such selective enforcement as cheating their part of the community out of adequate services.

By cheating is meant the feeling that someone else is receiving "our share" of police services. This in turn related to how visible the selective enforcement program is made.

When selective enforcement in a given area of the community takes on the form of high visibility, yet another paradox frequently occurs. The cruisers and walking beat are often welcome to the point of actual enforcement, but once the actual enforcement begins, the welcome and unwelcome segments divide. Criticism of police often follows this confrontation.

The Officer's Decisions: Need for Community Awareness

Police officers have no choice but to acknowledge the *possibility* that every stranger could be an escaped convict, or someone who has just robbed or murdered, or for any number of reasons, be a person prepared to assault the officer, perhaps with deadly force. Community leaders need to know that it is often in this context that discretion must be used, that decisions for action must be made or *not* made.

Of great influence even after the situation demands a decision be made is the locality, that is, the kind of neighborhood in which the situation occurs. The officer's discretion functions differently in a wealthy neighborhood where the crime rate is low than in a high risk neighborhood where crime and assaults on police officers are common. In terms of selective enforcement, the officer is likely to have far less backup available in the low-crime area, because (through selective enforcement) efficient use of police resources would require the strength to be in the high-crime area.

Yet discretion is more likely to favor slower, more deliberate decision making when the situation develops in the low-crime area. This point is often lost on police critics.

This phenomenon brings our attention back to the matter discussed early in this chapter: police discretion as a further argument for community support—or at least acceptance.

Officer's Decisions: Need for Community Acceptance

Not every police official would agree that there are major advantages for law enforcement in involving community leaders in police business. Insofar as such involvement in any way impedes the police mission, such reluctance is appropriate. There nevertheless remains an overriding need for police to acquaint the community with a number of factors that impinge on the enforcement of law. Among these is the officer's decisions, the officer's discretion, as noted earlier in the chapter.

In the suggested format of Chapter 14 on public relations, every effort should be made to acquaint the community with some of the realities of police work. For example, police officers have no choice but to acknowledge the possibility that strangers and even people known to the officer may have just committed an offense unknown to the officer — may in reality be prepared to assault the officer with deadly force. Community leaders need to know that it is often in this context that discretion must be used, that decisions for action must be made or *not* made.[9]

Perhaps more sensitive but nevertheless valuable in the general community awareness is the influence of the kind of neighborhood in which the officer must make decisions. As we already noted, police alertness and police discretion necessarily differ in high-risk neighborhoods, compared to the neighborhoods with low-crime rates. This reality could have controversial ramifications if the community is not aware and thereby not accepting of the officer's decisions and the context in which they are made. Community leaders should be made aware that in neighborhoods with high rates of assaults on police officers the officer is obliged to be far more alert and to exercise discretion differently, and selectively, than in neighborhoods where assaults of any kind are unheard of. The added reality is that discretion may be used more slowly in a low-crime area; decisions are usually less urgent.

These decisions and nondecisions occur continuously, day and night, in every jurisdiction in America. Any one decision has the potential to be scrutinized by the entire legal system as well as by civil law processes.

Returning now to the discussion of factors involved in community enforcement priorities, let's consider crime patterns.

PATTERN AND/OR TIME OF DAY

Figure 4–1 depicts daily crime frequency rates which can be made into *local* time-of-day "forecasts." They are an obvious aid to selective enforcement policy. Yet another aide to setting selective enforcement policy is pattern, which is fairly easy to clarify to community leaders; crime patterns are usually easy to understand once

[9]The literature on police discretion has been rich for many years. In addition to other citations in this chapter, see also Herman Goldstein, "Police Discretion: The Ideal Versus the Real," *Public Administration Review,* Sept. 1963. Also Wayne R. La Fave, "Arrest: The Decision to Take a Suspect into Custody." Boston: Little, Brown, 1965. Also Jerome H. Skolnick, *Justice without Trial,* 2nd ed. New York: Wiley, 1975. Also B. Atkins, and M. Pogrebin, (eds.), *The Invisible Justice System: Discretion and the Law.* Cincinatti: Anderson Publishing, 1978. Also John Finckenauer, "Higher Education and Police Discretion," *Journal of Police Science and Administration,* Spring, 1975, pp. 450–457.

explained correctly. In the individual case, the suspect's pattern may not be for media release. But when crime patterns have to do with the type of victims and style of offenders, the public is generally supportive of selective enforcement. Chapter 9 will have as the main topic the prevention of crime with an emphasis on community support. Selective law enforcement by pattern or by time of day can be a meaningful link between the community and police both in terms of mutual agreement on a need for selectivity in enforcement and in the actual prevention or at least controlling of crime and delinquency.

SPECIFIC CRIME

The use of task forces in many jurisdictions has to do with specific crimes in most cases. Typical of these crimes are:

> Serial homicides
> Serial rapes
> Serial arsons
> Drug trafficking
> Kidnapping
> Serial armed robberies
> Gang activities

Aiding police in gaining the support of the community for law enforcement in this variety of selective enforcement categories is positive media coverage. In Chapter 14 public relations and community relations will be elaborated on in this regard.

What may be missed all too often is the opportunity police have to clarify other selective enforcement policies when media attention is brought to bear on task forces dealing with specific crimes.

Whether by "task force," exhaustive detective work, or by alert patrol effort (most likely all three), when police effectively deal with a widely publicized crime problem, there is a golden opportunity to undertake what our later discussion of public relations and community relations will define as "PR."

If nothing more than emphasizing the need to "get back to other police priorities," law enforcement can influence publicity after a major success dealing with specific crime — even during the concerted effort to cope with a specific crime.

CITIZEN DEMAND

We have already noted elsewhere in this volume the complexity posed by the contradictory demands on police made by the public. In the absence of apparent crime, citizens are apt to prefer a low profile for police activities — to do more deterring than enforcing. This can be perplexing for the police since they occupy a dual role in the first place, both as enforcers and symbols intended to deter crime. This perplexity increases with the reality that, on the one hand, laws are passed that see the individual as responsible for his or her choices; police are then the enforcers. On the other hand, political pressures and some laws demand that recognition be given to social and economic conditions that foster crime. Here police are seen as part of a justice system that rehabilitates rather than punishes the offender; great concern in this category is addressed to the offender's rights.

Add to that the shifting tides of how high the enforcement profile should be in any given neighborhood. On the one hand, a high profile presumably deters crime, at least some crime. On the other hand, a low profile is desired by many who see the police as evidence that their neighborhood is not a good one.

Nevertheless, citizen demand is or should be a major consideration in setting policy for selective enforcement. It is common in many parts of the nation for crime to spring up in a manner that offends many citizens simultaneously. In such a situation, citizen demand is usually reasonable and readily understood by the police. As already noted, conspicuous drug dealing generates widespread citizen demand. In certain situations, rampant prostitution in a given neighborhood may generate the same response. As noted in Chapter 3, *due process* requires police to take enough time to ensure that an accused is presumed innocent until proved guilty. This reality includes the recognition that the prostitute on the street or the drug pusher on the corner is often the employee of someone who will simply replace him or her if arrested, a significant factor in police effort to gain community support of law enforcement.

While police deal with these time-consuming realities, critics (unfortunately including the media) often point out the number of traffic tickets given to citizens, while nothing is done about real crime, which is defined as whatever the critic perceives as the desirable priority.

In jurisdictions where street gangs form but do not actually violate law, a similar breakdown between police and the community can evolve; the mere sight of the gang generates a demand that the police "do something."

As the student of judo is aware, energy hurled at you aggressively can be used to great advantage. Inviting an articulate (or even an inarticulate) critic of the police operation to discuss the perceived problem with police officials can do wonders. Frequently, such a positive and innovative approach is the first step toward enlisting help for law enforcement from the sector of the community represented. Moreover, in a surprising number of instances, a severe critic of police practice, when given the opportunity to spell out the problem, proves quite receptive to explanations of *due process* and other matters taxing the resources of police.

Publicly reviewing police problems risks the appearance of seeking sympathy, so great caution is needed when deliberately dealing with the media regarding criticism of the police. But inviting the critical citizen to aid in solving the problem perceived has the potential to shape the media attention toward a positive vein; criticism may turn into praise, an old judo principle.

PUBLIC PERCEPTION OF UNFAIRNESS

Public perception of selective law enforcement is influenced and sometimes controlled by the implications of this line from Anatole France's *Crainquebelle:*

The law, in its majestic equality, forbids the rich as well as the poor to sleep under bridges, to beg in the streets, and to steal bread.

Paraphrasing a reverse situation, a hypothetical law against high speeds for Cadillacs would with "majestic equality" forbid both rich and poor to speed in a Cadillac. Anyone wishing to demonstrate the unfairness of selective enforcement has at their disposal these kinds of analogies.

On the one hand, police can *try* to ignore such evidence of unfairness and risk loss of public and political support. On the other hand, police can *try* to respond to criticisms and risk failing in their mission to enforce as much of the law as police resources permit. The least destructive middle ground for dealing with such conflicting variables has to do with discrimination in persecution.

Perhaps a brief note is needed on the varied philosophical reactions police experience when confronting problems of discrimination or persecution, the main subjects of later chapters. Police organizations, much like the military, establish strong traditions and encourage conformity, a requisite to a stable organization, as noted earlier in this volume. Also noted earlier was that such stability in traditions can be a problem. But police personnel, like personnel in many organizations, vary in their level of conformity. These variations have been described in terms of three kinds of police personnel: One who causes problems, others who solve problems, and ones who do not cause nor solve problems.[10] Solving or at least trying to solve such problems as perceived discrimination may well be one of the main problems to be solved, by those willing to try. It is these kinds of problems that are most often in conflict with strong police traditions. When the subject of attitude, prejudice, bias, and discrimination is discussed in later chapters, the ramifications of the contention between traditions and need for change will be elaborated on. In the present context, attention is addressed merely to the *perception* of discrimination or persecution. This by no means suggests that an irate public *perceiving* discrimination is not a police problem. On the contrary, some forms of *unfounded* perception can generate more hysteria and turmoil than straightforward documented cases. For the present discussion, however, the main point is that selective enforcement *can* be perceived as persecution, as prejudicial discrimination against those who are singled out or think they are singled out by the selective enforcement policy.

SELECTIVE ENFORCEMENT AND THE PERCEPTION OF POWERFUL POLICE

In regulating human behavior, police are empowered to arrest suspected law violators. *Arrest is simply taking a person into custody as specified by law.* The actual specifications of the law of arrest are extremely complex and are subject to constant change through court decisions and legislative acts, as we have already noted. But the *power* to arrest remains essentially the core of police ability to regulate human

---

[10]John P. Mathews and Ralph O. Marshall, "Some Constraints on Ethical Behavior in Criminal Justice Organizations," in Frank Schmallenger, and Robert Gustafson, *The Social Basis of Criminal Justice: Ethical Issues of the 1980's.* Washington, DC: University Press of America, 1981.

behavior after other approaches fail. This *power* is essential to maintain the social control necessary to provide the orderly environment. This power, however, is not the sole influence that police have on behavior. Police power should be the last government alternative to social control and is used only when all else fails. Ultimately, however, if everything else does fail, then police power is the only means of social control.

The problem for police, however, is that the existence of even *potential* power tends to exaggerate public reaction to selective law enforcement. The possibility the police may assert power, particularly what is perceived as unwarranted power, is likely to generate concern in certain parts of the community where the selective enforcement policy is salient. Both informal and formal police power entail police discretion that must be measured in the context of "human nature" in a democratic society. It might be useful to review briefly what was presented earlier as the need for police to have this authority, the reality that some members of the community at times overlook. Social control is actually both *formal* and *informal* enforcement of law. But whether the control is formal or informal, the power of arrest is fundamental. Indeed there are ever increasing pressures for police to restrict the use of power even under severe stress, particularly the use of lethal force. Moreover, sophisticated police training now focuses more and more on innovative alternatives to using power. Again, however, the formal and informal police powers of arrest underpin virtually *all* applications of law as an instrument of social control.

Yet *social control* is the absolute requisite of the orderly environment discussed in previous chapters. The individual's personal safety, property security, and freedom are at stake. Without police power, these will be short lived at best.

Yet is remains abundantly clear that the police need, indeed must have, the support of the community. To whatever degree the perception of power impedes such support, it is incumbent on police to devise methods to clarify the *essential* nature of power, whether in selective enforcement on a broad scale or in the individual discretionary application of power in the individual case.

A final note on selective law enforcement has to do with questions about the permanence of the laws being enforced. The question of permanence has to do with the democratic process that evolves by majority vote, within a constitutional framework, to become law, only to have the law removed by further legislative acts. Even those laws that seem to have both community and national support may be subject to this lack of permanence. Recall the opening discussion on drug enforcement as an exception to the risk of selective enforcement; it was stated that there is a nationwide demand for stricter enforcement of drug laws. In this regard, bearing in mind the concept of *permanence,* consider the following comments made by a retired United States chief probation officer:[11]

> We need to repeal all laws that impinge on the free flow of opium and coca derivatives and marijuana. Cocaine, heroin, morphine, opium, and marijuana should be produced or processed by recognized legitimate pharmaceutical companies and should be

[11]Merril A. Smith, "The Drug Problem—Is There An Answer?" *Federal Probation,* Mar. 1988, pp. 5-6.

available without prescription to all adults. Purity and potency should be subject to the same government standards as applied to other pharmaceuticals, and prices should be controlled to assure that no one need seek illicit sources.

Would such a course produce an increase in drug use? Not likely. *The nation is now awash in illicit drugs.*

Whether or not drug laws wind up like prohibition laws, the selective enforcement of law clearly must stay attuned to changes in the community and the nation, the main goal of efforts to gain support for law enforcement from the community.

ADDITIONAL FACTORS IN SELECTIVE ENFORCEMENT

Although we have covered thus far in this chapter many of the main considerations in approaching the selective enforcement of law, there are many more. Indeed, when the intent is to involve the community in the development of a consensus, where possible, in selective law enforcement, there is a wide range of additional considerations. Consider, for example, the potential entanglements when the limitations on police resources encounter community demands to increase the reserves. Reserves are volunteers who are *unpaid* civilian *part-time* police officers intended to augment the police function in many police agencies.

Reserves

The concept of *reserves* to increase police resources has great appeal to many. Students of police history are quick to note that Sir Robert Peel's Metropolitan Police Act was founded on the principle that police are paid to do what the rest of the population is responsible for doing without pay, philosophically a kind of mutual responsibility for law and order. Budget-minded taxpayer groups see the advantage of not paying volunteers. Certainly the goal of gaining community support for law enforcement can be aided by recruiting volunteer citizen reserves. The concept both makes sense and has general appeal. But applying this concept to eliminating the need for selective enforcement has problems. Even reducing the need for selective enforcement by recruiting reserves is difficult in the best of situations and impossible in most.

The ever increasing demand for expanding areas of police expertise makes the police officer's job far more complex than when Sir Robert Peel conceived of law enforcement. In jurisdictions that recognize the high liability of permitting officers to lag behind in professional training, police work and police training combine for a *full-time* occupation; part-time help is just that—part-time help.

Although training reserves to the highest level that their part-time status allows is cost effective in most cases, it is far from the professional levels sought and needed in coping with crime in a democratic society. Furthermore, such training is *not* free; the volunteer is not a cheap approach to expanding police resources if the volunteer is trained to an adequate level of competence.

There remains the cohesive influence that joins community support when volunteers assist in law enforcement, and this is reason enough to continue the practice of recruiting and maintaining reserves.

Private Security Patrol

Not long ago the use of *private* security services was mostly among commercial operations; larger corporations had their own security forces. In recent years, private security services have expanded dramatically; patrolling and guarding affluent residential neighborhoods and various housing projects is the primary area of growth. Although the use of private security patrols is an obvious acknowledgment that police are too shorthanded to provide such service, there is extremely wide variation in the training and qualifications of private guards.

Presumably, reserve police officers would have to meet the same, or at least similar, qualifications as career police officers. This is not the case with private patrols; they may or may not meet high standards.

Independent of the level of competence, private patrols are *not* law enforcement; private patrols must call on the *official* enforcement agency when enforcement is required. The public image of private patrols may be tarnished by unfavorable media attention.[12] Unfavorable reports on private patrols may be unfair to security services that maintain high standards of training, education, and other important qualifications. Unfair or not, it remains a reality that even the most qualified private patrols cannot substitute for law enforcement. On the other hand, the pressure to selectively enforce law is reduced when good, competent private patrols reduce the pressure on police patrols.

Another factor worth consideration in examining the subject of selective enforcement is organized crime.

Organized Crime

Selective enforcement, as we have noted, is called for in a variety of circumstances. But an additional consideration sometimes not perceived as selective enforcement has to do with criminal activities that are organized.

In many jurisdictions, police work against organized crime is a specialty and is coordinated with the activities of state enforcement agencies, as well as the FBI and other federal agencies. But in the sense that these specialists are officers *selectively* working on organized crime, this too is selective law enforcement. At a minimum, police officials can cite the necessity of selectively working on organized crime in cases where it is necessary to convince doubters that selective enforcement is necessary. Let's take a brief look at organized crime in that context.

By organized crime is meant a coordinated approach to gain money and power by unlawful means; it usually includes the involvement of legitimate business to

---

[12]For example, the CBS television program "60 Minutes" on Dec. 11, 1988, broadcast an unfavorable feature on residential security guards. For elaboration of this subject, see, for example, J.L. Sullivan, "The Moonlighting Police Officer," *Journal of Security Administration,* July 1987.

"launder" the monies illegally gained. Violence, graft, and corruption are often associated with the organization that coordinates criminal activities.

This phenomenon is by no means new. The mobs of the 1930s have been fictionalized, even glamourized, by early motion pictures. Nevertheless, the organized approach to crime has existed for a long time. In the 1960s and 1970s, a more serious look was given to the problem of organized crime. Part of the problem is that much of the activity of organized criminal is not illegal:

> it is not illegal for a person or people to plan, establish, develop or administer an organization designed for the perpetuation of crime — any more than it is illegal for detective story writers and university students to sit around trying to invent the "perfect crime". . . .[13]

Selectivity dealing with organized crime, then, must go beyond simply addressing persons who plan, establish, develop, or administer an organization designed for the perpetuation of crime. In that regard, during the same era, the president's commission on law enforcement and criminal justice noted:

> Organized crime, because of its inherent nature and structure, and because of the scope and complexity of its criminal operations, presents a special challenge to all levels of law enforcement. It is a society that seeks to operate outside the control of the American people and their governments. Its actions are not impulsive but rather the result of intricate conspiracies, carried on over many years and aim at being in control over whole fields of activity in order to amass huge profits.[14]

The concept of police reserves and selectively dealing with organized crime are but two of many additional factors that farsighted police officials can utilize in increasing the communication with community leaders. Even in situations where the nature of the police program prohibits full and candid disclosure of the details of police activity with regard to such problems as organized crime, community leaders are at a minimum entitled to be made aware that police have prioritized correction of such problems. This can serve to enhance the awareness of community leaders in other areas of selective enforcement policy.

It remains in the best interest of police, as well as the community, to keep the community as fully informed on all police activity as police security will allow. Police are, after all, *part* of the community and must function accordingly if community support is to be achieved and maintained: "Community relations are seen as the police being part of the community they are policing, rather than simply the speechmaking of a special unit."[15] Recognizing this, a police agency can deal

[13]Donald R. Cressy, *Criminal Organization*. New York: Harper & Row, 1971, p. 81.

[14]President's Commission on Law Enforcement and Criminal Justice. *Task Force Report: Organized Crime*. Washington, DC: U.S. Government Printing Office, 1967.

[15]Edward A. Thibault, Lawrence M. Lynch, and R. Bruce McBride, *Proactive Police Management*. Englewood Cliffs, NJ: Prentice-Hall, 1985, p. 6.

with selective enforcement, and all police operations, on the basis of "our community":[16]

> "Community relations is not just relegated to a public relations department in the police agency, but becomes the personal responsibility of each officer. . . .
>
> "An effective law enforcement support team can create a department deeply concerned with helping each citizen in the community. . . ."

This is important not only to selective enforcement, but to law enforcement in general, particularly in the context of the Chapter 5 discussion of social change and community tensions.

Law enforcement agencies that gear themselves to community need are *necessarily* in a far better position to cope with social change as it occurs. Entire police organizations have successfully adopted the community orientation.[17]

In Chapter 5 we will examine the social change related to these closing remarks.

SUMMARY

This chapter noted that there are risks in selective law enforcement, including the risk of appearing discriminatory. An exception was noted in terms of the epidemic drug problem sweeping American culture. It was further noted that there are simply not enough police to enforce all law at all times. Selective law enforcement was related to the limitation on police resources and in turn discussed in terms of the need for further professionalization of the police field. Selectivity of enforcement was discussed in terms of priorities emphasizing that crimes that were not prioritized were not to be simply ignored; prioritization was the emphasis point. Selective enforcement was elaborated on in terms of related factors such as the laws themselves, jurisdictional standards, crime statistics, and the efficient use of police resources.

The problem of selective enforcement appearing unfairly discriminatory was elaborated in terms of a rationale based on severity, crime rate, pattern, specific crime, and citizen demand. The potential of the public perceiving selective enforcement as unfair was further elaborated on in the context of the contradictory influences that require selectivity while at the same time recognizing that selectivity generates criticism. Police personnel and organizational considerations were examined in this context.

Police power was discussed in terms of its potential to damage police image, as well as in the context that police must have power to ensure the orderly environment.

[16]Ibid. p. 66.

[17]James McClure, *Cop World: Inside an American Police Force.* New York: Random House, 1984. A description of the San Diego Police Department community-oriented police program written from the patrol officer's point of view.

The chapter closed on the observation that laws are subject to change, which in turn controls the prioritization of which laws to enforce.

DISCUSSION TOPICS

1. Elaborate on the risk involved in selective law enforcement.
2. Present two reasons that selectivity in law enforcement is necessary.
3. Discuss the categories presented in this chapter for prioritizing enforcement policy.
4. Why is there a risk of appearing discriminatory in selective enforcement?
5. Distinguish between police discretion at the line officer level and at the policy-making level.
6. Present the ramifications of police power in the context of selective law enforcement.
7. What is the significance of the chapter's closing observation regarding the *permanence* of law?

Relevant Problems for Discussion

The main problems with selectively enforcing some laws were included in the chapter itself. Related to these problems is the fragmentation of the criminal justice system that was noted in Chapter 1. When the police seriously undertake to improve community relations by involving community leaders in selective enforcement policy, the odds of community support are greatly improved. This is not merely a good idea; it is essential for police success in the long run.

But developing mutual goals with community leaders does not always allow the police the latitude to prioritize the goals of other components of criminal justice. Indeed, there is the possible risk the police–community goals could even conflict with other components of justice. As an example, consider the problem for all concerned with a parole or other community-based correctional program that uses "freedom in the community" as an incentive for convicted offenders. If police in that community have reached an agreement with community leaders regarding selective enforcement of some *particular* law that the correctional offenders have broken, the ingredients of further justice fragmentation are present. They are not necessarily active ingredients, but nevertheless present.

Politically, it would be foolish for police to risk the police–community relations program—politically risky and ultimately risky to police success in their omission. But professionally, the challenge remains to try to reconcile such differences, to integrate such conflicting variables.

In the case of community-based corrections, the reality is that the overwhelming majority of offenders will return to the community in any event, and the question is the nature of the supervision, rather than the question of whether the offenders are in the community. In such matters the police have an opportunity to assume a leadership role in bringing the officials of the correctional system into contact with community leaders. While more difficult, problems with prosecutors and judges rejecting certain community priorities can also be approached on the basis of open discussions between community leaders, police officials, judges, and prosecutors.

While such simplistic approaches are far more politically difficult in some jurisdictions than in others, the severity of the problem frequently dictates the need to at least try.

PART TWO

Unrest from Social Change: Present, Past, and Future Impact

---

1. *Social Change and Community Tension*

2. *Community Unrest: Some Historical Background*

3. *Continuing Struggle for Equality: Impact on Police*

The general purpose of Part Two is to acquaint the reader with present and past community tension and the continuing problem.

In the context of limitations on police presented in Part One, Part Two will relate community unrest that can be reasonably handled to the potentially dangerous community tensions that demand stronger police-community relations. The violent history of American civil disorder will be reviewed and emphasized. Factors indicating that sources of community tension are likely to continue will be presented in terms of the impact on police.

Another purpose of Part Two is to afford the reader a better understanding of both the controllable and uncontrollable sources of community unrest and to establish the historical tendency toward violence when tensions are not controlled. This in turn is intended to strengthen the contention of Part Three that the police and community must work together to avoid disastrous problems. This in turn is intended to support the Part Four contention that problems confronting better police-community relations can and must be overcome.

5

Social Change
and Community Tension

In recent decades, law enforcement has encountered an ever-increasing demand to cope with *change* in many forms:[1]

> The rate of doubling all human knowledge — once measured in years, can be measured now in months. Other previously long-term cycles are increasingly short term, repeating themselves monthly, weekly, even daily. . . .

> For police professionals working in this setting, a disciplined effort to hold a broad view of culture and people is not a matter of professional elegance; it is a matter of operational survival.

> Human relations practiced in this fast-paced community environment must account for previously unexpected possibilities, combinations and opportunities. . . .

Change, particularly social change, is the subject of this chapter. The specific orientation of this concern with change has to do with various forms of tensions, particularly community-wide tensions that develop as a result of change. This concern with tensions in turn relates to the crucial need for police to acquire and retain the community's support in law enforcement if law enforcement is to succeed.

[1]Los Angeles Police Department, *Human Relations in the Police Service.* Los Angeles: LAPD, 1988, p. 35.

Without an understanding of the tensions generated by change, the ability to gain such community support is weakened.

In terms of such support, it must be acknowledged that the community and the police alike feel threatened by many forms of social change, a mutual feeling of threat that provides yet another reason to prioritize understanding these tensions and ensuring the continued support of community. In this regard, the cliche "we're all in this together" can be made to be very meaningful.

Let's quickly examine this common bond between police and the community in the area of mutual fear of change. Take, for example, the mutual recognition of social change that can occur in trends that are discernible to all observers.

Social change, and to some degree the related tensions, are made up or caused by events that many times are part of a trend. Events that can be identified as part of a trend are events that many believe are easier to predict, to plan for, to anticipate.

Unfortunately, from a community relations point of view, there is very little evidence that such events can be *accurately* predicted, even when the trends are clearly identified; there are simply too many variables involved. Nevertheless, one of the most important segments of police gaining community support is the mutual recognition by police and community leaders of trends in social change. Even more important is the anticipation and planning needed to cope with the problems associated with change. Success in dealing with community problems before the problems develop is, to say the least, a powerful incentive for community support of police and for police to seek the support.

The mere effort of police attempting to gain community support in heading off problems is often a catalyst to improved community relations, even when the problems cannot be avoided. In many instances, even mutual effort on the part of community leaders and police who deal with problems that were *not* accurately predicted affords a very successful relationship between law enforcement and the community.

To achieve such success, however, a fuller understanding of social change and related community tension is necessary. Let us begin by considering the concept of change, perhaps starting with how the idea of change affects most people.

CHANGE AS A THREAT

As already noted, just the *idea* of change is experienced as a threat by many people in the general community and in police work as well. The appeal of the predictable status quo seems to gain strength whenever change evolves into awareness. Students of behavior refer to this as fear of the unknown in most situations. Later chapters will also explore the impact of change on certain biases and prejudices.

Change can be extremely positive or extremely negative. When change reduces or even eliminates destructive prejudice, then change is positive. Other positive changes are the scores of improvements in medicine, in food production, and in the many inventions that improve our quality of life. But often change produces negative impact, the fear of the unknown posing a *threat* to those facing change.

When dread and fear dominate people's reaction to change, there is often a tendency to *blame* someone or some group for the uncomfortable feeling. As in the case of police becoming scapegoats for problems that *anger* a community, so also can certain other groups become the scapegoats for the fears associated with change.

On closer examination, this fear of change can emerge anywhere, even within a police agency. In many ways, an organization feels far more organized when there is a status quo atmosphere, when everyone feels that he or she "knows where you stand." This kind of homeostasis gives members of the organization the security of believing that at least within the organization everything is *predictable*. In this atmosphere, it should not be surprising when major unrest follows relatively minor changes. Nevertheless, many police chiefs have been astonished with the reaction to the mere rumor that administration is "evaluating the current shift assignments" or similar rumors. The threat associated with such *possible* change can prove devastating to morale. Change can definitely be experienced as a serious threat in the mind of the individual.

Whether a source of fear or not, change is not optional; change is a physical reality on our planet and a social reality in our culture. From the perspective of police interest in change as a source of community tension, it can generally be stated that the slower the pace of change, the lower the threat to most people; the slower the pace of change the less the unrest. Put another way, when social change occurs very slowly over a long period of time, there is far less risk of tension in the community (Fig. 5-1).

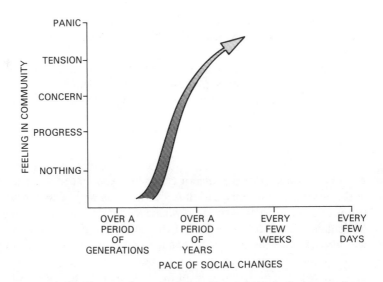

Figure 5-1 Significance of pace in change. Uncertainties in the community as social changes occur tend to be tolerated better when change is at a slow pace. When changes take place faster than one or more community groups can tolerate, community unrest involving police often follows.

Social Change and Community Tension   Chap. 5

But, like change, tension is also inevitable. When it is a part of the excitement of positive motivation, tension generates desirable achievements. But when negative community tensions and associated unrest flow out of change, police problems usually increase.

Improving the police ability to gain community support for law enforcement then requires a fuller understanding of change, particularly social change and the resulting community tensions.[2]

SOCIAL CHANGE[3]

We have already noted that *change* is *not optional*. From the physical dimensions of the planet it can be observed that the Grand Canyon is becoming deeper at the rate of 1 inch per year, whether people approve of this change or not. Scotland moves toward Ireland about 8 feet annually, and Europe and the United States are moving about 1 foot apart each year. London sinks a fraction of an inch annually, while the North Pole moves southward one-half foot.

When you note these changes in the tangible physical world, then changes in the social world should be no surprise. Any difference in human behavior over a period of time is change, and differences in human behavior are constantly observable, particularly in a constitutional form of democratic government.

But change may not always be of a positive nature. A brief discussion of leisure may illustrate this.

Leisure

Most of us would agree that leisure has a great number of positive factors. The discovery of tools and the use of animals along with numerous other sources of energy placed prehistoric people on a path that ultimately led to enough free time for the creation of the arts and sciences, neither of which were conceivable until sufficient leisure was available.

In this context, leisure tends to gain a favorable connotation, probably because it can be equated either with *recreation* or productivity. But not all leisure is recreational or productive, and herein lies a source of community tension. Among the unemployed and underemployed in most of America's ghettos and barrios, leisure may mean only having more time in which to get into trouble.

If you examine American buying habits, however, it might seem the increasing leisure of affluence has been dominated by recreation, but not all Americans enjoy sufficient affluence to translate leisure time into recreation. Many feel that adversity, including such adversities as exist in ghettos and barrios, is simply the consequences of "progress"—whatever happens to be meant by the term progress. To

[2]See, for example, the exceptionally well written publication, *Human Relations in the Police Service,* Los Angeles: Los Angeles Police Department, Aug. 1988, p. 35.

[3]Parts of this discussion are similar to some passages published earlier in A. Coffey, E. Eldefonso, and W. Hartinger, *Human Relations: Law Enforcement in a Changing Community,* 3rd ed., 1982. Passages from pages 69–74. Reprinted by permission of Prentice-Hall, Inc., Englewood Cliffs, NJ.

accept such a view without challenge is to question the possibility or at least the advisability of programs geared to alleviate the adverse consequences of social change. But if community tension is to be reduced, the negative results of social change that produce increased leisure *must* be conceived of as correctable. Correction, however, depends on a number of variables relating not only to the constitutional factors discussed in an earlier chapter, but on a number of social and economic factors that will be discussed in later chapters.

At one time, police were concerned also with aspects of the leisure time of those who were *not* in ghettos and not unemployed, the American middle class. This happened when entertainment, in both movies and night clubs, for example, became increasingly permissive. Middle class men and women became able to spend more of their leisure time in pursuits that in most jurisdictions often generated massive police response. However, the laws restricting what were then considered immoral exhibitions have since been greatly relaxed on the grounds of Fifth Amendment's guarantee of freedom of expression. Entering the 1980s, middle-class leisure has expanded even further, and in many instances so has permissiveness. It is notable that leisure time did once relate to law enforcement in recreational areas outside the ghetto, when what we now refer to as "adult movies" and other then frowned upon social conduct of the middle class were of direct concern to the police.

In and out of recessions, the middle class of the United States has enjoyed an extremely high standard of living, concerns about the recessions and inflation notwithstanding. But not everyone has enjoyed this affluence to the same degree, and some not at all. Segments of any affluent community that are deprived of comparable increases in affluence would, on a commonsense basis, appear to be perfect breeding grounds for the kinds of tensions with which police should be concerned during periods of social change.

This particular problem will be elaborated on in Chapter 6 and in the discussion of a continuing struggle for equality in Chapter 7, as will the significance of educational opportunity. In the context of social change, however, suffice it to say that negative tensions emerge when changes require greater education without providing access to education.

Let us give some consideration to the tensions that are generated by social change.

COMMUNITY TENSION

We have noted that change can either be experienced as positive or negative. When fear and dread are part of change, negative consequences follow. So it is with *tension*. Tension can be either positive, as in the case of line police officers preparing for the sergeant's exam, or it can be negative, as in the case of explosive personal outbursts over trivial annoyances.

What we mean here by tension is the subjective feelings of unrest that create tenseness in some part of an individual's life, part of the time or all of the time, when the individual is interacting with others or when alone. When such unrest is widespread, it can be generalized as group unrest or community tension.

Many potential crimes can be associated with an individual under severe tension; explosive violence is the worst case. But here we are addressing the widespread unrest that potentially leads to problems for police in broad areas of the community. Put another way, we are addressing the negative kinds of tensions, often associated with threatening social change, that somehow permeate large segments of the population of a community.

There are numerous causes of community unrest not necessarily associated with social change as such. Many of these causes lie beyond the scope of law enforcement or criminal justice. There is nonetheless a significant relationship between law enforcement and certain aspects of unrest. Symptoms or signs of unrest frequently foreshadow direct intervention by police. Moreover, law enforcement may become involved in various causal aspects of community tension, for example, the selective law enforcement discussed previously. The relationship of police to such community unrest has been placed in a category of high priority in the training program of many police academies and related training programs. It appears obvious that every effort must be made by police to avoid, where possible, permitting their activities to generate the very unrest that frequently leads to major problems. However, unrest might be thought of as a reaction to the method of enforcing conformity to a system that creates or permits inequality — reason enough for police effort to avoid this appearance if at all possible. Determining what is to be thought of as the most effective method in enforcing law without the appearance of generating tension is not easy; it may not even be possible in many instances. But to whatever degree law enforcement is able to achieve a system having these attributes, to at least that degree is community tension likely to be reduced and community support gained.

The significance of such reduction is probably most perceptible in distinguishing between a demonstration and a riot. Throughout this book emphasis has been placed on human relations as an approach to law enforcement. It then seems reasonable to generalize that rioters, from a human relations point of view, rarely conceive of law enforcement as friendly. In contrast, possibly many demonstrators do not riot simply because they believe the police have nothing to do with the social conditions and social changes that are generating the tension and unrest. Obviously, this is not always true. As we have already noted, there are many instances where police have borne the brunt of violence erupting out of demonstrations protesting social change and unrest. But it remains a valid area of conjecture that at least the degree of violence relates to the attitude of the rioter toward police.

The significance of attitude is the main subject of Chapter 10. But, in the present discussion, it may be useful to consider one of the major influences that worsen negative attitudes: overdramatization and often distortion of problems, called sensationalism.

Sensationalism

The sometimes astounding phenomenon confronting police is that a seemingly minor incident can escalate into a major source of dangerous tension. Part of the astonishment is that the incident may not have even happened, it could have been totally fabricated. Even when not fabricated, the distortions, exaggerations, and hysteria that often accompany a seemingly minor incident create the appearance that the incident was made up, at least in so far as police perception is concerned. Figure 5-2 illustrates the relationships between factors and motives in making certain events or situations seem more sensational.

The process in "making a mountain out of a mole hill" is sensationalism. This is *not* to say that all incidents, real or imagined, that are sensationalized are minor incidents. Indeed, there are extremely serious incidents that sensationalism makes even worse; fatal shootings involving police officers are one of the extreme examples. Sensationalism that plays on negative attitudes and prejudices frequently poses major problems for police. The potential police problem is twofold: first, the sensationalism may inflame or worsen problems between community groups, and, second, sensationalism frequently generates negative feelings toward the police themselves.

Sensationalizing problems and problem causes tends to aggravate community tension not so much through the distortion of facts as through the distortion of *perspective*. In view of the fact that over half a million men and women serve as police officers in America, it is not surprising that in the numerous contacts with all segments of the public, some abuses of police power are real, but many are mere fantasy. And yet both are frequently reported by the media (the media will be discussed in Chapter 14) without conscientious effort to distinguish between the two, at least in many reporting situations. Factually, media reports on police abuse

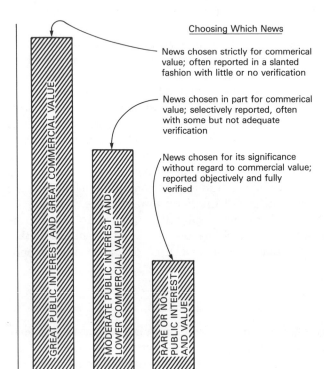

Choosing Which News

News chosen strictly for commerical value; often reported in a slanted fashion with little or no verification

News chosen in part for commerical value; selectively reported, often with some but not adequate verification

News chosen for its significance without regard to commercial value; reported objectively and fully verified

Figure 5-2 Certain types of sensationalized news can create dangerous tensions in the community. Police must recognize the factors that motivate sensationalism.

are generally correct insofar as what is *reported*. Distortions in perspective occur through a failure to examine the validity of the reports received by the media.

At the heart of the problem of perspective, however, is the media adage that "a dog biting a man is not news, but a man biting a dog is news." Police are far more available and visible than any other symbol of government authority. But like "the dog biting the man," police authority used to support an orderly society is expected and therefore of little news appeal. But "like the man biting the dog," police brutality, real or fantasy, is not expected and is therefore of great news appeal.

The sensational news of brutal police officers may serve two functions; law enforcement should be aware of both in its struggle to gain the support of a community for law enforcement. First, sensational news is probably of high commercial value. Second, there is great attention-getting value in sensationalism to any group seeking relief from actual or imagined social ills. Indeed, if government social programming accelerates in areas that have a history of civil violence, then a motive to sensationally discredit police is readily discernible and indeed may be the seeds of riotous conditions.

As already noted, community tensions in large measure reflect social changes over which the police have no control. There is nonetheless a significant relationship between law enforcement and certain aspects of unrest.

Tension Producing Change: By Chance and by Design

It becomes patently obvious to police seeking to gain the support of their community that many of the tensions creating social change are by design—tensions created deliberately for a specific purpose.

Even the most peaceful demonstration is usually organized with the thought of drawing negative attention to something, someone, or some group, a *planned* source of tension for those who oppose the particular point of view or law being protested.

Rhetoric to the contrary, deliberate civil disobedience is almost invariably designed to *create* tension, indeed aggravation, producing stress on some primary thing or group and secondary stress on the police. But there remain a wide range of tension-producing changes that are not planned. By not planned, we mean that there are numerous changes that occur in the lives of every individual as well as the life of a community. These sudden changes can be shocking and leave individuals and large groups grief stricken; unexpected deaths are but one of the many unexpected changes. In Chapter 6, at least some of the violent upheavals in American history had elements of all, to some degree, spontaneous causes. In many respects, the violence and unrest of the 1960s was unplanned.

From the perspective of law enforcement interest in community support, the tensions associated with unplanned change are less severe, although they can lead to serious police problems. In this context, death, injury, and property destruction can follow extreme instances of planned or unplanned community unrest.

Deaths and injuries are not the sole measure, in human terms, of the cost of community tensions that evolve into civil disorder. For example, there is a vast dislocation of families and individuals, as well as the human cost of fear, distrust, and alienation from the community. Indeed, even a relatively low level of violence and damage in absolute terms can very seriously disrupt a small or medium-sized community in a manner that may take years to correct.

Whether planned or unplanned, community unrest that develops the potential to explode into violence should be anticipated wherever possible. Here is yet another strong argument for law enforcement to conscientiously seek the support of the community. Such support is essential in both situations: the spontaneous or unplanned community tensions that lead to serious disorder, but, more importantly, *planned* community unrest.

Gaining the support of the community for law enforcement is in reality at two separate levels. First, when dealing with either planned or unplanned efforts to bring about some kind of change, community support of law enforcement is needed. The other level is when there are deliberate efforts to exploit the police themselves, to make the police the focal point of unrest. There are degrees of severity involved. The comparative volatility of a riot in progress is more serious than a group chaining themselves to a trespassed building. In both cases, community support is needed for law enforcement activities. Independent of the comparative severity, the support of the community is necessary even more so when the police themselves are targeted for *planned* tension.

Planned Tension

By planned tension we mean the deliberate creation of unrest and aggravation by a specific design, or at least an attempt at a design. Insofar as police involvement is concerned, the design generally includes the deliberate violation of law so blatantly that there *must* be police response and preferably arrest. In the extreme, violence is intended as part of the effort to generate community unrest. In other situations, the *stated* intent is to avoid violence, to bring police to grips with the frustrating and often confusing problem of civil disobedience.

Civil Disobedience

When an issue becomes a source of frustration for an individual or group, the alternatives to the peaceful mode of resolving the issue are usually examined. To some, all the alternatives must remain within the confines of law. To others, the options include the planned and deliberate violation of law — usually, but not always, violation of the very law considered wrong — making the symbolic gesture of civil disobedience more attractive to those with a zeal for public attention. By no means anarchy, civil disobedience is a confrontation with the values of the majority in a specific, limited area, usually with the express intent *not* to create violence.

Confusing the problems for police trying to cope with the deliberate violation of law posed by civil disobedience is the fact that any police choice can be seen by some as wrong. If arrests are made, then the demonstrators get the publicity they want and the incentive to continue violating laws to gain publicity. This publicity is directly at the expense of the police image. If police do not respond to the violation of law, they are not enforcing law. The civil disobedience concept is yet another of the many *damned if you do damned if you don't* situations confronting contemporary law enforcement.

In approaching this particular dilemma from a slightly different perspective, an argument has been made that dissent is not only a right, it is a catalyst of progress, presumably indicating a very positive view. This same point of view, however, points out that acceptable dissent is difficult to define constitutionally.[4] Regardless of the purpose and even justification of dissent, when law is violated, police are expected or *should* be expected to perform police duty. This brings up the question of amount of force needed in dealing with civil disobedience or any other form of law violation.[5]

The force necessary to effect an arrest in a riotous demonstration is likely to be far greater than the force necessary to arrest a chained demonstrator. Yet in both cases, the police *power* of arrest is the focal point once the encounter begins; this power retains the potential for negative interpretation, as previously discussed.

The social changes sought by the demonstrators have far greater potential for creating negative tension once the use of police force begins — any degree of force, if it becomes necessary. The reality is that some situations require force. Obviously, then, the *planned* tension and aggravation may well be accompanied by the hope that *excessive* force is used, that force beyond that which is required will bring even greater attention to the *planned* tension. If the force can be made to appear excessive, the potential for higher tension is created and there is a better chance to bring about the sought after social change. As in all confrontive police situations, professional training pays off — sufficient force to ensure necessary arrests, but no more force than absolutely necessary.[6]

Returning the discussion of social change and community tension to police seeking support of the community, we should note that the *"not always obvious problem"* continues to exist — the not always obvious problem that police cannot actually deal with unrest until the law is violated.

LIMITATIONS ON DEALING WITH UNREST[7]

We have thus far presented a number of reasons for the police needing to gain and retain the support of the community for law enforcement. The "not always obvious

[4]Pamela D. Mayhall, *Police Community Relations and the Administration of Justice,* 3rd ed. New York: Wiley, 1985, pp. 336–337.

[5]See, for example, W.R. Olin, "Tactical Crisis Management: Challenge of the 80's," *FBI Law Enforcement Bulletin,* Nov. 1980. pp. 20–25.

[6]See, for example, Lawrence W. Sherman, "Perspective on Police and Violence," *The Annuals,* Nov. 1980. See also Joseph D. Sax, "Civil Disobedience: The Law Is Never Blind," *Saturday Review,* Sept. 1968.

[7]See, for example, H. Jerome Miron and Robert Wasserman, *Prevention and Control of Urban Disorders: Issues for the 1980s.* Washington, DC: Law Enforcement Assistance Administration by Police Technical Assistance Project, Aug. 1980. See also James Q. Wilson, "What Can Police Do About Violence?" *The Annuals,* Nov. 1980, pp. 13–21.

problem" of police being unable to deal with unrest until law violation occurs is yet another strong argument in favor of community support.

Most veteran police officers recognize the potential for major problems when negative tensions develop, particularly when tensions rise at a rapid pace. The more volatile the situation generating the tension, the higher the risk of violence and other matters with which police are forced to deal. Although later chapters will address the variables involved in gaining the communities aid and overcoming this limitation, it is appropriate to point out that, in the context of social change, knowing *which* variable has the strongest influence on tension is important.

The present author likes to include in lecture what has been coined the soda analogy. Simply stated, one risks an erroneous conclusion when observing people drinking whiskey and soda, then gin and soda, and finally vodka and soda; it could be erroneously concluded that it is the soda that is making them act strange. After all, the soda is the only consistent variable.

Knowing which is alcohol and which is mix is far easier than isolating the factors that escalate social change into negative community tension. Some are convinced that the answers lie in the social ecology of the community.[8] Such variables as age, population density, sex, housing, and various economic factors underpin this approach. Still others debate the pros and cons of *predicting* violence, noting that there are variables that can indeed be predicted, but also raising the question of whether or not violence should be predicted, that is, raising ethical questions regarding the moral consequences of predicting.[9]

As a practical matter, isolating the factors that escalate social change into negative tensions vary in many ways from one community to another. Thus, again as a practical matter, Chapter 14 will deal with the subject of public and community relations and with the uniqueness of each community in terms of approaching the isolation of key variables in community tension.

A final note on the limitations placed on police in dealing with unrest. Even when the demonstrators force police to use arrest power, there is virtually no certainty that the courts will even hear the cases, and in cases that are heard the penalties imposed may not appear to justify the arrest, if indeed any penalties are imposed whatsoever. The confusing part of all of this is that in most of the situations in which arrest occurs there is absolutely no question that the law was violated and the demonstrators literally forced police to use arrest powers, leaving absolutely no alternatives.

But these limitations aside, police must cope with unrest and tension and in many instances use their powers of arrest. In this process, it is probably a truism that antagonisms will emerge toward the police for performing the very arrests that the planned tension called for, as well as antagonism from those in the community who may feel that not enough force was exerted. These antagonisms can be thought of as a kind of spillover from the pent up emotions and vague community tensions that

---

[8]See, for example, J.M. Byrne and R.J. Sampson (eds.), *The Social Ecology of Crime.* New York: Springer-Verlag, 1986.

[9]See, for example, Fernando N. Dutile and Cleon N. Foust (eds.), *The Prediction of Criminal Violence.* Springfield, Il: Charles C Thomas, 1987. See also, Harold V. Hall, *Violence Prediction: Guidelines for the Forensic Practitioner.* Springfield, Il: Charles C Thomas, 1987.

become crystallized in the tangible enforcement of the law—the visible, often widely publicized arrest of demonstrators.

Yet other arrests during such periods of community tension tend to trigger overreaction among the citizenry, also a kind of spillover from vague community tensions during social change.

Community Tensions as Spillover

Recalling the earlier discussion of selectively enforcing law, a case was made for prioritizing which laws *can* be enforced, given restricted numbers of police officers. During periods of high community tension and unrest, these selections tend to be noticed more and resented more. This is especially true during times when planned tensions and demonstrations are in progress.

A citizen cited for a traffic violation is more likely to question the citation, more likely to inquire why the officer is not either chasing real criminals or quelling some demonstration. Routine arrests of ordinary offenders such as shoplifters generate questions about police failure to apprehend those responsible for defacing schools with spray paint, and so on.

In short, when community tensions run high, the most routine police business is likely to be perceived in a more negative manner by many members of the public, and generally in a more emotional manner. It is almost as if it were the fault of the police that tension exists. And this spillover from tension in the community to police work is not restricted to the controllable levels of antagonism. As we will note in Chapter 6, such spillover and heightened tension evolve and can even erupt suddenly into civil disorders.

When tensions created elsewhere spill over into police contact with the public, the enforcement of law is strained, to say the least. As we have noted in various discussions of *police professionalism,* there is a tendency to unfairly blame police for problems often beyond police influence, certainly problems that are totally beyond police control. We have also noted a tendency of the police to withdraw into the police organization, to establish a kind of "we-they" approach to a sometimes dangerous public.

> When asked at a party what he does, the police officer says that he is a government worker. When he is pressed, he walks away. Why does he do this? As many officers have said, "If I tell them that I am a cop, they'll want to give me a hard time about some traffic ticket they got. Next will come some bull concerning police corruption and then they'll hold me personally responsible for some court letting some killer loose on the street. What do you want me to do, spoil all the parties I go to that have civilians there, spoil these parties for myself and my wife? It's really better if you stick to your own." And stick to their own, they do.[10]

The spillover of community tensions into police–public contact no doubt compounds these sentiments. Understandably, efforts at professionalizing may be

[10]Edward A. Thibault, Lawrence M. Lynch, and R. Brice McBride, *Proactive Police Management.* Englewood Cliffs, NJ: Prentice-Hall, 1987, pp. 27-28. Reprinted by permission.

more apparent than real when such pressures accumulate seemingly without end over long periods of time. Thus it is certainly understandable when the professionalism that is popularly discussed in law enforcement circles is in some cases rhetoric.[11]

But understandable though such reactions to continued tensions may be, the period of highest tension is the *very* period requiring the highest commitment to developing professional approaches. Indeed, if the *need* for professionalization of law enforcement is placed on a scale, equated with general tension, it is an absolute certainty that the greater the tension on the scale, the greater the need for continuing to develop the professionalization of law enforcement.

SUMMARY

Social change and related tensions were introduced in terms of the desirability of predicting trends. A further community relations observation was made that prediction is not always possible. It was noted that the mere effort of attempting to predict for the purpose of heading off community troubles will often gain the support of community leaders. Such anticipation and planning were presented as a cohesive force, likely to not only gain but to maintain community support for law enforcement.

Change as a concept was presented as inevitable and social change was elaborated as a concept; emphasis was placed on fast-paced social change likely to generate tension.

The power that people believe police hold in order to maintain social control was presented as a catalyst toward negative tensions in the community, with the potential to mar police image. Specific factors related to social change were discussed in terms of the tensions created. Tensions were also discussed in terms of deliberate effort to create antagonism and tension for some social purpose; civil disobedience was discussed as one of the planned tensions in the community. Community unrest during periods of change was elaborated on as a police problem. The limitations on police dealing with unrest were presented in the context of law violation and in the context of a rationale for developing community support for law enforcement. Also discussed was the spillover of tensions in terms of the continuing need to professionalize the police function.

DISCUSSION TOPICS

1. Discuss the advantage of police and community leaders cooperating in efforts to reduce the problems created by community tension.
2. Relate the concept of social change to community tension.
3. Elaborate on the concept that some community tensions and antagonisms are deliberately planned.

[11]See, for example, Michael Steinman, and Chris W. Eskridge, "The Rhetoric of Police Professionalism," *The Police Chief*, IACP, Feb. 1985, pp. 26–29.

4. Elaborate on what this chapter presented as the likelihood that police arrests will enhance the publicity for a dissident group.

5. Discuss the significance of the *degree* of police force in making necessary arrests.

6. Elaborate on the limitations on police dealing with unrest prior to the violation of law.

7. Discuss what the chapter concluded was a spillover of tensions that do not include law violations into enforcement functions involving law violations.

8. Relate this to the need for police professionalism.

Relevant Problems for Discussion

The chapter identified the problem of community tension spilling over into areas of law enforcement not directly associated with community unrest. A related problem has to do with the subtle, yet powerful strain this generates on a personal level for the police officer.

Such stress can be created by the subjective feeling of the officer of being caught between two conflicting forces. On the one hand, prudent police officials will insist that officers remain professional and objective even when dealing with the hostility involved in community unrest. Beyond that, an even greater demand is placed on the officer to conduct his or her duties in a professional manner when functioning outside the area of unrest. Qualified, trained professional officers should have no problem with this. The strain begins when the citizens themselves allow the community unrest to spill over into unrelated contacts with the police, to draw attention to the police scapegoat status.

While no serious problem exists if such spillover is on a limited scale, a big problem for the individual officer can develop when this is encountered consistently and intensively over a period of time.

Chapter 13 discusses police image and Chapter 14 discusses public and community relations, both subjects potentially a source of police stress, which will be discussed in Chapter 15, when the spillover of public hostility is continuous and intense. Although subtle, the stress generated from the grind of striving for good image and public relations when encountering an *excessive* barrage of uncalled for hostility can be debilitating to the individual. We are noting here the *excessive* spillover of hostility; some hostility is inevitably a part of successful law enforcement, as every career officer knows.

This problem can unwittingly be compounded somewhat by the dilemma of the conscientious official. On the one hand, the official is responsible for the morale of the officers. On the other hand, the police are responsible for professionally enforcing the law. If the official allows it to appear to the officers that the stressful bind somehow excuses unprofessional conduct, the officer may feel more support from the administration, but the question of professionalism and the police mission is raised. But in the absence of police administration acknowledging this bind, some officers may experience a feeling of being unsupported.

Like so many problems facing law enforcement, the emergence of this one during periods of community tension must be confronted without the availability of easy solutions, yet another of the many arguments for professionalism in law enforcement.

6

Community Unrest: Some Historical Background

The levels of intensity of community tension can be thought of as dangerous and not-so-dangerous. The community tensions discussed in Chapter 5 would fall into the not-so-dangerous category for two reasons: First, many community tensions posed no threat of law violation nor threat to peace and order, and, second, even those tensions that would threaten law violation were, in the context of the Chapter 5 discussion, controllable.

There are, however, varieties of community tensions that generate unrest that is literally waiting to explode into violence, which in some instances can be virtually uncontrollable. These would fall into the dangerous category and are the focal point of the historical discussion in this chapter.

Police–community relations programs in many jurisdictions include some type of accommodations for the not-so-dangerous category of community tension. Such things as police policies for handling civil disobedience coordinated with community leaders are but one example. However, the threat of a major eruption of violence is often shunned by community leaders, leaving it almost entirely up to police to deal with both *before* and *during* (but not after) a riot occurs.

Since police wind up having to confront the dangerous disorder, some community leaders reason, why shouldn't police handle the whole problem, at least the before and during? Moreover, police often agree, being grateful not to have to explain the intricacies of plans to control a dangerous riot. Once a riot starts, such reasoning appears vindicated; the police have to deal with it without civilians helping. But in most instances civilian "help" is immediately forthcoming *after* the riot in terms of challenges to whatever law enforcement decisions were made.

From the perspective of the human relations approach to law enforcement, the question must be asked: *Could* the riots have been prevented? Such a question is mainly used to *place blame* when asked *after* the disorder. But when asked *before* a riot, such a question has the potential to strengthen a community relations program.

One problem is that many, perhaps most, tend to doubt that a dangerous riot is even a possibility. These doubts are often strengthened by doom-sayers who continually cite the threat of disorder for political reasons, giving the threat of violence a kind of "cry wolf" appearance. But the truth of the matter is that community unrest *has* in fact exploded into violent civil disorders that took many lives, left countless thousands maimed and injured, and destroyed billions upon billions of dollars worth of property.

So consistently have such outbreaks marred American history that a pattern of sorts is discernible. The consistency and pattern are both valuable concepts in the sense that *complacency* is more difficult once this historical characteristic of community unrest is understood.

WHY BOTHER?

In those fortunate communities where the problems usually associated with unrest are minimal, the urgency of examining civil disorders is reduced, but not eliminated. Even in such fortunate communities, the ability to recognize the early signs and early stages of the problem are important, and this begins with recognizing that violent disorder has erupted throughout American history.

In those communities with the painful experience of violent disorder, dealing with it in the context of something that has repeated itself over and over again in American history affords a broader perspective in approaching corrections for the problem.

In all those communities that are somewhere in between, some mixture of both the ability to recognize early stages of the problem and accept the historical perspective is definitely indicated.

We emphasize that we are not studying the *details* of any one incident, but rather the historical consistency that forms a kind of pattern.

WHAT CAN BE LEARNED?

Since entire sections of major libraries are needed to store the literature on this subject, what can be learned from a brief overview of only the highlights of selected civil disorders? First, we must note that it is *not* our intention to learn all of the details surrounding each major disorder. This by no means is intended to discourage any reader from pursuing any one of the disorders in far greater detail; careful analysis of details provides much greater learning with regard to avoiding mistakes as well as discerning mistakes.[1] But while any reader is encouraged to pursue any area reviewed in this chapter in greater detail, it is the intent of this chapter to establish a *pattern* — to establish in the mind of the reader the *consistency* with which violence has erupted over and over again throughout our relatively short history.

By examining even a cursory review of our violent past, the conviction should develop that police–community relations in America should *always* acknowledge the possibility of civil disorder, and even of violence.

Recalling the Chapter 5 discussion of constitutional government, it should be noted that dissent is not only a right, but implicitly encouraged in many ways.

While the community unrest that has exploded into violence varies in many ways, the common thread remained throughout history that each of these riots and disturbances occurred in a nation that has a *continuing* history of violence. If the condensed review of our violent past does nothing more than establish the pattern of the *repetition* of violence, it will have served its purpose.

Role Police Played

A thoughtful analysis will be greatly enhanced if we examine the exact role that police played or failed to play in each of the outbreaks of violence. Some of this detailed analysis is available in historical literature, some is missing. In any case, there is not sufficient space in a single chapter to even approach compiling all the data related to the police role in our violent past. However, it still might be helpful to evaluate this role in a *speculative* manner.

In other words, an effort to "imagine" the role played by police before, during, and after a riot, for example, is at least *exercising* the right thought processes. It is very likely that the kinds of matters that the reader might use for such speculation are similar, or perhaps even identical, to at least the *categories* of things that are important for the human relations approach to law enforcement. In effect, speculating about the role of police in a disorder is a way of disciplining the approach to conceiving of the human relations approach to law enforcement.

Admittedly, this is nothing more than a simple "guessing game" in terms of how a situation might have been better or worse by different police activity or greater sensitivity to warning signs and the like. Although far more complex than suggested by the proposal to follow, communication and the absence of communication between police and the majority, as well as communication between police and minority groups, afford a sort of "framework" for *speculating* about the role of police. Consider Fig. 6.1.

"Guesses" about how things might have been better or worse are neither right nor wrong; the object is to simply develop the habit of critically evaluating situations in which very little is known, as will be the case in the following briefest of reviews of the many disturbances that have marred American history.

[1]As one of the many examples, see Belinda Swanson (ed.), *Journey from the Gallows: Historical Evolution of the Penal Philosophies and Practices in the Nation's Capitol.* Lanham, MD: University Press of America, 1988.

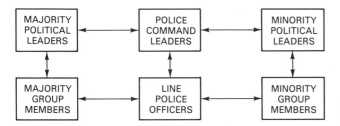

Figure 6.1 Communication breakdown.

SELECTED EXAMPLES OF UNREST IN THE PAST

Civil disobedience traces back to the earliest times in American history. Obviously, the Revolutionary War was a massive civil disobedience insofar as the British were concerned. There is well-documented evidence that the defiance of authority existed well before this revolution and has existed continuously ever since.[2] This unrest has been marked all too many times by severe violence.[3]

Let's now briefly review the more salient outbursts of major and violent disturbances.[4]

EIGHTEENTH CENTURY

1765. The Stamp Act Riots in the colonies were over the British appointing a stamp distributor. These riots were particularly violent in Boston. Headed by a group known as the *Sons of Liberty,* a mob destroyed a stamp distributor's home. The county sheriff and chief justice were stoned by this mob. Later the rioters destroyed the admiralty records and yet additional homes, including the home of the chief justice. Noteworthy is that most of this destruction and violence followed a police

[2]See, for example, David R. Weber, *Civil Disobedience in America: A Documentary History.* Ithaca, NY: Cornell University Press, 1978.

[3]See, for example, Willard A. Heaps, *Riots U.S.A. 1765-1965.* New York: Seaburg Press, 1966. See also Joseph Boskin, *Urban Violence in the Twentieth Century.* Beverly Hills, CA: Glenco Press, 1969.

[4]In compiling this selected list of major disturbances, the author relied heavily on a variety of resources, but primarily the following: Willard A. Heaps, *Riots U.S.A. 1765-1965,* New York: Seaburg Press, 1966. Thomas J. Fleming, "Revolt in America," *This Week,* Sept. 1, 1968, pp. 2-8. Joseph Boskin, *Urban Violence in the Twentieth Century.* Beverly Hills, CA: Glencoe Press, 1969. V.G. Stretcher, *The Environment of Law Enforcement: A Community Relations Guide.* Englewood Cliffs, NJ: Prentice-Hall, 1971, pp. 35-49. N.S. Watson (ed.), *Police and the Changing Community.* Washington, DC: IACP, 1965. J.L. Flinn, *History of the Chicago Police.* Chicago: W.B. Conkley Publisher, 1887, pp. 72-79. Edward H. Savage, *Police Records and Recollections.* Boston: John P. Dale & Co. Publisher, 1873.

Some of the historical material was published earlier in A. Coffey, E. Eledefonso, and W. Hartinger, *Human Relations: Law Enforcement in a Changing Community,* 3rd ed., 1982, pp. 111-117 and part of Appendix A. Reprinted by permission of Prentice-Hall, Inc., Englewood Cliffs, NJ.

officer reading to the mob what was known as the Riot Act. The rioters also forced the local jailer to release the half-dozen arrested rioters.

1786. Shay's rebellion resulted from Massachusetts' court plans to convene to hear foreclosure cases from debts that had accumulated in the depression of that time. Daniel Shay, a veteran officer of the Revolutionary War, led 1500 farmers in blocking attempts at such foreclosure. Once the mob got out of control, officials were abused and homes were looted. Shay fled when the governor called out the militia.

1771 to 1784. During this period major disorders occurred known as "the regulators in 1771," "the burning of the Gaspee in 1772," "the resistance to the Boston Port Bill in 1774," and "the revolt against North Carolina in 1784."

1788. The doctor's riot, or anti-dissection riot, erupted in New York when a medical student chased away a curious boy by brandishing a human arm (from a recent dissection). The medical student attempted to frighten the boy further by telling the lad that the arm belonged to the boy's mother, who by grisly coincidence had died recently and been buried. When the boy's father discovered that the mother's grave had been recently opened, a mob of over 1000 destroyed the medical school. A sheriff was able to rescue four medical students, but was later overpowered. The rioters grew to over 5000 and at least seven were killed during confrontations with the military units called in.

Eighteenth-century Law Enforcement

Even before the eighteenth century, demand for law enforcement in the new land was great. Following the pilgrim's 1620 landing, the Dutch West India Company set up a major operation in New Amsterdam, later to be known as New York. Shortly thereafter, it became necessary to appoint a peace officer. By 1631, Boston found it necessary to follow the lead of the Dutch West India Company, appointing not only one peace officer but six assistants as well.[5] This practice was quickly followed by most of the early settlements, with the inclusion of justices of the peace, modeled after Great Britain.[6]

Eighteenth-century law enforcement was ushered in with Philadelphia's "Watch and Ward" police coverage of both day and night.[7] A comparable system was set up in New York and called the "Constable Watch." Among other early names for police functions were "Town Watch," "Marshall's Watch," and "Town Crier."

The term watchman was the more common identification for early peace officers, and in some cases these watchmen were selected more or less at random.[8] The British influence, as presented in Chapter 3, prevailed in the style and approach

[5]E.H. Savage, *Boston Watch and Police,* 2nd ed. Boston: Edward W. Savage, 1865.

[6]R.B. Fosdick, *American Police Systems.* New York: Century Publications, 1920, p. 59.

[7]Ibid.

[8]H.O. Sprogle, *Philadelphia Police Past and Present.* Philadelphia: Howard O. Sprogle, 1887, pp. 24–27.

of early American law enforcement. Enforcement of law at *night* was the main characteristic of the eighteenth century.

NINETEENTH CENTURY[9]

American law enforcement in the nineteenth century began evolving more clearly toward modern systems, although retaining much of the early characteristics. In 1807, Boston separated the city into two separate police districts, continuing the *night* enforcement coverage only.[10] In 1837, seven years prior to the 1844 riots that will be presented shortly, Boston experienced its own version of civil disorders, drawing even greater attention to the configuration of the enforcement function.

Prior to 1860, some jurisdictions around the land passed laws requiring that police officials be voted into office, a reaction to an increasing image of police corruption. The influence of Sir Robert Peel, as noted in Chapter 3, was salient in developing metropolitan areas. Elsewhere in rural America, combinations of the British-style justice of the peace and sheriffs and other innovations prevailed during the nineteenth century. The United States marshalls, sheriffs, and the United States Cavalry enforced the law on the rapidly expanding western frontier, in many instances experiencing the violence depicted in motion pictures and written fiction covering that era.

The episodes of violence of the nineteenth century, however, that have been selected for this discussion are primarily in the metropolitan police areas, the increasingly urban sections. However, the discussion will begin with violence erupting in a relatively small, urban area of the United States.[11]

1831. Nat Turner was a slave. Among the many factors that make Nat Turner's revolt significant is a similarity in some respects to the Miami area riots, which will be reviewed later, part of the similarity including what is thought by many to be an intent to injure or kill whites.

Nat Turner's revolt began on the night of August 21, 1831. Turner and a relatively few other slaves in South Hampton, Virginia, murdered several farm families in the area and attacked many other farms. The militia was summoned and before the carnage ended at least 40 slaves were killed in the fighting and 12 were executed, including Turner. Approximately 57 whites were killed.

1844. As referred to in the discussion of nineteenth century law enforcement, the 1844 riots were particularly significant to the evolution of American police. The police role, as well as the absence of a clear definition of the police role at the time, may or may not be crucial in history. It is nevertheless clear that a similar situation these days would have much more early police involvement than may have been the case in 1844. The "anti-Catholic" riots began when a large mob of

[9]See footnote 4 for sources.

[10]J.L. Flinn, *History of Chicago Police*. Chicago: W.B. Conkley, 1887, p. 52.

[11]See footnote 4 for sources.

"native" Philadelphians gathered in the middle of the immigrant Irish section of town, following years of bitter contention over the years that Irish Catholics were loyal to the Pope rather than to the American government. The ensuing riot included gunfire and eventually cannon fire, as a sheriff's posse and the militia fought the rioters. Up to 24 were killed and over 100 seriously injured. One person was arrested.

1849. The Astor Place riot began when a mob of "native" New Yorkers rioted outside the Astor Place Opera House, following police removal from inside the theater of a group of "nativists" who had come to repeat an interruption of British actor William MacReady. The ill will toward the actor had to do with anti-American articles written by British travelers. The rioters attracted a large crowd, which included a group of thugs who escalated the disorder into greater violence. Police, joined by militia, fought the rioters without gunfire until a police officer was hit by a rioter's pistol shot. Many deaths and injuries occurred before the mob was dispersed by the threat of two cannons loaded with grape shot.

1855. Revolt of the German tavern keepers resulted from 200 of them being arrested for violating a previously unenforced Sunday closing law in Chicago, Illinois. The ensuing trial was disturbed by 500 Germans demonstrating against the arrests, as well as counterdemonstrations favoring the arrests. Police cleared the streets and made arrests, followed that night by a bloody gun battle between police and a mob seeking to free those arrested. Nearly all the cases of those arrested were dismissed following the funerals of the riot's victims.

1851 and 1854. Riots occurred in San Francisco known as the "Committee of Vigilance" and riots in Kansas known as the "Struggle over Slavery."

1863. The conscription riot or draft riot broke out when a Boston wife attacked two marshalls she mistakenly believed had come to take her husband to the army. She was promptly joined in the attack by a large crowd of people aware of the unfairness of the congressional law passed at Lincoln's request for conscription, which allowed wealthy men to "buy off." Police were badly beaten by the rioters during the four days of violence that ended only when militia was forced to use point-blank cannon fire and eventually a full-scale military charge.

1871. The anti-Chinese riot began when a Los Angeles police officer trying to intervene in a gun fight between Tongs was wounded. The incident was publicized as Chinese "killing whites wholesale" and a mob gathered in the Chinese section of town. In spite of the marshall's deputizing and deploying guards, one Chinese was lynched and another 18 shot, then hung after being shot, in various locations in Los Angeles. Later, others were hung and mutilated; some 23 were killed before the riot ended. Of the ten brought to trial, eight were convicted and given life sentences, which were then overturned by the California Supreme Court.

1871.   The Orange riots in New York began when a shot was fired at the Orange, or Protestant, Irish who were parading through the hostile Catholic Irish section of the city. Police and military units were accompanying the parade and opened fire without orders as soon as the shot was fired, killing 33, including a police officer, and wounding 91 on the very first volley.

1877.   The great railroad strike was in response to railroads announcing paycuts after four years of severe economic depression. Workers refused to work and seized railroad yards in Baltimore, destroying freight and buildings during a riot that ended only with the threat of federal troops intervening. In Pittsburgh, the rioters fought state militia, who killed 25 of the rioters. The strike turned into violent riots in city after city, until the combination of state militia, local police, and federal troops brought all the rioters under control.

1892 to 1899.   Additional bloody labor-related conflict erupted during the steel lockout of 1892. Nonunion strikers joined union strikers in Homestead, Pennsylvania, on July 6 of that year and fought a bloody and pitched battle with Pinkerton Detective forces, who had been hired by the steel companies; more than 30 were wounded and 2 killed with the very first shots fired. In 1894, the "Chicago Phase" of the pullman strike also proved destructive to the railroads and bloody to the strikers. The same was true for the miner's riot in Shoshone County, Idaho, starting on April 29, 1899, causing more bloodshed and destruction before the close of the nineteenth century.

TWENTIETH CENTURY

1913 and 1919.   The Ludlow massacre in 1913 killed more than 50; the Chicago race riot of 1919 left 38 dead and 537 injured.

1917.   Although an estimated 1800 black people have been brutally lynched in America in the twentieth century, the 1917 race riots in East St. Louis, Illinois, eclipse all brutality and savagery.

During a May 28 city council meeting, hate mongers joined union organizers in crystallizing resentment of blacks who had been brought to East St. Louis to replace striking whites. Rumors of a black shooting a white during an alleged robbery were embellished with stories of blacks abusing white women. A violent mob of 3000 rioted through the black district, virtually unopposed by police; the worse was yet to come.

On July 1, a black shot a white, and this was followed by whites firing into the homes of blacks, and blacks then firing on and killing a police detective investigating. A mob of whites then formed and initiated a new riot by marching to the black section of the city, shooting, clubbing, and stoning black men, women, and children. White women beat black women with fists, stones, and sticks. Shacks in which blacks lived were burned and terrified occupants shot when trying to flee. The water hoses of the fire department were cut, as the shooting of mothers and children alike continued. Lynchings were added to this ghastly carnage. Soldiers finally brought the riots under control late in the evening of July 1, with at least 39 blacks and 8 whites dead, many seriously injured, and many more without homes.

1919. The police strike in Boston, which lasted from September 9 to 12, evolved into a major riot. Juvenile troublemakers were the first to take advantage of the absence of police by various forms of malicious mischief. Later a gang smashed a plate glass window and started looting the store. Crowds gathered and continued smashing windows and looting stores throughout the city day after day. Rioting mobs defied state guardsmen who had been called in to replace the striking police.

Finally forced to retreat, rioters fired on the guardsmen, who returned the fire, eventually gaining control of the city, but only after 9 rioters had been killed and another 23 seriously wounded.

1919. Also in the year of the Boston police strike, the Chicago race riot killed 38 and injured 537.

1921 to 1952. The Tulsa race riot of 1921 killed 30 and injured several hundred more. The Detroit race riot of 1943 killed 34 and injured 700 additional people. Also in 1943, the Los Angeles "Zoot Suit" riots erupted between military personnel and members of the Hispanic "Zoot Suit" gang who had been preying on military personnel on leave in Los Angeles during World War II. The widely publicized prison riots in Jackson, Michigan, erupted in 1952.

"Old-time small town" police. (Courtesy of Santa Cruz Police Department)

1954 to 1965. Violence against civil rights marchers and other activists occurred.

1964. Riots erupted in Harlem and Brooklyn, New York; Rochester, New York; Jersey City, New Jersey; Patterson, New Jersey; Chicago; and Philadelphia, all with considerable bloodshed and property destruction.

1965. The Watts section of Los Angeles erupted into protest riots by blacks, leaving 34 killed, 1032 injured, vast homelessness, enormous damage, and 3952 arrested.

1967 and 1968. The Detroit riots of 1967 were similar to the riots in Los Angeles. In 1968, Chicago riots during the democratic party's election convention were also violent, ending in allegations of the police using excessive force and overreacting.

1968 and 1969. Far more violent than earlier "Free Speech" demonstrations that got out of hand, campus radicals and student activists opposing the Vietnamese War added to the problems police were having with violent social movements such as the Black Panthers. Focused at San Francisco State University and the University of California at Berkeley, protests spread throughout the land, threatening to repeat the tragic Kent State violence.

1973. On July 29, a mass memorial march for the slain Santos Rodriguez through downtown Dallas, Texas, erupted into chaotic violence that included the burning of police motorcycles and destruction of store windows.

1980. The Miami area riot of May 17, 1980, in some ways differs from other American riots. Five major cases, probably related to police, have a bearing on the explosive and deadly riot.[12] All five of the cases left much to be desired as far as police image is concerned. One case, the Arthur McDuffie case, proved to be the explosive "straw that broke the camel's back." For the first time since pre-Civil War slave uprisings, blacks were to spontaneously rise up with the sole purpose of beating or killing whites.[13]

Reaction to an all-white jury's acquittal of four officers accused of beating McDuffie, a black, to death, ultimately resulted in 18 riot-related deaths, 7 nonriot deaths, 1300 riot arrests, and upwards of $125,000,000 in damage.[14]

This tragic occurrence may well have been the very type of thing that was dreaded most when police community relations training "got organized" nearly half

[12]H. Miron, and Robert Waserman, *Prevention and Control of Violent Disorders: Issues for the 1980's.* Washington, DC: U.S. Department of Justice, LEAA, by Police Technical Assistance Project, University Research Corp., Aug. 1980.

[13]Marvin Dunn, and Bruce Porter, *The Miami Riots,* Report commissioned by the Ford Foundation, 1981.

[14]Miron, op. cit.

a century ago, when Chicago professor Joseph D. Lohman started his college course in community relations in the early 1940s.

Sadly, other violence has been reported in Miami itself in the years since this major outbreak. One recent example of such reported racial violence is again related to police activity. On January 16, 1989, Martin Luther King Day, television news and press wire services reported that police fired shots during the chase of two black men suspected of armed robbery, a chase ending with the fatal injury of one of the suspects. The crowds that gathered after the incident were reported to have burned cars and looted, as well as thrown rocks at officers.

Major police effort restored an uneasy calm that lasted until the following day when rioting, looting, and shooting again required massive police effort to restore yet another uneasy calm. With the international press gathered for the National Football League's 1989 Superbowl scheduled nearby less than a week away, a steady stream of news reports of new violent outbreaks in Miami continued for some time.

The Miami area is not the only scene of community unrest that exploded into violence during the 1980s; there is also Philadelphia.

1985. In many ways unlike the destruction reviewed thus far, the violent confrontations in Philadelphia in 1985 nonetheless have many common factors, at least from a police point of view. The radical group calling itself MOVE entwined itself into political controversies that were not directly related to law enforcement, but nonetheless evolving toward confrontation with law enforcement. The violent confrontation grew to disastrous proportions when MOVE fortified a house they had been ordered to evacuate. An armed confrontation erupted when police moved to enforce the eviction order. Violence escalated steadily and on May 13, a bomb was dropped on the fortified house from a helicopter.

The bomb created a fire that killed 11 members of MOVE, destroying the house, but also destroying an additional 61 nearby homes.

A few days after the bombing, the civic official responsible for the city's position on MOVE resigned. Of far more significance to police–community relations was the November 14, 1985, *New York Times* report that the police commissioner also resigned after 18 days of public hearings on the incident.

In some ways, this tragic disorder is more like police dealing with a gang than with one of the social problems alluded to earlier. Yet it crossed all the same community-problem lines of community relations efforts to gain and hold support for law enforcement. On November 21, 1985, the *New York Times* reported that a former Philadelphia police chief who had served as mayor planned to run against the mayor who was in office at the time of the bombing. The paradox of police finding it necessary to cause harm to prevent harm has been noted in the literature, as has virtually every facet of police involvement in violence and force, including the 1428 justifiable homicides by police from 1975 to 1979.[15]

---

[15] For elaboration on police force and violence, see for example the following: Kenneth J. Matula, *A Balance of Forces.* Gaithersburg, MD: IACP, 1982; see also *The Police Chief,* May 1983; Lawrence W. Sherman, "Perspectives on Police and Violence," *The Annuals,* Nov. 1980; Arnold Binder and Peter Scharf, "Deadly Force in Law Enforcement," *Crime and Delinquency,* Jan. 1982. See also *The Annuals,* Nov. 1980, James A. Wilson, "What Can Police Do about Violence?" and Arnold Binder and Peter Scharf, "The Violent Police–Citizen Encounter."

Another Look at Why the Past Is Important

Now that we have examined the highlights of violent disorders in the past, it might be wise to pause and reflect on our original intent in reviewing this history of American civil disorders. Perhaps the first consideration should be *speculation* about communication breakdown between police and community groups. Recalling the suggestion at the beginning of the chapter, the reader is encouraged to critique the "imaginary" communication between police and the community.

Next it might be helpful to take yet another look at why *past* civil disorders deserve attention when it is the present and future of law disorder that should be of primary concern. Put another way, it might be wise to once again raise the question of why review the past when, by its very nature, police–community relations deals with the present and future. This subject will again become germane in Chapter 14. But it is also relevant in the present context of considering the violent past of America.

The well-known authority on police–community relations, Louis Radelet, has noted that this subject includes, among other things, confrontations between the powerful and the powerless, politics, sociology, psychology, anthropology, theology, and ethics.[16] In Chapter 14 we will see that the uniqueness of every community indeed brings a wide variety of variables into play. But there is yet another factor that influences or should influence the police effort to gain community support; the factor is the *risk* of civil disorder and violence that is established by *history,* meaning that history is indeed another facet of community relations.

Examining history is worthwhile even when general interest is the only motive. This is why readers are encouraged to pursue in depth any particular area highlighted in this chapter. But in the human relations approach to law enforcement, history can provide a sound rationale for taking community relations seriously; history can establish that indeed there is a consistency in violence in the United States.

The history reviewed also supports the thesis that social change and the resulting tensions, as discussed in Chapter 5, are anything but new. If the conquering of America's western frontier may be thought of as social change, and it should be, the most salient characteristic of that change at many times was the extreme violence. And the prohibition era was marked by extreme gangster violence. Social unrest, tension, and violence are indeed part of America's history.

Violence per se is not the point of emphasis here. Our attention is on the violence resulting from uncontrolled tension. The past serves as a *warning*: uncontrolled tensions can mount to a point of violent disorder, a warning for the future.

WHAT ABOUT THE FUTURE?

It is imperative that a police department prepare long before violence occurs. Indeed it is crucial that preparations begin before even the signals of tensions and disorders begin to emerge. Police officials must begin to assess the possibility of outbreaks of

---

[16]Louis A. Radelet, *The Police and the Community,* 4th ed. New York: Macmillan, 1986, p. 3.

violence and even the staging of nonviolent demonstrations long before they happen; preparations and plans must be in place *before* they are needed. These plans for action should, where police intelligence requirements permit, be integrally involved with the community relations program; community relations may well depend on community leaders having awareness of and confidence in the police approach to such matters. Once the problem begins to emerge, planning is over; action is generally the requisite. Tensions in these situations rise rapidly, and even the responsible leaders on both sides of the contention have little control once disorder begins to take place. This lack of control exists even though responsible leaders on both sides of the contention may be fully aware of the building tension and emerging disorder. Law enforcement must learn to *sense* these problems in advance, even when the intelligence system breaks down. But emphasis should remain on sophisticated intelligence techniques to ensure that surprises do not occur that could evolve into the disastrous civil disorders reviewed earlier in this chapter. Possibly the evolving law enforcement problem with *gangs* might clarify the increasing need for sophisticated police intelligence that can be integrated with community relations.

Gangs: Challenge of the Future?

Against the historical background of violent disorder that this chapter has thus far reviewed, a glance at the future should address the growing problem of gangs, in many jurisdictions and across many jurisdictions.

Reports of gang activities spreading across the land are not confined to law enforcement intelligence channels; increasingly the media calls this problem to the public's attention. For example, *The New York Times* reported from Omaha, Nebraska, that two California gangs are "fanning out along the interstate highway system, spreading a sophisticated pattern of violence and drug-dealing across the country."[17]

Although gang activity differs in many ways from the civil disorders reviewed earlier in this chapter, gangs nevertheless pose a constant threat of violence both between gangs as well as between gangs and the communities. Law enforcement specialists across the land differ on the numbers of gangs and the numbers of members of gangs. Nevertheless, gang activity continues to increase and is worthy of attention when considering the future of law enforcement. Indeed, problems created by gangs more than justify the *effort* to develop intelligence techniques. Early warning is needed for more than simply knowing when general street crime is involved; the potential for explosive violence between gangs dwarfs these relatively routine police problems.

Jurisdictions fortunate enough not to be exposed to this enforcement nightmare would do well to strengthen community relations efforts as an investment in keeping the problem at bay. Those unfortunate jurisdictions now struggling with gang problems usually rely heavily on community relations to help cope.

[17]*The New York Times,* "California Gangs Selling Drugs Across U.S." Byline and dateline Nov. 25, 1988, Omaha, Nebraska, carried by wire service in the *Santa Cruz Sentinel* as a front page headline.

Regressing slightly to give perspective to gang problems, consider an incident reported by the *Los Angeles Times* on June 20, 1987. In the Harrison Park incident, four people were shot at a church meeting; quoting the head of the Pomona Police Crimes Against the Person Division, "It seems like lately nothing is sacred to the gangs. They just don't care."

Members of the Los Angeles community could scarcely be shocked by reading this; gang incident reports have been all too common in the media recently in the Los Angeles area.[18] Gang incidents are not only common but are far more complex than many would like to believe.[19] Law enforcement is in definite need of *full* community support in areas where the problem exists, and continuing law enforcement vigilance is required in jurisdictions not yet confronted with gangs.

The unfortunate reality is that gang behavior is perhaps moving across *all* jurisdictions. The constant potential of strongly organized gangs to create violence comparable to the civil disorders we've reviewed is reason enough to continue learning as much as possible about gangs. Appendix E elaborates on the gang problem, and it might be useful to present now, a brief description of gang characteristics:[20]

> A youth gang is a group of individuals between the ages of 14–24 years who associate on a continuous basis. The gang is without formal organization, and has as its leader its strongest or boldest member. The gang has a name, claims a particular territory or neighborhood, and directs its criminal activity towards rival gangs and the general population.
>
> Gang members are usually males who join the gang by either committing a crime or undergoing an initiation procedure wherein they are beaten severely by fellow gang

[18]Selected at random here are some other *Los Angeles Times* gang incident reports: Jan. 1, 1987: Gang Members Held for Threatening Safety of District Attorney; Jan. 4, 1987: Programs to Reduce Gang Killings; Jan. 6, 1987: Editorial on Gang Related Violence; Jan. 7, 1987: Police Investigate Connection between Nationwide Asian Gangs and Killing of Vietnamese Immigrant; Mar. 5, 1987: Police Arrest Gang Members to Break up Cocaine Network; Apr. 13, 1987: Gang Shootings Result in Death; May 1, 1987: Charges Against Gang Members for Courthouse Brawl; June 20, 1987: Meetings Called to Study Ways to Stop Gang Killings; June 25, 1987: Gang Violence Kills Child Bystander; June 25, 1987: L.A. Unified School Officials Say They're Powerless to Battle Gangs; July 10, 1987: State Prison Officials Believe Prison Gangs Conducting Crimes outside the Prison; July 30, 1987: White Supremist Gang Admits Abuse of Black Woman; Nov. 30, 1987: Community Youth and Gang Services Unit Unable to have Gang Truce Stop 6 Killed and 4 Wounded in "Drive-By" Shootings; Dec. 6, 1987: Two Youths Arrested for Murder.

[19]Review of the literature on gang behavior supports the position of complexity, even when the crimes of gangs are relatively simple. For an interesting review of some of the factors involved, see, for example, D. Bernstein, "East L.A.'s Gang Project: Prevention or Bribery?" *Police Magazine,* 3, 1980, pp. 46–51. See also L. Breen, and M.M. Allen, "Gang Behavior: Psychological and Law Enforcement Implications," *FBI Law Enforcement Bulletin,* Feb. 1983, pp. 19–24. For an older, yet still relevant examination of some of the factors in gang behavior, see Carl Werthman, and Irving Pilivan, "Gang Members and the Police," in David J. Bordua (ed.), *The Police: Six Sociological Essays.* New York: Wiley, 1977.

[20]*Gang Characteristics,* excerpts from training material compiled by Gang Activities Section, Los Angeles Police Department Detective Support Division, for the Gang Awareness School, 1988. Courtesy Los Angeles Police Department.

members to test their courage and fighting ability. Their motivation for joining gangs is varied, but usually falls within one of the following categories:

1. **Identity or recognition:** Being part of a gang allows the youth gang member to achieve a level of status he feels impossible outside the gang culture.

2. **Protection:** Many members join because they live in the gang area and are, therefore, subject to violence by rival gangs. Joining guarantees support in case of attack and retaliation for transgressions.

3. **Fellowship and brotherhood:** To the majority of youth gang members, the gang functions as an extension of the family and may provide companionship lacking in the gang member's home environment. Many older brothers and relatives belong, or have belonged, to the gang.

4. **Intimidation:** Some members are forced into joining by their peer group. Intimidation techniques range from extorting lunch money to physical beatings. If a particularly violent gang war is in progress, the recruitment tactics used by the gang can be extremely violent, even to the point of murdering a nonmember to coerce others into joining the gang.

Many times, the term "low rider" has been used synonymously with youth gangs. This is unfortunate, since Low Rider car club members do not normally involve themselves in gang-type incidents.

The term Low Rider is used to describe a modified motor vehicle which has been lowered so that it is only a few inches off the ground. The vehicle is usually adorned with other special items such as small steering wheels, "mag" rims, etc. Although many gang members drive low rider types of cars, true members of low rider car clubs are infrequently involved in any violation of laws. They have put a great deal of time, money, and effort in their vehicles, and will not become involved in gang-related incidents wherein their vehicles could be damaged. They hold fund-raising activities, as any established club does, and are law-abiding individuals.

In larger cities, police departments sometimes sponsor low rider car clubs. Normally, in the State of California, low rider car clubs do not present a gang-related problem to law enforcement.

The causes of youth gang violence are many and range from revenge for a real or imagined wrongdoing to competition for control over a particular criminal enterprise such as extortion. As youth gangs have become more sophisticated, the types of weapons used have evolved from fists, feet, and knives to handguns, automatic weapons, and sawed-off shotguns. Most firearms are either stolen during burglaries or purchased through a "fence."

Although no formal structure exists within most youth gangs, there does exist a system of crime specialization. One member of a gang may engage in illegal activity at which he is proficient, such as burglary, robbery, extortion, etc. The proceeds from this activity are expected to be shared with his fellow gang members.

Many gang members consider themselves the "soldiers" of the neighborhood and consider it their duty to protect it from outsiders, usually rival gang members. Encroachment of their territory cannot be tolerated or the gang will lose face, and thus many gang wars have their beginnings.

The most frequent violent crime committed by youth gangs is the "drive-by" shooting. Members from one gang will seek out the homes, vehicles, or hang-outs of a rival gang and, using an assortment of weapons, will drive by and shoot at members of that gang. Usually, the "suspect" gang member will yell out the gang name or slogan so that the "victim" gang will know who was responsible. The gangs thrive on notoriety and *want* the other gang to know who shot at them. Of course, this type of incident leads to more shootings when the "victim" gang retaliates and drives by at a later date. Many "drive-by" shootings into residences or in which gang members receive only minor injury will not be reported to police agencies.

Although most gangs are formed along racial or ethnic lines, violence between gangs is normally black gang versus black gang or Hispanic gang versus Hispanic gang. Conflicts between ethnic groups have been known to occur, but they are rare.

Youth Gang Structure

The structure of a youth gang can range from a loose-knit group of individuals who know one another and commit crimes together to a formal organization with one leader or ruling council of several members having written rules and regulations that delineate expected behavior and disciplinary action to be taken against their own members or against members of the community. The leaders within a gang usually acquire their positions of power through one of two methods—either by being the "baddest" guy around or possessing leadership abilities.

Before proceeding, perhaps an explanation of the typical youth gang structure is in order to clearly define the components of a youth gang. The structure or involvement by members is generally broken down into these areas:

1. **The Hardcore:** Those few who need and thrive on the totality of gang activity. The gang's level of violence is determined by the hardcores and their ability to orchestrate the gang as a vehicle to manifest their own violence. The hardcore are generally the leaders, the most violent, streetwise, and knowledgeable in legal matters. They may participate in violent acts or encourage others to commit the violence. They are usually liked and respected by the gang members and tolerated by outsiders.

2. **The Associates:** Those who associate with the group for status and recognition. They wear club jackets, attend social functions, and may even have tattoos. This association fulfills the emotional need of belonging.

3. **The Peripheral:** Those who move "in and out" on the basis of interest in the activity or activities.

4. **Cliques:** The gang is further broken down into "cliques" or groups, which are usually determined by age or geographical areas. This term may also be used synonymously with the term "gang," "barrio," or "neighborhood."

Types of Youth Gangs

Youth gangs in California are usually organized along ethnic lines and are comprised of Asian, black, Hispanic, or white groups. Although they tend to organize themselves according to ethnicity, the gangs (who constitute a very small segment of the population) are not representative of the ethnic community of which they are a part.

In Chapter 7 we will examine the continuing struggle for equality, which it is hoped will no longer include the violence reviewed in this chapter.

SUMMARY

The violent disorders that have marred American history were reviewed in this chapter for the purpose of placing the *need* for police–community relations in the context of urgency.

In spite of the brevity of each of the violent descriptions of various disorders, it was recommended that the reader attempt to evaluate through speculation the role that police did or did not play in each. A communications-breakdown schematic was proposed for that purpose.

Selected American disorders were briefly reviewed from the period prior to the American revolution through the 1980s, with particular emphasis placed on the examples of the Miami area riot in 1980 and the Philadelphia problem of police confrontation with a militant group in 1985.

The implications for police of these disorders were considered. The question of the role of gangs in future disorders was considered, and a brief review of gang unrest was presented.

DISCUSSION TOPICS

1. Considering all the bloody confrontations between those enforcing law and American citizenry, describe the most salient characteristics of the evolution of American police.
2. Elaborate on the value of attempting to assess the police role even in brief descriptions of violent uprisings.
3. Contrast the differences insofar as law enforcement is concerned of the Miami area riots of 1980 and the Philadelphia police effort to evict a militant group in 1985.
4. Discuss what this chapter presented as the potential of gangs to generate further massive violence in the future.

Relevant Problems for Discussion

Acknowledging that America has had more than its share of violent unrest in its short history is necessary for all those pursuing a professional career in law enforcement. To overlook the obvious is a costly mistake in virtually all professions, law enforcement included.

While it is important to understand our violent history, a potential problem exists in certain kinds of generalizing about the consistency of violence in this nation's development. To recognize the ever-present threat of violence is helpful, but to operate on the basis that violence cannot be avoided may be a serious overgeneralization that impedes necessary police effort.

Police must be prepared for violence; that is the lesson of history. Violence is a constant threat in many of the police contacts with the public; to ignore this threat would be foolhardy. So also, as we have noted, violence on a large scale is also an ongoing threat. But overgeneralizing this threat creates an additional problem. When preparation for violence exceeds police–community efforts to head off violence, it is conceivable that the risk of violence has increased rather than decreased. Put another way, the problem exists when training for dealing with violence *after* it starts exceeds training in methods to prevent violence in the first place.

When the violent history of American unrest is considered, just as when the violent encounters that a given officer has had are considered, the question is raised: What can be learned from this? The problem is reduced when the answer to that question takes these two directions: First, we must learn to deal with violence effectively, and, second, we must learn how to prevent violence whenever possible.

Violence of any kind has an extremely destructive impact on the community, whether it be the individual homicide, the barroom brawl, the large-scale riot, or the gang-war variety of violence; all are destructive in their impact on the community. But to overgeneralize to the point of assuming that such violence cannot be prevented, or at least reduced, is a serious mistake.

7

Continuing Struggle for Equality: Impact on Police

At the portals of America's Supreme Court is engraved the words EQUAL JUSTICE UNDER LAW. The question of equality remains problematic when criminal justice is discussed, justice under the law having little meaning to many members of our society.

Aside from the inscription over the Supreme Court portals, minorities in America face the reality that, in spite of the hard-fought civil rights battles, serious questions continue with regard to equality in general, not just "under the law."

Consider, for example, what many perceive as the current status of black males in America:

> In Africa, he was free. In America, he was a slave. Today, the black man is struggling with shackles of his own and society's making.

> Once his problems could be blamed clearly on slavery and racism. But today, civil rights successes make it difficult to single out prejudice as the culprit, social experts say. For example, at a time when the number of black elected officials are almost doubled — from 3,503 to 6,681 during the past 12 years — almost half the black men in America are out of work. . . .

Too few people see the correlation between the problems of black men — unemployment, drugs, crime, violence — and the problems of the black community. . . . [1]

From a police–community relations perspective, this viewpoint is crucially significant; its ramifications may well apply to most minority communities. In particular, when the *overall* problems of any minority group are separated from such things as "unemployment, drugs, crime, violence," solutions are not likely, and neither are successful police–community relations in this area.

But if civil rights have been significantly improved, what, then, is the struggle all about? Why is the struggle continuing?

First, there has been little *actual* change in the long-held perception of police work in ghettos and barrios as "dirty work," in some ways not unlike the infamous SS of Nazi Germany.[2] This harsh observation is an extension of a concept that perceives American society as *needing* occupations that insulate the majority of citizens from unpleasant or distasteful work such as garbage collection, the work of morticians, or unpleasant work of any kind.[3] The observation is made that the "respectables" want all these functions performed but are less concerned with the particulars of how the "dirty workers" go about getting the unpleasant jobs done.[4] When police are *perceived* as dirty workers, the question of equality under the law becomes even more cogent — whether or not the question is justified or even fair in the individual case.[5]

Later chapters will address avenues for the police to deal with such unjustified perceptions. But in this discussion of the probability that the struggle for equality will continue well into the future, these observations about police in the ghetto and barrio are very significant.

In the many years that have passed since these observations were made in the literature, claims of progress have been made. To evaluate the progress claimed, it may be helpful to examine the rank-ordered grievances that were documented, city by city, in the violent 1960s.[6] See Table 7-1.

[1] Keith L. Thomas, "Struggle with Social and Economic Shackles Lingers On," from the Cox Newsservice series *The Black Male: A Stranger in His Homeland.* Santa Cruz, CA: *Sentinel News,* Jan. 15, 1989.

[2] Lee, Rainwater, "The Revolt of the Dirty Workers," in J. Skolnick, and E. Currie (eds.), *Crisis in American Institutions,* 2nd ed. Boston: Little, Brown, 1973. For a broader context of this concept in criminal justice, see also James A. Inciardi, *Criminal Justice.* New York: Academic Press, 1984. See also Richard E. Sykes, and Edward E. Brent, *Policing: A Social Behaviorist Perspective.* New Brunswick, NJ: Rutgers University Press, 1983.

[3] Richard N. Harris, "The Police Academy and the Professional Self Image," in Peter K. Manning and John Van Maanen (eds.), *Policing: A View from the Streets.* Santa Monica, CA: Goodyear Publishing, 1978, p. 273. For an added perspective on this issue, see also D. Smith, "The Upsurge of Police Repression: An Analysis," *The Black Scholar,* Jan–Feb. 1981, pp. 35–36.

[4] Harris, op. cit.

[5] See, for example, Lois G. Forer, "The Law's Excessive Promise and Inadequate Fulfillment," *Crime and Delinquency,* Apr. 1978, pp. 197–206.

[6] Taken from *The Report of the National Advisory Commission on Civil Disorders.* Washington, DC: Government Printing Office, 1968, p. 81.

TABLE 7-1   Intensity Level of Grievances

First Level of Intensity

1. Police Practices
2. Unemployment and Underemployment
3. Inadequate Housing

Second Level of Intensity

4. Inadequate Education
5. Poor Recreation Facilities and Programs
6. Ineffective Political Structure and Grievance Procedures

Third Level of Intensity

7. Disrespectful White Attitudes
8. Discriminatory Criminal Justice
9. Inadequate Federal Programs
10. Inadequate City Services
11. Discriminatory Consumer and Civil Practices
12. Inadequate Welfare Programs

From the law enforcement perspective, the only grievance in the first, and highest, level of intensity that police could deal with happens to be about the police themselves — and happens to be the very highest grievance.

POLICE PRACTICES

Fortunately, few would argue against the proposition that, in general, this particular grievance has been dealt with — at least reduced in significance — with the exceptions noted regarding the events of the 1980s in Chapter 6.

Second-level grievances were and have remained beyond the control of police. But the first two listed under the lowest level of intensity have remained crucial matter for many police training programs in years since that report. "Disrespectful white attitudes" and "discriminatory criminal justice" have been under strong emphasis in both police training and police literature. But what has been the result?

We will discuss attitude, bias, prejudice, and discrimination in the following chapter and later in further chapters. Here we need only reflect on the reality that an overwhelming disproportion of nonwhites are arrested, convicted, and imprisoned.[7]

[7]See, for example, Joan Petersilia, *Racial Disparities in the Criminal Justice System,* National Institute of Corrections, U.S. Department of Justice, R-2947, June 1983.

It can be argued that police arrest more blacks and Hispanics than whites because blacks and Hispanics commit more crimes. This same argument adds that the socioeconomic factors that contribute to the disparity are beyond police control —valid arguments in most jurisdictions.

In spite of the validity of this argument in most cases, it remains a police problem to deal with groups who see police as the *symbol* of all that may be wrong, whether or not police can control the problems involved.

THE CONTINUING STRUGGLE FOR EQUALITY[8]

The civil rights movement is customarily written about and discussed as something that began about a half-century ago. There is no question that the period following World War II saw the strongest, most visible, widespread, and organized national effort to bring equal opportunity to all Americans. To fully appreciate the probability that the struggle for equality will continue, however, acknowledgment must be made of the reality that the time span began well before the Civil War, not with the civil rights marches.

Given the perspective on how long it has *actually* taken to achieve whatever degree of success is claimed at this point, it appears likely that law enforcement will face the related problems of this struggle well into the future.

The gains made thus far may well change many of the features of this struggle. It will bode well for all if politics replace violence in this struggle, in the sense that the political arena is far safer for police and far more appropriate for democracy. But in hoping for political measures to replace violence, it must be remembered that those struggling for equality are in the *voting minority,* not just in the racial and ethnic minorities.

As minority voters, gaining the political power to bring about equal opportunity *depends* on the willingness of majority voters. Such willingness may or may not continue on a scale that permits police to become complacent. Frustrating the achievement of equal opportunity, or even the perception that equal opportunity is frustrated, could easily bring back much of the community tension that underpinned a great deal of the violence reviewed in Chapter 6. Since the perception of progress and failure in the struggle is important, consideration should be given to some of the factors that lead to such perceptions.

PROGRESS: SELECTED FACTORS

Not much has been done to change the perception that police send poor people to jail; police remain a symbol of all criminal justice and the power of society.[9] The judicial segment of this is worth further consideration.

[8]The general context in which this discussion takes place is related in greater detail in the U.S. National Advisory Council on Criminal Justice, *The Inequality of Justice: A Report on Crime and the Administration of Justice in the Minority Community.* Washington, DC: U.S. Government Printing Office, 1980.

[9]An interesting peripheral support for this negative view is reflected in Jeffrey H. Reiman, *The Rich Get Richer and the Poor Get Prison,* 2nd ed. New York: Wiley, 1984.

The great majority of people accused of crime in this country are indeed poor. The system of criminal justice under which they are judged is rooted in the idea that arrest can be made only for good cause and that those arrested are presumed innocent until proved guilty; recall the discussion of previous chapters. By and large, the accused are entitled to pretrial freedom to aid in their own defense. A plea of guilty should be voluntary, and the allegations of criminal behavior are to be submitted to the adversary system of American justice.

The importance of the courts is underlined by the fact that, even though relatively few criminal matters reach trial, the cases that do often set the rules for later cases by precedent; court cases thereby become even more the key factor. All this notwithstanding, police still remain the *symbol* of the entire system to many minority groups, a symbol to blame.

Most obviously, the impact of the court is one very important factor in the continuing struggle for equality, even if unseen. Consider, for example, the court ruling in the Dred Scott case. In 1857, the Supreme Court held that Scott, because he was a slave, was not a citizen. Consequently, he could not even sue in court. This decision quite plainly indicated that a little under 150 years ago people of a minority group had no rights whatsoever in a country proclaiming EQUALITY UNDER

TABLE 7–2 The Power to Bring About Change: Three Types

I. *Power of the Majority Vote*
   - Mainly in the hands of voting majority
   - Mainly out of the hands of voting minority

II. *Conforming Alternative Power*
   - Moral persuasion of voting majority
   - Power of the courts and the Constitution

III. *Nonconforming Alternative Power*
   - Peaceful demonstration and dissent
   - Confrontive demonstration
   - Violent uprising

It is hoped, but cannot be taken for granted, that the continuing struggle for equality will remain in the second type of power effort, the conforming type of power to bring about change. Although largely out of the ability of police to deal with as a social problem, law enforcement must remain alert for signs that frustrations are developing in the conforming alternative, signs that may have gone unheeded prior to the violence reviewed in Chapter 6.

LAW. Passage of the Fourteenth Amendment to the Constitution in 1868 clearly established that members of minority groups were to be treated equally under the law. However, for many years following this, the courts interpreted the law in the light of a doctrine known as "separate but equal" rights. In the case of *Plessey* vs. *Ferguson,* the Supreme Court, in 1896, upheld this "separate but equal" rights doctrine as it related to the civil rights of American negroes. In many areas, especially regarding schools, this doctrine of separate but equal rights remained, the conspicuous inadequacy of the "equal" separated facilities notwithstanding. More recently the Supreme Court has made some rulings that should change a good deal of this. One of the first landmark decisions regarding the quality of justice was *Shelley* vs. *Kraemer* in which the Supreme Court struck down certain restrictive covenants in housing. Theoretically at least, this decision enabled members of a minority to legally buy a residence wherever they wished to; but from a practical standpoint, it was necessary to resolve each issue with new litigation.

However, part of the reasoning in the case lead to another landmark case, *Brown* vs. *Board of Education.* In 1954 the court found that the separate but equal doctrine was unconstitutional. This particular ruling by the Supreme Court began, finally, the process of correcting injustice to minority group members in pursuit of their education. It should be noted that segregated schools for Mexican-American youngsters were earlier found to be in violation of due process and equal protection of the law guaranteed under the Fifth and Fourteenth Amendments, in 1947 in California and in 1948 in Texas.

Essentially then, "separate but equal" schools have been ruled inappropriate for *all* minority groups. Another important court decision that affects minorities, principally Spanish surnamed minorities, was a 1974 decision in *Lau* vs. *Nichols.* The case concerned a Chinese youth who spoke only Chinese dialect. Because of this, it was impossible to educate the youth in the San Francisco public school system. The Supreme Court ruled that he must be provided an education in his primary language, rather than in English. The long-range significance of this ruling to the Spanish-speaking minority can only be estimated, but continuing and increasing attention has been focused in this regard.

In 1978, the famous Bakke decision in *Bakke* vs. *California* found that race and ethnic background *alone* cannot be used for setting a quota for admission to college. The decision did say that race–ethnic background could be considered. From a practical standpoint the decision was not important, but from a philosophical standpoint it was somewhat a setback for those struggling for equality.

More important has been the Affirmative Action programs as American companies attempt to deal with the struggle for equality in a more equitable manner. During the 1970s, Affirmative Action began to have some effect in the workplace. The result was more and more minority members getting jobs.

Continuing efforts are made to overcome inequities. These efforts have come from people who have been involved in organizing consumer-protection agencies, among others. Although consumer protection has generally been a concern of the middle class in America, it certainly has great importance to the poor, presumably greater importance to the poor. Its implications are such that continued review of its progress, as well as some knowledge of where a person might go for redress of grievances, would probably be quite useful to police in general and patrol officers in particular. If they were able to direct people with grievances of this sort to the appropriate agencies, this in itself could be a well-appreciated community relations gesture.

Good community relations gestures should not be passed by, even though changes in the law may be reducing at least some tensions.[10]

> The extension of the protection of law—to women, children, non-whites, the elderly, laborers, migrant workers, the poor, the mentally ill, and the convict—has been achieved through bitter and often bloody struggles.

It is these "bitter and bloody" segments of the struggle for equality that should be avoided if at all possible. What are the factors?

Recognition That Things Remain to Be Done

While progress has indeed been made, an important factor in keeping the struggle for equality from becoming "bitter and bloody" is to acknowledge that more progress is needed. To deny this is to add to frustrations and risk a return to the violence reviewed in Chapter 6. While police cannot deal with unemployment, underemployment, lack of education, poor housing, or a host of other social problems, it would be foolish *not* to acknowledge the existence of these problems, even though there is disagreement on whether or not such socioeconomic problems actually cause crime.[11]

It is in this context that we now consider the continuing fact that brothers from the same family, living in the same ghetto home, will often respond differently to these causes: one goes to college without violating any law, the other chooses a life of crime, a problem elaborated on in Chapter 8.

But in terms of a struggle for equality, the point is that for the police to seem to be indifferent to those problems that are beyond police control is not in the police interest. Sensitivity and awareness are definitely indicated. So even the matters beyond police control are of interest.

Employment[12]

In June of 1984, the Supreme Court ruled on a case involving Memphis Fire Department personnel. The court held that an Affirmative Action plan cannot

---

[10]Forer, op. cit.

[11]The argument supporting the theory that such conditions may cause crime can be found, for example, in Allen D. Calvin, "Unemployment among Black Youths, Demographics and Crime," *Crime and Delinquency,* Apr. 1981, pp. 234–244. For the point of view that such problems are merely a part of a larger complex, see for example, Michelle Sviridoff and James W. Thompsons, "Links between Employment and Crime: A Qualitative Study of Pikers Island Releases," *Crime and Delinquency,* Apr. 1983, pp. 195–212.

[12]Employment of racial minorities and women in police work has increased through Affirmative Action as well as through conventional Equal Opportunity. Law enforcement literature reflects a good deal of interest in this subject. See, for example, S.H. Decker and R.L. Smith, "Police Minority Recruitment: A Note on its Effectiveness in Improving Black Evaluation of Police," *Journal of Criminal Justice,* Aug. 1980, pp. 387–393. Nicholas Alex, *Black in Blue: A Study of the Negro Policeman.* New York: Appleton, 1969. Sam Walker, "Employment of Black and Hispanic Police Officers," *Review of Applied Urban Research,* Oct. 1983. Merry Morash, "Understanding the Contribution of Women to Police Work," in Louis A. Radelet, *The Police and the Community.* New York: Macmillan, 1966, pp. 290–294.

disrupt seniority systems to save the jobs of minorities protected by Affirmative Action, provided that the seniority system was unbiased.

This particular factor in relating law enforcement problems to the continuing struggle for equality is twofold. First, Affirmative Action is an avenue by which the frustrations of minorities might be reduced. Second, court rulings regarding civil service or public safety civil service, including police departments, brings the matter directly into the police agency. The Supreme Court decision on Affirmative Action no doubt caught the attention of all minorities, in particular, those who have gained their employment through Affirmative Action programs.

The ebb and flow of political forces in America make risky any speculation about the future of Affirmative Action. Indeed, change in the membership of the U.S. Supreme Court alone could influence Affirmative Action one way or the other.

But in terms of police interest in possible unrest in the future, it is worth note that Affirmative Action brings into focus the very essence of the struggle for equality by paradoxically placing majority job seekers in the position of experiencing discrimination, or "reverse discrimination" as it is sometimes called. This unquestionably does not contribute to the acceptance of minorities by the majority in many cases.

In discussing the rationale for Affirmative Action, Louis Radelet writes: "Lack of opportunity produces lack of accomplishment, which in turn is cited to confirm the original prejudice, or to engender new ones."[13] Radelet goes on to warn of the risk of "re-igniting the flames of violence—the communication of despair."[14]

Let's return to the factor of Affirmative Action bearing directly on police recruiting.[15] Recommendations to strengthen Affirmative Action in police hiring have been made. These recommendations were based on the findings that the police still did not have at the time of the investigation sufficient numbers of minorities and women in their ranks (from 1976 to 1981).[16] Recommendations to improve police training in human relations, improve procedures for dealing with citizen complaints, and revamp personnel selection standards were also included.[17] But in the present context of considering *employment* as part of the continuing struggle for equality, the recommendations to strengthen Affirmative Action is our focal point.

Law Enforcement Promotions and Assignments

A September 30, 1988, finding by a U.S. District Court is of particular significance to law enforcement. The court found that a class action suit filed by Hispanic members of the FBI was valid in that the FBI discriminated against Hispanic agents in both career promotions and field assignments. There are other court cases pending around the nation, and it appears likely that minority personnel will call on

[13] Radelet, Louis A., *The Police and the Community,* 4th ed. New York: Macmillan, 1987, p. 213.

[14] Ibid. p. 214.

[15] U.S. Commission on Civil Rights, *Who Is Guarding the Guardians? A Report on Police Practices,* Oct., 1981.

[16] Ibid.

[17] Ibid.

the court for redress in the future as well. It is clear that recruitment and personnel selection are not the only areas of continuing struggle for equality, even within the criminal justice community itself.

Education

The typical college textbook has many reports and findings from agencies responsible for studying, analyzing, and reporting significant matters. Also typical is that such findings usually become more the "property" of the college student's studying, much more so than the general public. References to academic findings appear in the press, but often without widespread interest — *unless* the report is that a problem has been solved.

This section of the chapter deals with a problem for those struggling for equality: the problem of access to education in a socially changing society that demands more and more education. Recalling that an important factor is to acknowledge that progress needs to be made, consider the following: On September 21, 1988, the U.S. Census Bureau released to the media the findings that over 75% of citizens 25 years old and over completed high school. The report further noted that nearly 20% finished at least four years of college. The Associated Press Wire Service reported a telephone interview on that same date with census demographer Robert Kominski:[18] "In the 1960's the civil rights movement added another level of opportunity. And expansion of college grant and aid programs in the 1960's and 70's allowed this to continue." The AP reported interview further reports Kominski as observing that part of the increase in educational levels was attributable to an "increasing share of black men pursuing their educations."[19] This media-publicized report, which was for the year 1987, noted Hispanic educational levels at 50.9% finishing high school and 8.6% with college degrees, which compares favorably with the 75% and 20% of the general population.

Using the media to publicize these findings is not a new practice; the Census and other services provide press information as a matter of course. But from the point of view of the residents of a ghetto or barrio feeling increased demand for education, it should be considered that such information is a kind of invitation to become complacent, to develop the feeling that everything has been corrected.

The subject of education brings up a variety of problems when discussed in terms of *fully* equal opportunities, the ratio of minority teachers to minority students, for example, which is particularly noteworthy in heavily populated states with large minority populations:[20]

> Minority children make up more than half of California's public school enrollment and their numbers are growing so fast that two out of three students are expected to be black, Hispanic, or Asian by 2015.

[18]Associated Press by-line, Sept. 22, 1988.

[19]Ibid.

[20]Aleta Watson, "Minority Teachers Sought," *San Jose Mercury News,* citing California Department of Education data. San Jose, CA: Ridder News, Jan. 1, 1989.

Yet many of these children may never have a teacher who looks like them, speaks their language, or understands their culture. . . .

In terms of the impact on law enforcement of the continuing struggle for equality, the focus should be on the frustrations and the perceptions of those groups involved in the struggle, not on the improvements perceived by those who already enjoy equality. This is probably an excellent rule of thumb for law enforcement in most areas, not just in terms of educational opportunities.

While educational opportunity has unquestionably increased as a result of the civil rights movement, we need only reflect on the continuing nature of ghetto and barrio life to see that the social gap is increasing between those gaining more and more education and those who do not. The significance of schools in a crime prevention context will be presented in Chapter 8. But in the present context of examining the impact on law enforcement of a continuing struggle for equality, education (or the lack of access to education) is even more significant. The gap that is developing between those acquiring more and more education and those who do not faces the risk of becoming greater in the future as technology continues to unfold.

A brief review of some aspects of ghetto and barrio life may clarify some of the dimensions of this increasing gap.

LIVING CONDITIONS

Before examining the problems of ghetto and barrio life, it should be noted that there is, in a real sense, the potential for struggle between cultures or subcultures in these areas of urban centers. This potential problem can be thought of as cross-cultural interaction.

Cross-cultural: A Potential Problem[21]

In recent years hundreds of thousands of refugees from Southeast Asia have come to America. Being from different Asian localities, their cultures differ, as do their native languages. Their struggle for equality includes the sad reality that they are vulnerable not only to the prejudice and discrimination facing other racial minorities, but must deal with exploitative criminals within their own cultural framework.

[21] The literature is rich in cultural matters relating to minorities. See, for example, U.S. Commission on Civil Rights, *Mexican Americans and the Administration of Justice in the Southwest.* Washington, DC: U.S. Government Printing Office, 1970. Also Nicholas Alex, *Blacks in Blue: A Study of the Negro Policeman.* New York: Appleton, 1969. Also National Advisory Council of Criminal Justice, LEAA, *The Inequality of Justice: A Report on Crime and the Administration of Justice in the Minority Community,* Washington, DC, 1980. Also P.B. Taft, Jr., "Policing the New Immigrant Ghettos," *Police Magazine,* July, 1982, pp. 10–26. P. Uhlenberg, "Marital Instability among Mexican Americans: Following the Patterns of Blacks?" *Social Problems,* Summer 1972, pp. 49–56. L.M. Stern, "Response to Vietnamese Refugees: Surveys of Public Opinion," *Social Work,* July 1981, pp. 306–312. See also other citations in this chapter.

Most share the cultural heritage of honoring parents, saving face, and shyness regarding physical contact.

Our later discussion of the plight of the Hispanic or Spanish-surnamed minorities in the barrios will include the same language barrier faced by Asian refugees. And the customs of the Spanish-speaking minorities vary for the same reasons as for Asians; like Asians, Spanish-surnamed minorities come from different areas: on the eastern seaboard, mainly from Puerto Rico, and in the southwest United States, mostly from Mexico. The black minority includes groups who have varying cultural standards, which in turn adds to the complexity in the struggle for equality — having in common certain goals but potentially perceiving each other as competitive.

Although the emphasis of this chapter is on the probable continuation of the struggle for equality, law enforcement appears to be facing up to at least part of the problems involved, the problem of cross-cultural communication as it relates to law enforcement.[22]

The police role in the broader societal perspective must of necessity be defined as primary; the mission of police is to "police society"[23]. In this broader context of the police mission on a society-wide basis, there are certain obvious criminological factors that must also remain a priority.[24] Yet even though the law enforcement mission encompasses a society-wide scope, the *potentially* explosive police problems in the seemingly secondary matter of trouble between minority cultures must remain a significant police concern. We need only reflect on the violence reviewed in Chapter 6 on civil disorders to establish the significance of this potential. So in our discussion of minorities struggling for equality, it should be continually acknowledged that there is a potential for struggle *between* minorities erupting as part of the process.

With this not so incidental consideration in mind, let us now address the subject of living conditions in the black ghetto and the Hispanic barrio.

The Black Ghetto[25]

There are many areas that are of concern when the problems of poverty confront the community; the barrios and black ghettos are not the entire story of minorities enduring the anguish of poverty. They are, however, largely concentrations of frustration and despair that should be of particular concern to law enforcement.

Every American city houses a major segment of the poverty stricken in a ghetto, and in many cities in a barrio; the barrio is the name given the separated,

[22]See, for example, G. Quintanalla, "Cross-Cultural Communication: An Ongoing Challenge," *FBI Law Enforcement Bulletin,* Feb. 1983, pp. 1–8.

[23]See, as examples of this broader perspective, the materials in W. Clinton Terry, III (ed.), *Policing Society.* New York: Wiley, 1985.

[24]A good example of the rich literature in this area is M.R. Haskell and L. Yablonsky, *Criminology: Crime and Criminality,* 3rd ed. Boston: Houghton Mifflin 1983.

[25]Parts of this discussion were published earlier in A. Coffey, E. Eldefonso, W. Hartinger, Human Relations: Law Enforcement in a Changing Community, 3rd ed., 1982. Passages from pages 30–46. Reprinted by permission of Prentice-Hall, Inc., Englewood Cliffs, NJ.

poverty-stricken area of Spanish-surnamed residents. The most salient characteristic of the ghetto is the increasing concentration of blacks, often within the central cities.

Here the discerning observer can recognize the severity of the plight of those struggling for equality. In recognizing this plight, the observer also recognizes the potential problems posed for police and the increasing need for police to seek the support of the community for law enforcement.

It is obvious that more and more of the black population has become urbanized during the past 75 years. However, so has most of the population of the United States. The difference is that most blacks have moved into and are concentrated in the inner quarters of large urban centers, whereas whites have moved more to the suburbs.

Furthermore, a very small percentage of the total population of the nation is made up of blacks. However, a large proportion of this group is concentrated in the ghettos of urban areas. Therefore, within the central city there is a high concentration of extremely poor people of a particular ethnic background — in this case, black people. It is speculated that the population shifts that have lead to the culmination of large black ghettos have been caused by three factors: (1) the migration of southern blacks to the cities in pursuit of employment, (2) the concentration of blacks in segregated big city neighborhoods, and (3) the rapid growth of the black population because of better medical care coupled with a high fertility rate.

In the mid-1960s, the period noted in Chapter 6 as related to a great deal of violence, approximately two-thirds of all black people who lived outside the South were residents of the 12 largest cities of the United States and lived mostly in the central cities. At that time, these cities were New York, Chicago, Los Angeles, Philadelphia, Detroit, Baltimore, Houston, Cleveland, Washington, D.C., Milwaukee, St. Louis, and San Francisco. For the most part, blacks moved into ghetto-type segregation. Like other migrants and immigrants, they first move into the older sections of the city. But unlike the case with migrants from Europe, the blacks' color historically barred them from leaving these poor neighborhoods even when they became financially able to do so. The predominantly white society that has absorbed the immigrant has, by in large, refused to absorb the blacks. Until quite recently, this segregation was effected by local housing ordinances and real estate codes coupled with violence and intimidation. Often when a black moved into a white neighborhood, whites moved out of the area, causing vacancies that were, in turn, filled by black citizens, and the whole character of the neighborhood changed. Unscrupulous real estate agents often used this "blockbusting" technique to increase sales and, consequently, real estate commissions.

Racial segregation has existed in American cities for most of this century. But during the early part of the second half of this century, it seemed to increase in every large city in the United States. It should be noted that the number of urban whites in substandard housing, generally known as slums, is about two and half times the number of urban blacks in such housing in most cities. However, the *proportion* of the black population in inferior dwellings is much greater. Put another way, even though more whites may live in these slum areas, the proportion of whites compared to the general white population is much smaller; a greater proportion of the black population occupies the slums, which are not only substandard overall, but overcrowded as well.

The overcrowding is directly related to the fact that blacks tend to get far less for their housing dollar than do whites. Often they cannot get housing similar to that of whites without paying much more for it, a situation that seems to prevail in most of America. This fact, plus the predominantly low income earned by black ghetto dwellers, results in a large percentage of family income being spent for housing.

Landlords often victimize ghetto residents by ignoring building codes, probably because they know their tenants are restricted, by economic or ethnic background, to live in the ghetto. Broadly speaking, these circumstances, along with others that will be expanded on later, are those that the minority groups refer to when they say they are being treated unjustly by society, a significant factor for law enforcement when it is recalled that police seem to *symbolize* society in general. There is some feeling that ghetto dwellers might have a better chance of leaving the ghetto if they were able to earn higher incomes. However, at least some blacks apparently feel uncomfortable moving away from their old neighborhoods; consequently, they stay in the black neighborhood even when they have the monetary resources to move. And these higher incomes are hard to come by: Ghetto residents have problems obtaining jobs. Unemployment and underemployment, as already noted in this chapter, are among the most serious and persistent problems of disadvantaged minorities. Perhaps just as important is the problem of the undesirable nature of many jobs open to blacks. While changing gradually in the culture, black ghetto dwellers nonetheless are often concentrated in the lowest-paying and the lowest-skill jobs in the economy. These jobs usually involve substandard wages, great instability, and uncertainty of steady employment. As a result, the income of black families has tended to remain below that of white families.

Because of these factors, residents of black ghetto neighborhoods have been subject for decades to social, economic, and psychological disadvantages. The result is a vicious circle of failure; the employment problems of one generation breed similar problems and worse for the following generation, and so on. The educational problems previously noted in this chapter are extremely severe in the ghetto. The one bright hope most Americans in earlier periods had for their future generations lay in the schools. A good education has traditionally been the means by which people have escaped poverty and discrimination and consequently from the ghetto. Therefore, education within the ghetto is particularly acute as a problem. By and large, schools in black ghettos have failed to liberate the people from their plight. This failure has caused resentment by the black community against schools, a resentment that is not wholly unfounded. Poor education is only one of many problems; the previously mentioned association with crime rates is also a factor. Whether or not such conditions can be proved to cause crime, criminologists have known that crime rates are always higher in poor neighborhoods, no matter what their ethnic composition. The black ghetto is no exception. The black resident's sense of personal security is certainly undermined by the frequency of crime in the big city ghetto. The ghetto may have as much as 35 times more serious crime per 100,000 residents as does a high-income white district.

Crimes in ghettos are committed by a small minority of the residents. Most of the victims are law-abiding people. It is difficult for middle-class whites to understand how insecure these law-abiding ghetto dwellers feel.

Because of this higher crime rate, many blacks have bitter feelings toward the police. The feeling that they do not receive adequate protection by law enforcement tends to be one of their principal grievances as we have already noted. Add to the general despair of the ghetto the reality that poor families are usually found to be on poor diets, inadequately clothed, and with poor medical care. The family structure itself is affected by residence in the ghetto. Because the men of the family often cannot obtain jobs in legitimate enterprises that enable them to support their wives and children, their status and self-respect are affected. Almost without exception, women are forced to work or go on welfare so that the family can be provided for economically. Women often earn more money than the men, and this too may affect the status or self-respect of their husbands. If the husband feels inadequate, the possibility of divorce or separation increases. This in turn leads to the fact that more and more ghetto families are being headed by females rather than males. A related factor is that welfare payments are often tied to the absence of the father from the home. Therefore, for the mother and children to survive economically, the father often deliberately absents himself from the home.

The Hispanic Barrio

The Spanish-surnamed minority (the Spanish-speaking minority) is the second largest minority in the United States. In many respects, the lot of these people has been similar to that of the blacks. By and large, the Spanish-surnamed minority lives in a separate residential district that has come to be known as the barrio. In the southwestern part of the United States, this is often a residential district separated from the rest of the population center by a highway or a railway track. Housing in the barrio, as in the ghetto, is dilapidated, aged, and substandard.

When discussing this minority group, it is necessary to remember that it is composed of several groups of people with somewhat different backgrounds. In the five southwestern states of Arizona, California, Colorado, New Mexico, and Texas, most of the Spanish-speaking people are Mexican-Americans. This means that they were either born in Mexico, rather than in other Latin American countries, or that their ancestors originally came from Mexico. The Spanish-surnamed population in New York and other eastern states, on the other hand, is largely Puerto Rican. And those with Spanish surnames who live in Florida generally trace their ancestry to Cuba.

Besides being from different countries, their racial ancestry tends to be different. They may be Caucasoid, Indian, Negroid, or any combination. They are sometimes referred to as Latinos or Hispanics. Also, because of their diverse backgrounds, they tend to be less organized than blacks.

The child learns Spanish as a first language in the barrio and often encounters a problem entering American public schools, where English is the language used. For a time in the 1920s and 1930s, Spanish-surnamed people were considered to be less intelligent because of their problems with school work. Since that time, however, an awareness has developed of the many different variables that affect school achievement, including health and nutritional status, as well as the obvious language problem.

The problem of overcoming the handicap of learning English as a second language, coupled with segregation of Spanish-speaking students in school, has had a negative effect. Until the late 1940s, there was segregation of the Mexican-Americans on a de jure (legal) basis in the Southwest as noted earlier with regard to court decisions. Today there is still de facto segregation of students within the school system. Such segregation due to residential patterns is under scrutiny in many western states.

Unfortunately, a member of the Spanish-speaking minority tends to have a problem receiving a good education in English, regardless of the school district's efforts. The result is that the person has problems selling his or her services on the job market, thus continuing the cycle of poverty.

But the solution to language problems is not rectified by a simple course in English. Many children with Spanish surnames, who are second- and third-generation American citizens, speak Spanish before they speak English. Many of them speak a combination of English and Spanish slang that is difficult for language instructors to deal with. That the Spanish-surnamed minority is not a heterogeneous group compounds the difficulty; the poverty to which Puerto Rican Americans are subjected is different in many ways from that of Mexican-Americans or Chicano minority members. Spanish-speaking blacks confuse the "Spanish-speaking" classification even further.

OTHER SALIENT PROBLEMS IN THE STRUGGLE

In the widening complex of social and economic factors influencing the struggle for equality, certain areas seem to be more salient than others, at least for the police, perhaps beginning with the visibility police have for minorities. If we are considering police visibility, acknowledgment should be made of the problem of America's homeless in this regard.

The Homeless

Although less of a law enforcement issue than many factors of the ghetto and barrio, the emerging problem of people without homes impinges on police. Police are asked to remove these people from the streets and parks and to enforce various ordinances relating to health and sanitation.

The homeless are no longer the group of vagrants that police have traditionally encountered. Although hobos are still among the homeless in America, many urban areas are witnessing the inclusion of women and children, even whole families, in this group.

This is not a simple problem. Among the homeless are those who *prefer* and deliberately choose to live on the streets. More in line with the theme of this chapter, however, are the homeless who are struggling to gain equality through programs to end the homeless situation.

Growing political pressure will continue to highlight this problem. It is conceivable that police will experience greater demands to involve themselves beyond the routine evictions from park benches.

Certainly every jurisdiction experiencing this problem needs to remain alert to any indication that the situation is evolving into the sphere of police responsibility, a definite priority in efforts by the police to gain community support.

Recruiting Minority Personnel

We have already noted that recommendations have been made to strengthen Affirmative Action and police recruiting. In support of this recommendation is a survey finding that the nation's 50 largest cities had underrepresentation of black and Hispanic officers in police agencies.[26]

The significance of the cited underrepresentation of black and Hispanic officers has to do with the *high visibility* of police, combined with the tremendous *symbolism* of police power—power perceived as control by the majority to the exclusion of minority influence.

Even the most sensitive, perceptive, and well-trained police officer symbolizes the minority society's loss. In this context, police are a reminder of how little power minorities have—a reminder that only a majority of votes can win an election or bring about wanted change, except of course when violence is used to bring about change.

Combine this variety of symbolism with the negative connotations of police as the enforcers in crime-ridden minority areas, and a clearer picture of the need for minority representation in the police force emerges. Even those minority members among the crime victims who want and need law enforcement develop their views in terms of seeing the police in the role of power.

Another salient characteristic in the struggle for equality is the ever-present contrast between the poor and the affluent.

Contrast with America's Affluent

The segment of population in countries who watch American television, particularly the "sitcoms" and commercials, would probably report a grossly inflated image of American affluence. This probably has to do with not having *actual experience* with the average culture in America. In many ways, poverty-stricken people are in the same situation. Without actual exposure to the real American society, the media image of general affluence is acceptable.

On a comparative basis, the affluence does exist. Typical middle-class lifestyles operate at a consumer pace that exceeds anything the typical poor family could hope for or even imagine without the media's help. When careful considera-

---

[26]Sam Walker, "Employment of Black and Hispanic Police Officers," *Review of Applied Urban Research,* Oct. 1983.

tion is given to this contrast, powerful images of affluence emerge, the image of all people outside the ghetto being rich and powerful. If this consideration is dwelt on for a period of time, it becomes astounding that the violence of the 1960s has not continued. For, indeed, in spite of great strides in coping with the gap between poverty and the rest of America, a visit to any slum area will show how great the gap remains.

The high visibility of affluence to the poor, combined with the high visibility of police, has always been a source of tension throughout the history of the ghetto. But this enormous difference in access to riches is far more threatening to all concerned if there is any belief that the enforcers of law are discriminating, a crucial subject in Chapter 4. The police officer willing to acknowledge the potential explosiveness of this very visible contrast must also acknowledge it seems likely to continue and even increase.[27] And as this contrast increases, even routine police practices may well increase resentment, which will increase the need for police seeking the support of the community they serve.[28] The final salient feature of the struggle for equality is intended to "roll up" several significant factors into one: Limitation on the police ability to correct problems they face.

THE STRUGGLE: LIMITATIONS ON THE POLICE

Obviously, unemployment and underemployment cannot be corrected by the police. Nor can poor housing, overcrowding, and poor educational opportunities. Continued police sensitivity to their existence is perhaps the only police response. But these are the *obvious* areas on which police are limited. Less obvious to many is that police cannot by themselves control the high crime rates of ghettos and barrios.

The conditions that make crime the primary alternative are far beyond police ability to deal with. This is not to say police can afford to ignore the criticism of underenforcement in the ghettos. Crime victims are victims regardless of the geographical area of the city. With this in mind, Chapter 14 will present police–community relations as including a communication network that at a minimum offers ghetto and barrio minority leaders information on where to seek redress from problems beyond police control.

Returning to what can and must be done for those struggling for equality, police must help reduce the *fear* of crime. There are many ways to do this. For it is this *fear* of crime in America that warps and distorts perception; the fear itself far exceeds the actual incidence of crime.[29] If this is the case in America overall, picture the amplified fear that must prevail in the crime-ridden poverty areas. The struggle for equality will not be won by police reducing the fear of crime. But the impact on the police of that struggle will be far more positive if effort is made to reduce fear, while reducing as much as possible the actual incidence of crime.

[27]For an insightful analysis of the difference affluence makes in the justice process, see Reiman, op. cit.

[28]Institute for the Study of Labor and Economic Crisis, *The Iron Fist in a Velvet Glove,* 3rd ed. San Francisco: Sythesis Publications, 1982.

[29]See, for example, *Report to the Nation on Crime and Justice, The Fear of Crime.* Washington, DC: Bureau of Justice Statistics, U.S. Department of Justice, March 1988.

In a related vein, Chapter 8 will discuss the theoretical causes of crime to provide a background for a later discussion of crime prevention, which is seen as the most powerful weapon against *fear* of crime.

SUMMARY

The struggle for equality was introduced as spanning the period that began well before the Civil War, with the prediction that the struggle will continue.

It was noted that the voting strength of minorities forces dependence on majority voters for continued improvements legislatively. It was also noted that there is risk of returning to disorder should the continuing struggle for equality be frustrated again. The selected factors of progress and failure of the struggle for equality were presented as including courts, employment (including Affirmative Action), education, and a number of social factors. These included the living conditions of underprivileged minorities, and a brief discussion of the black ghetto and Hispanic barrio was presented.

Salient problems for police were considered in the area of high police visibility, along with related social matters involving such problems as homelessness in America.

The impact of American affluence on the perceptions of the poor was considered. The limitation on the police role in correcting socioeconomic problems was presented in terms of what the police must do in the areas that impinge on law enforcement; citizen fear of crime was cited as one area in which positive police efforts could be made to improve the chances of gaining community support for law enforcement.

DISCUSSION TOPICS

1. Elaborate on this chapter's contention that the struggle for equality began well before the Civil War.
2. Discuss the point made in this chapter that minorities depend on majorities for changing legislation by the voting process.
3. Elaborate on the implications of the police being a symbol of society while at the same time being unable to correct many social problems.
4. Relate American affluence with potential police problems in the ghetto as discussed in this chapter.
5. Discuss the *fear* of crime as presented in this chapter.
6. Elaborate on this concept in terms of the ghetto crime rate.

Relevant Problems for Discussion

In the sense that the major theme of this chapter is *problems,* the main problems have been presented. The related problem of coming to grips with the *continuing* nature of the problems presented, however, is worth note.

With the positive incentive of building a better community, combined with the negative incentive of avoiding a repeat of the violence reviewed in Chapter 6, good police–community relations include integration of factors relating to the struggle for equality.

A potential additional problem can emerge when community leadership is divided into two points of view: first, a point of view that the community should set a goal that is realistic, measurable, and achievable; second, that there is no actual goal, and the struggle for equality will continue until everyone achieves the same level of affluence. Put another way, the community leaders reflecting the viewpoint of an affluent majority may, in good conscience, wish to set a specific measurable goal to be achieved in a specific period of time. Minority leaders may instead perceive the need to approach the matter on an open-ended basis, allowing the goal to be measured by the achievement of equal affluence for everyone rather than by a particular time frame.

Fortunately, most would agree that competition in society will always distribute affluence at different levels and that it would be totally unrealistic to attempt to equally distribute affluence. Nevertheless, there remains in many instances a difference in the perception of what is realistic and achievable.

To keep such a problem a minor one, to keep it "more apparent than real," the goals in police–community relations that deal with equality should focus on equality of *opportunity*. Achieving the opportunity to gain equal affluence and the related equal power is presumably a far more achievable goal than seeking the utopian equal distribution of all affluence. Obviously, police have very little actual influence over such philosophical points of view among community leaders. It is nevertheless worthwhile to seize every opportunity to exercise whatever influence is possible in creating this meeting of the minds. When opportunities present themselves, emphasis must remain on the continuation of competition as an economic reality during the continuing struggle for equality. In simpler terms, gaining an *equal chance to compete* is an achievable goal, whereas equal affluence for all is an economic impossibility.

This problem can be either more apparent than real and virtually not worth considering or a major schism in the community; the intensity of differing values and the presence or absence of leadership will make the main difference. This variation is also part of the rationale in Chapter 14 for describing every community as unique, each requiring a unique approach to police–community relations.

PART THREE

Law Enforcement and the Community

Part Three contains the subjects most emphasized in this volume. Its general purpose is to acquaint the reader with police programs that help and problems that hinder police-community relations.

The complexity of how crime and delinquency are caused is presented as a foundation for reviewing some of the strategies for community efforts to prevent crime. Such strategies are presented as dependent on police leadership in the community. The problems of attitude are related to community relations in terms of intergroup problems. The impact of prejudice, bias, and discrimination are related to these same police-community relations problems. Police responsibilities for domestic crisis and juvenile problems are related to the factors that both help and hinder efforts to improve police-community relations.

Another purpose of Part Three is to combine with Part One and Two to form strong support for the final section of this volume, Part Four's presentation of the requirement of community support for law enforcement to succeed.

8

The Causes of Crime and Delinquency

Previous chapters have emphasized, in various contexts, the need for law enforcement to gain and keep the support of the community. One of the more compelling reasons for the police to seek community support had to do with the restrictions placed on enforcing law in constitutional government, combined with the reality that in most jurisdictions there are from 4,000 to 15,000 people for every *one* uniformed police officer on duty; community support *is* needed.

One of the most constructive approaches to gaining the support of the community is the cooperative efforts of police and citizens in trying to *prevent* crime and delinquency, the subject of Chapter 9. In such a cooperative venture, police of necessity must take the leadership role. But when law enforcement takes the initiative in setting up programs for community crime prevention, the subject of the causes of crime and delinquency will certainly come up.

Understandably, community leaders usually expect police officials to know what causes crime and delinquency. Police are, after all, the community's own crime problem experts. Why not have the police simply explain what causes the problem, then go out and prevent it? Very simple—right?

Actually, there *are* approaches that do effectively reduce crime sufficiently to claim successful crime prevention. But these usually have more to do with *reducing the opportunity for crime* than with the complex causes of criminal motivations. There are those that contend that the opportunity is a *cause* of crime. But in the context of bringing community leaders and police officials together for the purposes of preventing crime, it appears useful to understand as much as possible about causes of crime other than mere opportunity.

Let us now consider what is involved in pondering the actual *causes* of crime and delinquency, beginning with the *prediction of crime.*[1]

CRIME PREDICTION VERSUS CRIME CAUSE

Although *comprehensive* research has not fully supported the belief, many veteran criminal justice personnel are convinced that they can predict future crime by certain offenders; some personnel make the claim for *all* offenders. These include police, probation, and parole officers, and in many instances they have been accurate enough often enough to perpetuate this belief. We might argue that such prediction has to do with the self-fulfilling hypothesis, the idea that, if a person is given to understand crime is expected of him or her, then crime is far more likely. Nevertheless, the personal intuition of veteran criminal justice personnel can often accurately *predict* crime.

Added to the personal acuity of veteran criminal justice personnel are the prediction devices used by various jurisdictions operating offender diversion programs or operating programs that screen offenders for release on OR (own recognizance). Psychological tests including projective technique as well as psychometric techniques, severity scales measuring the seriousness of the offender's behavior, and security scales are included in the various approaches used to *predict* whether or not crime will be committed by an individual offender.

But here we are talking about offenders who have already been "caused" to commit offenses. While it is true that preventing *further* offenses is still prevention, it is not the kind of prevention that can involve the whole community, assuming the entire community does not wish to be screened. Valuable though such prediction approaches may be to criminal justice programs, they are of little practical use to the community in terms of community *participation* in crime prevention.[2]

But prediction does relate well to a matter that can lead to further understanding of *causes,* that is, the matter of offender classification.

---

[1]Many jurisdictions that use offender-diversion programs employ a wide range of "severity scales" and "risk predictors," as do probation and parole programs. For literature on crime prediction, see, for example, Ferdinance N. Dutile and Cleon N. Foust, (eds.), *The Prediction of Criminal Violence.* Springfield, IL: Charles C Thomas, 1987. See also Harold V. Hall, *Violence Prediction: Guidelines for the Forensic Practioner.* Springfield, IL: Charles C Thomas, 1987.

[2]For discussion of the criminal justice use of this concept see, for example, John Blackmore and Jane Welsh, "Selective Incapacitation: Sentencing According to Risk," *Crime and Delinquency,* Oct. 1983, pp. 504–528.

CLASSIFICATION OF OFFENDERS

Once an accused person is *classified* as an offender, many further classifications occur. As in the case of *prediction* of crime, a variety of severity scales and risk scales, along with psychological and even sociological scales, is used by adult and juvenile detention as well as correctional programs. These various efforts to accurately classify the offender may be motivated by security concerns with how to distribute the offender population to ensure maximum security. Other motivations may be various correctional treatment concerns or rehabilitation, or both. But virtually all detention and correctional programs have *some* form of classifying offenders, if nothing more than by the nature of the crimes committed.[3]

Traditionally, when classification was intended as an all-inclusive method to explain crime causes, it was called *typology*.[4] Typologies in the broader application were intended not only to classify the criminal but to account for criminal motivation and define methods to correct or rehabilitate the offender.

Among other approaches to classification was the concept developed for the purpose of assessing the offender's level of maturity.[5] This approach may serve to give background for our discussion of crime causes.

Level of Maturity Classification

As it is commonly used in criminal justice circles, the term *maturity* generally embraces not only certain attitudes but also such variables as intelligence, demeanor, propriety, and even politeness. For purposes of classifying some of the more significant characteristics of offenders, however, maturity is better defined without reference to any of the many variables mentioned. Intelligence, for example, is not always associated with mature judgment. In other words, from a criminal justice point of view, maturity level has to do with the overall maturation process.

As it applies to the classification of criminal and delinquent offenders, the maturation process is concerned with what can be thought of as an awareness of others. The infant is relatively unaware of others: the mature adult, on the other hand, is aware of both others as well as himself. In a classification of maturity, this is the continuum referred to, the range of levels of awareness of others stretching between the two extremes of absolutely no awareness of others to a point of total

---

[3]Parts of this and later discussions in this chapter were published earlier in A. Coffey, *Prevention of Crime and Delinquency,* 1975. Passages from pages 28–49. Reprinted by permission of Prentice-Hall, Inc., Englewood Cliffs, NJ.

[4]During the 1960s, this approach was thought by many to hold the promise of major improvements in criminal justice. For an excellent explanation of the concept, see, for example, Julina B. Roebuck, *Criminal Typology.* Springfield, IL: Charles C Thomas, 1967.

[5]A great deal of literature was generated on this subject by M.Q. Warren and D.C. Gibbons. In particular, see Marguerite Q. Warren, *Correctional Treatment in the Community Setting: A Report of Current Research,* N.I.M.H./HEW, Pub. No. HSM 72-9129, Washington, DC, 1972, pp. 1–5. See also California Youth Authority, *The Community Treatment Project after Five Years.* Sacramento: CYA. See also Don C. Gibbons, "Differential Treatment of Delinquents and Interpersonal Maturity Levels Theory: A Critique," *Social Service Review,* Mar. 1970.

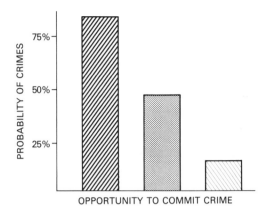

PROBABILITY OF CRIMES

75% —

50% —

25% —

OPPORTUNITY TO COMMIT CRIME

Crime-prone individual exposed to the psychological, sociological, and physiological crime causes, plus conditions noted in Chapter 7.

Crime-prone individual exposed to significantly fewer of the crime causes and living in better conditions.

Crime-prone individual without exposure to crime causes and with adequate living conditions.

Figure 8–1 Maturity level and crime causes. The concept of maturity level can aid police in explaining crime prevention strategies to community leaders. For example, the extremely crime vulnerable I-2 probably varies greatly in response to opportunity to commit crime, in terms of the presence or absence of the crime causes presented in this chapter, as well as the presence or absence of conditions noted in Chapter 7. (Source: California Youth Authority)

awareness of self and others, an extremely significant consideration in criminal attitudes and motivations.

Within this conceptual framework, an extremely sophisticated system known as the I-level (interpersonal maturity level) was developed and tested during the 1960s. Whether or not a given jurisdiction would subscribe to implementation of such a classification system, the principles involved are extremely important to understanding the complexity not only of the classification but of the causes of crime and delinquency as well.

The I-level classification system sought to take into account the fact that not all offenders perceive reality in the same way. To illustrate with a common example, some offenders may perceive police as just doing their job, while other offenders may perceive the same police as persecuting the offender.

The object of the classification system is to differentiate between the perceptual differences of the offenders. In this regard, the system identified seven stages along a continuum of personal development. Levels 2 through 5 included subtypes distinguishing certain behavioral or perceptual characteristics that varied within a given perceptual level. Levels 1, 5, 6, and 7 are not pertinent to this discussion in that level 1 is so infantile that the individual would require permanent institutionalization if an adult, whereas levels 5 to 7 are *by definition* too mature to be involved in offenses requiring criminal classification, the maximum maturity being a method of defining a "noncriminal." Consider the description given the maturity level 2 by the California Youth Authority:[6]

> Maturity Level Two (I-2). The individual whose personal understanding and behavior are integrated at this level is primarily involved with demands that the world take care of him. He sees others primarily as "givers" or "withholders" and has no conception of interpersonal refinement beyond this. He has poor capacity to explain, understand, or predict the behavior or reactions of others. He is not interested in things outside himself except as a source of supply. He behaves impulsively, unaware of anything except the grossest effects of his behavior on others.

The behavioral subtypes I-2 are the asocial, the aggressive, and the passive individuals. These subtypes add an interesting dimension to discussions between veteran police officers on offenders who are continually arrested without apparent understanding. Consider now the California Youth Authority description of the I-3:

> Maturity Level Three (I-3). The individual who is functioning at this level, although somewhat more differentiated than the I-2, still has social–perceptual deficiencies which lead to an underestimation of the differences among others and between himself and others. More than I-2, he does understand that his own behavior has something to do with whether or not he gets what he wants. He makes an effort to manipulate his environment to bring about "giving" rather than "denying" response, He does not operate from an internalized value system but rather seeks external structure in terms of rules and formulas for operation. His understanding of formulas is indiscriminant and oversimplified. He perceives the world and his part in it on a power dimension. Although he can learn to play a few stereotyped roles, he cannot understand many of the needs, feelings, and motives of another person who is different from himself. He is unmotivated to achieve in a long range sense or to plan for the future. Many of these features contribute to his inability to accurately predict the response of others to him.

The subtypes for I-3 are the immature conformist, the cultural conformist, and the manipulator, each of which has great significance in criminal justice; each classification is apparently associated with a different style of crime. Consider now the California Youth Authority description of the I-4:

> Maturity Level Four (I-4). An individual whose understanding and behavior are integrated at this level has internalized a set of standards by which he judges his and others' behavior. He can perceive a level of interpersonal interaction in which individuals have expectations of each other and can influence each other. He shows some ability to understand reasons for behavior, some ability to relate to people emotionally and on a long term basis. He is concerned with status and respect, and is strongly influenced by people he admires.

The I-4 subtypes, neurotic (either "acting out" or neurotic-anxious), situational emotional reaction, and cultural identifier are also geared to criminal justice problems. The I-4's concern with status and respect and the vulnerability to excessive

[6]California Youth Authority, The Community Treatment Project after Five Years. Sacramento: CYA, 1968, p. 3.

influence from people the offender admires should be of particular interest to law enforcement jurisdictions coping with gang problems.

There are many other classifications systems, many as intricate as this example. This particular example, however, provides a conceptual framework through which to approach the wide and varied theories of crime causes that we will now review.

CAUSES OF CRIME

There are two different views of criminal justice in America. Probably most veteran practitioners consider the criminal justice process more art than science. There are, however, those who consider criminal justice a science.[7] But even among those conceiving of criminal justice as science, there would probably be agreement that the precise *causes* of crime are not *actually* known. This reality is not always acknowledged; there are many explanations of crime, some by excellent scholars. In the press, it is not uncommon for the public to be advised that crime can be explained by a combination of biological and social influences.[8] The many factors that can be isolated and linked to crime, such as age, poverty, sex, race, and overcrowding, are also thought to explain crime.[9]

Another factor linked to crime is the disproportionately high percentage of minority persons who are arrested, compared to the size of the minority population.[10] But linking factors must be consistent to be useful, and consistency is where the problem emerges.

Confronting all serious effort to narrow down the vast array of factors to anything useful is a common problem: why a cause or causes do not *always* cause crime. This inconsistency in causes is generally known as the negative case.

The Negative Case

For centuries, serious students of human behavior have speculated, theorized, and researched the fascinating question of the causes of crime. This concern grew to its peak following World War II.[11]

[7]See, for example, James R. Davis, *The Science of Criminal Justice,* Jefferson, NC: McFarland and Co., 1986, p. 183.

[8]See, for example, Richard L. Hernstein and James Q. Wilson, "Are Criminals Made or Born?" *New York Times Magazine,* Aug. 4, 1985.

[9]See, for example, J.M. Byrne and R.J. Sampson, (eds.), *The Social Ecology of Crime.* New York: Springer-Verlag, 1986.

[10]Joan Petersilia, *Racial Disparities in the Criminal Justice System.* Washington, DC: U.S. Department of Justice, June 1983. For further elaboration of the concept of crime itself, see *Report to the Nation on Crime and Justice, What Is Crime?* Washington, DC: Bureau of Justice Statistics, U.S. Department of Justice, March 1988.

[11]Following World War II, considerable scholarly effort was expended on criminological theory. Among the outstanding recommended classical readings are H.E. Barnes and N.K. Teeters, *New Horizons in Criminology.* Englewood Cliffs, NJ: Prentice-Hall, 1960. Also, Paul Tappan, *Crime Justice and Correction.* New York: McGraw-Hill, 1960. Also G.B. Vold, *Theoretical Criminology.* New York: Oxford University Press, 1958. Also A. Vollmer, *The Criminal.* New York: Foundation Press, 1959. Also T.N. Ferdinard, *Typologies of Delinquency.* Berkeley: University of California Press, 1969.

All branches of modern behavior science have studied and researched deviant behavior, especially the deviant behavior of criminals and delinquents. Many profoundly eloquent theories have evolved through sociological, psychological, physiological, and anthropological approaches to studying crime. But the frustrating problem confronting earlier theorists, and to some degree modern theorists, is the negative case, the case in which the theory cannot account for the exceptions.

The negative case is that group, usually a majority of the population supposedly exposed to the theoretical cause, that does *not* become criminal. Put another way, if poverty causes crime, why do *most* poor people *not* become criminals? Likewise, if family problems or any other problems cause crime, why do not all people exposed to the same problems become criminals?

When the negative case demonstrates a flaw in the theory, behavioral scientists tend to adjust assumptions and blend one theory with another, hoping to account for the exceptions. Some theorists do better than others, but the truth of the matter is that neither police nor community leaders can to this day approach the crime problem with *definitive* information on crime causes; human behavior still remains too complex to provide such certainty.

Nevertheless, in spite of the failure to produce definitive causal explanations of crime, there remains a great deal to be gained through understanding some of the more classic examples of theoretically explaining crime. Medical research into mental disorders may soon fill in some of the missing pieces that have thus far frustrated most theoretical approaches.

Medical, Biochemical, and Pharmaceutical Theories

Many believe that psychiatry is on the verge of a major breakthrough in treating mental disorders. This belief is primarily founded on research into genetic and biochemical influences, the possibility being that many disorders previously treated by psychotherapy may in reality be a physical problem. It seems reasonable to assume that such a remarkable breakthrough in the information about human behavior would have some application to criminal conduct as well. This alone appears reason enough to reach some degree of understanding of the classical theories about crime causation. For, just as the negative case frustrated other approaches to crime causes, the genetic and biochemical theories may encounter the negative case as well. However, with a fuller understanding of many of the well-researched classical theories of crime causes, the total picture could be at hand; older classical theories may account for the negative cases of newly discovered genetic and biochemical theories, and vice versa.

This raises a question that cannot be answered at this juncture but should be noted: Are humans self-determined?

Are Humans Self-determined?

The philosophy of self-determinism holds that the individual has complete control over his or her behavior; crime and delinquency thus represent free choice. But what if it were to turn out that genetically and/or biochemically there is no free choice?

The laws that govern the land operate on the premise that individuals are self-determined.

The philosophy of determinism, on the other hand, holds that the behavior of an individual is determined by forces over which she or he has no control, an implicit assumption in many of the explanations of crime causes.

Societal regulation of individual behavior through laws and social constraints is grounded in the philosophy of self-determinism. Laws would be pointless unless individuals are free to choose to obey them. The orderly environment we have discussed would be impossible unless citizens are to some degree held accountable or responsible for their actions. Nevertheless, it is becoming increasingly clear that social control depends upon *both* deterministic and self-deterministic factors, a frustrating yet very real problem for modern police. This is yet another reason for the police seeking community support for law enforcement to have a fuller understanding of the theoretical explanations of crime causes, which virtually all assume some degree of determinism rather than self-determinism.

With this in mind, discussion will be now directed to some selected examples of the theories about crime causation: psychological, sociological, and physiological.

Psychological Theories

The two examples of psychological theories used to account for crime causes will be ego-state theories and personality-disorder theories.

Ego-state theories. A good starting point for examining the ego-state theories intended to account for criminal behavior is recognition that modern social science has repeatedly challenged the validity of a great deal of psychoanalytic theory. It is not our intent to examine psychoanalytic theory validity but rather to examine the conceptual framework that does indeed illuminate many of the complex variables involved in criminal careers. It was Sigmund Freud, the brilliant physician of his day, who devised the system known as *psychoanalysis,* a theory conceiving of personality as composed of three parts: the *id,* the *ego,* and the *superego,* a construct that will be useful in our later consideration of attitude. As will be noted in the discussion of attitude, the *id* was conceived of as a source of all basic drives, such as hunger and sex. The *ego,* developed through infancy and childhood, provides the *id* with a conscious avenue to acquire satisfaction for its drives. The *superego* is roughly equivalent to a conscience and tends to inhibit the immediate satisfaction sought by the *id.* In terms of crime and delinquency, the *superego* is the most significant of these structures; offenders with *no* superego are presumably the most dangerous or at least the most criminally inclined. The use of ego-state psychology to explain delinquency and crime hinges on the notion of conflict, at least in the case of Freudian psychoanalysis. For example, conflict occurs when basic *id* drives prove incompatible with civilized existence, as defined by the *superego* or conscience. Conflicts between these two ego states are more subtle when the need for success is combined with a limited avenue for success; some sociological theories hold this to be an important cause of delinquency and crime, as will be discussed later in this chapter.

This theoretical conflict presumably contributes to delinquency and crime through the discomfort it generates, although the offender is unaware of the source of this mental discomfort. He or she seeks only to reduce the ensuing anxiety, usually experienced as tension.

Reduction of anxiety is theoretically accomplished by substituting fantasy or other unreal activity for the conflicts, usually called mental illness when taken to an extreme. If instead an individual acts out the conflicts in overt behavior, criminal and delinquent activity may be included. From this theoretical orientation, the criminal activity is seen as an effort to resolve the conflict existing between the id and the superego.

Because the desires of the id are often in conflict with society's demands and standards of behavior, the impulses of the id must frequently be *repressed*. In effect, this means that a person unable to adequately repress his id drives will probably become a criminal or a delinquent.

Even when repression is successful, the id drives continue to seek expression, producing continued conflict and anxiety, which may eventually explode. A more subtle variation is when these drives increase the guilt feelings to the point that an individual will *seek* and desire punishment for the forbidden impulses and may indeed commit a crime for the purpose of being caught and punished.

A modern extension of ego-state theory is the *transactional analysis* of the late Eric Berne. Transactional analytic theory accounts for criminal and delinquent behavior, and virtually all human behavior, in terms of psychological games that people play.[12]

The *transaction* is, in its simplest form, a kind of psychological stimulus and response: one person's acknowledgment is the stimulus, and the other's reaction is the response. Transactional analysis describes three ego states of the human personality: the parent, the adult, and the child. The ego state known as the *parent* might well be compared to the superego in that it influences the ego state of the *child* toward a moralistic conformity. The *child* functions in part as does the id, contributing impulsive charm, pleasure, and creativity, as well as spontaneous delinquency in some cases. The *adult* is often oversimplified as simply being the same as the Freudian *ego* since its function is to regulate a person's activities. In transactional analysis, crime and delinquency are seen as a kind of game that serves, among other things, to substitute for real living. Real living involves an emotional risk by requiring exposure to genuine intimacy, which is fearful for many because it may carry the threat of various forms of rejection. Since a game reduces the risk of rejection, it replaces real living.

Transactional analysis also includes such concepts as rackets and trading stamps to explain human behavior. A trading stamp is something that happens to a person that can engender either good feelings (gold stamps) or bad feelings (brown stamps). Comments from a police officer perceived as insults are brown stamps that can be saved until the offender is entitled to either assault the police officer or commit another crime, thereby cashing in his book of brown stamps.

---

[12]Although intended as a popular book rather than a criminological theory, many criminal justice practitioners in the 1960s virtually adopted the concept of *transactional analysis* and the principles of Berne's book. Eric Berne, *Games People Play*. New York: Grove Press, 1964.

Delinquency and crime involving assault and battery may be related to such a brown stamp collection in general. Brown stamp collecting becomes known as a racket when the collection of bad feelings is used to justify the crime and delinquency, in a not infrequent phenomenon according to the criminal justice personnel who subscribe to this theory.

Criminal and delinquent behavior, according to transactional analysis, are caused by motivations or rewards called payoffs, such as cashing in brown stamps. Such payoffs operate as a kind of secret reason for playing the game; the secret may be kept not only from others, but from the offender's own adult ego state. This suggests that the cause of crime and delinquency may be unconscious.

Typical games include "lets you and him fight," "cops and robbers," "kick me," and "court room."

Now let's consider the theories of personality disorder.

Theories of personality disorder.   Criminologists tend to disagree on the relation of personality disorders to crime; this disagreement has continued for many years. While some consider personality disorder to be a cause of at least certain types of crime and delinquency, many others hold that such disorders are of little influence on criminal behavior; again the negative case strongly influences such opinion.

One personality disorder that is sometimes held to be related to crime and delinquency is *mental deficiency*. Mental deficiency describes a condition in which a person's mental attitudes have failed to develop to a normal degree. It is contrasted to psychosis and other disorders in that it involves *sub*normal, rather than abnormal development. Certain forms of mental deterioration associated with psychosis may produce mental deficiency, but fundamentally the feeble-minded person is usually *under*developed. Conceivably, the I-1 of the classification system reviewed earlier might fit this particular description.

Mentally deficient persons sometimes do commit delinquent or criminal acts. Such delinquency and crime, however, usually can be attributed to a lack of adequate supervision. Most individuals afflicted in this matter are not offenders. The negative case is extremely strong in this regard, and yet there is enough crime for many criminologists to continue to consider this a causal factor.

Personality disorders such as psychoses and neuroses are actually related to the ego-state theories that we have already discussed. There is literally no consistent way to determine how many criminals are *treated* as mentally ill or how many mentally ill persons are treated as criminals; the tremendously overcrowded prisons and the log-jammed criminal justice system simply cannot cope with the challenge of making such distinctions on a systematic basis. As the discussion of constitutional government indicated, mentally ill persons who are known to be incapacitated cannot be convicted of a crime in most jurisdictions, at least until they have sufficiently recovered to stand trial.

The personality disorder known as *psychopathy* or more commonly known as *sociopathy* is considered by many criminologists to be a direct cause of a great deal of crime and delinquency. The obvious question that emerges immediately is what *causes* sociopathy. A sociopathic personality can be defined in terms of the ego-state psychologies discussed previously; the person lacks a superego or conscience, or a *parent* ego state. The sociopath is hostile and aggressive toward others. He or she demands immediate satisfactions of his or her desires and needs and most of the sociopath's behavior is concerned with satisfaction; recall the previous discussion of the interpersonal maturity level classification I-2.

The key question of how the sociopathic personality is formed has developed little consensus among criminologists. The most common explanation of how such a personality arises centers on the individual's childhood experience. A sociopathic individual grows up in an environment in which parental love is lacking. Since the child does not have his parents' love in the first place, she or he has nothing to lose by behaving antisocially.

In the Chapter 9 discussion of prevention strategies, the significance of the family will be reviewed, an extremely significant factor in successful police–community efforts to prevent crime. The prevention of criminal offenses by offenders who have become sociopathic is virtually impossible in some cases; the prevention of individuals from becoming sociopaths may also be difficult but probably less so than coping with sociopaths once their personality has developed without conscience.

Let us now turn to a few of the sociological explanations of crime causes.

Sociological Theories

As in the case of the psychological theories just discussed, considering sociological theories will draw on the rich literature that developed following World War II.[13] The theory classifications selected will be ecological, cultural, and social.

Ecological theory. We have noted in many different contexts throughout this volume the application of social ecological theory to *dealing* with crime and delinquency. The theory continues to have application in approaches to *correcting* what is believed to be the causes of crime. Early ecological theorists, as much intent on discovering the causes of crime as correcting the crime problem, have contributed greatly to the understanding of criminal behavior in America. The ecological theory of crime and delinquency is concerned with the areas in which crime and delinquency seem most likely to occur. Many criminologists in the past have cited the work of Clifford R. Shaw as the most significant contributor in this area.[14] Shaw studied crime and delinquency statistics recorded in Chicago between 1900 and 1927. Over 55,000 juvenile delinquents and some criminals were found to live in certain zones of the city. Shaw concluded that many of the law violations recorded were

[13] The richness of literature on sociological crime causal theory developed rapidly after World War II and particularly in the 1960s. See, for example, R.A. Cloward and A.K. Cohen, *Delinquent Boys.* New York: Glencoe Press, 1955; D. Downes, *The Delinquent Solution.* New York: Glencoe Free Press, 1966; D. Matza, *Delinquency and Drift.* New York: Wiley, 1965; T.L. Stotbeckt, *Group Process and Gang Delinquency.* Chicago: University of Chicago Press, 1965. Then see in particular C.L. Shaw, *The Jackroller.* Chicago: University of Chicago Press, 1942; F.M. Thrasher, *The Gang.* Chicago: University of Chicago Press, 1963; Donald Gibbons, *Delinquent Behavior.* Englewood Cliffs, NJ: Prentice-Hall, 1970; and finally T. Hirschi, *Causes of Delinquency.* Berkeley: University of California Press, 1969.

[14] Shaw, *The Jackroller,* op. cit. Shaw also wrote *The Natural History of a Delinquent Career.* Chicago: University of Chicago Press, 1942, and *Delinquent Areas.* Chicago: University of Chicago Press, 1942.

acceptable behavior within the specific zone in which the offender lived, that the offender was in effect *conforming* rather than nonconforming.

About 26% of the male juvenile delinquents came from a single zone, whereas in another zone virtually no male juvenile delinquency occurred, or at least none was recorded. The negative course applies here in that 74% of the male juveniles were not delinquent, but the significance of Shaw's findings were nonetheless astounding.

The higher delinquency rates in certain zones were then attributed by Shaw to three factors: the deterioration of some neighborhoods due to the invasion of industry and commerce; a subsequent reduction of interest in appearance or moral reputation; and, finally, a reduction of social control through neighborliness. Also cited was the influx of immigrants whose customs tended to conflict with local norms and in turn ultimately produced a secondary conflict between first- and second-generation immigrants.

Another criminologist, Frederick Thrasher, studied over 1000 Chicago gangs and he too found that they were concentrated in zones of factories and railroad centers, radiating from Chicago's loop district outward toward the city's exclusive residential areas, an "old finding" that continues to have startling relevance in many jurisdictions throughout the land.

Cultural theory.   Still another theoretical explanation of criminal and delinquent behavior attempts to isolate the subculture of the delinquent or criminal in the urban setting.[15] The variance of criminal or delinquent gang subculture is in part attributable in this theory to "significant different social worlds," a concept developed by criminologist Albert Cohen. Before pursuing this any further, it might be useful to define the terms culture and subculture. Insofar as crime and delinquency are concerned, culture might be considered to be simply the pattern of behavior, ideas, and values that are accumulated as a tradition. A subculture, then, would simply be a group whose characteristic behavior, ideas, and values distinguish it from the broader culture. The cultural approach to crime and delinquency conceives of a given age group as a subculture. While a subculture need not be at variance with the more general culture, it is obvious that in the case of a delinquent or criminal subculture such a conflict does indeed exist, and continues to this day to be an extremely significant factor in many urban jurisdictions.

The variance between culture and subculture referred to here might be thought of in extreme cases as being at odds with the culture. Beyond the violation of the laws of the culture, the very value system on which laws are based is called into question in the criminal subculture, according to this theory.

In this regard, whatever causes a person to conform to the subculture norms is the *cause* of crime and delinquency because the norms are crime and delinquency. As the working class individual experiences frustration in achieving culturally desirable goals, he or she becomes aware of the alternatives to legal methods of achievement that are already available, at least in the criminal and delinquent subculture, thus becoming aware in many instances of the "norm" to be delinquent or criminal.

[15]Cohen, *Delinquent Boys,* op. cit.

According to this and the ecological approach, working class children and adults as well are caught up in a frustrating struggle between means and ends; while they strive competitively for material symbols of wealth, they find themselves unfairly denied access to these symbols because of their subcultures. Criminal and delinquent behavior provide an illegal means of achieving the desired goals, but the significance of illegal is weakened by the norm of the subculture.

An interesting expansion of this particular explanation of crime and delinquency was developed by the noted criminologist Edwin H. Sutherland,[16] In his *differential association* theory, Sutherland held that crime and delinquency flow from excessive exposure to certain values that prove conducive to such behavior, that a criminal or delinquent has been *differentially* associated with such values. In the context of the negative case, those who are not criminal in a given area were not "as differentially associated" with the causation influences.

Certain implications of the concept of differential association have been examined by another criminologist, Walter Reckles, who noted that a child growing up where she or he learns the techniques and justifications for crime may well respond to this influence in the same manner that a middle-class child responds to the influence of culturally acceptable behavior. In other words, Reckles went beyond Sutherland's initial premise to point out that the process by which a child acquires the behaviors and values of the accepted culture is identical to the process by which the child acquires the behaviors and values of the delinquent subculture; only the content of the culture that is acquired is different. From this perspective, a delinquent child is not deviant.

Even though differential association does a better job than certain other theories in dealing with the negative case, the negative case nevertheless poses a problem—the failure to account for persons who do not commit criminal offenses even though they *seem* to be exposed to the same influences as persons who become criminals and delinquents. The unanswered question, obviously, is *why* is this differential association experienced differently?

Social theory.[17]   One of the first beliefs to emerge from the early experience of juvenile courts was that divorce and parental desertions were the cause of most of the crime and delinquency at the time. This belief no doubt stemmed from the observation that about half the known criminals and delinquents were from broken homes.

Criminologists Clifford Shaw and Henry McKay concerned themselves specifically with this question but found that only 42.5% of known criminals and delinquents came from homes disrupted by divorce or desertion. They interpreted their

[16]Probably the most widely acknowledged theoretical effort to deal with the negative case from a sociological type of framework was Sutherland's *differential association*. Directly and indirectly, the principles and concepts of Sutherland's *differential association* continue to clarify many frustrating facets in the study of crime and delinquency. E.H. Sutherland and D.R. Cressey, *Principles of Criminology*, 8th ed. Philadelphia: J.B. Lippincott, 1970.

[17]See footnote 11 for sources. See also Clifford Shaw and Henry McKay, *Juvenile Delinquency in Urban Areas*. Chicago: University of Chicago Press, 1942; and Sheldon Glueck and Eleanor Glueck, *Unraveling Juvenile Delinquency*. New York: Commonwealth Fund, 1950.

findings as evidence that broken homes, although significant, could not be the major cause of crime and delinquency.

Although later studies failed to confirm broken homes as a *cause* of delinquency, there nevertheless appeared to be some kind of relationship between family status and juvenile offenses. For example, some 44,000 children who were studied in Philadelphia appeared less inclined to become delinquent when living with both parents. With such findings, refinements in this causal theory expanded to include the *nature* of the broken home—the nature of parental separation in terms of divorce and desertion as opposed to death of one parent or other causes.

Still another social variable that has been related to crime and delinquency is the lack of recreation. In Chapter 9 the family and the availability of recreation will be cited in the discussion of strategies for prevention. These factors have been associated with the crime problem for some time; studies have indicated that criminals and delinquents seek exciting diversions, sometimes on dark streets or in railway yards as well as vacant lots and buildings. In this approach, delinquency and crime are viewed as recreation that leads in turn to additional crime. This notion that criminals and delinquents seek excitement and recreation may lack comprehensive research and validation, but is a belief held by many veteran police officers.

The problem of poverty has been associated by some social ecologist theories to crime, more so by social theorists attempting to account for crime. The late Paul Tappan, noted criminologist of his time, questioned the relationship between delinquency and crime and poverty, noting that the overwhelming majority of poor families do not become involved in crime and delinquency.

One other social factor often linked to crime is the school, a major subject in the Chapter 9 discussion of strategies of prevention. As a primary agent of the socialization of children and adolescents, the school is clearly related in many ways to the attitudes and conduct norms developed by students.

Physiological theories

This third category of theories on the causes of crime concentrates on the *physical* characteristics of the offenders. These theories can be broadly divided into three groups: hereditary, biochemical, and anthropological. Discussion of the biochemical in this chapter will be confined to the earlier theorists; the ongoing genetic research noted in the beginning of this chapter will not be reviewed.

Hereditary theories.[18]   Early proponents of the hereditary theory of crime and delinquency may not have envisioned the current research into the genetic influences on human behavior. Indeed, such research, combined with the research into the biochemical influences on human behavior to be discussed next, may ultimately prove the most enlightening of all explanations of crime, as well as the

---

[18]This discussion of earlier research on hereditary "causes of crime" is drawn primarily from R.R. Bell, *Social Deviance.* Homewood, IL: Dorsey Press, 1971; W.E. Schafer, C. Olexa, and K. Polk, "Programmed for Social Class: Tracking in High School," and K. Polk and W. Schafer (eds.), *Schools and Delinquency.* Englewood Cliffs, NJ: Prentice-Hall, 1972, pp. 43–44; and particularly M.F.A. Montagu, "The Biologist Looks at Crime," *The Annals,* Sept. 1941, pp. 45–51.

most challenging in terms of constitutional rights, civil liberties, and the other factors discussed in Chapter 3.

Proponents of the heredity theory of crime held that the tendency toward criminal behavior is inherited much the same way as other genetic characteristics. Studies of three families, the Kallikaks, the Nans, and the Jukes, in which criminal behavior appeared in members of successive generations, are generally cited as evidence of the hereditary cause of criminality. This brief reference to theories on crime causation that relate directly to heredity has more to do with the widespread acceptance of such theories by the general public than to its acceptance among criminologists. Indeed, the majority of criminologists would likely contend that heredity is *not* a major crime causation, at least pending a great deal more evidence than currently exists from genetic research and other physical considerations.

The hereditary explanation of crime, in contrast to sociological theories, tends in most instances to disregard the influence of the environment on crime and delinquency, or at least relegate such influence to a secondary position. The greatest support for this approach to explaining crime was probably the noted biologist M.F. Ashley Montagu, who sought to combine the sociological theories and hereditary theories by acknowledging those cultural factors that are indeed influential in delinquency, while at the same time giving primary emphasis to the genetic endowment of the offender. In the context of continuing research, Montagu's theory may ultimately prove far more useful than currently believed.

Current genetic research indicates that at least certain types of behavior can be abnormal as a result of genetic variables, for example, the complement of sex chromosomes. As more intensive research continues in the future, hereditary explanations may prove to have a far greater significance in approaching the prevention, or at least the control, of crime and delinquency.

Biochemical theories.[19]   The influence of secretions of the endocrine glands on human behavior was first set forth in *The Glands Regulating Personality* by Louis Burman, published in 1922. Since that time, findings on the ways in which various hormones effect behavior have been woven into a kind of biochemical explanation of crime and delinquency. Surprising to many is the relative acceptance of this theory, the acceptance of a notion that "ductless glands" can cause criminal behavior, whereas heredity cannot.

According to the biochemical explanation of crime, different individuals show varying levels in the body of such hormones as the estrogens and androgens, thyroxin, parathryn, cortin, and adrenalin, and these variations produce corresponding differences in behavior.

Endocrinologists, biologists studying the functions of the ductless glands, continue research in this area, and their findings are proving increasingly useful in psychiatry, as noted earlier, and may ultimately revolutionize many segments of psychiatry.

[19]This brief discussion of earlier approaches to explaining crime causation biochemically is drawn primarily from the literature cited in footnote 18 and A. Podolsky, "The Criminal Brew of Criminal Behavior," *Journal of Criminal Law, Crime, and Police Science,* 1955, pp. 675–679; and A. Snodgrasse, "Crime and Human Constitution," *Journal of Criminal Law, Crime, and Police Science,* Spring, 1951 pp. 19–27.

Anthropological theories.[20]   The widely held notion that all fat people are jolly is evidence of the common belief that persons with similar physiques share certain personality traits. Some scientists and theoreticians have a tendency to develop systems that would directly correlate specific physical features with certain behavior, suggesting that a certain type of physique might *cause* crime.

The nineteenth century Italian physician Cesare Lombroso sought to identify the physical features that could be directly linked to criminal misconduct. Drawing heavily on the then popular beliefs of phrenology (which holds that the configuration of the skull is related to personality), Lombroso described certain physical characteristics comprising the "stigma of degeneration" which he held to be shared by all criminals.

Advancing Lombroso's "lantern jaw and pointed ears" concepts further, William H. Sheldon, an American psychologist, developed a widely recognized classification system that relates body shape to personality. Sheldon, building on a somatic typology formulated two decades earlier by Ernest Kretschmer, identified three basic physiques: *endomorphy* (rotund, with excessive fatty tissues), *mesomorphy* (muscular), and *ectomorphy* (lean, angular).

According to this system, the fatter endomorphs are affectionate and gregarious and therefore less likely to become criminal. The muscular mesomorphs are held to be reckless, to seek physical adventure, and to need activity when troubled, and are thus considered prone to crime deviance. Finally, the tall, lean ectomorph is described as shy, aloof, and often nervous and therefore unlikely to become criminal or delinquent.

It would be difficult to argue that physical characteristics such as height, weight, skin tone, and physical attractiveness do not *influence* the social experiences of children in many ways that help to shape their behavior. This fact may well account for the persistence of the anthropological approach to delinquent and criminal behavior, the fact that many fat people are not jolly and many muscular people are not adventuresome notwithstanding.

This will conclude the review of the selected theoretical explanations of crime causation. Let us now turn to concepts that may make such theoretical explanations of value in approaching police–community crime prevention, the subject of Chapter 9.

PERCEPTION OF OTHERS AND THE CAUSES OF CRIME

Early in the chapter we reviewed a classification system known as the interpersonal maturity level. The concept on which that was based had to do with an increasing awareness of others.

Since it has become clearer that no one theory or even any group of theories is fully adequate to explain the causes of crime, the significance of this *continuum* of

---

[20]This brief discussion is drawn from a wide range of literature, but in particular the earlier writings of criminologists H.E. Barnes and N.K. Teeters, *New Horizons in Criminology.* Englewood Cliffs, NJ: Prentice-Hall, 1960, Chapter Six, "Prescientific Theories of Causes of Crime;" Paul Tappan, *Crime, Justice, and Correction.* New York: McGraw-Hill, all chapters under the section "Causation." Also contributing were S. Sheldon, A. Hartele, and M. McDermott, *Varieties of Delinquent Youth.* New York: Harper & Row, 1949.

awareness of others is a valuable concept. Indeed, each time a negative case undermines an explanation of crime, it may well be related to the variation in the awareness of others and, more importantly, awareness of the needs of others.

Awareness of Needs

To identify the combination of causes that are relevant in a particular case of crime, some understanding of the individual's perception of *needs* may be important, the perception of the needs of self and the needs of *others*.

Human beings vary in their awareness of the needs of others. For example, a teen-age boy may find himself overwhelmed by certain sexual needs that he relates to self. Yet he may be all but unaware of the needs of his female peers for warmth, security, and affection. If he commits sexual assault, this delinquent act may theoretically be described as caused by a combination of physiological factors and psychological factors, compounded by the absence of social influence due to the lack of awareness of others' needs. If this teen-ager has a brother who is not sexually assaultive, it may well be that certain differences exist in how the same psychological and physiological factors are perceived by the two brothers, perception influenced by a different level of awareness of others' needs. For example, the second brother may have a greater awareness of the needs of others, which leads him to replace sexual assaults with sexual seductions. That is, because he is more aware of others' needs, psychological and physiological influences lead him to seek sexual gratification by simply exploiting the needs of others rather than aggressively committing a violent and illegal act.

This oversimplified illustration falls far short of acknowledging the complexity of juvenile delinquency[21] and obviously does not address the scope or extent of juvenile delinquency.[22] In spite of these limitations, the implications of this illustration *may,* on reflection, increase the understanding required to bring police and community closer in dealing with crime. For one thing, the differences in perceptions noted in this illustration are remarkably similar to the variations in perceptions between various groups in the community, including the variations in perceptions between community leaders and the offenders who are of concern to the police.

It is therefore advisable to consider the wide variation in people's understanding of the needs of others when attempting to relate some of the possible causes of crime to the subject of Chapter 9, police–community crime prevention.

SUMMARY

This chapter was introduced as a foundation for the Chapter 9 discussion of community crime prevention. It was noted that community leaders tend to regard

[21]See, for example, Marvin E. Wolfgang, Terrence B. Thornberry, and Robert M. Figlio, *From Boy to Man: Delinquency to Crime.* Chicago: University of Chicago Press, 1987. See also Steven M. Cox and John J. Conrad, *Juvenile Justice,* 2nd ed. Dubuque, IA: William C. Brown, 1987.

[22]See, for example, Jay S. Albanese, *Dealing with Delinquency.* Lanham, MD: University Press of America, 1985.

police as experts on the causes of crime and expect leadership in this regard when crime prevention programs are developed. Crime prediction was contrasted with crime causes in terms of community prevention needing as much understanding of *cause* as possible and prediction having to do more with the responsibilities of police and other criminal justice components.

The classification of offenders was illustrated with the example of maturity levels.

Earlier classical crime causation theories were reviewed, with examples from psychological, sociological, and physiological/hereditary theorists.

Review of these earlier theories was followed by a discussion of the perceptual differences, with emphasis on the wide variation that exists between individuals in terms of an awareness of needs of others.

The negative case was emphasized throughout the discussion, and the promise of continuing genetic and biochemical research was noted.

DISCUSSION TOPICS

1. In what ways can the understanding of earlier crime causation theories aid understanding of future research?
2. Discuss the classification of offenders as presented in this chapter.
3. Describe the continuum of increasing maturation as discussed in this chapter.
4. Distinguish between the three categories of classical theories presented: psychological, sociological, and physiological.
5. Elaborate on the significance of the negative case.
6. Relate the discussion of differences in the awareness of others' needs to the negative case.
7. Discuss ways in which police–community crime prevention can be enhanced through recognizing both the theories presented and the negative case problem.

Relevant Problems for Discussion

We noted in this chapter that citizens tend to expect police to know the *causes* of crime because police are the community specialists in dealing with crime. We also noted that many veteran police and other criminal justice personnel do in fact seem capable of predicting further crime for certain offenders.

In Chapter 9 on community crime prevention, it will be pointed out that a kind of self-fulfilling hypothesis takes place when people are *expected* to be criminal; people often do precisely what they are *expected* to do.

When the *concept* of what causes crime becomes part of police–community programs, extreme care is needed to ensure that all concerned remember the *negative case*. Entire neighborhoods can often fit crime-causal categories when the negative case is overlooked. This is only a short step away from entire neighborhoods being expected to be criminal and treated as though they will become criminal. And no matter how many *are* criminal in even the most crime-ridden neighborhoods, at least some are not.

Regardless of how expedient it may be to utilize crime rates to bolster crime-causal categories to prove an entire neighborhood fits, police will add to the number of criminals by following this path, not reduce the number.

The pressures of life and of law enforcement problems tend to create a kind of demand for simple answers that make such expedience attractive in some cases. Such temptation should be resisted and the causes should be considered as factors associated with crime, never as proving an entire neighborhood should be expected to be criminal.

This position is very easy to hold as long as the negative case is remembered.

9

Police and Community Crime Prevention

We have discussed in Chapter 8 some of the classic theories on what causes crime and delinquency. Now let us address the police–community effort to prevent crime, since prevention is the greatest incentive for community support of law enforcement.

The complexity of our society and human nature, in general, will not allow complete prevention of crime or delinquency. But with the combined efforts of law enforcement and the community itself, enough crime can be prevented to make controlling the rest much easier, and gain community support for police in the bargain.

This approach will not relieve police of their enforcement responsibilities. But good enforcement deters at least some crime and that too is "prevention."

PREVENTION OF CRIME: SOME DEFINITIONAL CONSIDERATIONS

The October 1988 issue of the *FBI Law Enforcement Bulletin* was devoted to crime prevention—five excellent articles on the subject. Let's consider one of the approaches used to define crime prevention in one of these articles:[1]

[1]George B. Sunderland, "The Community: A Partner in Crime Prevention," *FBI Law Enforcement Bulletin,* Oct. 1988, p. 7.

Community crime prevention can mean many things to many different people. J. Edgar Hoover, while Director of the Federal Bureau of Investigation, once stated that crime prevention begins in the high chair and not in the electric chair. To others, crime prevention means the elimination of social and economic inequalities.

The community can be the most effective vehicle for the reduction of the kinds of crime that bother individuals the most — the "opportunistic" crimes.

Opportunistic crimes suggest the kind of definition of prevention that removes or reduces the *opportunity* to commit crime. In this context, consider the following:[2]

Risk avoidance (avoiding known areas of criminal activity or placing valuables in a safe deposit box);

Risk reduction (reducing the level of exposure to an acceptable level, e.g., when a storekeeper reduces amount of cash on hand to cover only immediate business transactions);

Risk spreading (applying security devices and procedures);

Risk transfer (purchasing insurance to cover crime losses);

Risk acceptance (when a merchant or individual determines additional crime prevention efforts are not worth the possible loss, e.g., valuable jewelry is placed in a safe at closing but inexpensive costume jewelry remains on display); and

Risk removal (placing valuables in a safe deposit box).

Conceiving of crime prevention in terms of opportunity greatly simplifies the concept, at least compared to the complexity of trying to apply the theoretical concepts of causes as presented in Chapter 8. But the main task is to involve the community, whether the definition of prevention is simple or complex.[3]

One of the smartest investments a local law enforcement agency can make is to help its community establish and sustain citizen-based crime prevention efforts. The job of law enforcement *is* to prevent crime, but it must be a task shared with community members.

Helping the community, we will note later, is the key; law enforcement is and must remain in the leadership role of accepting total responsibility for dealing with crime in the community. But that part of the crime problem allocated to prevention efforts must have community support. Some believe this is not too difficult:[4]

Establishing a community organization as a cooperative venture with law enforcement agencies is not difficult if the community perceives a need and if the crime prevention practitioner is persuasive in convincing the participants that crime can be reduced.

[2]Ibid.
[3]Jean F. O'Neil, "Crime Prevention Pays," *FBI Law Enforcement Bulletin,* Oct. 1988, p. 14.
[4]Sunderland, op. cit., p. 9.

There have been such astronomical increases in common street crimes in recent decades that most communities will participate once they believe they can do something about this "hopeless" problem.

There are others who propose approaching the establishment of a cooperative venture between law enforcement and the community on the basis of challenging questions to the citizens of the community; the questions were intended to challenge the citizen to recognize that community help is essential to combat crime in the following case, as related to drug abuse:[5]

> Are you just watching . . . while drug-related crime invades your community? What are you doing to combat the problem? What would you be willing to do as a responsible and concerned member of your community? How much local drug abuse and related crime finally becomes too much? How many deaths from drug overdose must occur before your community becomes concerned and preventive action is taken? Are you prepared to support and participate in law enforcement programs which are designed to protect you, your loved ones, and your possessions?

Defining crime prevention in a manner that permits all forms of crime to be considered indeed brings complexity in much the same sense as did the theoretical causes reviewed in Chapter 8. But such expansion also allows attention to focus on areas where police input could and should be used, but usually is not:[6]

> The well-worn cliche coined by Benjamin Franklin, "An ounce of prevention is worth a pound of cure," seems an appropriate way of introducing a new role for law enforcement agencies in supporting the public and private activities of communities. Law enforcement agencies are the only major community and governmental service not included in the review and approval process of planning, zoning, traffic, and environmental design decisions.
>
> Why is it that a law enforcement officer who is visiting another city can automatically pick out the problem neighborhoods and business areas? The answer is simple—they learn to associate certain environmental conditions with social, economic, and crime problems.

Chapter 14 has as its main subject the concept of police–community relations. Here we are concerned with police *leadership* in efforts to prevent or at least control crime. Law enforcement input into planning, zoning, traffic, and environmental design may, in many communities, be a significant factor in crime prevention or at least crime control. It is therefore worthy of consideration in any discussion of prevention.

Crime prevention has the potential of bringing about a great deal of community support for law enforcement, a great deal of police–community harmony. Such harmony is the natural result of sharing the common goal of preventing as much crime and delinquency as possible and controlling the rest. Chapter 14 deals with the broad concept of gaining community support. Here we are addressing the specific

[5]Drug Enforcement Administration, *Drug Abuse Is a Community Problem,* Washington, DC, U.S. Department of Justice, 1988, p. 1.

[6]Timothy D. Crowe, "An Ounce of Prevention: A New Role for Law Enforcement," *FBI Law Enforcement Bulletin,* Oct. 1988, p. 18.

subject of gaining at least some of the needed support through efforts to prevent crime and delinquency. Support for law enforcement is encouraged by the actual participation of citizens; members of the community actually perform activities that are intended to prevent or at least reduce crime.

About Citizen Crime Prevention Strategies

What needs to be emphasized is that we are not here examining what *police* must do to prevent crime. Special characteristics of the police patrol and other police programs are addressed to that particularly. Here we are considering citizens and groups of citizens that might play a key role in preventing crime and delinquency.[7] In selecting the community groups for discussion as possible crime prevention resources, it is assumed that the police must play a strong leadership role or, at a minimum, a strong advisory role.

In performing the leadership role, police officials must take whatever steps are necessary to ensure that what police officials say is what line officers actually do. Veteran police officers, as well as the literature, attest to the problems of agency policy and police behavior being two different things.[8] Police officials who recognize this as a problem might consider involving line officers in the leadership role with both community leaders and community groups.

Presumably, when line officers are functioning as consultants or advisors rather than being on patrol duty, there is a better chance of an open and honest exchange of views and ideas. The officer should both *teach* and *learn* — teach citizens the realities of the crime problem and learn the value of citizen support. At least in the proverbial best case, this approach should reduce the problem of the community having to deal with two stories, what the administration says, and what line officers do.[9]

With emphasis placed squarely on the activities of citizens, let us now consider a few crime prevention strategies or, more accurately, consider some citizen groups that might play key prevention roles.

STRATEGIES OF CRIME PREVENTION IN THE COMMUNITY[10]

Strategies to prevent crime and delinquency can take two basic focuses: efforts to prevent first offenses or efforts to prevent the repetition of criminal and delinquent

[7]See, for example, J.T. Duncan, *Citizen Crime Prevention Tactics: A Literature Review and Selected Bibliography.* Washington, DC: U.S. Department of Justice, April 1980. See also M.A. Greenberg, "Volunteer Crime Prevention Program: A Proposal to Survival in the Third Century," *The Police Chief,* Apr. 1977, pp. 60–61, for a differing perspective. And for an interesting view of police–citizen contact, see P.H. Schnabel, "Park, Walk and Talk: Bridging the Gap," *FBI Law Enforcement Bulletin,* Feb. 1983, pp. 15–18.

[8]See, for example, Michael K. Brown, *Working the Street: Police Discretion and the Dilemmas of Reform.* New York: Russell Sage Foundation, 1981, p. 286. See also Peter K. Manning, and John Van Maanen (eds.), *Policing: A View from the Street.* Santa Monica, CA: Goodyear Publishing, 1978.

[9]Ibid.

[10]Parts of this and later discussions in this chapter were published earlier in A. Coffey, *The Prevention of Crime and Delinquency,* 1975. Passages from pages 26–47 and 53–91. Reprinted by permission of Prentice-Hall, Inc., Englewood Cliffs, NJ.

acts; these are the prevention of contact with the justice system in the first instance and the prevention of the *penetration* of the justice system after contact has been made.[11] Successful efforts of law enforcement with community aid in preventing crime generally include both type of strategies.

Effective prevention strategies must also take into account the *causes* of crime that were discussed in Chapter 8.[12] When conditions are consistently associated with crime, prevention requires effort to correct those conditions even when they cannot be proved *the* cause of crime.[13] Many of the influences perceived by some as causes of crime are totally beyond the control of police. Nevertheless, such matters must be at least understood in the dialogue between police and the community served.

In planning prevention strategies, especially delinquency prevention programs, four general approaches can be singled out: (1) development of programs of behavior modification, (2) improvement of institutional services for offenders, (3) creation of new services for both offenders and potential offenders, and (4) development of programs to counteract the influences that propel children, as well as adults, into violation of law.

Prevention activities under the second and third approaches fall more within the purview of correctional institutions and suggest the involvement of that segment of criminal justice in the dialogue between the police and the community. But the approaches of behavior modification and programs to counteract influences toward crime and delinquency offer clear opportunities for the citizen in the community; in this case, law enforcement plays a supportive role for the community. Provision of community recreational activities to divert juveniles, as well as adults, away from violation of the law is but one example of how communities might enjoy such strategies in prevention work.

The prime requisite for the success of any prevention program is the support of the community in which it is being carried out; we repeatedly make this observation. And community support begins with concerned, committed citizens who recognize that crime prevention is *everyone's* business and who are willing to take individual as well as collective action to help prevent crime and delinquency.

Encouraging Citizen Participation

Few persons concerned with crime prevention would disagree with the contention that success in reducing crime requires a willingness on the part of the community to

[11]These diversion programs can be controversial. See, for example, William L. Selke, "Diversion and Crime Prevention," *Criminology,* Feb. 1982, pp. 395–406. See also James Austen, and Berry Krisberg, "The Unmet Promise of Alternatives to Incarceration," *Crime and Delinquency,* July 1982, pp. 374–409.

[12]Recall the Chapter 8 discussion of the negative case in crime—members of the same family reacting differently to theoretical causes. Yet beliefs abound. See, for example, Francis F. Cullen and Karen E. Gilbert, *Reaffirming Rehabilitation.* Cincinnati: Anderson Publishing, 1982. See also Vincent J. Hoffman, "The Relationship of Psychology to Delinquency: A Comprehensive Approach," *Adolescence,* Spring 1984, pp. 55–61, and Vri Bronfenbrenner, "Doing Their Own Thing," in Andrew Parizeau, *Parenting and Delinquent Youth.* Lexington, MA: Lexington Books, 1980. See also J.M. Byrne and R.J. Sampson (eds.), *The Social Ecology of Crime.* New York: Springer-Verlag, 1986.

[13]See, for example, Robert L. Green, "Future Trends in American Ethnic Relations," *National Forum,* Summer 1984, pp. 11–15.

participate. Fortunately, most communities have at least a few citizens who are willing and able to confront the crime problem:[14]

> The elderly are more likely than younger crime victims to be attacked by strangers. Not surprisingly, surveys indicate a high rate of fear regarding street crime. But many seniors are not sitting around worrying about crime. They are addressing the issue head on, helping educate people of all ages in crime prevention and founding new community service programs.

Noteworthy also is that among the elderly who are willing to "address the issue head on" are retired police officers and other people with considerable relevant expertise. Unfortunately, there are often more citizens who are apathetic about preventing crime than there are citizens who feel motivated to participate. Apathy of this kind is often associated with widely held beliefs that crime is caused by enormous social problems that are too vast for the individual to make a difference.

Recalling the Chapter 8 discussion of crime causes that fail to account for the *negative case,* effective police leadership in community crime prevention should include efforts to convince citizens that much crime can be prevented by citizen effort; there are far too many *negative cases* for each cause of crime to believe otherwise.

Citizens who are allowed to believe that all crime is the result of abstract social forces totally beyond the control of citizens are unlikely to seek ways in which they themselves might contribute to the war on crime and in effect often fail to recognize any role for individual citizens in crime prevention. Pointing out to these citizens that the majority of poverty-stricken Americans do not engage in criminal behavior and that criminals may be found in all classes of society may bring them to realize that the causes of crime are both more complex and less removed from the community than the citizen may have believed. Here again the police can play a strategic role in bringing this knowledge to the forefront.

Thus, correcting misconceptions as to the causes of crime is an important step in gaining greater citizen participation in crime prevention. Reminding citizens that crime affects every member of society, directly as well as indirectly, may also increase their willingness to engage in preventive activities.

Not all law violation is considered intolerable by the community. It should be evident, therefore, that only preventive efforts that focus on those law violations that are not tolerated by citizens can hope to overcome public apathy and indifference and gain adequate citizen participation.

A wide range of activities readily lend themselves to citizen participation, many of which will be elaborated on in various contexts throughout this volume. Some of the more obvious have to do with reporting crime or even suspicious circumstances that call for police investigation. Less obvious, but nevertheless significant, are the citizen activities to bring about better lighting in high-crime areas or public parking lots. The *participation* of the individual citizen in *any* activity that reduces the risk of crime is the prime requisite of successful prevention programs.

[14]Leonard A. Sipes, Jr., "The Power of Senior Citizens in Crime Prevention," *The Police Chief,* IACP, Jan. 1989, p. 35.

Police officer briefing business owners. Part of the police leadership role in community crime prevention can be as simple as helping educate community businesses and employees in crime prevention concepts. (Courtesy of Santa Cruz Police Department)

Relevancy through Agreed-upon Prevention Priorities: Severity

How severe crime is in a community is *not* always a point of agreement. Recalling the Chapter 4 discussion on *selective* law enforcement, part of the problem is that one group in a community may actually favor illegal gambling, for instance, while another group demands strict enforcement of gambling laws.

Severity is also a question of numbers—how many offenses how often. An occasional car exceeding the speed limit in a quiet residential district is one thing, but daily drag races are quite another.

There is, however, a generally agreed upon scale of severeness that uses the crimes themselves. We noted earlier that felonies are more severe than misdemeanors and assaultive crimes more severe than property crimes. This concept can be put on a scale for crime prevention priorities. Figure 9–1 shows such a scale, which includes *both* crime and juvenile delinquency.[15] When severity is conceived of in this manner, citizen perception of *relevance* is far easier to gain.

Ensuring that prevention programs are relevant to the community is not sufficient, however. Initial bursts of citizen enthusiasm have too often faded without providing a permanent base of community support for law enforcement; this is primarily due to the lack of strong leadership capable of maintaining public interest in crime prevention. We will return to this problem of inadequate leadership later in this discussion.

[15]Alan R. Coffey, *Prevention of Crime and Delinquency.* Englewood Cliffs, NJ: Prentice-Hall, 1975, p. 5.

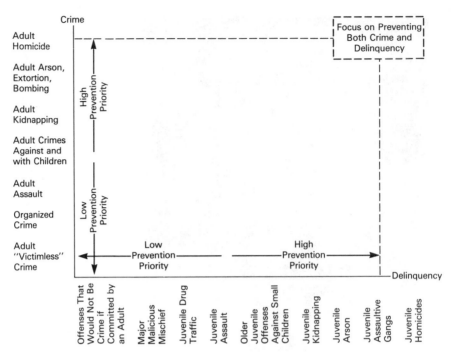

Figure 9-1 Crime/delinquency/prevention. (Alan R. Coffey, *Crime and Delinquency,* Englewood Cliffs, NJ: Prentice-Hall, 1975, p. 5. Reprinted by permission)

The citizen who has been made aware that crime is a problem touching all members of society and who has recognized the citizen's responsibility for, as well as the effectiveness of, individual involvement can find many opportunities for constructive action. Nor are these limited to community-wide prevention efforts. There is a great variety of independent actions the individual citizen can and should take; for example she or he should report crimes, serve willingly as a juror or witness, vote for candidates of integrity, and assure that her or his conduct at home and at work is well within not only the letter but also the spirit of the law.

Admittedly, this approach is exceedingly idealistic and likely to stir the cynicism of many veteran police officials. Nevertheless, it constitutes the core of what can and should be accomplished in the combined effort of the police and community in preventing crime.

Such combined effort is the basis of the widely adopted Neighborhood Community Watch program:[16]

The Neighborhood Watch Program operates on the concept that effective crime prevention requires citizen cooperation with law enforcement. In most cases, residential crime can be reduced when individuals, instructed by law enforcement agencies, take

[16]Betsy Cantrell, "A Commitment to Crime Prevention," *FBI Law Enforcement Bulletin,* Oct. 1988, p. 2.

positive steps to make their property more secure. Neighborhood security can be improved when a majority of the citizens become more vigilant and concerned about illegal activities in the community.

"Law enforcement officers cannot significantly impact crimes of opportunity such as residential burglary and vandalism without help from citizens," says the Executive Director of the National Sheriff's Association (NSA). "By taking steps to protect their persons, homes, and property, watching over that of their neighbors and reporting criminal activity, citizens can help their law enforcement agencies reduce neighborhood crime. This is what Neighborhood Watch is all about."

The conceptual framework from which prevention is approached by community watch applies to other areas in which citizens can provide an enormous amount of help in preventing crime; consider the following scenario:[17]

It was 11:00 P.M. when Martha, a 36-year-old business executive, pulled into a convenience store parking lot, which was deserted and poorly lit. Preoccupied with what had transpired throughout the day, she parked her late-model luxury car, complete with temporary tags, and hurried into the store, unaware of the man who was watching her from the shadows. Martha had left her car's engine running, her doors unlocked, and her packages in plain view on the passenger's seat — after all, she was only going to buy a carton of milk. Martha was about to become a victim, and if she was very lucky, only her car or her recent purchases were in jeopardy.

PREVENTION IN FAMILIES

Chapter 12 has as its main subject police intervention into family crisis. In this context, however, we are addressing the supportive role the family unit plays in a strong community-based crime prevention program.

Because a person's strongest emotional and psychological ties are generally to members of his or her family, the family possesses the greatest potential for shaping the behavior and attitudes of the individual. (Chapter 10 discusses attitudes, prejudice, and bias.) The potential of families for improving the plight of law enforcement goes beyond simple crime prevention, as will now be discussed; the influence on attitudes that affect intergroup relations, which in turn affect the police, is also a factor.

Family-related prevention efforts have two major focuses: (1) to prevent crimes precipitated by family crisis, and (2) to exercise social control within the family to discourage both criminal and delinquent behavior on the part of its members, thus reducing the possibility that family members will encourage other families to participate in crime and delinquency.

Noteworthy here is the reference to delinquency *and* crime. The relationship between family and criminal offenses may well be just as significant as between families and juvenile delinquency. The specific relationship between the family and

[17]Bobbi J. Cotter, "The FBI's Dual Approach to Crime Prevention," *FBI Law Enforcement Bulletin,* Oct. 1988, p. 25.

offensive behavior, however, may be easier to examine in the context of juvenile delinquency, even though it is extremely relevant to adult crime as probational officers and parole agents will attest. For this reason, delinquency will receive slightly more emphasis, but only for the sake of clarity. The exercise of social control within the family to discourage criminal and delinquent behavior is primarily the responsibility of the family itself, even though many families ultimately turn to the community for help. While family influences may inhibit criminal behavior by adult members and reduce the likelihood of violence provoking crisis situations, the primary role of the family in internal preventive action concerns parental control over children to prevent juvenile delinquency and the exerting of family influence over adult members turning to law violation.

In terms of the relationship between the family and the prevention of crime, it can be conceived of in yet another context. When any family member actively participates in another prevention strategy within the community, that individual holds the potential to influence his or her family to assist in the prevention of community crime. In this regard, the family unit increases the span of the total network.

In connection with the potential of the family to assist in prevention efforts, most parents of delinquent children wish to know why their children are delinquent; many have exhausted the literature attempting to find an answer. The Chapter 8 discussion of *causes* noted that family problems have been associated with delinquency. Care is needed not to create parental resistance to prevention programs. When both police and community leaders approach the problem of delinquency on the basis that parents would welcome assistance, at least in most cases an entirely different dialogue is possible. The dialogue conceived of by those who theorize about parental responsibility for delinquency does little more than foster guilt feelings among parents.

The emergence of experts in the family causes of delinquency has been facilitated by the parental *preference* for asking someone else how to solve the conflict between parent and child. It is definitely in the interest of serious community efforts to prevent or at least reduce delinquency in crime to take advantage of this preference by providing a supportive service wherever possible and by understanding the parental position when juvenile justice remedies become necessary. This is in the community's interest, if for no other reason than the most effective control over juveniles is parental control; building the parental capability to exercise such control is an ultimate investment in the entire social milieu of the community. In matters involving police in juvenile delinquency, the subject of parental control is frequently a major factor. Let's give brief consideration to the subject of parental control.

Parental Control

The amount of parental control that can be exercised over a child's behavior varies in a number of ways, not the least of which is the child's age. The infant's survival depends on parental control of all facets of the infant's life. As the child grows, it becomes more independent and self-sufficient; as it learns to do things for itself, the parents allow the child greater freedom to determine its own behavior. But because the child must still depend on its parents to supply basic physical needs and because its judgment is too immature to allow it to always recognize its own best interest, parents must retain some measure of control over the child's behavior. Finally, by the time adulthood has been reached, the individual has become fully capable of providing his or her own needs and assuming the responsibilities of an adult and is completely free of parental control, but *not* free of parental influence.

With regard to criminal and delinquent behavior, parental control can be directly related to the concepts of responsibility and accountability. Laws generally hold adults *responsible,* whereas children on a sliding scale can be considered *accountable.* An eight-year-old juvenile, for example, can be held accountable for law violation only to the degree that he or she can be expected to comprehend the consequences of his or her action, the behavior that society expects of its members, and the responsibilities that will be placed upon him or her upon reaching adult status. And because the child's understanding is limited and because the child is not fully accountable for his or her actions, parents must control the child's behavior to assure that the child does not harm others or itself. When the child reaches 14, he or she has a somewhat better understanding of the behaviors that society considers appropriate and can be held even more accountable by juvenile authorities.

In terms of *responsibilities,* parents are responsible to assure that the behavior of the child is within the limits of conduct acceptable to society. This responsibility, however, may be impeded by many influences beyond the control of the parents.

In the past, when societies changed little from generation to generation, the wisdom gained through age remained relevant for succeeding generations, and parents could pass on intact to their children the knowledge acquired through the experience of living. The parents in modern America find themselves raising children in a world very different from that of their own childhood, and particularly different from that of the childhood of their own parents. Indeed, the world to which parents must now help their adolescents adjust may be startlingly changed to the point that parents themselves depend on the children to explain the technical education they are receiving. The parent's own experience therefore may offer them few, if any, guidelines for the technical education of their children. This awkward turn of events may well inhibit parents from trusting the "maturity" their years have provided.

To whatever degree law enforcement and community leadership can support parents in this frustrating, often confusing distortion within the family itself, to that same degree are the community crime and delinquency prevention efforts served, as well as the community's overall welfare.

The family and the subject of parental control do not cut across all groups of the community; there are many other groups and individuals. Bearing in mind that the family group has tremendous potential for crime prevention and is often the most dominant group in a community, attention now is shifted to the entire range of community groups and individuals who may provide a strategy for preventing crime and delinquency.

Prevention in Families

COMMUNITY-BASED PREVENTION

Approaching community-based prevention strategies may best be served initially by considering the recruitment of individuals to assist in prevention efforts. Problems in recruiting range from minimal in some communities to all but insurmountable in many others. In large urban cities, it is unrealistic to hope to gain widespread support in the ghettos and barrios. And yet, because of the high crime rate, there are individuals living in the crime-ridden areas who would readily serve if confidence in the prevention program existed. Some communities enjoy the collective trust and confidence of virtually all citizens. In such communities, the urgency of crime prevention is rarely the case; generally the cohesive effort between law enforcement and community exists so conspicuously that the existence of crime and delinquency is minimal. In other communities, citizens find themselves unable to even communicate with other citizens, and the prospect of collaborating with citizens with whom they do not wish to talk is highly unlikely.

Nevertheless, successful crime prevention requires that every effort be made to overcome these obstacles. This is necessary because the active support and participation of community-based prevention activities determine success or failure. Indeed, even the most rudimentary criminal justice activities depend for their success on community involvement and success.

Again, the actual approaches to reaching the community will be covered in Chapter 14. Here, we must acknowledge that public acceptance of the law enforcement function is a necessity; but, beyond that, participation in efforts to prevent crime and delinquency are a requisite for success in that regard. One avenue that might prove successful in overcoming some of the barriers to participation is law enforcement efforts to gain citizen cooperation in simply reporting crime or reporting suspicious circumstances.

Many communities have enjoyed a widening support for prevention efforts simply by initiating a *Neighborhood Watch* program. The ever increasing utilization of the 911 emergency telephone system has enhanced such approaches to the point where citizens become willing to utilize a nonemergency number in many instances.

The point here is that the key to gaining community participation may be a matter of how simple or complex the effort is; starting simply may be the key.

But even more critical than the simplicity or complexity of a program is the *leadership* of the program.

Leadership

Leadership is primarily a matter of accepting responsibility for taking the initiative in bringing people together at all levels within the community and creating community awareness that a concerned citizenry is a prerequisite to a successful prevention program. This leadership is best served by a community leader rather than by police. (Law enforcement efforts in support of such leadership will be reviewed in Chapter 14.)

Such leadership is customarily characterized by effective communication leading to tangible citizen participation based on an ever increasing awareness of the need for and the potentials of community-based crime prevention.

Unfortunately, much of what currently passes for leadership in the field of prevention reduces to little more than political manipulation. In some instances, even those working as professionals in the field of crime and delinquency prove as interested in political power as do the nonprofessionals involved in many prevention operations. This sad situation, regrettably, often generates a tremendous amount of cynicism and creates further barriers for subsequent prevention efforts. In other words, the continual subordination of effective community leadership in prevention to maneuvers that are designed to gain political power does far greater damage than simply retarding prevention efforts. For this reason, police officials would do well to remain alert for any evidence of such political manipulation and drop out if at all possible in the early stages and reserve their support for an effort that promises higher yield.

This is *not* to suggest that politically based power is unnecessary for prevention; on the contrary, it is probably a prime requisite for success. But until the activities practiced in the name of prevention and the choices taken on its behalf are made consistent with the stated goal, disillusioning false starts are likely to continue; the quality of the political involvement is the key.

The failure of community prevention programs to achieve continuity of effort or consistency of results is often due to failure to establish clear lines of accountability, another facet in hidden-agenda politics. Perhaps, if the inadequacy of leadership did not force the delegation of prevention responsibility to inappropriate groups, the problem of who is responsible for doing what would not arise, but in all too many cases it does.

Even the most enthusiastic citizens tend to approach crime prevention more in terms of the objective to be attained than in terms of the concrete courses of action necessary to achieve this objective. While affirmation of the goal of crime prevention and the determination of immediate objectives that will lead to the achievement of such goals are indeed essential, the effective organization of collective citizen participation in crime prevention requires strong emphasis on the *specific techniques* and *activities involved;* each individual must clearly perceive his or her particular role.

As might be expected, the specific methods and types of activities required for preventive efforts to be successful vary from community to community. This difference exists even though the goals and objectives may be the same from city to city. Unfortunately, too much of the existing literature on preventing delinquency in crime implies a kind of uniformity or at least creates conceptual parameters for communities in the type of preventive efforts that will prove effective. The truth of the matter is that radically different approaches succeed among communities in spite of identical goals and objectives.

The importance of strong community leadership becomes apparent here as well. Without adequate leadership, citizens may become bogged down in discussions of goals and objectives without ever developing the specific techniques and activities necessary to get a prevention program moving. For example, a program geared to having marked houses for children to run to if strangers attempt to approach them may never come into existence if repeated meetings are called to discuss the philosophies and rationale for such houses.

Failure in initial prevention efforts carries the high risk of the loss of future citizen's work and thus the blocking of subsequent efforts to cope with crime. Careful planning that keeps in view the overall crime picture as it relates to the entire community, the county, and the system of criminal justice is therefore of paramount importance. Here police can play a strategically important role.

In virtually all cases, specific methods and techniques, as well as specific activities, are worked out only with strong leadership that pushes group interest past the philosophical and theoretical rationale for activities. Once there is agreement on goals and objectives, immediate emphasis should shift to priorities and thence to specific activities and techniques, with the delegation of volunteers with specific assignments.

This is not to say that the discussion of the philosophical rationale for such techniques is unimportant. However, continued discussion is frequently the preference of a leaderless group.

Citizens who are mobilized for specific prevention activities may lose interest once the immediate objective has been attained. In a sense, the passing of a sense of crisis tends to bring about complacency. The role of police in acquainting community leadership with the actual crime picture can be useful. A high level of citizen enthusiasm can be maintained only if the broad nature of the problem is continually emphasized with credible data and support. Strong prevention leadership is required to balance citizen awareness of the scope of the task with recognition that the only effective approach is to concentrate on specific aspects of the problem. As an example, citizen efforts to bring about lighting in parking lots where crimes have occurred can be followed by these same citizens bringing about lighting in yet other parking lots once the initial objective has been achieved.

Effective community prevention programs are generally found to share a number of ingredients. For example, the press and the media are supportive. Successful press relations are usually *explicit, tangible, candid,* and in some kind of formula. In this case we are discussing more the relationship between community leaders and the press than between law enforcement and the press (law enforcement public relations will be discussed in Chapter 14). In favorable press for community-based prevention, things of significance are pointed out in terms of accountability, a clearly delineated picture of "who is doing what." Spelling things out, regardless of the complexity or uniqueness, contributes to maintaining citizen enthusiasm. By far the most critical factor in preventing crime and delinquency is the establishment and maintenance of citizen enthusiasm for community participation, but *all* factors must be clear to both the press and the individual citizens participating in the prevention effort.

THE PREVENTIVE ROLES OF SCHOOLS AND SOCIAL AGENCIES

Schools and social agencies reach a large segment of the population with a variety of services ranging from formal education, to personal counseling and guidance, to opportunities for creative and productive use of leisure time, which is of particular importance in the prevention of crime and delinquency in many jurisdictions.

The American Association of Retired Persons (AARP) has been a leader for many years in providing communities with crime prevention guidance and material. These comic strips are only a small part of the extensive materials that AARP's Criminal Justice Services provide.

Because they are able to influence the behavior of their clients in important ways, schools and social agencies must take an active part in all *successful* community-wide prevention programs; lack of their assistance is a serious deficit.

Such institutions and organizations normally play a supportive role in preventive activities by participating in programs initiated and directed by community leaders. These programs are frequently enhanced considerably by sophisticated police input of law enforcement perspective on the need for a particular prevention concept.

When effective general community leadership is lacking, however, and this is all too often the case, schools and social agencies themselves, in conjunction with the local law enforcement, can still contribute a great deal to the community effort to reduce crime or delinquency.

The greatest obstacle to effective prevention work is the readiness of *all* groups in society to downplay the importance of their own efforts and to shift to the enforcement of law as the primary focal point of crime control. Law enforcement alone, however, cannot solve the crime problem; the community is absolutely needed. Once again we state that this is a mutual problem in which police need the support of the community to perform their function.

The Preventive Roles of Schools and Social Agencies

Burglars can be deterred in many ways. Consult your local law enforcement agency for home security advice.

Don't take the law into your own hands. Crime prevention and the reduction of criminal opportunity are not vigilantism.

Verify the credentials of strangers before admitting them to your home. Don't admit them unless you're absolutely certain they are who they say they are and that their purpose is legitimate.

Some people use only first initials with their surnames for telephone book, mailbox and other listings. This can provide women a special measure of security.

The primary mission of law enforcement is to control crime and to the extent that it is forced to commit all available resources to this crucial function, to that same extent is the support of the community absolutely necessary. This rationale more than justifies recognition that schools and social agencies can play a vital part.

The community at large, and specifically schools and social organizations, must assume responsibility for much of the work of prevention in order to allow law enforcement to focus on its primary mission of controlling crime that has not been prevented.

Our knowledge about crime and delinquency prevention is less than complete, and, unfortunately, much of what needs to be learned is not even being addressed in a systematic manner. Yet many tangible approaches to the prevention of crime and delinquency have worked and continue to work. Programs to increase the lighting in high-crime areas and to improve the security in homes as well as the security consciousness of citizens are but two of the many successful prevention methods. Beyond this, schools and social agencies have the potential to greatly influence the attitudes of citizens toward crime, as well as influence the attitudes of those willing to commit crime.

The School

The school is the one social agency that directly impinges on every child. *For this very reason, it would be an excellent idea if every community and police agency, as a matter of course, were to assign an officer to arrange a class discussion with primary grade children.*

Independent of the potential for law enforcement to develop an *early* positive image by police officers arranging with primary grade teachers for a discussion with their classes, the liaison established between police and the schools in such a process has a positive yield in its own right.

Returning to the school's own potential in crime and delinquency prevention, the school can and frequently does have enormous impact on the behavior and conduct of the child, rivaling in many instances the influence of the family. Because of this unique position, the school is the prime institutional focus for identifying child and youth problems and initiating corrective action, as well as for motivating law-abiding behavior among children and young people.

The role of the school in the socialization process becomes even more crucial in view of the increasing inability of many parents to exercise as much control over their children as was possible in the past. As the effects of rapid social change and increasing urbanization erode parental authority and influence, the school may well be forced to assume an even greater share of the burden of the socialization of children. This fact carries broad implications for prevention work and points up the responsibility of the school to provide leadership in the prevention of crime and delinquency.

Unfortunately, schools have typically often been slow to recognize their obligation to guide the social as well as the intellectual development of their pupils. Concerted law enforcement effort to orient school principals and teachers in the vital role that they can play, *without adding a great deal to their work load,* can remedy a great deal of this problem in most communities.

If the school is to exercise leadership in preventing delinquency and even some crime, it must accept its responsibility for influencing children and young people away from delinquent behavior. This entails modifying many of the programs in a manner that incorporates education geared to building *respect* for law and order. This task is much easier for a school teacher who has been acquainted with the specific problems of crime and delinquency in the community in which the school is located, an obvious law enforcement responsibility.

One of the most important ways in which the school can influence students away from delinquency is by providing paths for students to achieve adequate preparation for careers or further educational challenges. The success of such a program in steering pupils away from illegitimate careers depends on the existence of occupational and educational opportunities and motivation for *all* members of the community. In this regard, it is important to recall our discussion of the continuing struggle for equality among many of America's minorities. This makes resistance to such efforts by the school particularly disturbing. School administrators who attempt to initiate creative programs in this regard encounter unfavorable reaction from those holding the narrow view that teaching a predetermined list of academic subjects is the only potential of a publicly supported school system.

The organization of recreational activities for students during nonschool hours is yet another concrete way in which the school can channel the energy of pupils away from delinquent behavior. More often than not, budget restrictions require that the use of volunteer parents be included, usually within the somewhat complex boundaries of state insurance and liability laws. Such recreational programs, regardless of their difficulties, have the potential to divert a great deal of youthful exuberance and energy into positive channels, without appearing to be delinquency prevention. School-organized recreation for children can have a significant impact as a model for other community agencies, which may organize similar activities to

Police sergeant meeting with high school class. Police leadership in community crime prevention can be enhanced by expanding the recommended visits of uniformed officers in primary schools to include intermediate schools and high schools. (Courtesy of Santa Cruz Police Department)

serve their more specialized needs. Providing recreational outlets for young people can be an important part of community prevention efforts, and the school can play a vital role in awakening the community to the value of such services.

Physical security is another area in which the school can carry out successful preventive action, as well as provide leadership to the community. For example, the installation of locks and fences, the institution of patrols, and other physical security measures that prevent such problems as vandalism, arson, and theft create a model for the rest of the community in physically preventing crime and delinquency. Such school initiatives can aid in heightening citizens' sensitivity to physical security methods as one element of the total community prevention program. Energetic efforts to plan effectively for school security might provide an effective model for similar needs virtually everywhere in the community.

Related to physical security is the problem of *vandalism*. A definition of the term is the deliberate defacement, mutilation, or destruction of private or public property primarily by a juvenile or a group of juveniles. Millions upon millions of dollars in such damage is endured by many communities. Public schools are one of the major targets. The steps to prevent vandalism provide school officials with an excellent model for preventing crimes of all types. But like most specific delinquencies or crimes, vandalism often involves a wide range of complexity.

In pursuing their preventive efforts, schools may fall into the unfortunate practice of labeling certain students, either implicitly or explicitly, as potential delinquents.

Branding Delinquents: Self-fulfilling Hypothesis

A paradox to many, the reality is that when prevention efforts include the identifying and labeling of delinquents, the delinquent behavior frequently increases rather than decreases. Labeling students in this manner can prove very detrimental to prevention activities. First, isolating a certain group of children as predelinquent may focus preventive efforts on these children alone, to the exclusion of the remainder of the student population. A school may thus consider its preventive obligations fulfilled by programs to discourage delinquent behavior among those children identified as high risks, while ignoring its broader responsibility to prevent delinquency and foster law-abiding behavior among all pupils.

In addition, school prevention efforts aimed at a small group of students may backfire. Pupils labeled predelinquent and treated as such may be tempted to fulfill these expectations. Some efforts to prevent delinquency may, in fact, *cause* delinquency, at least in this context.[18]

To stop preventive measures from themselves becoming a cause of delinquency, schools must recognize this danger and take steps to ensure that such a risk is minimized. Law enforcement can play a critical role in this regard. It is extremely

---

[18]It has been argued that, independent of prevention efforts causing delinquency by branding juveniles as delinquent, virtually *all* juveniles commit offenses. See, for example, J.G. Albanese, *Dealing with Delinquency*. Lunham, MD: University Press of America, 1985. See also Marvin E. Wolfgang, Terrance P. Thornberry, and Robert M. Figlio, *From Boy to Man: From Delinquency to Crime*. Chicago: University of Chicago Press, 1987.

impressive to have a veteran police officer discuss the sophisticated concept of *self-fulfilling hypothesis*. It has been this author's experience that teachers, customarily with Master's degrees and considerable experience with young people, are very receptive to a veteran police officer pointing this potential out. And it is only by confronting the problem head on that schools can erect a protective buffer to keep prevention activities from being sabotaged through inappropriate labeling and self-fulfilling prophecies.

One attitude in prevention work that is common to both schools and other social agencies is the tendency to transfer behavior problems to another segment of the community. American frontier justice provides a ready example of such a transfer approach. Law breakers and troublemakers were simply run out of town; in effect, crime was neither controlled nor prevented but simply moved elsewhere. Towns with the nasty sheriffs had less crime.

Urbanization, population growth, and mobility have made the transfer of crime problems in the modern day less obvious, but often just as real. For example, the parents of a child who misbehaves may depend on the school to correct his or her behavior. The school, encountering difficulties in controlling the child, may look to law enforcement to deal with delinquent tendencies. The police, in their turn, may shift the responsibility to the juvenile court, the court to the probation officials, and so on. Rather than confront the child's behavior problems and take active steps to correct them and prevent further problems, each segment simply shifts responsibility to another. In fairness, the statutory definition of liabilities as well as the specific delineation of functions is a factor in this regard, at times precluding confronting the delinquent problem and forcing a "passing of the buck." Nevertheless, it is critical that everyone involved recognize the negative impact of "passing the buck."

To avoid such transfer and accomplish the purpose of preventive efforts, the efforts to prevent crime in one segment of the community must serve as a model for the rest of the community, rather than a substitute that invites transfer. Such a model must encourage the necessary preventive practices in many segments of a community accustomed to viewing either criminal justice or the school as having total responsibility for coping with the crime and delinquency problem.

Communities that are fortunate enough to have strong leadership in preventive activities need to depend on the schools to demonstrate the impact of effective planning in this area. Schools in such communities can concentrate their efforts on teaching their students and give prevention a secondary priority without sacrificing prevention success. Unfortunately, most communities lack effective leadership, and in such a case the school may be forced to devote more attention to preventive activities if the success of the community prevention is to be achieved; in the process, the school's primary responsibility of education is weakened.[19] Obviously, schools are unlikely to remain enthused about their prevention efforts if it is at the expense of their primary mission.

[19]See, for example, Steven M. Cox, and John J. Conrad, *Juvenile Justice,* 2nd ed. Dubuque, IA: William C. Brown, 1987.

SOCIAL AGENCIES

As pointed out earlier, there are two types of preventive activities: (1) efforts to prevent offenders from engaging in further criminal activity, and (2) efforts to prevent potential offenders from committing criminal acts in the first place.

Social agencies, defined here as any organization whose purpose is to serve social needs or deal with social problems, play a significant role in diverting offenders away from the criminal justice system and in preventing actual offenses. Many, if not most, of the alternatives to criminal justice involve influencing clients not to commit crimes—or influencing clients not to commit *additional* crimes. Once minor offenses have been committed, social agencies can serve to *divert* the offender from the justice system. Elsewhere in this volume, it has been pointed out that there is considerable question about the effectiveness of such diversion. Nevertheless, when police and probation agencies carefully evaluate each case referred, such an approach is certainly worthy of consideration.

But beyond contributing alternatives for certain law violators who are not considered in need of formal criminal justice, social agencies can always prove instrumental in preventing potential offenders from committing criminal acts in the first place. The role of social agencies may involve more the exercise of subtle influence than actual crime prevention as such, but it can be a key to successful community prevention nevertheless.

Before exploring the role of social agencies in preventing crime, it would be useful to examine just how social agencies have traditionally related to the control of crime. The concept of the welfare model has often been uppermost in the minds of social workers.

What many refer to as the welfare model is actually a variation of criminal justice diversion. The more vigorous advocates of the welfare model suggest that all functions of the juvenile court must be replaced or that, at least, alternatives that operate in lieu of juvenile court must be provided; juvenile justice is seen as punitive when social work is perceived as the appropriate alternative. Many cite what they consider the success of Scandinavian countries (particularly Sweden) in operating without juvenile courts. This particular philosophy advocates a system in which a child is neither accountable nor responsible for offenses until he or she reaches a specific age, whereupon the child assumes complete responsibility for criminal acts.

One argument against this philosophy compares such an arrangement with the situation in which a child is given unlimited money throughout his or her minority and then at maturity is suddenly required to earn all the money he or she spends. Many opponents of the welfare model argue that a wiser course is to establish a system whereby the accountability of the child for his or her behavior gradually increases, contingent upon his or her maturity, until the child reaches adult years and then becomes fully responsible. It should be noted that this welfare model conceives of juvenile delinquency largely as a symptom that reflects other social problems. It is not uncommon to hear opponents of this philosophy sarcastically refer to the most violent of criminal offenders as "a victim of his environment."

For these and other reasons, the social work philosophy as presented here and the stronger philosophy toward increasing the accountability of young people should be distinguished. The juvenile justice system is concerned primarily with public safety and secondarily with treatment of the delinquent, and the reverse, to some degree, may be true in the welfare model. This *distinction* makes it possible for law enforcement to carefully evaluate the diversion of minor offenders.

Recreational Function of Social Agencies

A community prevention program of necessity has to address the subject of leisure time. The amount of leisure time enjoyed by Americans has been steadily increasing. But while most would agree that leisure time has a great many positive factors, not all leisure time is productive nor recreational; recall our discussion of the leisure time of the unemployed.

Some consider increased leisure to be a contributing factor in the growth of vandalism; it is argued that vandalism consisted in little more than Halloween pranks until young people began to enjoy increased leisure, which gave them time for more destructive mischief.

Psychologists and psychiatrists, who approach the problem in terms of pent-up aggression and similar concepts, tend to support such a viewpoint. In particular, the clinical problems confronting the psychiatrist may relate to how the patient uses his or her time, or *fails* to use it, to avoid boredom, depression, or other emotional symptoms. This by no means suggests that people who are not goal oriented or do not structure time always have psychiatric problems or commit crimes. Nevertheless, it would be foolish to ignore the reality that many acts of vandalism would not have been committed were the children (and adults in some instances) not in a leisure situation.

Organized recreation addresses such problems. In determining the degree to which organized recreation can successfully resolve these problems, it is important to remember that recreational programs are oriented toward an extremely wide range of goals, which have considerable influence on the extent to which the programs can be brought to bear in prevention. Boy Scout and Girl Scout programs have multiple goals, which easily qualify as direct delinquency prevention. Little League Baseball and Pop Warner Football emphasize successful competition, a goal some critics contend can be carried too far regardless of the program's success in structuring leisure time. Nevertheless, by the criteria used in this discussion, these activities are all potentially successful. Conversely, the less complex, even noncompetitive recreational programs of many municipal recreational agencies are virtually without goals other than simply using leisure time nondestructively. These programs also have high potential in the context of this discussion.

Religious Institutions

Overlapping such recreational programs as dances, popular music concerts, games, sporting activities, and other program efforts of social agencies specifically concerned with leisure time are the social activities of various religious groups.

While many believe that the potential for crime and delinquency is lower among those seeking out religious experience than among other population groups, the very fact that many churches provide recreational activities as a matter of tradition suggests that the churches themselves do not take this for granted. And to the degree that religious groups provide a model of wholesome recreation for the wider community, they are potentially influential beyond their own membership and can offer valuable leadership in prevention activities.

Neighborhood and Service Clubs

Service clubs, such as the Rotary Club, Kiwanis Club, Lion's Club, and Optimist, subsidize many recreational activities as well as other programs that provide constructive alternatives for using leisure time. As in the case of religious groups, service clubs (perhaps acting in unison with religious institutions and others) can be influential beyond their immediate program efforts through helping to create a general community atmosphere that promotes the positive use of leisure time. Grass-roots neighborhood recreational programs often gain a sense of direction from successful activities such as summer camps and pack trips sponsored by service clubs.

The willingness of local businesses to sponsor athletic teams or social events in neighborhoods is often the direct result of service club activity. *The willingness of local businesses and even the service clubs to provide such sponsorship is frequently a result of the initiative of local law enforcement.*

People living in a neighborhood in which a successful pancake breakfast or raffle is held to raise funds for neighborhood sports equipment are customarily far less reluctant to participate in neighborhood improvement programs *including* crime delinquency. And any neighborhood improvement on its own merit contributes toward the prevention of crime.

In short, organized recreational activities may promote the neighborhood cohesiveness needed in preventive efforts, a fact that carries great significance in view of the absence of community leadership in all too many instances. For it is the cohesiveness of neighborhoods throughout the community that permits and then sustains citizen enthusiasm to commit the necessary energies for preventing crime. Reflecting back on what we have discussed as a strategy for prevention, it can be said that this would be an ideal for the police, and perhaps, to many, far too idealistic. Nevertheless, even the law enforcement effort to influence the development of such an approach will of necessity improve the police chances of gaining community support for law enforcement, a reward worthy of the most aggressive integration of community relations in police values.[20]

None of this permits the police to relinquish any part of their responsibility to control crime. In effect, it is proposed here that responsibility be combined with community efforts to prevent crime. In terms of combining prevention with the apprehension of offenders, police have a great number of options in how, for example, *patrol* is to be accomplished. Such innovations as foot patrol in selected

[20]See, for example, Lee P. Brown, "A Police Department and Its Values," *The Police Chief,* Nov. 1984, pp. 24–25.

neighborhoods are most likely to have public support, provided there has been community involvement in the plan to create a foot patrol. Such involvement of the community is bound to increase the likelihood that the public will perceive the foot patrol as a great deal more than simply increasing the number of officers walking the beat.[21] Such an approach may conceivably improve the problems some have cited regarding rookie policemen evolving into cynical veterans with a great number of negative feelings regarding police gaining the support of their community.

Reducing the risk of creating cynicism among police officers improves the police services for the community they serve.[22] This too is a contribution to police–community relations.

It is beyond the scope of this chapter to elaborate on the potential community relations yield from devising methods to bring community leaders into innovative prevention–control programs, but the potential is tremendous. Perhaps the only universal word of caution is the financial cost of many "great ideas."[23] But this caution need not be a major impediment. Full involvement of the community necessarily will include those familiar with the availability of funds, and full involvement is (or should be) the goal. This *goal* is not the only significant goal in the human relations approach to law enforcement.

Community Goals: Law Enforcement Objectives

Goals and objectives will be discussed in a later chapter, as having considerable significance in successful police community relations. Beyond the significance of mutual agreement between community leaders and police in prevention goals, general agreement between law enforcement and the community served is essential for the overall success of law enforcement in general.

When leaders of community groups agree with police officials on mutual crime prevention goals, law enforcement objectives are invariably heeded.[24] These objectives, being measurable components of goals, can be a variety of matters deemed significant by the police, among which is successful public relations.

Public relations will also be discussed in Chapter 14 as having a great deal to do with the relationship between the media and law enforcement. In terms of that relationship, both the problems and the advantages of media influence on the police image become far easier to negotiate when there are mutual crime prevention goals

[21]Robert C. Trojawowicz, *An Evaluation of the Neighborhood Foot Patrol Program in Flint Michigan.* East Lansing, MI: Michigan State University Press, 1983.

[22]For a full discussion of this subject, see, for example, Lawrence Sherman, "Learning Police Ethics," *Criminal Justice Ethics,* Winter–Spring 1982, pp. 10–19.

[23]For an excellent discussion of competing needs and limited finances, see Edwin W. Zedlewski, *The Economics of Disincarceration.* Washington, DC: National Institute of Justice Reports, U.S. Department of Justice, May 1984, pp. 4–8.

[24]This point of view is held from many perspectives. See, for example, R. Mellard, "Crime Preventions: A Workable Alternative," *The Police Chief,* March 1982, pp. 18–23. See also K. Krajick, "Preventing Crime," *Police Magazine,* Nov. 1979, pp. 7–13. Also A.F. Brandstater and Louis A. Radelet, *Police and Community Relations: A Source Book.* Beverly Hills, CA: Glencoe Press, 1968.

established by police and community leaders.[25] The possibilities for mutual goals can go beyond prevention to include the whole range of goals for police service.[26] When media cover favorably the goals that reflect community and police agreement on preventing or at least controlling crime, law enforcement effectiveness increases along with law enforcement image.

In a sense, community prevention programs form the most significant underpinning for successful police–community relations; in many jurisdictions successful community crime prevention programs *are* the community relations program.

In the following two chapters we will discuss matters having great influence on community problems: attitude, prejudice, and bias.

SUMMARY

Crime prevention was introduced in the context of a variety of definitional considerations. The need for community involvement was emphasized. The advantages to police of developing support from the community was also noted.

Acknowledging that police retain the primary responsibility for controlling as well as preventing crime, attention was shifted to the leadership role that police can play in organizing citizen efforts to assist in preventing crime. It was noted that the ability to control crime was enhanced by citizen efforts to prevent crime.

Strategies of crime prevention were approached from the orientation of combined police and community effort. Emphasis was placed on encouraging citizen participation as well as community-based programming. The strategic prevention roles of schools and social agencies were examined against the background of the significant role played by the family.

Control of crime was related to prevention efforts, but placed primarily in the police area of responsibility.

Also emphasized was the cohesive influence between police and community when crime and delinquency prevention are successful; the role of the media and the police image were also discussed in this context.

DISCUSSION TOPICS

1. Elaborate on the contention of this chapter that prevention of crime is a major incentive for the community to support the police.
2. Relate police policy setting as discussed in this chapter to community relations.

[25]See, for example, Arthur F. Hehrbass, "Promoting Effective Media Relations," *The Police Chief,* IACP, Jan. 1989. See also V.F. Sacco and R.A. Silverman, "Crime Prevention through the Mass Media: Prospects and Problems," *Journal of Criminal Justice,* Feb. 1982.

[26]See, for example, Marcia Cohen and Thomas McEwen, *Handling Calls for Service: Alternatives to Traditional Policing.* Washington, DC: Report of National Institute of Justice, U.S. Department of Justice, 1984, pp. 4–8. See also Research and Forecasts, Inc., *The Figgie Report. Part IV: Reducing Crime in America—Successful Community Efforts.* Willoughby, OH: Figgie International, 1983.

3. Discuss the strategies for community crime prevention.
4. Discuss the strategic prevention roles of schools and social agencies.
5. Relate the concept of family to crime prevention.
6. Discuss common goals as a cohesive force.

Relevant Problems for Discussion

This chapter cast police in a leadership role and presented the community, rather than the police, as the source of crime prevention effort. It is doubtful that anything else is nearly so powerful in cohesing the police and community toward a common goal—the prevention or at least the reduction of crime. But if the leadership role of the police weakens ever so slightly, the responsibility for enforcing law can be obscured; the limitations on citizen involvement cannot be blurred.

On the surface, there is a tremendous difference between citizens involved in coordinated and planned police–community crime prevention and, say, vigilante groups. But the difference is made up mostly of police leadership and clearly defined limitations, leadership that never obscures the main responsibility for *who* enforces the law. Without police leadership, situations can evolve where less and less difference is discernible between citizen prevention and vigilante groups.

Indeed, citizen motives may be similar or even the same in both cases. Such things as climbing crime rates, unsafe streets, and seemingly ineffective criminal justice may well be the underlying motivation for the citizen either assisting in a program or joining a vigilante group; both acts seek to make the community safe. Police leadership is necessary to channel these motivations and to establish a *clear* division of labor between citizen activity and police activity.

```
┌──────────────── 10 ────────────────┐
│                                     │
│                                     │
│          Attitude and               │
│      Intergroup Relations           │
│                                     │
│                                     │
└─────────────────────────────────────┘
```

It is not uncommon for discussions of the subject of *attitude* to encompass the entire range of topics that might be considered as part of police–community relations. In this chapter and Chapter 11 the subject of *attitude* will be distinguished from the subjects of *prejudice* and *discrimination* and discussed as an individual factor and important factor, but only one of many factors in successful police–community relations. Before moving on with that discussion, however, it might be useful to clarify what will later be defined as that attitude:[1]

> A mental position or emotion about people or events influences the approach to those people or events, and that approach influences outcome. A positive approach tends to produce a positive outcome; a negative approach tends to produce a negative outcome. The quality of human relations is affected accordingly. . . .
>
> There is a big difference between what a person thinks and what a person does. Everyone is entitled to his or her thoughts. These include police officers and all the people they serve. . . .
>
> However, problems occur when people lose awareness of the boundary between their thoughts and the objects of those thoughts. . . .

[1] *Human Relations in Police Service.* Los Angeles: Los Angeles Police Department, 1988, p. 3.

Losing awareness of this boundary is the main problem when attitude becomes a negative influence in police work. Awareness is the key, because *all* personalities incorporate attitudes.

By personality we mean those parts of a person's character that are obvious, as well as aspects that are hidden deep inside, perhaps hidden so well that the individual is not aware. Psychologists tend to refer to personality in terms of various modes of perceiving, feeling, needing, and behaving in a fairly consistent manner. From a law enforcement perspective, the Greek word *persona,* meaning theatrical mask, may be a worthwhile addition to this definition. Much of the human interaction of law enforcement involves people who consciously hide their personality for criminal reasons. But for purposes of this chapter, the visible and the invisible facets of personality are approached on the basis that there is nothing *necessarily* malicious or dishonest in either, at least in terms of what we will define and discuss as *attitude.*

Since this is not a discussion of theoretical approaches to understanding attitude per se, a relatively simple concept is needed. There are so many theories about personality that it is difficult to choose any particular approach.[2] One theory that permits easier clarification of the attitudinal dimensions of personality became popular early in this century and has remained more or less "conversational" since, the Freudian notion that children are born without consciousness. Freud speculated that consciousness emerged through *stages,* which could be arrested or fixated in a way that impeded further development of many personality variables.

We discussed earlier Freudian crime causes in terms of the *id,* an *ego,* and a *superego,* each developing (or failing to sufficiently develop) in a sequence. The infant's consciousness expanded in relation to this sequence. Students of human behavior readily recognize the similarities between these Freudian concepts and Eric Berne's popular transactional analysis, with the *child,* the *adult,* and the *parent* making up the human personality.

In any event, the infant ideally passes through the stages of development having to do with id, ego, and superego. Freud called the stages *oral, anal,* and *genital,* each reflecting Freud's view of body functions as dominating the gradual consciousness of the infant.

Id has to do with hunger, thirst, and physical comfort. *Ego* deals with conscious links between id needs and behavior needed to satisfy those needs, the key factor in the individual behaving or not behaving the way society dictates.

The infant's acquisition of guilt feelings is one of the functions of the *super-ego,* another concept relevant to law enforcement in that sufficient guilt feelings may deter the commission of a crime. This notion of how personality emerges could be diagrammed as in Fig. 10–1.

The somewhat complex explanations of the problems in getting through the three stages are not particularly valuable to this discussion, nor are all of the *learning* and *conditioning* psychological theories that fill dozens of volumes. What is being emphasized here is the reality that at least *some* learning is involved in personality development. The precise mixture of genetic variables and the learning

---

[2]See, for example, T.W. Adorno, *The Authoritarian Personality.* New York: Harper & Row, 1950. See also Gordon W. Allport, *The Nature of Prejudice.* Reading, MA: Addison-Wesley, 1954.

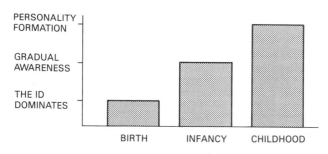

Figure 10-1 Perceiving self and then others.

process is not crucial to this discussion. What is crucial is the reality that attitudes are at least in part formed through learning that occurs since infancy.

It is not important that we agree with all of Freud's thinking. It is clear that, regardless of how unique every individual may be, the power of the culture's *folkways* and *mores* are learned with some degree of uniformity following the early acquisition of learning skills that occurs after birth.

This is important in approaching the relationship of attitude to intergroup relations. The impact of attitude on intergroup relations is the main subject of this chapter. This concept of *learning* attitude also applies to the Chapter 11 discussion of *prejudice;* prejudice is also *learned,* in many cases is too deeply ingrained to be modified.

Returning briefly to what we have noted as the seen and the unseen segments of personality, the point is made that attitude, as well as prejudice, may be hidden either from others or from the self or even from both until a situation arises that brings the learned prejudice forth. From this perspective on personality, let's now consider the relationship between attitude and the interaction between community groups. Such consideration is essential to Chapter 10's discussion of police-community relations programming.

The program title that any given police agency might give community relations is of relatively small importance. What is important is that the program integrate the reality that the community is made up of many different *groups,* which may or may not get along well together. Moreover, the police themselves, even in smaller agencies, vary in their feelings and perceptions about the community's groups.

One reason that police should be concerned with the relations between the community's groups was discussed earlier in terms of major civil disorders, the violence that has erupted throughout this nation's history. This chapter will discuss intergroup relations in the context of the *attitude* of majority groups, minority groups, the individual, and the police.

In approaching this discussion, we will take the position that because attitudes are learned, attitudes can be unlearned. We will not take the position that it is absolutely necessary to change attitudes to achieve successful community relations. On the contrary, we will take the position that demonstrations of negative behavior stemming from attitude must be controlled.

Furthermore, we will define attitude as far less ingrained than *prejudice,* so the unlearning attempted should be far easier.[3] Although no one is born with either

---

[3]See, for example, Milton Rokeach, *The Open and Closed Mind: Investigations into the Nature of Belief Systems and Personality Systems.* New York: Basic Books, 1960.

Attitude and Intergroup Relations

attitudes or prejudice (both are learned), attitude allows the individual to function more open-mindedly than prejudice, so attitude is not only easier to unlearn, it is also less threatening.

Before moving on to a definition of attitude, it is reemphasized that neither attitude nor prejudice must be unlearned to avoid bias and overt discrimination. Bias and overt discrimination can be banned even when poor attitudes and prejudice remain. Let's now define these terms for this discussion.

MEANING OF ATTITUDE

Whatever an individual believes is real at a given time is strongly related to a complex mental and physical process called *perception*.[4] To the extent that perception is accurate, and it may not be accurate, the belief *may* be accurate. But perception may go through certain filters of the senses. These filters are not limited to the physical limitations of what can be accurately seen, heard, felt, smelled, or tasted. In addition, many psychological filters operate in all of us. Asking a child to concentrate on studying is a form of filtering perception, in this case, completely blocking out perception and stimuli that are extraneous to the child's studies.

But although perceptions may be filtered, they are the basis for most human behavior; thus consideration must be given to the influences on perception.

In the context of police–community relations, the important influences over perception are *attitude, prejudice,* and *bias,* with discrimination being the result of these factors in most cases. What a person *perceives* can create attitudes and prejudices, but here we are concerned with the influence over perception from already formed attitudes and prejudices.

Let's begin by defining, for this particular discussion, the meaning of these terms.

Definitions of Attitude, Prejudice, Bias, and Discrimination

The terms attitude, bias, prejudice, and discrimination were used in so many contexts during the 1960s and 1970s that the literature of the 1980s tends to either omit their use or use the terms almost interchangeably. Compounding this communication problem is the distortion of these terms in newscasting and reporting. For purposes of this volume, the terms are intended to have the following meanings when used.

Attitude.   The influence on human thought processes that is longlasting and includes perceptual, motivational, and emotional influences on how other persons or objects are perceived. Attitude can be positive or negative, and attitude may or may not be apparent in human behavior.

[4]This concept is elaborated on in a wide range of contexts throughout the literature of behavior science. See, for example, Jozef Cohen, *Sensation and Perception, Eyewitness Series in Psychology.* Chicago: Rand McNally, 1969.

Prejudice. Like attitude, prejudice influences human thought processes, but the person or object perceived is *precategorized;* that is, whereas attitude *influences* the individual's perception, prejudice *controls* the perception of a person or object. Like attitude, prejudice may or may not be apparent. Prejudice can exist without discrimination, and discrimination can exist without prejudice. Moreover, prejudice can be *learned* by practicing discrimination as a folkway or more simply as a group norm.

Bias. Bias is intended to mean tangible demonstrations of prejudice, where overt communication or action clearly establishes the biased perception or prejudice of the individual.

Discrimination. *Discrimination* is any action, or failure to act that clearly impedes the struggle for equality (violates civil rights) or systematically denies access to appropriate redress of legitimate grievance; any of these on a *selective basis* is discrimination for purposes of our discussion.

This volume's approach to police–community relations allows for recognizing that prejudice and even bias may be extremely undesirable, but do not necessarily violate the law, as long as such bias or prejudice do not *impede* the struggle for equality we have discussed earlier. Discrimination can exist without prejudice; the discrimination is simply "the way we've always done it."

Another point must be made, having to do with changing attitudes.

CHANGING ATTITUDES

In view of our definition of attitude, it is possible to place *change* in the exact context of enforcing law. Laws can and do prohibit a wide range of discrimination as defined here, in housing, in employment, in transportation, and so on. So strong are most of the laws that police need not even examine whether the discrimination was on a *selective basis;* that was implicit in creating the law.

Clearly, discrimination can be changed and continues to be changed in terms of enforcement of the laws. Changing the attitudes and the prejudices that generate the discrimination, however, is another matter. But whether or not attitudes and prejudices can be changed, the law requires that many forms of discrimination be changed.

The law also requires that certain biases be regulated, whether changed or not. When prejudice emerges in a tangible form, by our definition here it is demonstrated as a bias. Where law leaves off, various codes of conduct take over, and bias can be controlled or at least reduced.

Regrettably, prejudice remains a private matter that, when not displayed, is not illegal. This is defined as unfortunate in the sense that its sudden display has far more destructive impact than prejudices continually displayed; "knowing where one stands" is usually an easier situation to cope with than being caught "off guard." Even when displayed, prejudice is not *necessarily* illegal; in many instances it is simply rude, insensitive, and uncivil.

In the final analysis, *direct* efforts to change deeply ingrained, negative prejudice may even strengthen the prejudice. Realistically, all that is likely to be enforceable is a requirement that prejudice be not translated into overt discrimination. It is, however, definitely in the interest of police–community relations that every effort be made to avoid any display of negative prejudices that might reflect on already strained relations between many of the community's groups.

But in a more positive situation, attitudes as we have defined them can and do change, even though it is not a requirement that they change. Let's examine the concept of attitude.

The Concept of Attitude[5]

There are two broad considerations in studying human behavior, study of the individual and study of the group. Both approaches overlap, since personality influences group behavior, but so does the behavior of the group influence the individual.

Behavior can also be viewed from two perspectives. The first, the *sociological approach,* focuses on group processes. The second is the study of the *individual,* or the psychological approach. These methods cannot be completely independent of each other; each has an influence on the other. Because humans are social beings as well as individuals, they are interdependent. To study the behavior of the individual, we must use the framework that sees social behavior as being influenced by others.

When social scientists wish to describe how a person perceives situations and objects and how his or her behavior is affected by these perceptions, they do so in terms of attitudes, at times ascribing a far more complex definition of attitude than is being used in this discussion. Let's review the definition used here for attitude: the influence of human thought processes that is longstanding and includes perceptual, motivational, and emotional influences on how other persons or objects are perceived. By this definition, prejudice is related to attitude, except that attitude merely influences perception, whereas prejudice controls it.

Attitudes may serve many functions. Generally, the individual's ability to react consistently in situations is made possible by his or her attitudes. These arise from a combination of many learned feelings and experiences that create a meaningful totality. How this comes about has been speculated on by many social scientists. Two theories that we will examine are the psychoanalytical theory and, to some degree, the learning theory. Our purpose in examining these theories is not to enlighten the reader on the two separate disciplines involved; the literature of both is rich and readily available. However, brief consideration may afford greater understanding of how attitude affects law enforcement problems; consider for example the development of attitudes by minority groups and/or ghetto residents.

[5]Parts of this discussion were published earlier in A. Coffey, E. Eldefonso, and W. Hartinger, *Human Relations: Law Enforcement in a Changing Community,* 3rd ed., 1982. Passages from pages 82–94. Reprinted by permission of Prentice-Hall, Inc., Englewood Cliffs, NJ.

Psychoanalytical Theory as Related to Attitude

We have already borrowed from Freud's notions of a child being born into the world without consciousness. The subsequent psychoanalytical theory was based entirely on the concept of the development of a person from early childhood, but combined with motivational conflicts that might occur at any given time. Basically, development is a kind of unfolding of sexual impulses, with certain transformations being the result. This theory emphasizes changes within a person, with a stronger emphasis on biological maturation than social and environmental influences. Greatly simplifying the matter, we can say that culture and experience affect sexual impulses, and these in turn affect behavior and attitudes, in contrast to the learning theories suggesting that culture and experience directly affect behavior and attitudes.

Recalling our discussion of the Freudian notion of expanding awareness, it may well be that many American citizens born in a poverty-stricken ghetto are virtually predestined to develop attitudes of resentment as their awareness expands to incorporate the affluent segment of society.

Some people who have been oppressed and treated as inferiors may accept this as a condition of existence, while others join what was previously discussed as the struggle for equality; in either case both are strongly influenced by the attitudes associated with the expanding awareness since their infancy.

Learning Theory

Learning theory, in its broadest sense, says that a person is born into a social environment, and his or her personality is shaped as a result of interaction with other human beings in this social environment. The distinguishing characteristic of a culture is that it contains a body of behavioral patterns such as skills, habits, and activities. Also, certain types of thought patterns may be as much a part of the culture as the behavioral patterns. Thus, it can be seen that attitudes and opinions may well be determined by culture and may in turn reflect the culture and/or subculture. The subculture of the ghetto tends to be made up of people in a low class by virtue of their inability to succeed economically. As we have already noted, this inability is not the fault of the ghetto resident in most cases. Recall our discussion of the continuing struggle for equality.

Given this theory of how attitudes are acquired, it can be assumed that attitudes toward law enforcement would be by and large hostile. Most of the studies and literature of the violent 1960s bore that contention out at that time. There is little reason to believe that similar surveys would not produce the same results if conducted today.

The reasons for this are obvious. If we learn from the group the attitudes that are taken into adult life, the group in poverty-stricken ghettos see police only in the context of enforcing the laws passed by those having affluence and political power. Reaction to this continuing perception, particularly without seeming recourse in many instances, is certain to have a negative impact.

In addition to frequently being a member of the lower class and being thoroughly indoctrinated by the values of that class, the black person has had experiences that have further alienated him or her from law enforcement. Moreover, the typical ghetto resident has witnessed both police and other ghetto residents in violent encounters with each other, and in some areas on a continuous enough basis to be routine. By and large, one of the more important contacts that black people make with white society outside the poverty-stricken ghetto is through the police officer, who personifies white authority. We noted in Chapter 3 that for much of American history, even after the emancipation of slaves, the "separate but equal" doctrine prevailed, in spite of overwhelming evidence that there was not equality.

Attitudes toward Police

Opinions are closely related to attitudes; opinions can be thought of as a kind of expressed reflection of attitudes. The term *attitude* implies a preparation to act, whereas *opinion* refers to what we believe is true. Because what we believe to be true affects our readiness to act in a certain way, it can be seen that opinions and attitudes are intertwined. Therefore, we will be concerned with both attitudes and, in a sense, opinions.

The voluminous studies and analyses during the 1960s reflected a highly negative attitude by many minorities toward the police; this has been repetitiously documented in the literature since the violent 1960s. In the sense that the opinions expressed can be assumed to reflect at least in part the true attitudes of the ghetto residence, most students of criminal justice conclude that attitudes toward police are extremely negative. The often cited and frequently quoted President's Commission on Law Enforcement and Administration of Justice, "Task Force Report: The Police" showed in 1967 that law enforcement suffered from an extremely poor image in minority sections of urban areas. There is a high probability that police still suffer from a poor image today, although it has improved in many ways (see Chapter 13).

However, it remains a reality that attitudes may *not* change, even though they are easier to unlearn than prejudices. For, indeed, the tragic reality is that *prejudice* may more accurately describe what is functioning not only among many ghetto residents against the police, but in the police perception of the ghetto as well. Nevertheless, further exploration of changes in attitude may be useful.

Changes in attitudes are brought about in various ways. Some stem from a change in an individual situation. An example would be a young man who develops a new attitude toward police when his brother becomes a policeman. Change in group membership, too, may cause a shift in attitude, as in the case of a youth who quits his gang to go to school. This may well change his attitude toward police.

Other changes in attitudes are brought about through education. Consider, for example, the education segment of the prevention programs reviewed in Chapter 9, particularly the role of the schools. As suggested there, law enforcement needs to be concerned with education, not only of the public in the broadest sense regarding police and community relations, but in the educational process of children developing their attitudes early in life. Representatives of the police need to meet with and talk to all manner of groups and organizations, particularly to primary grade children. An alert, forward-looking police administration will make arrangements to see that this type of public education and community relations is carried out.

At the same time, there may also be room for improvement in the police officer's own attitudes toward the people that they serve. Once again reiterating that it is not a prime requisite to change attitudes, it is nevertheless appropriate to at least evaluate attitudes. Police officers need to appreciate the fact that the majority of their time is spent not strictly in law enforcement, but rather in what could be broadly called a social role; here, if attitudes are to change at all, is the most likely place. In all beginning training courses of police and in all retraining courses, the subject of attitude should be reviewed. Through the very process of reiterating that it is not necessary to change attitudes, change of attitude is more likely. And it should be noted in terms of modifying attitude that a person receives education not only through formal schooling but through interpersonal relationships. This is the kind of education that a police officer can make use of to affect attitude changes or at least encourage attitude changes. Each member of law enforcement should realize that he or she has some positive effect on the public's attitude toward the police, and that treating every person as humanely as possible under the circumstances, which may be quite trying, to say the least, is the best method of cultivating positive attitude. This is education of the best sort.

Conceiving of education in a slightly different context than the "informal," attention is now directed to the subject of police training.

POLICE TRAINING

The FBI conducted a nationwide study of law enforcement training needs as perceived by law enforcement personnel themselves.[6] For whatever reason, police did not choose "community relations training" as a priority. While this conceivably may indicate that police *assume* community relations to be a priority, its absence from a well-documented priority list should be of concern to police administrators, at least to those administrators who recognize the critical need for community support for law enforcement. In other words, the absence of priority for police–community relations[7] may flow from the *perception* that police are already well trained and already providing adequate performance. Without a comparative study that isolates this particular factor, speculation is the only thing possible.

Training in community relations matters, however, is important whether or not listed as a top priority. Consider, for example, that the sixth highest priority for police training is "promote positive public image." Later chapters will deal specifically with police image problems and with public and community relations.

But in the present discussion of the absence of community relations in the priorities, the significance here is that there apparently exists some sensitivity to the *need* for communities to accept law enforcement. Community relations not only

[6]Robert G. Phillips, Jr., "Training Priorities in State and Local Law Enforcement," *FBI Law Enforcement Bulletin,* Aug. 1988, pp. 10–16.

[7]Ibid., pp. 10–11.

generate such acceptance, but go beyond to the point of gaining full community support.

Community relations training, then, is an important priority. And the approach to training in terms of whether specialized units or training for all sworn personnel is not the crucial issue. Put another way, the approach to training a few specialists in an agency in community relations, as opposed to training all personnel, is not, at least initially, crucial. Ultimately, successful community relations requires that all personnel fully appreciate the significance of the program, but the specific approach is not the main consideration. As noted earlier, the process of learning more factual data can change attitude — perhaps even change prejudice if learning were to actually occur.

Major differences exist in police training formats. In general, the professional preparation and continuing development of professionalization is gained through one or more of the following formats geared either to the individual specialist in the agency or to the entire staffing pattern:

1. College and universities, preentry
   (a) Conventional classroom/lab courses
   (b) Practicum-type experience courses and internships
2. Police academies, preentry: combinations of academic of law and procedure and practicum training (in personal combat and related matters, vehicle and firearms) usually geared to graduation leading to sworn officer status
3. Departmental training, postentry: Combinations of OJT, academic workshops, field exercises, personal combat and legal matters, policy, and overall proficiency maintenance
4. College and universities, postentry: Advanced study and degrees

In much the same manner that practitioners of probation credit Boston shoemaker, John Augustus, as being the father of probation in the last century, so also do enforcement personnel feel that police–community relations' formal training was organized by Joseph D. Lohman as a sociology course at the University of Chicago. In that same year, 1942, Gordon W. Allport designed a similar course for the Boston Police Academy. Significant training has continued since, motivated largely by the negative influence of breakdown in police–community relations to the point of major problems.

In terms of the relationship of attitude to the continuing development of police–community relations training, the role of police *ethics* is important.

Police Ethics

All criminal justice components, not just police, "need to develop an ethical awareness which can guide them through these troubled times."[8] The significance of this

[8]Robert K. Gustafson and Frank Schmalleger (eds.), *The Social Basis of Criminal Justice: Ethical Issues for the 80s.* Washington, DC: University of America, 1981, p. iii. See also Gerald M. Caplan (ed.), *Abscam Ethics: Moral Issues and Deception in Law Enforcement.* Washington, DC: Police Foundation, 1983.

observation emerges when one reflects on the frequently cited difference between the police subculture and the efforts to professionalize police, the difference between administrative police and the group norms of police behavior.[9] The emergence of police unions bears on this difference.[10]

The idea of including *ethics* in police training does not truly fit what may be the trend in higher education. It has been noted that whereas moral philosophy was the mainstay of medieval universities, the emerging dominance of science and technology has greatly changed the format of higher education.[11]

Were training courses in police ethics to be called something like *Rules of Self-discipline in Law Enforcement,* the stifled academic atmosphere might well be reduced, particularly if they were integrated with the usually straightforward training in law and department policy.

With or without such preparation, police must deal with the consequences of *attitude* in intergroup relations. The attitudes of the groups in contention and the attitudes of the police themselves are critical, and *ethics* plays a crucial role. Let's now turn to consideration of the community in terms of its groups; we first consider the group behavior that the police must at times confront.

GROUP BEHAVIOR[12]

Investigation by scholars into civil disorders has given rise to concern with the ways knowledge and the theories of the behavioral sciences can be applied to training programs and community relations programs. Because methods of handling civil unrest are of great importance, a brief look at some behavioral patterns might suggest alternatives to physical force in controlling unrest.

Traditionally, mob behavior has been interpreted in two widely different ways. One has emphasized the group itself. This interpretation suggests that groups are more or less independent of the individuals of which they are composed. The other emphasizes the behavior of the individuals who make up the crowd.

Were it possible to actually *know* which theory prevails in a riot, for example, this information might be vital to police. In truth, there is no practical way to

[9]See, for example, Michael K. Brown, *Working the Street: Police Discretion and the Dilemmas of Reform.* New York: Russell Sage, 1981, p. 286. See also Maurice Punch (ed.), *Control in the Police Organization.* Cambridge, MA: M.I.T. Press, 1983, as well as D. Smith, "The Upsurge of Police Repression: An Analysis," *The Black Scholar,* Jan.-Feb. 1981, pp. 35–36, and finally Richard E. Sykes and Edward E. Brent, *Policing: A Social Behaviorist Perspective.* New Brunswick, NJ: Rutgers University Press, 1983.

[10]For more elaboration, see, for example, C.A. Salerno, *Police at the Bargaining Table.* Springfield, IL: Charles C Thomas, 1981. See also D. Forcese, "Police Unionism—Employee Management Relations in Canadian Police Forces," *Canadian Police College Journal,* Feb. 1980, pp. 79–129.

[11]See, for example, Douglas Sloan, "The Teaching of Ethics in American Undergraduate Curriculum, 1876–1976," in Daniel Callahan and Gissila Bok (eds.), *Ethic Teaching in Higher Education.* New York: Plenum Press, 1980, pp. 2–9. See also Lawrence Kohlberg, *Essays on Moral Development,* Vol. II. New York: Harper & Row, 1984.

[12]Parts of this discussion were published earlier in A. Coffey, E. Eldefonso, and W. Hartinger, *Human Relations: Law Enforcement in a Changing Community,* 3rd ed., 1982. Passages from pages 209–218 and 230–236. Reprinted by permission of Prentice-Hall, Inc., Englewood Cliffs, NJ.

determine whether the individual is being influenced by his own personality, the crowd, or both; police must deal with the behavior on the basis of the actions exhibited. Nevertheless, it would probably be of considerable use to give some consideration to the concept of crowd and to crowd behavior, regardless of the precise motivation affecting such behavior.

The Crowd

Behavior scientists generally refer to people in mass as a *collectivity*. They use this term to denote crowds, groups, classes, and the public in general. Practically all group activity can be thought of as collective behavior. Group activities consist of individuals acting together in some way: in the action there is some fitting together of different lines of individual conduct.

Because the collectivity that police are most concerned with is the crowd, let's now examine some of the structure and function of crowds and later address some attention to the individuals within the crowd.

Crowd Types

In the limited context of examining the impact of attitude on inner group relations, it is not necessary to examine all the sociological ramifications of crowd topologies. For our purposes here, crowds can be thought of as either groups of people walking along the street or looking in store windows with no apparent connection; groups of people at a sports stadium mutually observing a sports event, but without any particular communication or mutual identity; or crowds with a purpose, particularly important to police when the purpose is some sort of violence or aggressiveness. This aggressive crowd can be thought of as a mob.

Let's give some further consideration to this particular crowd, because of its relevance to law enforcement.

Formation of the Mob

Most social scientists are in general agreement regarding phases of formation of a crowd becoming a mob. An exciting event, which catches the attention of people and arouses their interest, seems to be the first step. In the process of being occupied with the event and the excitement generated by it, a person is likely to lose some self-control. Characteristically, impulses and feelings are aroused that tend to press on to some type of action. A number of people stimulated by some exciting event, therefore, are inclined to behave like a crowd, *but not necessarily like a mob.* Young people being entertained by certain types of musical concerts exhibit this behavior.

A second phase in the formation of a mob involves a milling process. People who are aroused by some stimulating event are inclined to talk to one another and/or to move about if this is possible. This tends to increase the excitement, since each person's excitement is conveyed to the other and then reflected back, thereby intensifying the whole condition. The milling process seems to generate a common mood among members of the crowd and also to increase the intensity of the mood.

Individuals are inclined to take on a common identity and are therefore much more likely than in other circumstances to act as a unit. To this point, the description could still fit the group of young people attending an exciting musical concert.

The formation of a crowd may be the culminating or the precipitating event in police concern with a group. Because the police objective is to avoid precipitating events, it becomes important for officers to handle crowd situations with good judgment. And because good judgment is much more likely if all the pertinent facts are known, it is of prime importance that police obtain as much information about the group as is possible beforehand.

In bygone days when patrolmen walked beats, a good officer knew the people who lived on his beat. He could predict where trouble was likely to occur and who would be involved in it. As often as not, he could prevent an act of violence and avoid the necessity of making an arrest. This in part may account for what some perceive as a returning trend toward walking beats, at least in some jurisdictions.

No one would suggest that we give up modern police organization and go back to the officer on the beat totally. However, as we continue to expand and refine law enforcement techniques and police use of intelligence, we become aware that efficiency may be impersonal. And although people appreciate efficiency, they resent impersonalization; this in itself may cause problems, particularly in the formation of a mob out of a crowd.

Let's consider further the formation of a mob.

The Hostile Outburst

Often, a hostile outburst occurs from within what was a crowd until the outburst, by design or by some spontaneous panic situation. A hostile outburst apparently occurs because people feel there are limited numbers of escape routes in a panic situation, or they are overwhelmed with anger, often combined with fear.

In the panic situation, the situation of strain is physical danger and fear. However, many situations of strain are socially institutionalized, such as strains resulting from differences in social class, in religious or political outlook, or, of particular significance to police, in race. (The subject of race will be elaborated on later.)

If the strain placed on a crowd is sufficient to induce hostilities, violent eruptions of emotions are likely to be forthcoming. Of considerable importance to police is the reality that these negative factors are a function of *communication*. This is important in terms of the ability of police to *control* hostile outburst; preventing the communication of the information that strains and provokes crowd members is an excellent method of controlling crowds.

When the explosive situation is deliberate and designed, it usually involves the spreading of half-truths and rumors among the group with the hope that these will be accepted and precipitate a violent reaction. If the crowd begins to believe the rumors and half-truths, then, given a reason, it may be ready for a hostile outburst. In terms of such a reason, a crowd that is dominated by *negative attitudes* or, worse yet, *negative prejudices* is extremely easy to manipulate.

Once a hostile outburst begins and people become aware that there is a crack in the social order that is conducive to the expression of hostility, an interesting

Crowd control. (Courtesy of Capital Newspapers Group, Albany, New York)

phenomenon takes place. A rash of hostile action appears, most of it motivated by hostilities that are not related to the conditions or even the immediate strain that gives rise to the outburst. This, in effect, is people capitalizing on the fact that an outburst has occurred and that their hostile acts may be somewhat anonymous. Police are accustomed to such hostile and violent outburst being followed by accusations of police brutality in attempts to control the situation.

It is often found that a mob contains not only a number of people who become involved because of the initial strain or grievance, but also some people with grievances that are independent of the condition that caused the mob to form. This probably explains why participants in a riot may shift their attack from one object to another.

Controlling Hostile Outbursts

Once behavior has erupted into a hostile outburst such as a riot, social control must be exerted. At the beginning of the crowd's formation, police isolating apparent leaders is one way of precluding the communication necessary to incite further hostility or a riot. Police academies and ongoing police training emphasize the need to break up the crowd wherever possible before hostilities begin, but certainly as soon as possible once hostilities begin.

More in the prevention mode, residents of a ghetto area, for example, are far less likely to riot in a situation where it is common knowledge that complaints about police are taken seriously and evaluated, as are other grievances that may exist in the minority community. While police may not control the avenues for redress in other social problem areas, certainly the matter of complaints regarding police practices is a matter that law enforcement officials can address. In other words, adequate means for registering discontent with police should be built into the police system and be so accessible that it is difficult to persuade a crowd that they do not exist. But this should never intimidate police in their appropriate use of authority once a crowd becomes a mob and the threat of violence is imminent. This is most important, for it has been found that the inadequate enforcement of law and order also tends to encourage mob violence.

Law enforcement would do well to encourage other social agencies to take the necessary action to correct *false beliefs* caused by the rumors and half-truths that are frequently the basis for inciting riots. In the context of this chapter's discussion of *attitudes,* every effort should be made to clarify that negative attitudes are unfounded as to matters subject to police control. With that in mind, let us close this discussion of changing attitudes with a few comments on how the inciters of riots are able to exploit the negative potential of attitudes on intergroup conduct.

How Leaders Manipulate Crowds through Attitudes

Often people conform on the surface in social circumstances, but they have within them the potential to act antisocially when the right types of stimuli are unleashed in a social response, particularly when their attitudes are negative in terms of the stimulus posed.

Most people have been trained to follow a leader in certain circumstances. Even the rules of a childhood game are based on this concept. However, people have also been taught to follow the crowd under a different set of circumstances. The example of children made to stay in line in school is an appropriate example, and also an example of how attitudes are formed. Presumably, in this case, the child develops a favorable attitude toward the teacher who insists on conformity with the group.

A person interested in inciting a riot is able to use these two factors. When that particular leader is aware of negative attitudes toward the object of the riot, the task at hand is much easier. The leader generally tends to be the center of attention by standing alone and speaking or yelling. Some leaders use repetition and rhythm to stir a crowd to a frenzy. Good examples of this can be found in old newsreels showing huge crowds of Nazis responding to Adolf Hitler at party rallies.

Crowd leaders use such tactics to get an emotional buildup rising in the crowd. If the intent is to create a mob out of the crowd and to generate riot and violence, the riot inciter may use emotion-laden verbal symbols such as "rape" or "wholesale attacks" or any number of derogatory racial and religious terms. These words can stir up high emotions, particularly when the negative attitudes exist in the first place. Not surprisingly, violent reaction is likely to be forthcoming and the crowd becomes a mob.

It has been said that individuals in a crowd do not critically evaluate the leader's use of rhythm and repetition for stimulation. To be critical, one must wait and evaluate a number of alternatives in regard to how a situation should be handled. Therefore, one means of law enforcement controlling a crowd before it becomes a mob is to introduce a debate with the crowd leader. This will create a pause for critical evaluation and may check the impulsive activity that can take place under the stimulation of repetition and rhythm within the shelter of a crowd.

However, the more ingrained the negative attitudes or worse yet the prejudices, the less likely is a favorable result for this debating technique. Nevertheless, it is worthy of consideration in view of the alternative.

Now let us further examine group behavior in terms of *intergroup relations*.

INTERGROUP RELATIONS

One definition of *community* might be the population of people living within a geographical area with a social dependence on each other. But the depth and breadth of social problems that ultimately affect law enforcement require recognition that there are wide variations in the dependence various groups have on one another.

If the community has more than one population and the enforcement goal is to find a method for anticipating behavior that does not correspond to law-abiding attitudes, the first step must be to identify each of the community groups sufficiently well to associate it with a particular *attitudinal* trait. Criticisms of stereotyping and generalizing notwithstanding, sophisticated police efforts to anticipate problems require recognition of specific group attitudes.

Although the overriding law enforcement goal of identifying each group has more to do with reducing community tension than with immediate control of crime, clearer identification of the citizen groups could, in many instances, also be of great use to crime control as such. But in the present context of anticipating rather than controlling criminal behavior, sensitive recognition of the characteristics of particular populations within the community is essential. This entails examining the relationship between the majority and minority groups.

Although the relationships between the majority and minority groups in the nation or in the community is critical, the minority group is cited here as deserving specific attention for law enforcement. After all, in a voting democratic society, the majority is presumably less motivated to pursue conduct that would require police intervention, since the availability of a majority opinion vote generally satisfies much of the stress of that group. In recognizing the significance of the minority group, meaningful dialogue between the police and the minority group is a prime requisite.

Meaningful dialogue is a requisite not only between police and the minority community, but among the groups of the community as well, particularly when the goals of the various groups might be in conflict. For example, the goals of the majority may be to simply maintain a status quo, whereas a minority group is likely to be pursuing the struggle for equality to the degree that such a difference in goals is likely to generate hostility; the intergroup relationships and their attitudes are of police concern.

As Related to Police

While it is true that the vast majority of relationships between the groups of the community are of little concern to police, it is also true that many intergroup relationships are of critical concern for law enforcement. Consideration of the groups that draw police interest is the rationale for this discussion.

One of the most consistent views police officers have of groups with whom they must deal is that such groups are often inherently criminal or inherently violent. This perception obviously flows from *attitude,* as discussed in this chapter. The negative perception is in most cases reciprocated manifold by the group itself.

When groups perceive not only the police but other groups in the community with hostility, the potential for considerable difficulty is evident. To consider the causes of problems when attempting to prevent them is good police practice. However, dealing with the unrest and tensions that police address necessitates giving attention to the problem itself—the attitudinal frictions of groups and between groups. Because of the nature of intergroup activities in a free society, police must deal with certain groups directly even when aware that the source of the problem may be elsewhere.

Consider, for example, police responsibility in the case of continuous high school fighting between students of different races. In these cases, it becomes severe enough to require police involvement; police intelligence, more often than not, is aware of the hostile philosophies of certain leaders that aggravate and play on the negative attitudes of the groups involved. Moreover, police intelligence is frequently aware of the aggravation long before such philosophies are transformed into violence. Beyond police intelligence gathering, law enforcement agencies can often provide a community relations program of sorts that tries to head off the potential problems. The two main weapons available to police to combat the growth of such negative attitudinal strife are public awareness and intense attention to the potential trouble spot. In a democratic society, police do not have the option of intervening with the "source" until the source is actually breaking the law. Of course, there are enforcement options when the source becomes explicit enough to provide a case for inciting riots and other violations of law.

Preventing or at least reducing the potential for violence between groups then becomes a matter of how well police use the two main weapons put at their disposal, public awareness and attention to the trouble spots. These two alternatives may be more than enough when public awareness leads to public education and when attention to the trouble spots leads to improved relations between groups, that is, leads to improved *attitudes* between the groups.

Finally, let us consider *interracial relations* in terms of attitude.

Interracial Relations

The term *interracial human relations* acknowledges a great deal more than the inherent frustration of membership in a regulated minority. Implicit in this term is the despair that accompanies the witnessing by generation after generation of the elevation of nearly all regulated minorities but theirs, and a system that inflicts severe socioeconomic penalties on those already penalized by a loss of dignity. To be meaningful, interracial human relations must involve the right of every person to be respected as a human being—to accept the legitimacy of the continuing struggle for equality.

Police in particular cannot afford to treat this as an option, for failure to acknowledge this right invariably leads to police problems, frequently violent police problems. Moreover, fundamental respect for humanity is a prime requisite of enforcing law in a society in which the only justification for police intervention is the violation of law. In recent decades, the police have made great progress in coming to grips with the reality that all human beings are the highest form of life and that only the *behavior* of people can be called good or bad. Bad behavior is subject to modification in proportion to the degree of human dignity accorded; treat a person inhumanely and modification of the unacceptable behavior becomes less likely.

This is not to say that the proper behavior by police will completely eliminate the need for force. Law enforcement is and will remain a *dangerous,* often deadly job in which violence may be thrust upon the police regardless of their sensitivity to the nature of human interaction. Nevertheless, it remains true that interracial human relations afford the police an avenue for reducing the magnitude of the enforcement segment of their responsibility and for improving the negative attitudes that worsen the situation.

In this sense, interracial human relations differs very little from intergroup relations. After all, both are intergroup human relations and both are severely stressed by negative attitudes. But a sensitivity to all the problems affecting intergroup relations is a good beginning for correcting the negative attitudes that all too often plague this aspect of law enforcement.

This brings us to the final consideration of this chapter, the composition of the community in terms of its groups.

Community Composition

The groups that populate the community, as we have seen, vary widely from many perspectives. Economic status influences many of the other variations, but it remains a fact that people of the same economic status may be liberals, conservatives, or radicals. And increasingly, fortunately, people of all races may be found in the higher economic brackets.

In Chapter 11 we will elaborate on the distinctions between the racial and ethnic characteristics of groups in a community. In truth, we will see citable differences are far fewer than the similarities once all of the groups of a community have been considered.

However, a community composed of different groups often develops a strong need for improved attitudes about intergroup relations, unless similarities are perceived to a greater degree than differences. While large differences may be perceived through the filters of negative attitudes and prejudice, human beings consistently prove to have far more in common than not.

So long as attitudes have not hardened into ingrained prejudice or at least so long as prejudice has not become so strong as to preclude peaceful interaction, there is reason to believe police–community relations will succeed, not in spite of the community (and the police for that matter) coming from divergent attitudinal situations, but *because* people's conduct can transcend the influence of even negative attitudes.

In Chapter 11 greater attention will be directed toward the main impediment to such community cohesion, racial and ethnic prejudice.

SUMMARY

This chapter noted that the community is made up of many groups who may or may not get along well. Influences against groups getting along well were discussed in terms of perceptions that may be distorted by attitude or controlled by prejudice. Discussion definitions were given for attitude, prejudice, bias, and discrimination. The impact of attitude on perceptions and behavior was presented as an influence, in contrast to prejudice, which controls perception.

The subject of changing attitudes was presented as a feasible possibility, but not a requirement. So also was prejudice presented as learned, but far more ingrained. It was emphasized it is not necessary to eliminate prejudice in order to eliminate discrimination.

Bias and discrimination were presented as overt acts, events that deprive someone of rights, that must be stopped, regardless of whether negative attitudes and prejudice are maintained. The general concept of attitude was explored in the context of influencing and improving attitudes, whether completely changing them or not.

Police training was considered in the context of community relations, with acknowledgment that in one study the subject was not considered one of the top 20 police training priorities. Also discussed was the high priority police give to police image training.

The formats of police training were discussed, along with the subject of police ethics. Group behavior and intergroup relations were examined in detail in the context of community composition and interracial relations.

DISCUSSION TOPICS

1. Elaborate on the significance of conceiving of the community in terms of intergroup relations.
2. Contrast attitude and prejudice.
3. Discuss changes in attitude.
4. Elaborate on the rationale for insisting that discrimination cease whether or not negative attitude is changed.
5. Discuss the influence on group behavior of attitude in terms of perception.

6. Elaborate on the concept of crowds evolving into mobs.
7. Discuss what the chapter presented in terms of methods for police avoiding the formation of a mob out of a crowd.

Relevant Problems for Discussion

Attitude is something that can be successfully hidden, even from the individual who holds the attitude. Levels of self-awareness vary widely, and few of us *actually* know how we "come across" to others. So it is that we observed in this chapter that it is necessary to *change* attitudes, but the goal is to avoid the *display* of negative attitudes, both by police and toward police. Seeking to avoid displaying bad attitude is the only realistic goal, since attitudes can be successfully hidden from all but the most painstaking and unrealistic psychological screening. Moreover, there are many personnel who, if their marginal attitudes are not displayed, make exceptionally fine police officers in *every* sense of the word.

A problem related to the position that bad attitude need not be changed, merely not displayed, has to do with the failure to establish rigid standards and definitions with regard to "not displaying" the bad attitude. For example, if standards for professional demeanor do not include being courteous, an unnecessarily wide range of interpretation of "displaying bad attitude" remains. Far more significant is the hostile police encounter where "courteous" is scarcely appropriate. In these situations, professional conduct must be defined in terms of *minimum force,* as well as clear definitions of professional demeanor. Emphasizing the minimum force necessary to control the situation and clearly defining the criteria for professional demeanor permit enforceable insistence on not displaying bad attitude. Without emphasis on these specifics, the subject of displaying bad attitude is too obscure.

There is not likely to be tangible evidence that such control of police attitude will always improve citizen attitude; police will continue to encounter people that veteran officers often describe as "failing the personality test." But the *professional* approach still requires minimum force, professional demeanor, and maximum effort not to display bad attitude.

11

Prejudice: Racial, Ethnic, and Others

The question of *why* police should be concerned with the subject of *prejudice* is the theme of this chapter. It is not a new concern; prejudice has been a focal point of the civil rights movement for a long time and will likely continue to be of concern to many minority groups well into the future. But new or not, there is considerable reason for law enforcement to be concerned with the *impact* or at least the potential impact of prejudice. Consider, for example, prejudice as defined in Chapter 10 in this particular case, prejudice *against* police:[1]

> A few individuals have an almost automatic negative response to police officers. The person in uniform is not seen as an individual but as a symbol. Badge, gun, and uniform may trigger guilt feelings and anger in people who have not resolved their own conflicts with authority. In order to feel more comfortable, they need to see an external authority symbol as a scapegoat. Officers as well as other groups fill this need for the scapegoat. In this sense, police officers serve without due recognition or thanks.

Prejudice against police is one reason to address the subject; prejudice by police is another:[2]

[1] *Human Relations in Police Service.* Los Angeles: Los Angeles Police Department, 1988, p. 18.
[2] Ibid., p. 16.

207

Every police employee, like every citizen, may have private biases and personal feelings. However, when these attitudes adversely affect the manner in which the employee deals with people on the job, then effectiveness is diminished.

Employees can be impaired by exaggerated attitudes about the superiority of their own race, sex, age, political or religious beliefs. . . .

In extreme cases, these attitudes can render the employee incapable of judging the significance of conduct which departs from their own standards and practices. . . .

The point at which attitudes stop merely influencing perception and start to control perception is how we have defined prejudice. When a human being is rendered "incapable of judging the significance of conduct," that individual's perception is controlled by opinion before the facts are known—prejudice. This can be more discernible in the context of *stereotyping:*[3]

Working hypotheses on past experience with people are an important and necessary part of the professional police employee. However, these working data should not be confused with stereotypes, which are exaggerated assumptions based largely on emotional feelings. Stereotypes are generalizations which automatically assign certain group characteristics to anyone who happens to belong to that group. . . .

The career police officer is often particularly vulnerable to the risk of "confusing working data with stereotypes"; the very nature of police work all but encourages cynicism:[4]

In police work, as in other professions, a certain amount of skepticism is healthy. It means alertness and not taking things for granted, even apparently routine situations. But exposure to crime and its aftermath can tend to harden and render insensitive an employee whose sympathetic understanding is needed to properly perform his or her duty.

Concern with prejudice should not be confined to prejudice toward and by police; law enforcement should also be concerned with the potential impact of prejudice of one group against another, at least to the degree that such intergroup feelings hold the potential for police problems.

It might be argued that police need only be concerned with prejudice among law enforcement personnel. After all, this argument could go, the law forbids only *discrimination,* not prejudice. Citizens can be as prejudiced as they want, so long as they do not transform their prejudices into illegal *discrimination.*

What this argument fails to recognize is that prejudice may instead transform itself into violence, even riots, not merely into illegal discrimination. There is no question that police *should* be concerned with prejudice as a more serious extension of the problem of negative attitude, which has already been discussed.

[3]Ibid., p. 14.
[4]Ibid., p. 15.

PREJUDICE[5]

Let's quickly review the distinction between *attitudes, prejudice, bias,* and *discrimination.* Attitude contrasts with prejudice in that attitude *influences* perception, whereas prejudice *controls* perception (through precategorization). Bias makes the prejudice discernible, and discrimination is overt acts that deprive someone of their civil rights.

The complexity of prejudice is such that it can exist without being discernible until certain combinations or factors come into existence. The complexity also includes recognition that *discrimination,* as defined for this discussion, can be the *source* of the prejudice; people can learn their prejudices by coming to believe there is something wrong with the victims of discrimination. Put another way, treating someone as inferior long enough leads to the belief that the person is inferior.

It is possible to discriminate without prejudice, but our concern here is prejudice that evolves into discrimination, into discernible overt acts that at one level can be simply illegal and at another level be extremely violent.

Let's consider prejudice further. *Prejudice,* by this definitional approach, is not merely an *influence* on perception and subsequent behavior. The precategorization process actually *controls* perception and exerts an extremely strong influence on behavior. In terms of the folk saying, "keep an open mind," a prejudice absolutely prevents open-mindedness. The person or people against whom the prejudice is directed are, in the mind of the prejudiced individual, precategorized regardless of the available facts, which are simply not discernible when the prejudice is strong.

Further consideration of this often destructive phenomenon is needed.

Racial Prejudice

We have all known people whom we can justly label prejudiced. Many of the readers of this book, in fact, are in all probability quite intolerant toward one or more of the ethnic or racial groupings. Prejudice and bias (bias is an important extension of prejudice because, if biases are not displayed, prejudices are not necessarily negative) toward outsiders is so frequent an aspect of American society, and of all known societies, that it is literally a universal phenomenon common in all cultures. Despite the contention of many racialists, however, prejudice is *not* inherent in humans; it is not a biogenic trait. Prejudices, like attitudes, are learned. To effectively probe how and why prejudice exists, then, it is crucial to recognize that, like stature or IQ, prejudice is not something that a person either has or does not have, but is a matter of degree and intensity. We cannot, for example, legitimately assert that a man whose height is six feet is "tall," whereas a man standing at five feet eleven is "short." Nor can we assert that a person with a recorded IQ of 140 is "near genius," while one whose IQ is 139 is merely "bright." Nevertheless, there are tall people, geniuses, and highly prejudiced persons. This discussion concerns the highly prejudiced, those

[5]Parts of this and later discussions in this chapter were published earlier in A. Coffey, E. Eldefonso, and W. Hartinger, *Human Relations: Law Enforcement in a Changing Community,* 3rd ed., 1982. Passages from pages 3–19. Reprinted by permission of Prentice-Hall, Inc., Englewood Cliffs, NJ.

who pose a potential threat to the orderly environment for which law enforcement is responsible.

Perhaps further elaboration on the definition already ascribed to prejudice for this discussion will be of assistance. Prejudice is, specifically, thinking ill of a person or a group without sufficient justification; a feeling favorable or unfavorable that is prior to or not based on actual experience. In terms of favorable or unfavorable, the context of law enforcement suggests that we focus on the unfavorable prejudices.

A prejudiced person will almost certainly claim to have sufficient cause for his or her views. But in most cases it is evident that these facts are both scanty and strained. Such a person typically resorts to a selective sorting of his or her own memories, mixes them up with hearsay, and then overgeneralizes. No one can possibly know all members of a group. Hence, any negative judgment of these groups as a whole is, strictly speaking, an instance of thinking ill without justification.

We can further elaborate on our basic definition of prejudice to include an avertive or avoiding or hostile attitude toward a person simply because he or she belongs to a certain group and is, therefore, presumed to have objectionable qualities ascribed to the group—"reason enough" to avoid them. Another essential attribute of prejudice is that of giving and applying a stereotype name or label, usually some extremely derogatory term intended to make the user of the term feel superior, and the target of the term inferior.

Targets of Prejudice

Historically, the targets of prejudice have been determined by the particular configuration of conflicting values and opposing groups, largely because of the cultural and social situation of the time and place. The most evident targets of prejudice have been those groups whose relationships with the prejudiced are marked by competition or other forms of opposition. Often a group has been singled out as a target for a period of time and then replaced by another group; recall our discussion of the continuing struggle for equality.

At the outset of American history, the targets of strong prejudice were the British, who opposed our efforts toward independence. But there was also a certain amount of sectional division among the states. As the struggle for the extension of slavery became more and more a factor in national politics, a split between the industrial North and agrarian, slave-geared South became evident. After the Civil War, the whole situation changed in the South, with the appearance of the colored-caste system, which still continues in spite of civil rights gains. Later, as blacks moved into the north in response to conditions at home and the lure of freedom and economic betterment, they came into direct competition with the northern urban whites. A certain amount of antiblack prejudice began to emerge in such places as Chicago, Detroit, Los Angeles, and New York City. Then, with the flood of immigrants fleeing poor political and economic conditions in Europe, new objects of prejudice entered the scene.

The black and immigrant groups constitute a handy set of specific targets of intolerance, discrimination, and prejudice on the part of native-born or long-established American citizens. Economic competition was a crucial factor in the earlier outbreaks of prejudice; immigrants willing to work for lower wages often eased American workers out of jobs in this era of rapid industrialization. But one of the symbols of hostility pertains to an ideological conflict between the Protestantism of most of the Americans and the Catholic faith of the immigrants. Recall our discussion of the violent riots from the last century into this century.

This problem was especially acute after 1890, when southern Europeans began to outnumber immigrants from Germany, Great Britain, and Scandinavia. The Protestant–Catholic friction, with native hostility less often directed toward Catholicism per se than toward the very different southern European brand of culture, erupted in the growth of native American or nativist movements. Foremost among these movements was the Klu Klux Klan.

To this point, we have considered prejudice as though it were a single style. Prejudice can actually take two forms.

Two Types of Prejudice

Granted that prejudice is so widespread that it is normal, who are likely to manifest the *most* prejudice? Put another way, the question is, where is prejudice most likely to pose a potential problem for law enforcement?

Although prejudice is essentially a matter of degree, there are two types that we can consider. As we evaluated attitudes in Chapter 10 in terms of group influence as opposed to the individual personality, so prejudice can be approached on the same basis.

Prejudices learned from the group or culture. Group-conditioned prejudice is primarily learned or acquired in the normal process of social interaction; the *folkway's mores* and general *norms* of a culture "teach" prejudice. Thus most people raised in an environment verbalizing antipathy toward a group assume prejudicial orientation, which in turn often translates into prejudiced behavior. In effect, it might be said that the individuals have been taught, deliberately, to be prejudiced. Underlying prejudices of this nature is the belief that the target of prejudice is inferior and presents some sort of perceived threat.

It cannot be overemphasized that typically the formation of prejudice is not a product of distorted personality development. Prejudice, or at least negative attitudes, as we have defined them for this discussion, are derived from group norms; to not have the prejudice, or at least negative attitudes, would not be normal. Within a group, when patterns of prejudice prevail, it is the person who *conforms* to the group that is most normal or well adjusted. Accusations of prejudice are particularly resented when the self-image of the prejudiced person is of ultimate conformity.

Once a small child accepts the prejudicial norms of his or her parents and, through osmosis, his or her schoolmates, the negative stereotypes become internalized; that is, they slide into the subconscious mind and become a functioning part of his or her personality. In adult years, when the individual feels an aversion for the outgroup, he or she will defend his or her attitude with all manner of "reasonable" rationalizations, and strongly, because they are "normal."

There are, however, differences in susceptibility to these cultured-conditioned brands of prejudice, even among people reared in the same general culture. This variation is similar to the earlier discussions of many families raising children in a "crime-causing neighborhood" only to find one child becoming a criminal and another becoming a clergyman.

Since prejudice is *learned,* in theory it can be *unlearned,* as discussed in Chapter 10. Unlike negative attitudes, however, prejudices that are culturally conditioned are generally deeply ingrained and extremely resistant to unlearning, particularly in the context that to be prejudiced is normal.

Nevertheless, the possibility of unlearning prejudice is of interest to law enforcement. Insofar as additional education that discredits the basis of the prejudice may in fact weaken the prejudice, the concept of unlearning remains relevant, if for no other reason than consideration in police training.

Yet the hard truth of the matter is that prejudice is generally deeply ingrained and difficult, if not impossible, to dispel. Because prejudice is not formed in a piecemeal way and usually is deeply ingrained within the personality structure throughout socialization, attempts to legislate prejudice out of existence are absurd; the only negative factor in this process that is susceptible to legislation is overt discrimination, as we have discussed.

To lessen prejudice with any degree of effectiveness, then, either we must change the basic values or attitudes of entire groups, or we must somehow transfer the prejudiced person's allegiance to another group. What we have discussed as the civil rights movement may eventually bring either or both of these about. But, for the immediate problem, the abolition of *discrimination* appears to be the only societal recourse; prejudice, as it exists among many citizens currently, may continue to exist.

Educating the young child is a far simpler undertaking than changing highly prejudiced adults; therefore, the future is where the hope for increasing harmony between the community's groups rests. Nevertheless, such educational programs must reach the child during the lower elementary school years and must be skillfully handled in the context of a child being socialized by parents that may be extremely prejudiced.

Prejudice as a function of personality development. Having considered some of the ramifications of how the group teaches prejudice, attention can now be turned to the individual acquisition of prejudice. This type of prejudice is firmly embedded in the personality makeup, and attempts to rid people of it must be far more formidable than the techniques of unlearning the group-conditioned prejudice just discussed. As will become clearer during this discussion, people with a prejudiced personality almost *have* to hate, and if one of their scapegoats or objects of venom is somehow eliminated from focus, they will inevitably seek out some other victim.

A psychologically prejudiced person is more dangerous than the sociologically or group-conditioned prejudicial person for two reasons. First, he or she is present in all areas of the population—among the educated, wealthy, and influential, as well as the poor and ill educated; and, second, he or she is more likely to be actively prejudiced and in a position to translate hatred into effective political or social action, or, worse yet, into overt violence. Postwar studies of the more avid Nazis and of potent native American fascists have uncovered all the earmarks of this kind of individual prejudice.

Like prejudice learned from the group, the individual psychological variety of prejudice has its roots in childhood. But unlike the group-learned prejudice, specific sets of prejudice are seldom acquired in early years. Rather, a basic outlook on life is learned during this formidable period, an outlook that will warp the entire life of the victim. How does the childhood of such a psychologically prejudiced person differ from the normal person's life? It differs at many crucial points, as the subconscious will affirm. We must recognize how vitally important the formative years are in shaping the entire personality; recall our discussion in Chapter 10.

It is abundantly clear that the more deeply prejudiced person, one who looks down on *many* minority groups rather than one or two specific outgroups, is marked by distinct personality problems. These people are "sick" in a very real sense. Their sickness is not of their own doing but rather the outcome of a strict and undemocratic upbringing. As a result, their entire lives will be marred by deeply embedded frustrations, vague hatreds, and insecurity. They are already targets of demagogues of the far right and far left. They will be unhappy with both the Republicans and the Democrats and can be satisfied only with a totalitarian order, one in which their hatred can be legitimized.

From the law enforcement perspective, the question needs to be asked, how do both of these forms of prejudice translate into problems for the police? Recalling our discussion of interracial relations in Chapter 10 affords an initial answer to this question.

The Forms Prejudice Takes

What is racism? The word has represented daily reality to millions of racial minorities for centuries, yet it is difficult to define the term precisely. *Racism* may be defined as predictions or decisions based on consideration of race. Furthermore, such decisions, or in some cases policies, are intended to subjugate a minority racial group for the purpose of maintaining or exerting control of that group.

Minority problems are problems of intergroup relations. The majority itself is made up of many minorities and, indeed, is sometimes but the dominant minority of a group of minorities holding key positions. When this majority group, however it is constituted, prejudges a minority group, the minority group is at a disadvantage to say the least. When this prejudgment is highly negative, even hostile, the potential for police problems exists. When this prejudgment entails routine *discrimination,* as an extension of the prejudice of the majority group, the risk is even higher.

Reducing Prejudice

It must be reiterated that the complete elimination of prejudice is virtually impossible; prejudice is deeply ingrained and resistant to change. Indeed, we have noted that even the elimination of negative attitudes is difficult at best. Nevertheless, it remains a consideration for law enforcement.

Because much prejudice is based on stereotype thinking, education in the matter of group differences, when they are found, should provide the necessary intellectual basis for a change of attitude. If attitudes can be changed, perhaps prejudices can at least be modified.

It is for this reason that various organizations like the National Conference of Christians and Jews, the National Association for the Advancement of Colored People, the Urban League, and the Anti-Defamation League carry on extensive educational programs, hoping to change negative attitudes and at least modify prejudice.

However, prejudice remains by definition an irrational attitude, that is, resistant to factual input. Knowledge is not enough. A change of attitudes conditioned by norms found acceptable by the group may well indeed ultimately at least modify prejudice. Several techniques have been found to be successful in achieving changes in attitudes; one is to change group norms, that is, change folkway mores and norms, through discussions, lectures, and the use of communication media—TV, newspapers, books, radios, and the like. The second is to encourage association of the prejudiced members of a group with the members of the group toward whom the prejudice is directed. Quite often, the removal or suspension of *discrimination* subsequently provides an opportunity for experiencing social interaction that may lead to a reconsideration of negative attitudes and perhaps eventually to modifying prejudice.

Because prejudice is largely irrational and emotional in nature, emotional appeals to the alleged values of democracy are usually ineffective in the long run, although in some instances they have a temporary impact.

The key variable, then, remains the elimination of discrimination—the elimination of the *practice* of prejudice.

Reducing Discrimination

Social scientists are generally of the opinion that the attempt to eliminate prejudice under conditions of widespread discrimination is destined to fail. To the degree that this view is accepted, it becomes obvious that discrimination must be eliminated to reduce prejudice at least to the point that it no longer constitutes the potential to create law enforcement problems.

Therefore, antidiscriminatory laws have been increasingly created and have proved to be increasingly effective. This effectiveness has not been achieved without major conflicts. There are some indications of an improvement in the conditions surrounding minority groups, particularly the black community. The U.S. Supreme Court has made several important decisions that we reviewed earlier in this volume. The effect of these decisions has been to strengthen the antidiscrimination movement.

Because blacks are becoming much more sophisticated politically and their vote is growing larger with every election, politicians are taking cognizance of the blacks' might. When a distinction is made between the predominantly peaceful civil rights movement and the intermittent violent outburst, the most discernible improvements tend to follow violence, a worrisome reality for police. Fortunately, the political power of such factors as "block voting" has also begun to emerge as a strong alternative for achieving change.

It is noteworthy that members of the groups that constitute the civil rights movement are now going beyond the earlier civil rights demands. Members of these groups have now demanded not merely the removal of legal barriers, but active *affirmative* efforts to open up opportunities to them to ensure that they will be in a position to take advantage of these opportunities; recall our discussion of *affirmative action* as part of the continuing struggle for equality. Returning the discussion to the context of prejudice translating into overt discrimination, brief consideration should be addressed to the avenues that discrimination takes—avenues that probably underpin the emergence of demands for full participation in society.

Discrimination can take several forms as it applies to minority groups. *Economic* discrimination involves unequal treatment in the economic sphere of members of certain minorities. *Educational* discrimination results in school segregation and inferior facilities for educating those who reside in poorer school districts. This is particularly true, as we have noted earlier, in the case of blacks and Spanish-speaking Mexican Americans and Puerto Ricans. Because of apathy in enforcement procedures, *political* discrimination is exercised against minority groups despite constitutional amendments designed to ensure all citizens the right to vote. There are many signs that this particular form of discrimination, *political* discrimination, will soon change. Nevertheless, political discrimination continues to exist and is particularly important because it is largely through federal legislation that minorities can expect to gain protection against other types of discrimination. Put another way, when political avenues are closed, virtually all avenues are closed, unless there is a return to the violence that occurred in the 1960s.

Another aspect of political discrimination is the manipulation of political boundaries and the devising of restrictive electoral systems. This particular technique is under increasing scrutiny in many parts of the land. In areas where there is a large block of minority residents, it is not unusual for the political machinery of the dominant group to jury rig such neighborhoods so that their true voting strength is not reflected in political representation.

Social discrimination is perhaps the most difficult form to eliminate through legislation, since many people believe strongly that it is their basic democratic right to associate with whom they please and to bar whom they please from membership and associations to which they belong. This is another context for the assertion that *prejudice* cannot be eliminated, only the overt extension of prejudice into discrimination. In the social area, this extension is particularly resistant to legislative efforts to correct.

For example, many fraternities will not admit members of certain minority groups. Also, restrictive covenants in housing operate to exclude minority groups from certain residential areas; the Supreme Court's decisions and legislation regarding such discrimination are still frequently circumvented by various techniques and ruses.

Perhaps the best approach to understanding the fallacy of this continued discriminatory practice in our culture is the consideration of the basis of prejudice, race and ethnicity.

RACE AND ETHNICITY

While more detailed explanations will be made shortly, it may assist in clarifying the notion of race and ethnicity to note at the outset that *race* is a biological/genetic type of a concept, whereas *ethnicity* is learned and is similar to the acquiring of attitudes and prejudices, as we have discussed.

The Myths

There are a number of strongly held beliefs about race and ethnicity; many are unfounded and most are myths. It is worthwhile to explore these widely held beliefs in the context of the reality that underpins the concepts.

Race

Race, as the term is popularly defined, evolves from several factors. First there is the notion of *mutations,* which are markedly different specimens that appear in a species for no apparent reason and then pass on their unusual characteristics to their offspring through hereditary forces.

Second, there is a concept known as *isolation.* Isolation refers to a geographical concept generally, which is self-imposed and results in the interbreeding of a particular species that tends to perpetuate and magnify the original characteristics. Finally, there is the logical extension of isolation, the *inbreeding* that genetically reinforces the mutations that are in isolation.

The most frequently used criteria for racial identification were skin color, hair color, hair form, eye color, racial nose width to nose height times 100, distribution of body hair and beard, and the projection of lower facial characteristics. These criteria were used because it was assumed that they are relatively stable; that is, they are more of less unmodified by the environment and essentially inherent in the genes, and, more importantly, are easily measured.

Yet in the study of the distribution of these characteristics in the human species, it has been discovered that there is a wide variation in each of them; thus human types range through every conceivable combination of these factors. Nevertheless, there is a continuing and widespread belief that human beings can be clustered into three categories. These three categories were identified by early theorists as Caucasoid, Negroid, and Mongoloid. In general terms, these classifications are roughly equivalent to the terms caucasian, negro, and oriental.

When groups of human beings did not fit these early theoretical classifications, the theorists usually chose to either overlook the group that did not fit, or squeeze them into one of the handy classifications, regardless of the lack of conformity.

In the context of understanding race as a basis for prejudice, it should be emphasized that racial theories usually depend on statistical averages of selected characteristics. The early theorists created rigid criteria for each of the three categories, elaborating what we have already noted in terms of skin color, along with head and body shapes, nose and eye shapes, height, hair characteristics, and so on.

And as we have already noted, people vary so much that no one group completely fits into any of the classifications that are defined by such strict criteria. It is easy to observe that large percentages of the white population have many of the same characteristics early theorists assigned to black people and to oriental people. A large percentage of black people have the same characteristics that were assigned to white and oriental people. Among oriental people and people who early theorists chose to squeeze into a classification, all the characteristics can be observed.

Prejudice based on race requires the prejudiced person to either overlook or minimize these similarities in favor of emphasizing whatever differences are discernible. But it is a myth that any group of people truly fit the rigid criteria that early theorists established for identifying the races.

Moreover, the *behavior* that is often cited by the highly prejudiced person as a racial characteristic is the result of learning, not race; behavior is learned, not inherited. And such learning occurs independent of the biological influences of race.

In the last analysis, more people do *not* fit these types of descriptions than do fit them. Most people are neither distinctly Mongoloid nor Negroid nor Caucasoid but show some mixture of all listed characteristics. Whether the origin of humans is multiple or single, biologists and anthropologists concur on one point; there is no *pure* race. A pure race could exist only if its people had lived throughout history in complete and total isolation, with no cross breeding whatsoever with other groups.

We find, then, that there are no pure races in any serious sense of the word and no large numbers of people who are reasonably identifiable as distinct types. We are left, therefore, only with the fact that many small groups may share in common certain genetic features by which they are identifiable or distinguishable. The biological fact of race and myth of "race" should be distinguished. For all practical purposes, *race* is not so much a biological phenomenon as a social *myth*.

We cannot, therefore, scientifically account for differences in group behavior in terms of differences in group biology. The events overwhelmingly point to the conclusion that "race" and "race differences" are not valuable concepts for the analysis of similarities and differences in human group behavior, a cogent observation in terms of enforcing law in a democratic society.

Let's now consider the concept of ethnicity.

Ethnicity

Whereas race refers to hereditary ties or genetic or biological concepts, *ethnic* means social and cultural ties; ethnicity is a *learned* process. Thus, when people confuse racial and ethnic traits, they are confusing what is given by nature and what is acquired through learning.

In the context of the law enforcement interest in prejudice that becomes a police problem, the question arises, what is ethnicity?

From the law enforcement perspective, what is often confused as racial prejudice is actually a combination of both racial and ethnic prejudice when a clear distinction is made between the biological factors of race and the behavior people learn independent of race. Put another way, racial hatred that evolves into a police problem is often mixed with behavioral factors along with the racial prejudice.

Careful analysis of the insulting terms that are applied to groups against whom racial prejudices are directed usually indicates confusion—that there is a *racial* along with a *learned* ethnic concept functioning. Considerable confusion over these concepts continues. Many racial insults, for example, refer to or imply behavior. Since we learn behavior, rather than inherit behavior, at least part of the insult is toward ethnicity as well as race. The insulted behavior could have been learned by any group, not just the group being insulted. This is true whether addressing behavior deemed positive or behavior seen as negative.

Even when prejudice is accurately aimed at ethnicity without regard to race, it is often technically inaccurate by virtue of the wide variation in behavior within an ethnic group. Prejudice operating on the premise that an ethnic group has a racial composition or even a great deal of cultural matters in common is conspicuously unfounded.

IMPLICATIONS OF PREJUDICE

The *impact* of prejudice that turns into discrimination, is the backbone of the civil rights movement. In criminal justice, it is not always clear whether actual discrimination has resulted from prejudice, and yet in many instances it becomes obvious that illegal prejudice has occurred.

For example, more than half of the 314,083 inmates of prison in 1979 were blacks, even though blacks are a minority.[6] The position is taken that the disproportionate inmate population traces to police community relation problems.[7] Put another way, police arrest more black residents of a community than white. Of interest to a discussion of prejudice, it is further observed that blacks are imprisoned eight and a half times more often than whites.[8] Finally, it is observed that, on the basis of socially threatening conduct, the law tends to criminalize black behavior while simply overlooking white socially threatening behavior; such comparisons are made between ghetto burglaries and to the pollution of rivers and lakes by large corporations.[9]

Does this meet the standard of discrimination as prejudice coming into view? The issue is not that simple. From the enforcement point of view, river polluters who violate law should be prosecuted in the same vein as ghetto burglars; both are law

---

[6]Norval Morris, "The Outlook for Criminal Justice and the Community," synopsis of a lecture on Oct. 21, 1980, to the 25th Anniversary of the National Institute on Police and Community Relations, cited in Louis A Radelet, *The Police and the Community,* 4th ed. New York: Macmillan, 1986, p. 204.

[7]Ibid.

[8]Ibid.

[9]Ibid.

violators whose conduct is socially threatening. But the inmate population still speaks to at least the *appearance* of prejudice turning into discrimination, which is significant because punishment itself may cause crime via alienating the inmate from family and community and fostering a "get even" prejudice of yet another kind.[10] "Get even" retribution tends to compound the complexity of arguments for and against punishment versus deterrents in crime control. Discrimination in how punishment is applied makes the matter even more complicated.[11] Put another way, there is not universal agreement on the rationale for imprisonment, even when imprisonment does not have an overrepresentation of a minority group.

Now add to this problem the reality that there are major inconsistencies in the law.[12] Inconsistencies exist between and within jurisdictions and the laws themselves and the manner in which laws are enforced.

Sadly, yet another problem emerges from time to time — corruption in industry and government, which does even more social harm than many of the crimes for which imprisonment is imposed.[13]

With these and many more negative factors impinging on the social damage done by prejudice, the *appearance* that blacks are discriminated against has an extremely high potential for police problems.

Clearly, the racial composition of the prison inmate population is not established by police alone. Differential arrest rates among minorities do exist, but so do differential crime rates. To the degree that we accept overrepresentation of black inmates as proof of discrimination, to that same degree are we obliged to include as causes for this overrepresentation the social and economic conditions. Prejudice *may* exist, but there are many other factors in this regard. Perhaps police can examine their practices for the presence of prejudice that has become discrimination, but police need the help of all society to root out the main social and economic conditions that *encourage* crime, whether or not they cause crime.

Prejudice, as a learned process, can be unlearned. The more deeply rooted the prejudice is the more unlearning that is required, conceivably too much unlearning for certain individual cases. Racial prejudice that exists before a black officer is partnered with a white officer rarely stays at the same intensity; and it often disappears completely after a period of time.

Criminal justice statistics keep the question of discrimination in focus for minority groups. But concerted police effort to eliminate prejudice, if possible, and eliminate discrimination whether or not prejudice is eliminated, could bring the statistics into the right context: *overrepresentation of minorities in prison reflects social and economic problems rather than police discrimination.*

[10]David Lovell, "What Is Punishment?" *Newsletter of Michigan Coalition for Prison Alternatives,* Spring 1984.

[11]Marcus G. Singer, "Judicial Decisions and Judicial Opinions: Relationship between Law, Justice and Morality," *Criminal Justice Ethics,* Winter–Spring 1983, pp. 17–30.

[12]See, for example, Frederick Elliston and Michael Feldberg (eds.), *Moral Issues in Police Work.* Totawa, NJ: Rowman and Allanheld Publishers, 1984.

[13]See, for example, Jameson W. Doig, Douglas E. Phillips, and Tycho Monson, "Deterring Illegal Behavior of Officials of Complex Organizations," *Criminal Justice Ethics,* Winter–Spring 1984, pp. 27–59.

The need to clearly establish that police are not prejudicial in their practices may evolve into a sense of urgency in many jurisdictions. The destructive impact of hate mongers may have been significantly reduced in recent years, but by no means eliminated.[14] Should the turmoil that follows the activities of such groups erupt into major violence, it is of critical importance that the community perceive their law enforcement as *professional* to the point of removing any question of prejudicial police conduct and permitting law enforcement to deal with any situation without the necessity of defending itself. This has to do with improving police image. In the same context, Chapter 12 will address subjects concerned with how the community perceives police, domestic crisis, and juvenile problems.

SUMMARY

This chapter noted that progress in racial and ethnic relations has been made, but not enough for police complacency. Indeed, the chapter closed by noting that there are continued signs of hate mongering and racial prejudice.

It was proposed that law enforcement remain aware and alert to potential problems growing out of racial and ethnic prejudice, regardless of the perceived progress made. Prejudice was discussed as a concept, in which virtual control over perception exists by prejudice that is learned.

Race and ethnicity were discussed in terms of science as well as myths—race as a genetic or biological concept in contrast to ethnicity as a learned or cultural concept. The implications of prejudice and some of its impacts were considered in the context of police problems.

The disproportionate numbers of black prison inmates were considered from the perspective of questions: Is it criminal justice prejudice turned into discrimination, or is it arrest rates that reflect social conditions that appear to induce higher crime rates among minorities, or both?

The *appearance* of prejudice forming into discrimination was considered in terms of posing great problems for police, even if the appearance is unfounded. It was emphasized that the appearance of prejudice can be as destructive as actual prejudice insofar as law enforcement is concerned. The appearance of prejudice was discussed in the context of relatively few arrests for societal damaging corporate crimes in contrast to major imprisonment for minority members committing crimes.

DISCUSSION TOPICS

1. Discuss why it would be a mistake to become complacent about apparent improvements in recent years in racial and ethnic relations.

[14]Wire Service of the Associated Press on October 30, 1988, Los Angeles, California, publicized a report from the Anti-Defamation League of B'nai B'rith, including the assertion that "skinhead" gangs have doubled. The report found that in 21 states these gangs are said to have ties to the Ku Klux Klan and the White Aryan Resistance. These gangs are said to be responsible for many "hate crimes," which according to the report "have a special emotional and psychological impact—thereby creating the potential for escalating violence and turmoil."

2. Discuss racial prejudice as a potential threat to the orderly environment for which law enforcement is responsible.

3. Elaborate on the ramifications of police appearing to be prejudiced.

4. Why is the appearance of prejudice potentially as great a problem as actual prejudice in some instances?

5. Discuss the reason for police needing to remove the appearance of prejudice.

Relevant Problems for Discussion

An extremely unpopular, yet related problem in terms of rooting out prejudice and discrimination is the sometimes *lingering ramifications,* the problems that at times hang on long after the main problem has been presumably solved.

Some veteran police officials whose careers span efforts to root out prejudice and discrimination have observed a similarity between the accusation of prejudice and the accusation of child molestation. When either case is buttressed with strong evidence, the matter is settled and dealt with properly. But when accusations are permitted without evidence, a kind of air of suspicion lingers on even after the allegations are proved unfounded. Peripheral problems having to do with debates about whether unfounded allegations were made in good faith or used as some kind of vindictive weapon tend to compound this lingering effect. But, in any case, an unjust penalty accrues to the accused, at least in instances when the allegations are proved unfounded. When the accused is a larger group, the risk of intergroup strife emerges.

Police officials are not in total control of allegations. However, clearly defined guidelines can be established with regard to the level of evidence required to gain official recognition of allegations.

When evidence is there and can be gathered in exactly the same manner that police gather all forms of evidence, the matter is dealt with in a professional way.

When politics, problems with police image, public relations, and police credibility force the matter outside the sphere of police administrative control, the involvement of community leaders *with* appropriate civil service personnel, police unions, and other interested parties may be the only arena available. But even in this turbulent context, police expertise on evidence should be the main factor, at least insofar as the police involvement in such a process is concerned.

12

Domestic Crisis
and Juvenile Problems

There is more than ample reason to be concerned with the problem of domestic crisis:[1]

> Domestic violence is a growing problem in both California and the United States. Statistics from the California Department of Justice reveal that in almost one-third of all willful homicides the victim was killed by a spouse, parent, or child . . . hundreds of thousands of Americans are harmed, not by strangers, but by those they trust and love. They are victimized not on the street nor in the workplace but in their own homes . . . most authorities agree that violence is a learned behavior . . . to tolerate family violence is to allow the seeds of violence to be sown into the next generation. . . .

This troublesome reality is by no means confined to California, it is recognized nationwide as a significant problem and increasingly a problem to law enforcement.[2] Domestic violence is part of the larger picture of criminal violence in America, which includes serial homicides, vicious rapes, and brutal child molesting and assaults on spouses.[3]

---

[1]*Guidelines for Law Enforcement Response to Domestic Violence.* Sacramento: California Commission on Peace Officer Standards and Training, 1985, p. 1.

[2]See, for example, U.S. Commission on Civil Rights, *The Federal Response to Domestic Violence.* Washington, DC: U.S. Government Printing Office, 1982.

[3]See, for example, Aleister Segerdal, *Assault on Violence: You Need Not Be a Victim.* Riverside, WA: Arcadia-Ford Publications, 1987.

The problem of juvenile delinquency has for many decades been recognized and dealt with as a serious law enforcement challenge. Juvenile problems other than delinquency, just as in the case of domestic violence, have not received such recognition until recent years. Increasingly, however, there is legislation reflecting the public demand that domestic crisis and such problems as child abuse be recognized as major problems demanding law enforcement involvement. Most veteran police officers have dealt with some form of both of these problems as part of their careers. Since the legislative trend is likely to continue, the involvement of police in such matters is likely to increase.

Whether incorporated in a generalized manner or performed as specialties, police work with domestic crisis and juvenile problems other than delinquency is usually thought of as very specialized. In a sense, both of these police matters are *thought* of by some as the same kind of special work performed by forensic technicians in a crime lab, or the highly skilled workers in a computerized identification system, and thus are considered "necessary" to police work, but not "real" police work. Such thinking is an error; police intervention into both family crisis and juvenile problems other than delinquency (often the same case) is very real and increasingly a more difficult variety of problem to deal with.

Moreover, in the context of gaining community support, *how* police deal with domestic crisis and juvenile problems has the potential for improving public image. Let's examine domestic crisis.

DOMESTIC CRISIS

A popular publication reported that China has 4 prison inmates per 10,000 population compared to 26 inmates per 10,000 Americans,[4] This is particularly interesting because, according to the article, China has 5 police officers to 10,000 population compared to 20 for the United States.[5] Possibly, if China had more police, more Chinese would be in prison, but the slant of the article was to the contrary. Among the additional considerations reviewed was a 4.7% recidivism rate of Chinese parolees, compared to a whopping 69% of American parolees convicted of additional crimes after release from prison.[6]

Many factors were cited in accounting for this astounding difference, in the sense that China's population is *far* greater than America's.[7] One factor was the significant role of the *family*. The family was cited as having powerful influence, even over prison inmates.[8]

In our earlier discussion of community crime prevention, the importance of the American family was presented, both in terms of parental control with regard to preventing juvenile delinquency and in terms of major support for other crime

[4]Robert Elegant, "Everyone Can Be Reformed," *Parade,* Oct. 30, 1988, pp. 4–7.
[5]Ibid.
[6]Ibid.
[7]Ibid.; 242 million in the United States and 1.02 billion in China.
[8]Ibid.

prevention activities. The *family* was presented as an important factor in preventing and controlling crime.

But there is another area of law enforcement concern for the *family*: family crisis that becomes verbally or physically violent. It is not only families that become violent enough to draw police response in terms of domestic violence. Couples and others occupying the same residence also experience strain in their relationships. When such strain evolves into verbal or physical violence, police are called.

What was once referred to by police as family fights has, in recent years, expanded to the category of "domestic disturbance." Many jurisdictions distinguish between "domestic disturbance" as "verbal" and "domestic crisis" as "physical assaults." For purposes of this discussion, the term domestic crisis refers to both, noting that "words" often lead to violence.

In spite of vast variation in the attitudes toward this type of police work, every police agency must deal with domestic disturbances in one way or the other. Some seek diligently to avoid such involvement altogether, and others try to minimize the involvement by attempting to refer calls to clergy, family counselors, or social agencies. In spite of varying degrees of success, police still become involved to some degree in one way or the other.

Attempting to minimize involvement is permissible when the domestic disturbance is verbal. But when the domestic disturbance turns violent and physically assaultive, police are obliged to take a more direct approach. And of little surprise to most veteran police, physical assaults by wives against husbands—"husband beating"—is included in the vast array of domestic difficulties encountered.[9] Beyond the phenomenon of husband-beating, there is seemingly ever increasing concern with wife-beating; warrantless arrests of spouse assaulters are covered in the penal codes of many states, and mandatory arrests in the statutes of a few states.

Child abuse, physical assaults, and sexual abuse will be discussed later in this chapter as part of juvenile problems. Of note in this context, however, is that the penal codes in most jurisdictions mandate explicit law enforcement involvement in these matters.[10]

The problem of domestic violence has gained federal attention as well.[11] A significant lobbying effort is continually being made not only in both houses of the Congress but in most state legislatures as well; laws will doubtless continue to emerge. But recognition is one thing, and acceptance of the responsibility to improve police services *may* be another. Before moving into this subject, let us quickly consider the notion of the police accepting the idea of gaining community support for law enforcement through better services in domestic crisis.

[9]Maureen McLeod, "Women against Men: An Examination of Domestic Violence Based on an Analysis of Official Data and National Victimization Data," *Justice Quarterly,* June 1984.

[10]As an example of early recognition of child abuse problems for law enforcement, see Richard Steen, "Child Abuse Units in Law Enforcement," *The Police Chief,* IACP, May 1978, pp. 38–39. See also Alan Coffey, *Juvenile Justice as a System.* Englewood Cliffs, NJ: Prentice-Hall, 1974, pp. 68–78.

[11]U.S. Commission on Civil Rights, *The Federal Response to Domestic Violence.* Washington, DC: U.S. Government Printing Office, 1982.

A consistent characteristic of criminal justice workshops and courses taught by the author of this volume is to encourage participants to share differences of opinion—to enrich the insight of the group with the point of view of the individual. This style has greatly enhanced the instructor's understanding and appears to have served its intended purpose for many students as well. One such difference of opinion that has bearing on the subject of this volume is a rather consistent view expressed by many experienced, dedicated police officers, including black officers and Hispanic officers. The view often expressed is that police have no business in community relations, often citing the enormous complexity of constitutional law "without getting bogged down in social work and politics." This view is frequently buttressed with the observation that good public relations would resolve any perceived difficulties for law enforcement.

Since the author has not only respect for these officers' opinions but empathy for their viewpoint, it has never been a pleasure to rebut the argument with the many factors that literally prove that community relations is *not* optional if law enforcement is to succeed. By whatever the name the program is called, the very survival of future police organizations depends on bridging the police–community gaps (see Chapter 15). "Better PR" will be noted, but better public relations must be combined with many other community relations factors.

The reason for noting this rather consistent expression of concern by a veteran police officer is to dramatize the absence of criticism of police involvement in family fights. In other words, while it has been the present writer's experience to encounter questions regarding the need for community relations, it has not been the writer's experience to encounter questions over involvement in family fights. Intervention into domestic crisis appears to be accepted as a police function.

If the present writer's experience reflects the general attitude of law enforcement, then the chances of improved community relations are greatly enhanced. In this regard, there appears to be evidence that police in general do indeed accept law enforcement responsibility to intervene in domestic crisis, at least if training priorities reflect general acceptance. Recent FBI research indicates that training in handling domestic disturbances is one of the top 20 training priorities of American law enforcement.[12] Included in this priority is the need for training in awareness of spouse abuse and child abuse.[13]

Beyond this recognized training need, there is reason to examine the causes of domestic problems in the context of community relations, for the "sake" of community relations.

Growing national concern with child abuse and spouse abuse continues to affect the justice system in every state; the agendas of meetings between community leaders and police officials are often devoted entirely to these subjects. If community leaders perceive police officials as being reluctant to deal with this problem, they are likely to withhold support for law enforcement in other areas.

[12]Robert G. Phillips, "Training Priorities in State and Local Law Enforcement," *FBI Law Enforcement Bulletin,* Aug. 1988, pp. 10–16.
[13]Ibid.

Far more dramatic than the community's withholding support however, is the violent, many times fatal, domestic disturbances themselves.[14] The typical family fight that explodes to lethal violence focuses attention on the dangers of this facet of police work. Domestic violence also poses the potential for risks to police image in the community; both are of concern, with the danger to the police being of higher concern.

However, the police image is important. Such image is often a reflection of how the media report police functions, including the handling of domestic violence. Citizens vary widely in how they integrate the massive number of influences that form the police image, but the effects of reports on family matters, with which the citizen can identify are probably long lasting. Because the citizens of a community have a personal affinity for the concept of family or at least domestic relations, how police intervene in this private area is necessarily a matter of interest for the community.

INTERVENTION INTO PRIVATE MATTERS

When a family moves into a new house or apartment, neighbors typically are more amused than outraged if the family is overheard "bickering." Respect for privacy is a powerful influence; embarrassment would generally preclude interference, at least during the initial period following the new neighbor's arrival. Out of respect for privacy, it is usually a matter of seeing the new family as "settling their differences" rather than "disturbing the peace." Even if the new family's fight is loud and annoying, there is generally a neighborhood tolerance, at least for a while.

We are not describing here the kind of domestic crisis in which neighbors are aware of the potential for extreme, even lethal violence. Were the neighbors aware of and no doubt fearful of such a potential, an entirely different perception would form. When the neighbors fear a serious injury or death, their interest in *privacy* gives way to their concern for law and order, with the likelihood of police being summoned.

Part of the problem is, however, that neighbors often have no way of knowing when the noise of a family fight is actually the warning signs of an explosive domestic crisis. There are many interspouse or parent–child arguments that can be heard throughout a neighborhood that are nothing more than letting off steam. Conversely, there are seemingly quiet, controlled arguments that are the prelude to murder–homicide cases, even barricades and shooting sprees.

When police are summoned to a domestic disturbance, the citizen calling may be convinced that the noise level not only is "disturbing the peace" but is proof that injury or death is imminent. When the police do nothing, the police image may be tarnished, at least in that neighborhood. In such situations, police image would be

---

[14]Some years ago the author published a book on domestic crisis for police academics and training programs. Emphasized was the violence and danger for police. There appears to be no reason to conclude that danger has lessened. See Alan Coffey, *Police Intervention into Family Crisis*. Santa Cruz, CA: Davis Publishing, 1974. See Chapter II, "Family Strife as a Danger to Police," pp. 18–40.

Police dealing with domestic crisis. (Courtesy of San Jose Police Department)

greatly enhanced if public awareness programs were designed to acquaint the community with the variables involved, not the least of which is the right of privacy.

These same neighbors may well be appalled when police intrude on a family that does not seem to be disturbing the peace. In cases where the neighbors perceive police as posing safety, health, or other problems to children or parents or both, there is sometimes little evidence available to the neighborhood that police are following the mandates of law. All too often the severest forms of abuse are not discernible to the neighborhood, but are perhaps discernible to school teachers or other police sources of information.

The point being made here is that the community's *perception* of the *need* for police involvement in domestic matters has a significant influence on the police image. Unlike the clear-cut *need* for police to be involved in settling a fight between bar patrons, intervention into domestic matters is judged on a scale of perceived need without common criteria to make such an evaluation. Each citizen retains a personalized criteria for judging the police as either intruding or intervening.

This alone would justify inclusion of domestic crisis in police community relations, but there is a far stronger justification. Increasingly, police are being required to deal with domestic problems that were once thought of as private matters. National attention to child abuse and spouse abuse spawns new laws, with growing community demand for enforcement; indeed, enforcement is mandated in many statutes. If ever there was an area in which police community relations could find common ground with much of the community, certainly domestic violence would qualify, since virtually everyone has some form of identity with the concept of family. Let's examine some of the main characteristics of domestic crisis.

Intervention Into Private Matters

POLICE CRISIS INTERVENTION TRAINING

The first thing to acknowledge and then emphasize is that intervening in a family fight can be and often is dangerous for police.[15] The trained officer is no doubt at less risk than the untrained officer. But what should be the training goal?

A real enhancement to any law enforcement community relations program is an adequately trained officer. In the case of domestic crisis, adequate does *not* mean training an officer to be a psychotherapist or even a family counselor. Yet a great deal of police work places the officer in a counseling role of some kind. Training should therefore include at least some of the skills recognized as needed in dealing with counseling problems, particularly serious family problems. Furthermore, even the process of encouraging a family to seek counseling is a counseling skill in itself.

From the purely enforcement perspective, training should also include, but not be limited to:

I. Sophisticated methods of recognizing abuse
   A. Spouse abuse
   B. Child abuse
      1. Physical abuse
      2. Sexual abuse
II. Sophisticated methods of recognizing child neglect
   A. Nutrition
   B. Shelter and supervision
III. Professional evidence-gathering standards
   A. Adult prosecution
   B. Juvenile court protective custody
IV. Precise application criteria for state and local law

Once these primary matters are handled by appropriate training, further training is desirable in the nature of family dynamics and the various methods families employ to cope with stress. Since the goal of such training is to equip the officer to *understand* the dynamics of family crisis, it can be taught in either of two contexts: (1) Handling Personal Stress, or (2) Dynamics of Domestic Crisis.

The same FBI research cited earlier listed as a training priority "Handling Personal Stress." Indeed, this category of police priority for training need was the highest priority of all.[16] This no doubt reflects the extreme emotional stress in police work. But it also underpins the possible double value of training in family crisis intervention; a police officer can gain a great deal of insight into the stresses he or she confronts personally by learning the techniques in successfully dealing with family crisis.

The title under which an officer receives needed training is not nearly as important as receiving the training, something worth exploring where there is

[15]Ibid.

[16]Phillips, op. cit.

reluctance to get "shrink training." When "shrink training" is resisted, perhaps a welcome mat would be put out for training in "stress management."[17]

A brief summary of generalized family stress may serve to illustrate how at least the "theory" can apply to police intervention and/or to personal stress management.

Those responsible for training must draw the parallel and point up certain differences. Nevertheless, the same training can be made to cover both areas if sophisticated and energetic effort is made by the trainers. The training can be handled in such a way that the officer learns a great deal about managing the personal stress that police work invariably generates while at the same time enhancing her or his professional skills in domestic crisis intervention.

POLICE AND DOMESTIC CRISIS INTERVENTION

Police programming in domestic crisis prevention requires police to intervene *during* a domestic crisis. This suggests the value of exploring briefly the *meaning* of domestic crisis, a meaning here referring to the counseling variables rather than the police definition per se. One approach to clarifying the meaning of domestic crisis is through the concept of stress.

Stress

Family *systems* and family *communication* are the key factors in family *process*. Family process is like the wind; it can be felt even though it cannot be seen, at least by family members. Thought of in another way, family activity patterned into various systems, which are discernible to family members if not to others. These patterns include various styles of communication through both word and deed. The family system of communication is molded in large measure by the nature of the *stress* encountered by the family. All human beings, families included, encounter stress. All humans deal with stress, and certainly families deal with stress. Many times families aid family members in stress but many other times, families worsen the stress, rather than help. When stress becomes too severe to handle, police may be called to intervene. This suggests a definition of domestic crisis:

Crisis exists when the family or its members lose their ability to cope.

Many situations are a crisis by this definition, but are not matters for police intervention. But many matters that are a crisis by this definition *are* police problems: suicides, family fights, and other domestic disturbances.

But in terms of a more typical police contact with domestic disturbance, this definition can be singularly useful. For, when police either knowingly or unknowingly intervene at the point of crisis, police *are* performing family crisis intervention in the sense that they are either knowingly or unknowingly influencing

[17]For a fuller review of police stress, see, for example, Hons Seyle, "The Stress of Police Work," *Police Stress,* Fall 1978. See also the April 1978 issue of *The Police Chief,* IACP.

Officer handling family problem. (Courtesy of Santa Cruz Police Department)

alternatives for one or more family members. This is singularly important in the context that the crisis is the point at which at least one family member has lost the ability to cope successfully with stress.

In terms of *danger* to the police, the question becomes whether or not police *know* that they are intervening in a crisis—whether or not police *realize* that their presence may be experienced as far more threatening than would appear on the surface. Thought of another way, this has to do with police recognizing when they are seen as *intruding* rather than intervening.

Police Intrusion or Crisis Intervention?

Recalling the Chapter 2 discussion on the nature of enforcement, police control of human behavior can be seen as intrusion no matter what else it might be called. For that matter, *intervention* is an accurate description of police control of behavior. For purposes of this discussion, however, it is important to distinguish between "unwelcome intrusion" as an invariably negative situation and "sometimes welcome intervention," which *may* be a positive situation.

This suggests the wide variation in not only the nature of police effort, but in the intended outcome as well. This wide variation appears to more than justify distinguishing between *intruding* for the purposes of enforcing law and *intervening* to prevent law violation. In short, the distinction between police intrusion and police intervention is a matter of the *intent* to enforce the law, as opposed to the *intent* to prevent law violation.

In the volatile situations into which police are thrown in this category of police work, these distinctions frequently lose their significance. The actions necessary by the police to stop violence in progress or to prevent violence when it is imminent obscure the *intent* of the officers in most cases. In such volatile situations, even the most sensitive intervention comes across as intrusion.

Recognizing the intruding nature of police involvement in family strife also affords a basis for defining the actual nature of police risk during such intrusion, even when police *intend* merely to prevent law violation.

The Family Feels Threatened

The main irony of police trying to help a family during crisis is that the family may feel threatened by the police. And even in families that fight a great deal, the feeling of being threatened tends to draw members together for common defense, which may be a significant danger to the police in some situations. Put another way, almost any group that comes to feel threatened by almost anything will be influenced in the direction of self-protection.

Police are at far greater risk when their involvement in domestic crisis is experienced as a threat to the group or the family. The family's feelings of self-protection are focused on the perceived threat of the intruders.

From the police officers' perspective, the *intent* may well be to intervene for the purpose of helping. And it would be ideal if the family or group also perceived the intervention as helpful. It would be even more ideal if a family in serious crisis welcomed helpful intervention.

In reality, the opposite is true. It is *not* common practice for families to invite police to participate in resolving family difficulties; police are usually perceived as outsiders. For this reason, the police must recognize that their safety is constantly in question in such encounters.

The idea of recognizing the potential risks and dangers of any situation is a value in *all* police work; these skills apply to virtually every encounter of police routine. Recognizing a well-disguised armed robbery in progress, and diagnosing the number of participants and the potential risks and dangers to all concerned is an obvious advantage in police work. Recognizing the implications of an automobile with mud obscuring the license plate number and muddy windows obscuring the view of the car's occupants, along with the fact that the vehicle is traveling in a residential district with a high incidence of burglaries is also of value to police.

But in the case of recognizing and diagnosing risk factors in domestic disturbances, a particularly significant addition to the police repertoire has been made. For unlike the "shoot out" and the "high-speed chase" in which the danger is overwhelmingly apparent, the risks and dangers emerging from domestic disturbances are frequently so obscure that they remain invisible to even the family members themselves. Training in the techniques of discerning such signals without the defensive threat of police power actually *enriches* police skills in literally all human relations, including confrontations with violent criminals.

Beyond reducing the risks and dangers of police work, then, learning what is required to recognize and diagnose potentially dangerous domestic disturbances may prove to be one of the most effective instruments for improving the police image.

Keeping the peace and enforcing pertinent law are tasks that are enhanced by having an understanding of such dynamics, so further pursuit of these subjects is not inappropriate. But with regard to police intervention and domestic crisis, an officer trained to recognize the *signs* of imminent emotional outburst is at far less risk. Emphasis is placed here on the reality that proficiency in *applying* this kind of training is limited to keeping the peace and enforcing pertinent law, or *preventing* violation of the law. The well-trained and skilled acuity needed to recognize domestic problems places police officers in an ideal position to establish a referral network that brings other community resources to bear.

Referral Network

Officers overloaded with calls may not have the time to settle minor domestic problems. The perceptive and trained officer will, however, discern matters that either require further investigation or perhaps intervention by some other agency. Networks of communication between medical, social, health, welfare, and child protective or counseling agencies and the schools are ideal when police actively participate.

From an investigative standpoint, many cases seem minor on the surface and without probable cause to investigate further. Yet the well-trained officer may perceive a number of signs indicating the need for further investigation. When under the pressure of additional, more serious calls, a network referral may bring an appropriate social agency into the picture or possibly even further criminal investigation.

Community relations programs that emphasize interagency cooperation provide a network that can both seek appropriate aid for stressed families and also provide investigative evidence should a criminal justice case emerge. For example, the alert officer leaving a minor domestic problem where he suspects but did not observe evidence of child abuse, can later alert whoever reports and centralizes the index of complaints—a school teacher twice reported a child appeared beaten, a social worker often reported the child appeared beaten, a local medical clinic twice treated the child for a broken arm.

Police, after educating themselves to the problem, must then educate the community. Take, for example, the school teacher who thought a little girl was just making up stories about being "touched" or the school nurse who thought the little boy broke his arms and ribs because he was accident prone. In short, every agency that the community brings to bear on social problems should learn what the police role is in domestic crisis—whether to provide aid to the family or to provide evidence needed to protect the child

In larger police agencies, the juvenile division trains specialists who utilize such a network as a matter of course.[18] The concept of crisis intervention itself is much more practical than police may believe.[19] But even in the largest jurisdiction, police community relations are bound to improve if this very sensitive, very necessary police activity is shown to the community in its best light of being handled by well-trained, professional officers who *intervene,* rather than intrude, whether they are perceived as intruders or not.

[18]For elaboration, refer to U.S. Commission on Civil Rights, *The Federal Response to Domestic Violence.* Washington, DC: U.S. Government Printing Office, Jan. 1982. See also Richard Steen, "Child Abuse Units in Law Enforcement," *The Police Chief,* May 1978, pp. 38–39.

[19] See, as one of many examples, J.E. Keogh, "Crisis Intervention: A Practical Approach," *The Police Chief,* Jan. 1980, pp. 56–57.

Police and juvenile contact. (Courtesy of San Jose Police Department)

Now let's consider juvenile problems as they might affect the juvenile justice system.[20]

JUVENILE PROBLEMS[21]

In our introductory chapter, we discussed the police as a component of the overall system of criminal justice. This same approach may be useful in considering juvenile justice. Consider Figure 12–1. The diagram is intended to illustrate the position of juvenile justice in American justice overall. Now let's consider the process of juvenile justice.

Process: Delinquency and Dependency

Police problems with juveniles include both the *delinquent* or law-violating child and the *dependent* or neglected and/or abused child. The term *child* often seems incongruent with the violent acts some 15-year-old, physically large youths commit. Nevertheless, when law violators are underage, they are juvenile problems.

[20]For elaboration of the juvenile offender, see, for example, Don Gibbons, *Delinquent Behavior,* Englewood Cliffs, NJ: Prentice-Hall, 1981. Regarding juvenile justice, see Alan Coffey, *Juvenile Justice as a System* and *Juvenile Corrections.* Both Englewood Cliffs, NJ: Prentice-Hall, 1975.

[21]Figure 12–1 and parts of this discussion were published earlier in A. Coffey, Juvenile Justice as a System, 1975. Passages from pages 68–72. Reprinted by permission of Prentice-Hall, Inc., Englewood Cliffs, NJ.

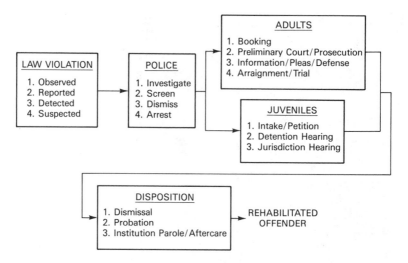

Figure 12-1 Adult/juvenile justice system. Alan R. Coffey, *Juvenile Justice as a System,* Englewood Cliffs, NJ: Prentice-Hall, 1972, p. 44. Reprinted by permission)

The neglected and abused minors who are known as *dependent* cases will be discussed later. Police handle these cases differently than *delinquent* children accused of law violation. Both types of juvenile cases are usually handled differently than adults (see Figs. 12-2 and 12-3).

One of the most consistent phenomena related to juvenile justice is the frequency with which it is overlooked in discussions of justice. During discussions of criminal justice, juvenile justice is often ignored. This is most unfortunate because juvenile delinquency remains a serious problem that should not be overlooked.[22]

Many reasons account for such oversight. There is an incredible fragmentation of juvenile justice between states and within states. Indeed, the diagram of the juvenile process in Fig. 12-2 would not fit many jurisdictions. For example, one jurisdiction may, *simply out of deference to a juvenile's age,* choose to totally ignore his or her offenses and delinquent behavior in favor of "dealing with the emotional problems." Another jurisdiction may treat the juvenile delinquent in virtually the same manner as an adult, totally ignoring both the juvenile's age and his or her immaturity. Little wonder, then, that the juvenile justice system rarely emerges as a significant variable in discussions of American justice.

Adding to the difficulty in understanding juvenile justice is the neglected or abused child. So significant has this facet of police work become that an overview of that area is indicated.

Neglected or Abused Child

One of the most dramatic and certainly one of the most complex aspects of police work involving juvenile problems is the neglected or abused child. Law enforcement

[22]See, for example, R.C. Trojanowicz, and M. Morash, *Juvenile Delinquency: Concepts and Control,* 4th ed. Englewood Cliffs, NJ: Prentice-Hall, 1987.

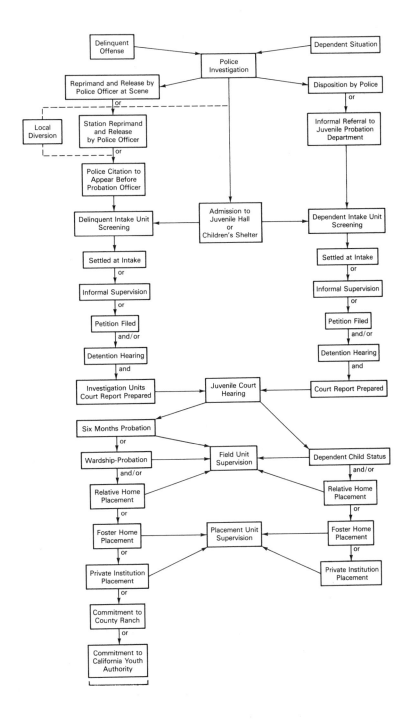

Figure 12-2 Flow process of juvenile justice. (Coffey, *Juvenile Justice as a System,* p. 46. Reprinted by permission)

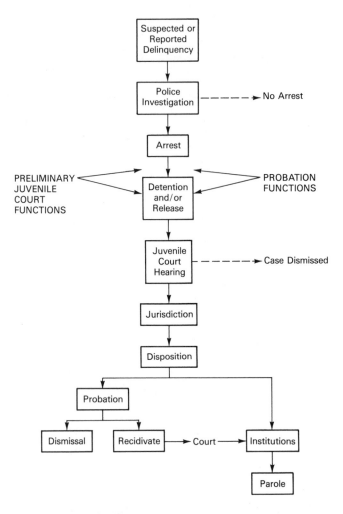

Figure 12-3 Juvenile justice system. (Coffey, *Juvenile Justice as a System,* p. 45. Reprinted by permission)

work in this area involves parents or guardians who, by virtue of the police involvement itself, are considered potentially unfit as parents and perhaps a matter of adult prosecution. The adult police officer and the adult parent generally agree that a delinquent child is in need of straightening out. If nothing else, the adults can agree that the delinquent is a "bad kid." But what happens when the police are not questioning the child's behavior but instead are questioning the behavior of the parent? What happens when evidence against the parents is collected instead of against the child? In short, what happens when the crime is not *by* the child but *against* the child?

These situations are by far some of the most sensitive in police work in the community. Police involvement with the neglected and abused child is almost invariably perceived as hostile to the parents rather than protective of the child. In this context, the police role is confusing and unrewarding, compounded by the sometimes shocking evidence of unbelievable abuse inflicted by some parents on their children.

There are three general areas in which police become involved in such matters: the neglected child, the battered child, and the sexually abused child.

There is at times an understandable reluctance on the part of police officers to deal with the problem of neglect. Although many investigations of reported neglect frequently reveal simple differences in standards for adequate care, cases of actual neglect are uncovered too often to merit discontinuation of police involvement. But any report of child neglect is difficult to handle and awkward to investigate, and the police tend to welcome assistance from well-meaning neighbors, relatives, and particularly social workers.

The police commonly issue an informal warning to parents about the consequences of continued misconduct. In most cases, these warnings suffice, particularly when embellished with the officer's personal recall of tragedies involving lost or abandoned children. The general success of these warnings no doubt relates to the impression made by the presence and manner of the police officer, who should exhibit a professional approach.

Most state jurisdictions have specific statutes covering a segment of the neglected child problem generally known as "inadequate supervision" or "unfit home." The unfit home may be unfit because it is filthy. But where does one draw the line between dirt and filth? How much filth is unhealthy? The five-year-old obviously needs more supervision than the twelve-year-old. But who is more neglected, the exceptionally responsible five-year-old or the careless, immature twelve-year-old? It is not uncommon for these situations to be intricately interwoven with domestic crisis.

The battered child is a particularly depressing experience for most police officers. Although all forms of child abuse are abhorrent to most personnel in law enforcement, the sight of a child who has been severely battered is appalling, even to veteran police investigators. Neglected children can be mistreated in many ways that are scarcely, if at all, visible to the untrained eye. Physical abuse is usually visible; in the case of the abused and *battered* child, it is especially shocking because typically the abuse is inflicted on a consistent basis, not just once in a while. Any child displaying frequent accidental bruises, burns, or the like should be regarded as a possible victim of the *battered child syndrome.*

Consider this example: Following reports of a child battering, a police officer began an investigation of a mother who had sandpapered her three small daughters' buttocks until they were raw and then poured acid on that area. When the children cried, their heads were shaved. Reports of abuse were not considered relevant by the social worker whose caseload included the parents themselves. The police officer obtained x-rays of each child's arms. They revealed the numerous "healed breaks" typical of the battered child and caused by continual and violent jerking.

Although the children's mother, on the advice of legal counsel, denied responsibility for the acid, head shaving, and previously broken arms, further evidence was found of the *battered child syndrome* in medical records; the mother had taken her daughters to *different* pediatricians each time a new injury was inflicted to increase the likelihood that each new doctor would believe her story that the injury was an accident. This behavior is generally a reliable indicator of the battered child syndrome.

Police are increasingly confronted with cases of child sexual abuse. For a number of reasons, these cases are the most difficult for law enforcement to pursue. Most sexual abuse is committed by a family member, and the shame of incest in this and most societies is such that the child's family often prefers to keep the crime a private matter, in spite of the increasing effort to educate the community, the schools, and parents.

The children in these situations are in a particularly precarious position. Raised to respect their elders, many of them simply never question the actions of a close relative, let alone a parent. If they do, they may receive some sympathetic understanding but little concrete help from another relative. The incident will be hushed up; the child will feel that he or she is a part of the whole shameful business and may assume that he or she also shares the blame or guilt. There is little possibility that the child will feel certain enough of his or her role as a victim to take the complaint outside the family.

Many jurisdictions have passed legislation that requires professionals, including physicians, social workers, and clergy, to report instances of child abuse. Such legislation may be helpful to the criminal justice efforts to cope with this problem once a situation is reported, but may have little effect on the family's willingness to share this kind of information with any of those required to report.

Law enforcement dealings with juvenile delinquency and even those who are considered "beyond control of their parents" are in a sense, relatively simple compared to the complexity of the neglected or abused child. In a sense, juvenile justice as a concept is relatively simple. Recalling earlier discussions of *responsibility versus accountability,* children gradually learn how to accept responsibilities as they mature. During the gradual acquisition of understanding, the juvenile is accountable only to the degree that he or she could be expected to understand these responsibilities. For this reason, police involvement with juvenile problems is more confusing than the relatively straightforward police activity with adults. While statutes generally are explicit in identifying the exact age at which a child is no longer a minor, ambiguity usually prevails in determining the degree of accountability a child has for a particular offense. Juvenile court judges vary widely in their assessment of this very issue, providing little clarification for police in this regard.

Although police work with juveniles is not as clear-cut as police work with adults, most law enforcement agencies establish fairly clear policies and procedures and many times specialists and specialized units. The literature of police management clarifies juvenile problems even further insofar as organizational considerations are concerned; the following will serve as an excellent example:[22]

1. *Investigation of juvenile cases.* This involves not only criminal cases where the suspects may be juveniles but also cases where juveniles are victims. Generally, cases involving adult crimes committed by juveniles are handled by

[22]Edward A. Thibault, Lawrence M. Lynch, and R. Bruce McBride, *Proactive Police Management.* Englewood Cliffs, NJ: Prentice-Hall, 1985, p. 128. Reprinted by permission of Prentice-Hall, Inc., Englewood Cliffs, NJ.

regular investigative and patrol personnel. When an arrest has been made, or a suspect has been brought in for questioning, the juvenile aid personnel should be notified. Those cases involving status offenses or child victims should be handled by the juvenile aid personnel. In many situations, cases of this nature do not involve a typical police response but demand patience, knowledge of referral agencies, family crisis intervention skills, and counseling techniques. The officer may need to handle child abuse. Or there may be cases of simple neglect. In one case, an officer walked into a home and saw a child being bathed on one side of a tub while there were feces on the other side. It takes a strong stomach to handle these cases. Normally, social agencies are available to work with these parents, but in the long night hours, immediate police action may be necessary.

2. *Screening of cases.* Cases that are forwarded to the juvenile aid division must be screened for a future course of action. The recommendations of the investigator or the patrol officer should be taken into consideration in view of their familiarity with the circumstances surrounding the case. It is at this stage that the juvenile aid officer may wish to divert the case away from the normal progression found in the criminal justice system into either a formal or informal mode of treatment. Such options include referral to a community agency, police counseling, or "station house probation," where the youth reports to the juvenile aid division on a regular basis to account for his actions during the week. The case may be disposed of if the situation warrants restitution and it is made or there are no grounds found for future action.

3. *Preparation of cases for juvenile court.* The necessary paperwork and evidence must be gathered by the officer if the case is forwarded to the juvenile court. The experienced juvenile aid officer will know how to present the documentation needed for the court as well as be able to keep track of when the case will be called. The officer should follow the ultimate disposition of the case, and advise the initial arresting officer(s) of the results.

4. *Community liaison.* This is an important aspect of the juvenile aid function. The police should be viewed as the experts in all areas of crime in the community, especially that related to youth. This will be important for the planning and funding of special programs undertaken by community groups for juveniles. At the same time, the police should maintain an active liaison with community groups that are involved with problems with juveniles, such as the YMCA/YWCA, Catholic charities, and the school district.
Another aspect of community liaison involves keeping abreast of community programs where children may be referred if there is a need for special treatment. These might include those programs involving youth employment, professional counseling, vocational training, and recreational activities.

Unfortunately, even when the activities and procedures of police juvenile work are clarified, the ambiguity of a minor's degree of accountability often creates police–community problems. Because of this ambiguity, police officials should involve community leaders in this segment of police work. Public reaction to what police are doing, or in many cases are not doing, can be extremely negative if formed out of the context of the complexity of juvenile justice. Involvement of community leaders in police work with domestic crisis and juvenile problems is essential. This involvement is restricted to areas that are *not* mandated by law; the police responsibility is first to follow these mandates. But even in mandated areas, if police officials acquaint community leaders with the expertise needed in handling juvenile delinquency matters, and acquaint community leaders with the extreme sensitivity required in dealing with beaten wives, sexually abused children, and cruelly battered children, it cannot help but enhance the image of police.

SUMMARY

This chapter introduced the subject of domestic disturbance and juvenile problems as significant to police–community relations. The dangers in dealing with domestic crisis were emphasized and discussed in terms of police training needs.

It was noted that police give a high priority to training in domestic crisis, and law enforcement intervention into crisis has many risks and gains for police–community relations. The distinction between intervention and intrusion was discussed in the context of the overall law enforcement mission.

Neighborhood perception and media coverage of police intervention were considered in terms of police image. Domestic crises were elaborated on in terms of the categories of police training needed, such as the sophisticated methods needed to recognize *signs* of child abuse and neglect as well as spouse abuse, and of the potential for violence. The need for training in pertinent legal matters was also noted.

Police intervention into domestic crisis was discussed as remaining outside the therapy role, but crucially involved in community referral networks, including referrals for further investigations and possible prosecution. The value of good police effort in domestic crisis was presented as a valuable community relations asset.

Juvenile problems were briefly discussed in virtually the same context of a potential for improved police image. The position of the juvenile justice system within the overall justice system was also presented.

DISCUSSION TOPICS

1. Contrast the difference between the danger facing police in domestic crisis and "obvious" armed robbery.
2. Discuss the concepts of intrusion and intervention as discussed in this chapter.
3. Elaborate on the significance of privacy in terms of intervention and intrusion.
4. Relate police training in family crisis intervention to personal stress management.
5. Elaborate on what this chapter presented as variations between jurisdictions in juvenile justice.
6. How can the involvement of community leaders in police activities in the area of domestic crisis and juvenile problems enhance the police image?

Relevant Problems for Discussion

The involvement of community leaders in police efforts to coordinate resources for family and juvenile problems has great potential in police–community relations. Although the law itself guides most of the police operations in these areas, there remains considerable latitude to at least ensure community awareness of this police function. In approaching this problem, police officials are likely to encounter, in the case of juveniles, problems in helping community leaders distinguish between adult crime and juvenile delinquency.

The obvious distinction, the age of the offender, tends to become blurred when the community relations program includes selective enforcement as presented in Chapter 4. In other words, when a particular crime is the target of selective enforcement, the *age* of the person committing the crime may prove far more important in law than in community understanding. We noted that unlike adult offenders who are responsible for their crimes, juveniles are usually held not responsible, but to some degree accountable on a sliding scale of accountability that ranges from early childhood to nearing adulthood.

As noted in Chapter 1, police officials who acquaint community leaders with how little control police have over the rest of justice are in a better community relations stance. In the case of juveniles, focus can then remain on apprehending the law violator and shifting other concerns to the law itself and to the juvenile justice system, a system largely beyond the control of the police after the juvenile is apprehended.

Since this is easily perceived as "passing the buck," police officials must do more than a cursory job in acquainting community leaders with the legal distinctions between adults and juveniles. This can be done without jeopardizing community-supported selective law enforcement as discussed in Chapter 4.

Discussion Topics

PART FOUR

Community Support Required
for Law Enforcement

The general purpose of Part Four is to acquaint the reader with Image Problems, Police–Community Cooperation, *and the* Importance of Communication.

The public image problems growing out of controversy over what role the police should play are related to the variety of roles that society demands that law enforcement perform. This in turn is related to factors that help or hinder improved public image, which in turn is related to community relations. Human relations and public relations are presented as separate concepts, and both are presented as functions of police–community relations. The need for good community relations is related to problems with communication, which are discussed in terms of potentially reducing many police problems.

Another purpose of Part Four is to bring together the discussions presented in Parts One, Two, and Three, and place them in a positive context for addressing the ever increasing need for good police–community relations.

13

Focus on the Problem of Police Public Image

Law enforcement is a unique profession concerned with the most sensitive aspects and issues of society, e.g., death, personal liberty, citizens' rights, etc. Even the day-to-day, seemingly routine decisions officers make about their own conduct and actions have potentially far-reaching consequences. Individual introspection about values, ethics/integrity, principles, and standards enhances law enforcement professionalism.[1]

Such a high-minded perception of the quality needed in police service is not uncommon; most will agree that law enforcement standards are now and must remain extremely high. With such high standards, the question of police image problems may seem incongruent.

Part of the difficulty and seeming incongruence relates to the very nature of a career in law enforcement:[2]

Locked in combat against the evil that some people do, police professionals risk becoming the evil they touch and that touches them. In encountering crime and violence, the police professional passes close to cynicism, feels the breath of prejudice,

[1]Norman C. Boehm, *P.O.S.T. Career Ethics/Integrity Training Guide.* Sacramento, California Commission on Police Officer's Standards and Training, 1988, p. ii.

[2]*Human Relations in the Police Service.* Los Angeles: Los Angeles Police Department, 1988, p. 43.

and the hand of provocation. These are dangerous enemies that must be defeated to accomplish the police mission.

Conceiving of police as battling these negative forces allows a clearer picture of how image is made. A good police image is one that has the police winning this battle; poor image is one in which police are *perceived* as losing the battle. Successful police–community relations depends on the public perceiving police as winning this battle, thus making police image a very significant factor.

There are other considerations in gaining an understanding of good and bad public image for the police. Among these is the reality that although *enforcement* in a democratic free society may be a necessity, it is never likely to be popular. The frustration this can bring to efforts to gain community support may well relate to a problem known in police management as personnel *burnout*.[3]

Put another way, frustration of seeking to be popular while performing unpopular tasks may well lead to a loss of enthusiasm for winning the battle with crime, violence, cynicism, prejudice, and provocation.[4]

But whether good image improves popularity or merely *respect,* it is clear that good public image is based on the public's belief that police do indeed win the encounters with crime. Good image is based on this perception.

Many believe that image is nothing more than an illusion created for the purpose of substituting for actual human interactions. But in the sense that image has a profound impact on the actual human interactions, sensitivity to how people perceive police is a very positive indicator. Among the many reasons that this is a positive indicator is the alternative available to police, which is to *insulate* themselves from public opinion rather than to seek more favorable public opinion. In other words, instead of prioritizing a positive public image, police could withdraw from the confusing frustrations facing law enforcement today, and thoroughly insulate themselves from concern with how the public perceives them. With this in mind, the priority assigned to public image is extremely encouraging. In Chapter 14, the high priority police place on public image will be considered.[5] Here we are concerned with the image that the public has of their police, the community's impression of those enforcing the community's laws.

There is a very convincing argument that the public image of the police is strongly related to the image that police have of themselves,[6] as well as how police *want* to be seen and how police believe the public *wants* to see them.[7]

[3]An exceptionally fine review of the cogent factors in police burnout is contained in Hillary M. Robinette, *Burnout in Blue: Managing the Police Marginal Performance.* Westport, CT: Praeger, 1987.

[4]Los Angeles Police Department, op. cit.

[5]It has been found that police place a high priority on public image. See, for example, Robert G. Phillips, Jr., "Training Priorities in State and Local Law Enforcement," *FBI Law Enforcement Bulletin,* Aug. 1988, pp. 10–16. This subject will be discussed in Chapter 14 in terms of police programs geared to gaining community support for law.

[6]Louis A. Radelet, *The Police and the Community,* 4th ed. New York: Macmillan, 1986, pp. 109–139; see also pp. 83–104, "The Self-Image of the Police Officer."

[7]Ibid.

Another factor in the public image of the police has to do with how criminal justice is perceived in general and associated with the police. Since the police serve as the *symbol* of American justice, it may well be that much of the public image of the police reflects their image of criminal justice overall. Also impinging on image are such matters as more affluent Americans appearing to receive preferential treatment in criminal justice.[8]

IMAGE AS A PROBLEM

An interestingly cogent observation has been made in the literature regarding the police and the community.[9] "Secrecy and institutional separation have ceased to be defensible positions for police to take in relationship to the community they serve." On reflection, very few police officials would argue this point.[10] And yet many, perhaps most, minority group members conceive of police as both separated and secretive, at least insofar as open and free dialogue with the police is concerned.[11]

This is a problem for police *image,* in terms of the overall perception of the police by the groups that make up the community. This image problem is aggravated by the reality that many minority people do not trust the police, and police do not trust minority groups, claims to the contrary notwithstanding. Recalling our discussion of *attitude, prejudice,* and *bias,* this difficulty may prove difficult to correct. But separation, secrecy, and distrust are not the only problems for police image. There is also *fear.*

The literature reflects considerable interest in the use of force by the police.[12] No doubt, this interest was kindled by the cries of police brutality in the violent 1960s. Nevertheless, such problems as the Miami area riots discussed earlier suggest that *fear* of the use of force by police is a definite image factor, one raising questions regarding the control of at least deadly force.[13]

Obviously, *force* is an absolute necessity in effecting resisted arrests. The question has to do with the *degree* of force. More importantly in terms of police

[8]Jeffrey H. Reiman, *The Rich Get Richer and the Poor Get Prison,* 2nd ed. New York: Wiley, 1984.

[9]Pamela D. Mayhall, *Police-Community Relations and the Administration of Justice,* 3rd ed. New York: Wiley 1985, p. 1

[10]In a generalized overall context to evaluate this observation, see, for example, H.H. Earle, *Police-Community Relations: Crisis in Our Times.* Springfield, IL: Charles C Thomas, 1980.

[11]For an interesting peripheral perspective on this subject, see D.C. Couper, *How to Rate Your Police.* Washington DC: Police Executive Research Forum, 1983.

[12]Among the many discussions of this subject are the following: Lawrence W. Sherman, "Perspective on Police and Violence"; Arnold Binder and Peter Scharf, "The Violent Police–Citizen Encounter"; Wilson, James, Q., "What Can Police Do About Violence"; Van Maanen, "Beyond Account: The Personal Impact of Police Shootings"; William Ker Muir, Jr., "Power Attracts Violence"; Peter K. Manning, "Violence and Police Role"; Carl B. Klockers, "The Dirty Harry Problem," all found in *The Annals,* Nov. 1980. See also H. Jerome Miron and Robert Wasserman, *Prevention and Control of Urban Disorders: Issues to the 1980s.* Washington, DC: Department of Justice, Aug. 1980.

[13]See, for example, Albert J. Reiss, Jr., "Controlling Police Use of Deadly Force, "*The Annals,* Nov. 1980, pp. 122–134.

image problems, the question has to do with how the degree of force is publicly perceived.

Compounding the image problems related to secrecy, separation, distrust, and fear are the image problems associated with the controversy over the role police are to perform, with and without the use of force.

Let's take a closer look at the controversy over the police role.

POLICE ROLE CONTROVERSY

We have previously discussed the confines on law enforcement of constitutional government. In that discussion we noted that a great deal of our attitude on orderly environment can be traced to English common law. This same heritage applies to modern police in the sense that they can be traced to the 1829 Metropolitan Police Act won from Parliament by Sir Robert Peel (Sir Robert is the source of the term "Bobbies").

Peel conceived of the police role as conspicuously community oriented, geared more to preventing or deterring than enforcing. He conceived of the police as an *alternative* to the repression of crime and disorder through military might and severe legal sanctions; this was the first of his famous principles. Peel's position was particularly reassuring to English citizens, who feared a loss of civil liberties when the Metropolitan Police Act was passed.

This same notion of the police role was transferred to America. But with the emergence of more and more statutory laws to *specifically* enforce, the role expanded beyond what we have discussed as maintaining an orderly environment, just how far it is difficult to determine. For one thing, as we have noted throughout this volume, American police do both; they keep the peace *and* enforce statutory laws. But it is this combination of role expectations that generates controversy, particularly with those who emphasize the peace-keeping segment of police work as opposed to actual *enforcement*.[14]

In the nation's large cities and in small cities and towns as well, the need for strengthening police–community relations continues to be a crucial factor. As the most visible representative of the society with which minorities continue to struggle for equality, pressure continues to mount for police to be scrupulously fair in their dealing with all concerned.

Even if fair treatment of minority groups were the sole consideration, police departments would have an obligation to attempt to achieve and maintain a positive image and good police–community relations. The fact is, however, much more is at stake. For police image has a direct bearing on the character of life in cities and on the community's ability to maintain stability and solve problems. At the same time, the police capacity to deal with crime depends to a large extent upon how the community's citizens perceive the police—what kind of image the police have.

[14]See, for an excellent example, Bruce J. Terris, "The Role of Police," *Annals of the American Academy of Political and Social Science,* Nov. 1967.

The last few decades have seen a great deal of criticism of the police, some of which has been without any validity at all. As a result, thousands of loyal, capable, and professional officers throughout the nation have become perplexed and apprehensive, even cynical. The complexity of contemporary law enforcement in conjunction with the rapidly growing problems has done little to improve the nature of the interaction between police officers and most citizens.

Police image cannot be viewed as an isolated problem, one confronting only those agents who have a vested interest in the administration of criminal justice. When we discuss the human relations problems of police image, we really have many things in mind. Because practitioners in the field of criminal justice are primarily concerned with working with people, each an individual in his or her own right, it is vital for police personnel, as well as those associated with judicial and correctional processes, to understand that there is a common denominator, a sharing of one very important feature. This is the awareness that every human being has his or her own aspirations, hopes, and standards of behavior. Police being perceived as recognizing this reality are police with a good image.

Yet a great deal of controversy exists today over the role the police should play in our contemporary society. The responsibility of the police officer is basically to protect life and property, regulate conduct, and minister to the needs of people from all classes of life, all of whom are equally entitled to the services of police. Other duties have fallen within the purview of law enforcement, but when carefully analyzed all of them are within the scope of these basic responsibilities.

The primary police–citizen contacts are, contrary to popular belief, with those members of society who request assistance and protection, those who seek contact with the police. These people turn to the police officer for assistance with problems that are extremely difficult and important, at least to the individual seeking police assistance. In analyzing the number and character of contacts the police officer has with members of the public during a tour of duty, we see that he or she spends very little time chasing criminals or locking people up. Let's consider roles of the urban police officer.

Variety of Urban Police Roles[15]

It may well be that the public image of public safety reduces to oversimplified stereotypes of the urban fire fighter and police officer. But this image of the fire fighter may be simpler than the police image because, although both perform more roles than are generally recognized, the police officer is playing many more roles than the fire fighter.

There appears to be little doubt that police roles are more varied, if for no other reason than that their responsibilities go beyond public safety; police deal with "morals" and with "peace and quiet."

The multiplicity of police roles is worthy of consideration for many reasons. Among the more significant is to make certain that evaluations of police perfor-

[15]Parts of this and later discussions in this chapter were published earlier in A. Coffey, E. Eldefonso, and W. Hartinger, *Human Relations: Law Enforcement in a Changing Community,* 3rd ed., 1982. Passages from pages 161–180. Reprinted by permission of Prentice-Hall, Inc., Englewood Cliffs, NJ.

mance are related to proper roles. For example, an assessment of a police officer's public relations role might not be appropriate in the performance of the officer's role in the arrest of a resisting felon.

More pertinent to the present discussion, an understanding of the variety of police roles is necessary for the overall understanding of law enforcement in the context of dealing with the public as humanely as possible. With this in mind, let us consider two broad enforcement rules, the keeping of peace and the enforcement of law.

At first glance, it might appear that those two roles are the same thing. But on closer examination it turns out that many, perhaps most, peace-keeping functions do not relate to actual law violations and usually do not lead to arrest or prosecution, whereas the enforcement of law generally does.

Thus police officers must be able to first recognize the differences in the two roles and then adjust the performance of their duties accordingly. Theoretically, police officers are recruited and trained on the basis of their ability to make such adjustments in their performance. Indeed, beyond these two relatively simple distinctions between peace keeping and enforcement, police have numerous roles that must be performed in virtually all jurisdictions, from the family counseling role to aiding fire fighters.

One of the two police roles may dominate in any given police jurisdiction; in one, maintaining order might dominate over enforcement; in another jurisdiction, the opposite might be observed. Let us consider an example. Consider the effect on the peace-keeping role if there were *no* enforcement rule. In such a circumstance, any refusal of citizens to comply with police efforts to keep peace would be in the same category as their refusing to obey their clergyman or their neighbors or their relatives. The *availability* of the enforcement role is the strongest enhancement of the peace-keeping role, even when the peace-keeping role is dominant. In the most negative case, the fear of arrest, even when an arrest is not threatened, is one of the strongest influences in the peace-keeping role. Ideally, police officers are recruited and trained in a manner that stresses reliance on communication rather than arrest. But when communication fails, something else is required if the community is to remain reasonably assured that order will prevail. That something else must of necessity be a potential for *enforcing* the law.

An apparent lack of threatened enforcement is deceptive when skilled officers keep the peace. That is, there are those who would argue that enforcement has nothing to do with peace keeping because police keep the peace without arrest or force of any kind in the majority of situations. Although such an observation might appear to be valid, we need only remove the police officer's authority to arrest to see how very dependent effective peace keeping is on the potential to enforce law. Indeed, many officers who are apparently able to maintain order through simple communication skills might become assault victims were they stripped of their enforcement authority.

Mutual Dependence of Roles

In much the same manner as the enforcement role complements and secures the peace-keeping role, many other police roles are mutually dependent. The police officer called on to deliver a baby in an emergency is in a role that depends for success on the overall role of public service. Officers attempting to prevent juvenile delinquency are in a role that may depend nearly entirely on the skills needed to perform the role of arbitrator in serious family disputes. Suicide rescues, hostage negotiations, and mob control require common skills in communication applied to different police roles.

The prime requisite is the police officer's ability to recognize varied situations and to draw on appropriate skills for the particular role required. Underpinning all police roles, however, remains the authority role of law enforcement. The more skilled the officer, the less visible the authority role, but the authority to enforce the law remains primary.

This leads us to the subject of police power.[16]

Police Image and Police Power

How an officer handles the inherent power of arrest authority is often a factor in the public's view of law enforcement in the community. Law must be enforced if civilized people are to survive. Society cannot depend completely on simple persuasion to induce law observance and therefore must require the *enforcement* of laws. This enforcement is necessarily a part of the police role. But, as we have noted, it is the *degree* of force or, more importantly, how the public perceives the *degree* of force used that is important.

Compounding the image problem for police is the reality that neither the media nor the typical citizen is trained sufficiently to evaluate the *degree* of force used, when force becomes necessary. This is not to say that there are not abuses of police power. But even the most sophisticated approach to determining the degree of power necessary runs the risk of being misunderstood by a public that is not trained in assessing violent situations. Understandably, this frustrating reality leads to a kind of "withdrawing" by many police officers, evolving into a "we and they" of the "police versus the public" situation. This problem involves more than a lack of understanding by the public regarding police activities. There is increasing evidence that Americans of all races, creeds, and income groups have reservations about the police, at least about the use of police power. Unfortunately, there are instances in which this mistrust is founded on bitter experiences. But even when the encounter with police is within all guidelines, the reality is that force used by police is an unhappy experience, whether the citizen is directly involved or simply a witness. Moreover, the citizen who avidly supports the police may resent a ticket for illegal parking or for driving faster than the posted speed limit. When police restrict their contact to the public to only those activities that "tend to agitate," police image will suffer. Here then is yet another reason to pursue the community relations programs presented in Chapter 14, and also a rationale for actively seeking an improvement in the public image.

Further reinforcement of the "we–they" feelings of police toward the public probably relates to the fact that police officers are a symbol not only of all of

[16]See footnote 12 for sources.

Officer, dog, and child. There are times when the simplest of activities can have great impact on the public image of the police. (Courtesy of Santa Cruz Police Department)

Arrest is a crucial segment of police image. (Courtesy of Santa Cruz Police Department)

criminal justice, but of the authority of the middle class. With the standard equipment of uniform, gun, insignia of rank, and baton, officers on occasion tend to think of themselves as part of a paramilitary unit, which is certainly not far from the truth. However, unlike the military, the police are required to keep good relations between themselves and the community they serve. Law enforcement is completely dependent on public support for success.

Crime and other police problems obviously are not restricted to any particular area in society. The *frequency* of certain types of crime tends to increase in certain areas. When that occurs, greater numbers of police officers are likely to have greater numbers of contact with those living in the area. When the area is one with which the officer personally identifies, the risk of misunderstanding is smaller. But when the area differs greatly from what the officer is used to, the risk of misunderstanding increases dramatically.

Statistically, the average police officer is likely to come from a middle-class community in which he or she lives a well-regulated life according to middle-class standards of ethics and morality. But these officers may work at law enforcement in an area populated by people who are largely alien to them. They may find their language, customs, and emotional differences with the minority groups, a difference they consider strange, hostile, and aggravating. The trend toward professionalism has not resolved this problem. Identification with fellow officers is reinforced, and unfortunately, a kind of mutual suspicion between minority groups and police emerges.[17]

There is no question that serious assaults on police occur with alarming regularity. Thus, confronted with hostility and fearing physical injury, the officer is constantly on guard. This contributes to the feeling of isolation and a view of the community as "they."[18]

> The idea of the symbolic assailant illustrates one of the two variables which make up the working personality of the police officer—reaction to danger. The other is his reaction to authority. . . .

It is paradoxical that the people who are the most victimized by crime are also the most hostile to the police, but it is not remarkable, because the police are the symbol of middle-class values from which many minorities have been excluded.

In a fundamental sense, it is wrong to define the problem solely as hostility to police. In many ways, the police symbolize much deeper problems. Responsibility for apathy or for disrespect for law enforcement agencies would be more appropriately attributed to "a social system that permits inequities and irregularities in law. . . ."[19]

The ongoing daily affairs of the people of the community are the result of the interplay of social, economic, psychological, and biological forces that influence the behavior of all citizens, whether clerics or criminal, educators or demonstrators,

[17]D.J. Dodd, "Police Mentality and Behavior," *Issues in Criminology,* Summer 1967, pp. 56–57.

[18]Ibid.

[19]R.L. Derbyshire, "The Social Control Role of the Police in Changing Urban Communities," *Excerptor Criminologica,* Fall, 1966, pp. 315–316.

merchants or police. Police problems are not unrelated to welfare problems. Drop-outs are obviously not solely the problem of school administrators. Unemployment, bad housing, discrimination, improper family structures, illegitimacy, and disease produce results that directly aggravate those problems more generally regarded as police matters—crime, violence, and the like. Moreover, to the extent that the people living under these conditions see themselves as victims of social oppression, the police can expect much of the hostility focused on them as symbols to continue.

Everyone certainly agrees that the police cannot be expected to solve all the ills of the community. Many do not realize, however, how directly the police are involved with the problems these ills generate, yet another difficulty in improving police image. Public recognition of the vigorous efforts of police to keep community tranquillity is needed.

It is easy to see how the police are involved when there is a demonstration, riot, or minor or major disorder, but the less spectacular day-to-day accumulation of social cost and police involvement, although not so dramatic, is nonetheless enormous and yet out of public view, a significant factor in the context of police image.

When disorders break out, everyone assumes that the role of the police is to stop them; but what is not generally understood is that in their daily performance the police, along with other government structures, inevitably tend to do the things in terms of community mores. Police in general go about their daily lives in a sort of unverbalized understanding that "this is the custom, this is the way things are." And for most people in most facets of their daily existence, it is comfortable to be able to rely on such things "the way they are." The police realize this, perhaps more so than most, because they are so close to the potential for conflict that accompanies pressures for change. The fact that the police do not take the initiative to change things is not just a case of not wanting to "rock the boat." The police alone are not in a position to change community mores even if they wanted to and knew how.

To a considerable extent then, the police are the victims of community problems that are not of their making. The police officer, as a symbol not only of law but of the entire system of law enforcement, becomes the tangible target for grievances against shortcomings throughout the system, which includes other segments of criminal justice totally beyond the control of the police.

When a suspect is held for a long period in jail because he or she cannot pay a fine, when the jail or prison is physically dilapidated or its personnel brutal or incompetent, when the probation or parole officer has little time to give to a prisoner, or when a prisoner is given inadequate counsel from a public defender, the police officer who arrested the citizen and started the process of criminal justice will probably be given a large share of any blame that is assigned. Improvement of police image of necessity must take this reality into consideration.

The police officer assigned to the ghetto is a symbol of an increasingly bitter social debate over law enforcement that has continued for four decades. Some blame police as agents of repression of those who tend to support defiance of law enforcement. Fortunately, to a lesser degree in recent years, the subject of brutality is less frequently included in discussion of this subject.

The subject of physical police brutality is invariably controversial. Police spokesmen protest angrily against such charges, noting the necessity to utilize force.

Critics invariably refer to excessive force. Regardless of the validity of police denials of brutality, many believe that accusations will continue because of a deep-seated suspicion that police sometimes practice a double standard in dealing with certain members of the community. In fact, the more intimate a person's knowledge of the ghetto, the stronger his or her feeling that brutality is a fact; and the converse is equally true. The consensus among authorities in the field of race relations is that, although there may be some cases of brutality with racial overtones, brutality, if it does occur, does not generally have such overtones. It is, however, often related to socioeconomic groups.

Press reports of police dispersal and arrest of demonstrators, whether for civil rights or over the controversy involving abortion, are said to reinforce in many people the view that the police officer is a defender of one group and an oppressor of another—a "can't win" situation for the police involved.

Harassment or discourtesy by police officers may not be the result of malicious or discriminatory intent. Many officers simply fail to understand the effects of their actions because of their limited knowledge of the group they are addressing. There is an obvious training need inherent in this observation, which has direct bearing on the police image.

It should be emphasized that most officers handle their rigorous work with considerable coolness and with no pronounced harassment, discourtesy, or racial prejudice. However, it has been noted by the late O.W. Wilson that

> The officer must remember that there is no law against making a policeman angry and he cannot charge a man with offending him. Until the citizen acts overtly in violation of the law, he should take no action against him. . . . [20]

These views are accepted by all responsible police officials. Although all departments have written regulations setting standards of behavior, in many departments these are too generalized. Where standards are violated, there should be a thorough investigation of complaints and prompt, *visible* disciplinary action where justified. Emphasis on the visibility of disciplinary action is an absolute requisite to improve police image.

THE PROFESSIONAL APPROACH[21]

Elsewhere in the volume we have addressed the trend toward *professionalism* in law enforcement and noted that the frequent comparison to medicine is not appropriate

[20] O.W. Wilson, *Police Administration,* 4th ed. New York: McGraw-Hill, 1976, p. 73.

[21] The literature is rich in this area. See, for example, C.E. Brown, "Professionalizing Police Practice," *The Police Chief,* March 1981, pp. 54–57. R. Chackerian, "Police Professionalism and Citizen Evaluations: A Preliminary Look," in J. Munro, *Classes, Conflict and Control.* Cincinnati: Anderson Publishing, 1976. Quinn Tamm, "Police Professionalism and Civil Rights," *The Police Chief,* IACP, Sept. 1964. Harold Wilensky, "The Professionalization of Everyone," *American Journal of Sociology,* Sept. 1964, pp. 137–158. Louis A. Radelet, "Implications of Professionalism in Law Enforcement for Police–Community Relations," *Police,* July–Aug. 1966.

because the body of knowledge and the standards of internship of law enforcement are not yet fully developed nor established.

Professional standards do exist, but a professional body of knowledge, such as in medicine, will not soon emerge. Indeed, it might be useful to quickly review key stages of development since Sir Robert Peel's victory in Parliament with the Metropolitan Police Act.

The famous Berkeley, California, Marshall, August Vollmer, established his police training school early in this century, sowing the seeds of a professional body of knowledge that have grown and flourished since. The era known as the Roaring Twenties temporarily retarded professionalism, but during the Depression of the 1930s, competition for police jobs raised the caliber of police recruits. With higher educated, more sophisticated police leadership, the 1940s witnessed increasing use of the technology developed during World War II. After the war, the emphasis on police science emerged as a catalyst for wider college curricula. By the time LEEP and LEAA came to bear in the troublesome 1960s, many police agencies were already requiring four-year college degrees that could be gained in police work. Evaluation of the growth of professionalism leaves one impressed, but still forced to acknowledge that the role of police must be more precisely defined before a *definitive* body of knowledge can fully underpin a profession.

But in the context of *image* problems, there is sufficient professional understanding of the principles of law enforcement to move forward. Indeed, the subjects reviewed thus far in this volume afford a professional perspective of human relations in police work; let's look at yet another dimension, how the individual officer conceives of her or his own role.

Police Officer's Perception

In many cases in which an officer is challenged, the challenger is trying to get the officer to step out of the professional role. It is as though the belligerent individual is saying, "Look, buster, you wouldn't be such a big shot if you didn't have that gun and badge." As the wielder of public power and authority, the officer is the dispenser of public discipline. In this capacity, he or she is required by law to exercise his or her authority according to the rules. These rules do not provide for the administration of punishment by the police. Vindictiveness or harassment by an officer is as much against the rules as are criminal actions. It is *imperative* that officers perceive their work in this manner if improvement in the police image is to occur.

A police officer is not an ordinary person, but a professional, whether or not a fully developed body of knowledge exists. Therefore, the officer's conduct must conform to the rules. It is offensive to be called a pig, but no retaliation can be permitted in violation of the rules, because this would threaten destruction of the very system the officer is sworn to defend. Moreover, to abandon the professional prescriptions for conduct is to walk into a trap, and this is the objective of the belligerent challenger.

The widely held concept of the police role overemphasizes the police–violator relationship. Seldom is a police officer thought of as a helper, even though a large part of his or her time is spent in rendering various kinds of services. The common concept of the role of fire fighter, to the contrary, emphasizes the helper notion. Unfortunately, it is unrealistic to expect that at any time soon we will be able to persuade people that the police officer is a *helping* person, despite the fact that each time a violator is brought to justice, the public good is promoted. What can be hoped for in the foreseeable future is public awareness that the enforcement role includes helping, an obvious need in police image.

Adopting the professional role as a model for conduct and conforming to it in the face of provocation, frustration, and temptation are not only correct but commendable; it is also a source of great strength for the police and tilts the balance of power in their favor. Officers who are constantly professional in conduct and bearing are in an advantageous position. They are clearly demonstrating their superiority, and, as a result, people give them the respect and admiration their professional behavior has earned.

It again must be emphasized that it is critical that the individual officer review the enforcement responsibility in this manner. Failure to do so risks creating the opposite of the desired result. For example, when an officer weakens and abandons a professional posture, the conduct that results may assume several forms, all of which are seen by the public as deserving of condemnation. Depending on the circumstances, nonprofessional conduct may consist of anything from vulgar language and petty abuse, to unwarranted physical punishment and harassment, up to outright criminality. Those who seriously challenge the police want them to shed their professional armament and to be reduced to their level. The best way to handle such people is to adhere steadfastly to the standards of a professional code.

Officers should not make threats they cannot or do not intend to carry through. To do so weakens their position and leaves a residue of animosity that will plague them and other officers in the future.

Every officer should be *constantly* aware that he or she is symbolically threatening to many people. The police are regarded as disciplinarians, wielders of power, people to be *feared*. Their very presence constitutes a threat to many people, even those who are doing nothing wrong. It is a common experience for people to slow down when they see a patrol car, even though they are not exceeding the speed limit. Undoubtedly, a lot of people immediately make a behavioral inventory—"Am I doing anything wrong?"—and become wary when they see a police officer approaching. This apprehension is part of the aura of threat with which the police are surrounded.

The fact that many people see the police as a threat has desirable consequences, in terms of deterrents and criminal conduct, and undesirable consequences, in terms of people seeking to avoid police. Another extremely unfortunate consequence is the refusal or unwillingness of many to cooperate. Others may see the police as enemies, which often produces overt aggressive behavior. It has been suggested that if we disarm the police, they would not seem to be so threatening. The present writer considers this suggestion ludicrous, even though it points out the reality that police do indeed appear threatening to many individuals in society.

The fact that police are regarded as threatening by law violators is legitimate; they *should* be a threat to such people. But law-abiding citizens and police should be pulling together in a common cause; police should have an image of being an ally rather than an enemy of the typical citizen of the community. What can police officers do about the problems growing out of human relations in which threats or challenges are significant issues? There are some human relations techniques that police can cultivate with good effect. Learning how to be an effective person is essentially a matter of developing skills in relating to others. *Skill in relating to others is what the human relations approach to law enforcement is all about.* It also proves to be the most effective tool in building a better public image for police.

Let's close this chapter on a word about dealing with the problem of a negative police image.

NEVER FOR IMAGE ALONE

It is the author's strong belief that action taken for the sole purpose of improving image invariably winds up hurting rather than helping. This is true in spite of what will be presented in Chapter 14 as public relations efforts designed to make police appear as acceptable as possible.

Figure 13–1 illustrates the variables involved in efforts to gain favorable public reaction to law enforcement. These image enhancements only work well, particularly in the long run, when they result from actual improvements in the police service. Such improvement can *include* such things as better media relations and generally better public relations, but even then they must be combined with good police service to be effective in establishing a positive image that endures.

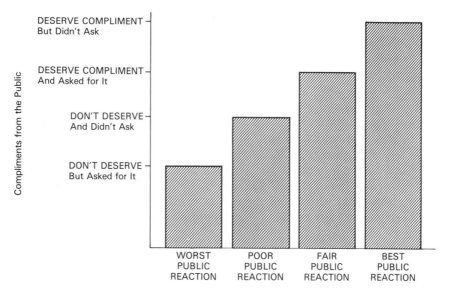

Figure 13–1 One of the many risks of trying to improve image for the sake of image alone is that it can work like compliments—the best ones are deserved but they are not asked for. Care is needed to be sure requested compliments are deserved.

Chapter 14 will discuss the uniqueness of every community in terms of its needs for good relations with law enforcement. This same uniqueness applies to the variety of agency improvements that may be needed to correct public image, which must be actually practiced, not just claimed.

Here are a few, by no means all, of the kinds of things that are worthy of evaluation when image problems impede gaining the support of the community.

- Response time to calls
- The agency's selective enforcement policy and/or patterns
- Relationships with other justice agencies and/or government services
- Proportion of minority or women police officers
- Training in ethnic, culture, communication, and sensitivity subjects
- Crisis management and crisis intervention techniques
- Citizen grievance procedures
- Follow-up disposition information on complaints
- Preferential treatment and/or rumors of graft or corruption
- Officer morale and related personnel considerations
- Juvenile programs
- Adequate patrol coverage
- Emergency response: disaster, SWAT, others
- Media relationships: specific agency contact personnel
- Organizational matters: specialities identified
- Management styles, methods, and techniques
- Community relations unit or agency-wide program

Many other matters might be considered before deciding on the area or areas of emphasis in preparing the agency to combine human relations with public relations as a basis for a community relations program that includes the improvement of police image.

Fortunately, the literature is extremely rich in all these areas, and many more. Most states provide local police agencies with guidelines for strengthening the areas defined as in need. Consulting expertise is often available via local universities, the federal government, and a variety of resource centers, in most cases subsidized sufficiently to meet budget requirements without serious strain.

In Chapter 14 we will address the combination of human relations in law enforcement with good public relations to form the basis of police–community relations, clearly the ideal image improvement.

SUMMARY

This chapter opened by noting the concern that the police have for public image. This was elaborated on as a positive indicator in that there remains a need for public support of law enforcement.

The problems of secretiveness, separation, distrust, and fear were considered. The role of *force* was also discussed.

The controversy over the police role was discussed from many different perspectives, including the officer's own image. Police professionalization was highlighted in relation to image problems. A variety of factors were evaluated in terms of enhancing or detracting from a better police image in the community.

DISCUSSION TOPICS

1. Elaborate on what this chapter presented as controversy over the police role.
2. Discuss what was presented in this chapter as the professional approach.
3. Discuss what this chapter presented in terms of police developing a "we and they" feeling.
4. Why is it difficult for the public to evaluate the correct *degree* of force used by police?
5. How is the combination of public relations and community relations potentially positive in terms of police image?

Relevant Problems for Discussion

Good police image can mean different things to different people. There are some who interpret the public popularity of the police as evidence that laws are not well enforced. This school of thought tends to build on the reality that there is bound to be at least some hostility and resentment when effective police activity takes place following law violation. It is not uncommon to extend this argument to the position of assuming the entire community will fear police for this reason, if police are doing an effective job.

Other viewers of law enforcement interpret public popularity as evidence that the nature of enforcement as discussed in Chapter 2 is both clear to the public and accepted by the public; everyone in the community realizes the necessity of enforcement and holds those involved in high regard—virtually "applauds" the enforcement. Since there is some validity to both points of view, a problem can arise when good police image is not defined in a manner to accommodate both.

Jurisdictions vary in the mix of these two viewpoints and vary accordingly in how and what to emphasize. This variation, along with many others, underpins the contention of Chapter 14 that every community is unique and needs a unique community relations program. But common to all approaches to defining good police image is the concept of *respect*.

When good image includes in its definition the concept of respect, the notion of popularity loses significance. Not many like to go to hospitals, but most *respect* the need for hospitals. When hospitals do their job, they may not become popular, but they remain *respected*.

Once out of the context of popularity, defining good police image in terms of respect emerges as a powerful support for all facets of police–community relations and affords a clear definition of what a good police image is all about.

14

Human Relations and Public Relations: Functions of Community Relations

In this chapter, we will address the specific subject of police–community relations. This discussion will be from the perspective of what we have already identified as human relations and what we will identify as public relations, the major components of police–community relations. Brief consideration of how the subject is perceived by the police may be useful. The policy statement of the Los Angeles Police Department is one of many excellent examples:[1]

> Community relations is based upon the principle that in a democratic society the police are an integral and indivisible element of the public they serve. Community relations is manifested by positive interaction between the people and the police and represents their unity and common purpose. . . .

Gaining unity and common purpose would certainly go a long way toward achieving the needed community support for law enforcement that has been emphasized in the 13 previous chapters. The obvious question is, what must happen for the police and community to achieve and enjoy such unity and common purpose? This question poses a challenge that must be met by modern law enforcement.

[1]*Manual of the Los Angeles Police Department,* Vol. 1, Section 310. Los Angeles: Los Angeles Police Department, 1988.

One complex dimension of this challenge is the often common assumption that police and community "automatically" enjoy unity and common purpose. Often, this assumption is in total error, which is often brought into focus by an unexpected crime wave, some disaster, or an outbreak of violence that brings into focus how far apart community leaders and police officials can be.

Yet another dimension of the challenge is that community relations are often perceived within police organizations as a specialty to be handled by select officers "good at making public speeches." When perceived this way, good community relations is simply "turned over to the specialists." Like the erroneous assumption that police and community automatically enjoy good relations, the perception of "the specialists" being able to create "unity and common purpose with the community" is also in error.

One way to modify the perception of community relations being a speciality is to simply rename community relations — call it something else. If the desire for unity and common purpose with the community is taken seriously, the "something else" that community relations might be called should sound like "real" police work. Such an approach could conceivably begin with something as simple as providing every police officer with a "public contact checklist" that supervisory and management personnel monitor closely.

Whatever the approach is called, a prime requisite for success is tailoring it to the *unique* community needs. Every community varies in many crucial ways when it comes to unity and common purpose and to an even greater degree in what is necessary to achieve this. What works well in one community may actually do harm in another; borrowing a program touted by another community as successful can backfire. Even when individual parts of another community's program are borrowed, the borrowed part should be carefully screened for local needs. Again, the approach may or may not be called police–community relations. What police choose as a title for this kind of program is not important. Here we call the program police–community relations, but it could function just as well under other titles.

While the title of the program is unimportant, the components of the program are very important. The essential components of successful community relations are a combination of what we have referred to as the *human relations* approach, plus what we will now define as *public relations,* combined within the framework of specific crime reduction goals and objectives.

Before defining public relations, let's review the concept of the *human relations* approach to law enforcement.

HUMAN RELATIONS

Throughout this volume we have referred to the *human relations* approach in terms of the many human interactions between police and the individuals with whom they come into contact. Here we add to these contacts with community residents the many interactions between police and other justice agency personnel and with people in other social and government agencies – in effect, all contact between police and people.

These interactions involve the attitudes and prejudices that we discussed earlier. The interactions also involve verbal and nonverbal communication between police and others. Physical contact is also involved.

The role played by *human relations* in successful community relations is that of gaining individual respect for the police through *personal* contact. Through their personal conduct and demeanor, individual officers can and must win the respect of the people with whom they come into contact.

Since the majority of situations in which most police make contact with people do *not* call for arrest, emphasis remains on making *most* personal transactions a pleasant experience insofar as is possible, while recognizing that a number of police situations will preclude this. Nevertheless, this is an emphasized priority – good human relations.

Police officer issuing citation. (Courtesy of San Jose Police Department)

The *goal* of the human relations component is to gain and hold the respect of the individuals within the community with whom individual police officers make contact. Perhaps even more importantly, the human relations approach calls on police officials to give high priority to this goal in their policy setting.

When achieved, the goal assists in achieving success with *public relations*.

PUBLIC RELATIONS[2]

Public relations are whatever police *through their agencies* say and do for the sole purpose of creating a positive public image. In other words, when what is said and

[2]Parts of this and later discussions in this chapter were published earlier in A. Coffey, E. Eldefonso and W. Hartinger, *Human Relations: Law Enforcement in a Changing Community,* 3rd ed., 1982. Passages from page 239-247. Reprinted by permission of Prentice-Hall, Inc., Englewood Cliffs, NJ.

Police sergeant in a TV interview. Whenever the particular situation allows, it is best to treat contact with the media as an opportunity to improve police image. Being as candid and responsive as the situation permits usually creates good-natured understanding in cases in which information cannot be released. (Courtesy of Santa Cruz Police Department)

done is *deliberate* and for the purpose of improving image, it is defined here as public relations.

Planned interviews with the media are the primary methods of public relations. But PR also includes speeches to service clubs, churches, and groups of all kinds, as long as the intent is primarily to create a positive public image.

However, when such public speaking and media contact have a *specific* crime-reduction purpose, then they become what we will define here as *community-relations* — anything geared to reducing a particular crime problem through contact with the public.

COMMUNITY RELATIONS

The main distinction of *community relations* programming is the existence of goals and measurable objectives having to do with specific crime reduction. Neither human relations nor public relations, as defined here, have *specific* crime-reduction goals. But as Figure 14-1 illustrates, both provide the basis for effective community relations.

For example, police officers in their activities when using the *human relations* approach can and should be able to build respect and individual goodwill, and thus support for law enforcement. A public agency effectively pursuing good *public relations* can enhance the image of the agency, also increasing the possibility for community support. But when these components are combined to achieve specific goals and objectives in the area of particular crime reduction, then it becomes community relations as defined here. *All planned activities to achieve specific crime-reduction goals and objectives are part of community relations.*

Developing, achieving, measuring, and modifying the goals and objectives are also a crucial part of police–community relations, at least in getting started and keeping it going. And the goals *must* be related to the mission of police, preferably the reduction or control of a *specific* crime problem recognized by the general community as significant.

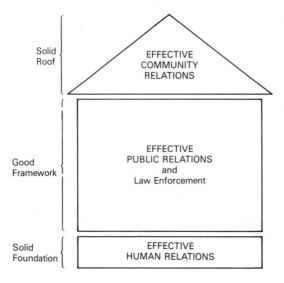

Solid Roof

Good Framework

Solid Foundation

EFFECTIVE COMMUNITY RELATIONS

EFFECTIVE PUBLIC RELATIONS and Law Enforcement

EFFECTIVE HUMAN RELATIONS

Figure 14-1 Police–community relations. A well-built structure provides a good analogy for the relation of human and public relations to community relations.

Goals and Objectives

The most cohesive force in police and community relations is a common goal or several common goals on which both police and community leaders agree. These goals must be related to the reduction, control, or ideally the prevention of some particular crime and/or delinquency. Police involvement in goals *outside* the sphere of police responsibility have a way of losing the support of police, thereby eventually losing the support of community leaders as well.

With goals there must be objectives, which are the tangible, measurable achievements that mark the path of success toward discernible goals. Both goals and objectives vary widely because of the uniqueness of every community. But all *effective* police–community relations goals and objectives have in common the crime control orientation of the goal and the tangible, measurable nature of the objectives.

Effective police–community relations programs also have in common the *commitment* of both police and community leaders. Here, in most situations, emerges a major difficulty to be negotiated, the reality that political support is needed for the continued success of any police program, and yet political support is often accompanied by political values.

The Dilemma of Politics

Every community has a political process that, like the community overall, is unique. One thing that all political processes have in common, however, is the political aspirations of community leaders. This has obvious implications for the police when attempting to gain community support for the reduction of a specific crime. The first step is to select crime or criminal problems that are perceived by the general community, or at least the community leaders, as important.

Friction usually comes from political leaders prioritizing the wishes of specific constituents over the police concern for a given crime problem. In the worst situation, police officials may be confronted by political leaders wishing to permit the continuation of a particular crime problem for an array of reasons. Fortunately, most differences of opinion between politicians and police officials are "purely political" and therefore subject to negotiation.

In every case, police officials must make the effort to involve community leaders in establishing the goals and objectives for the community relations program. One approach that is generally successful in this regard is emphasis on an obligation of the police to respond to the needs of *all* citizens, while at the same time respecting the constituency of each political leader's value system.

The laws themselves do not permit police officials to approach this subject without controls; many enforcement policies are virtually mandated by statutes. Nevertheless, negotiating the dilemma of politics is critical, if for no other reason than in most jurisdictions the political leaders also control the police budget. It would be asinine to downplay this potentially destructive factor in attempting to tailor community relations programming to uniquely local needs.

While no strategy can be devised that would fit all jurisdictions (or even any two), the style and approach can influence the political approach. The style of operating police agencies *professionally* with professionally trained personnel reduces the problems of capricious and potentially destructive political undercutting. The approach of giving high priority to human relations in all policy making is by far more difficult to subvert than policies made to the exclusion of such concerns; the public is unlikely to overlook the wishes of a well-respected policy agency. This style and approach of thinking fit the large police agency, with all of its complex specialties, including PR, designed to generate better image.

Yet, if it is believed that citizens would *rather* have effective police, that belief can be formed into a political power of its own, even in the smallest police agency. Perhaps this begins when citizens become confident that their police officers have adopted the human relations approach to law enforcement.

UNIQUE PROGRAMS

Programming for gaining and keeping the support of the community in specific crime control objectives is the intent of community relations programs. Programs by this definition must be geared to the local *uniqueness* of the community if they are to succeed. It must be acknowledged that every community is unique. There may be general areas in which trends outside the community may prove germane—ethnic relations for example.[3] Indeed, the concept of trends may be worthwhile considering.[4] For those starting from scratch conceptually, there are guidelines that can be helpful.[5]

[3]See, for example, Robert L. Green, "Future Trends in American Ethnic Relations," *National Forum,* Summer 1984, pp. 11–15.

[4]See, for example, Kenneth E. Boulding, "The Fallacy of Trends: On Living with Unpredictability," *National Forum,* Summer 1984, pp. 19–20. See also John Naisbitt, *Megatrends.* New York: Warner Books, 1984.

[5]For a comprehensive set of guidelines for future community relations programming, see Chapter 21 of Louis A. Radelet, *The Police and the Community,* 4th ed. New York: Macmillan, 1986, pp. 514–524. See also Pamela D. Mayhall, *Police-Community Relations and the Administration of Justice,* 3rd ed. New York: Wiley, 1985, Chapter 1.

Whether such material is helpful, depends on the local needs of the community—the uniqueness of the community. If recognition of the uniqueness of every community is a serious consideration, and it should be, then there are *no standards;* the only standard is that the goals and objectives should relate to a specific crime reduction purpose.

No Standards: Local Uniqueness

If there were a standard or even a set of standards for establishing community relations programs tailored to each unique community, the balance of this chapter would be devoted to such standards. But in truth, programs that succeed in one community may have little chance for success in another; merely the point of *emphasis* of a given program or different personnel or political leaders is all it takes to thwart the success of a particular transplanted program. This is because of the incredible variations and needs, realities, and circumstances among cities, counties, and states that prevent standardizing community relations programming, the impressive literature that could be cited to the contrary notwithstanding.

In spite of this, some common factors are worthy of consideration. Future law enforcement careers will experience even greater emphasis on the relations between law enforcement and the community served; there is literally no choice. Programs that are administered for the specific purpose of improving such relations are likely to grow, perhaps in some jurisdictions to the point that all police careers will at one time or another include active experience in a community relations program such as we are describing in this chapter. It is already standard police practice to acknowledge that public relations possibilities are critically important to police administration. And we have already observed that public relations is a crucial component of successful community relations.

In a sense, any effective police program could be made to serve as good public relations. From the discussion of police image in Chapter 13, good image is a prime requisite to successful law enforcement. But community relations programs must have in common an intent to go further than image.

Ideally, community relations programs afford the police the opportunity to *anticipate* law enforcement problems and, more importantly, gain public support in heading them off before they develop. The process through which such ideal community support occurs so thoroughly intertwines, at times, with PR that it is difficult to separate them. Nevertheless, effective community relations programs have in common that the goal of particular crime reduction is inherent in community relations; good public relations to enhance the image merely facilitate achievement of this goal.

The distinction between community relations and public relations is sometimes discernible only in the *intent.* Public relations intend to enhance police image, whereas community relations assumes good police image and intends to anticipate and control crime problems. Both PR and effective community relations programs have to do with improving the police image, but PR is *designed* for this purpose and good community relations achieve better image only as a consequence of achieving crime-reduction goals. Community relations go further by seeking to head off police community problems over approaches to enforcing the law; recall the discussion of selective law enforcement in Chapter 4.

Another distinction between PR and community relations has to do with change or improvement. PR programs assume neither change nor improvement in police activities; the intent is to enhance the image of the police in performing existing duties. In other words, the task of PR is merely to present a more favorable image of what police activities are. Community relations, on the other hand, assume an *improvement* in the police function and subsequent change in the severity of the crime problem.

It is not necessary to emphasize this change or improvement. Successful community relations programs frequently achieve the improvement without any emphasis at all. In such cases, public relations emphasizes the successful anticipation and correction of a police problem as good police work and capitalizes on the image improvement, thereby using PR to further enhance the success of goal-oriented community relations.

It is true that some police agencies retain a good public image without vigorous community relations programming, but it is not true that good public relations anticipates and prevents major police problems. On the other hand, good PR can be just as useful as a good community relations program in the important area of, for example, recruiting qualified candidates for police careers, a common concern in many jurisdictions.

Recruitment

Successful recruitment of the most qualified personnel often requires a combination of PR and sophisticated community relations programming, since highly qualified candidates are unwilling to settle for either poor image or totally reactive law enforcement, as opposed to a far-sighted, future-oriented approach to law enforcement.

As the trend increases toward college-prepared police careers, the sophistication of the police recruit also increases. As we have noted earlier, police in a democratic society react to crimes already committed far more often than they actively anticipate and prevent crime. The locally tailored community relations program emphasizes the anticipation and prevention or at least the control of crime. More and more today, police education includes this concept of relating to the community in such a manner that at least some of the causes of crime can be altered by anticipation and correction, even in this democratic society.

The sophisticated candidate readily recognizes the advantage of working in an agency actively seeking a reduction in police problems and also recognizes programs for community relations as one of the more effective methods to reduce these problems.

This personnel consideration is likely to become an increasingly significant factor in tailoring community relations programs to the local community. It would be scarcely realistic to hope to attract the most qualified candidates in the future without addressing this very real recruiting influence.

The community relations programs of a particular agency may not function under the title of community relations; it is the concepts we are discussing that are important in attracting qualified personnel. The program may take the form of a policy that every police officer perform a particular task, or that a group of specialists handle most of the tasks, or some combination of both. Even the most knowing career candidate might be amazed at the variety of approaches to community relations.

Focus on the Difference

Often a PR program is mistaken for an agency's community relations program, which suggests the need to reemphasize the difference. Once again, programs designed to improve the public's attitude toward police can be thought of as PR. Programs designed to anticipate problems and to avoid them through vigorous community work can be thought of as community relations, at least when goal-oriented toward the reduction of a crime problem. The combination of human relations and public relations is the basis of what we are calling police community relations.

It should be reemphasized that the problems addressed should be those that are of significance to law enforcement and not those over which police have no influence or legitimate concern. Furthermore, the crime problems should be recognized by community leaders as significant. Put another way, any police program intended to deal with the community should do so on the basis of potential police problems rather than political or unrelated problems

By confining the problems to which police address themselves to the area of law enforcement, community relations efforts can be more sharply focused and geared to specific problems; and, just as importantly, progress can be measured. This not only focuses more clearly on particular goals but also affords a method of determining whether too much or too little police effort is being expended. The all-inclusive political or economic problems afford no reference points; specific community relations goals for the reduction of crime are the essential difference between community relations and public relations.

BREAKING AWAY FROM EARLIER STANDARDS

Problems relating to crime vary as much from one community to another as the penal statues vary from one state jurisdiction to another. But just as there is considerable similarity in penal codes, there can be great similarity in the goals of community relations programs if a "boiler plate" approach is used. That is, if reviewing the success of other communities influences the establishing of goals for a given community, success is not likely to be forthcoming. This is because differences between communities' problems, resources, economics, and politics form unique situations that must be addressed.

The question of whether optimal success is to be achieved requires further consideration from the point of view of future efforts to create successful community relations programming.

During the emergence of widespread police interest in community relations a few decades ago, there were more similarities than dissimilarities between programs. This is understandable because, as a new concept, recognition of the uniqueness of every community was not apparent. This seeming uniformity among widely separated jurisdictions also had to do with the massive federal and in many cases state funding for local law enforcement agencies during the turmoil of the 1960s.

Government grants for nonexperimental purposes frequently required that the program funded follow certain guidelines, and the result is often a kind of inbreeding in which most successful applications for funding have a great deal in common, at least in writing.

Not all early community relations programs were funded, and innovative approaches were taken to tailor the effort to local needs. Even in these situations, however, when success was cited and publicized, a kind of model emerged, generally followed by a deluge of analysis in the literature. Not infrequently, such successes wound up being not only models, but absolute guidelines for obtaining grants in other jurisdictions.

Similarities, to perhaps an inordinately high degree, continue to this day and often exclude the critical ingredient in successful planning, tailoring the program to the local uniqueness of the community. Fortunately, there are indications that such similarity is no longer massive nor *necessarily* perpetuated, as when federal funding created the general appearance of uniformity. Gradual but steady change continues in the salient characteristics of community relations and law enforcement in general.

A reasonable argument can be made that there never was an actual uniformity in anything other than certain training, certain techniques, and certain organizational characteristics of community relations programs. Jurisdictions vary widely not only in size, economy, and crime problems, but even more widely in political and economical characteristics. Moreover, two seemingly identical communities may have an entirely different perception of criminal behavior, with one community tolerating crime a great deal more than the other, a critical factor in the incentive for law enforcement to be concerned with community relations.

Most would agree that the never-ending conflict between the orderly environment for which police are responsible and the individual rights, noted in our discussion of constitutional government, continue to be a strong influence on what is called community relations. Much of what was once identified and labeled as community relations a few decades ago is now frequently performed by the police without a specific label, leading some to believe that community relations no longer exist in certain jurisdictions. On the contrary, where this evolution has occurred, community relations has advanced significantly; the evolution of a special program into the routine police activities is the most effective form of community relations.

Similarly, police administrators who claim to have done away with the early programs have, in many instances, merely integrated them into staff training programs, that is, moved them from a small group of specialists into the mainstream of police operations by using staff training. Far from doing away with community relations, such a powerful move to integrate them into overall law enforcement is the optimum application of the concepts dealt with throughout this volume. In effect, this approach takes the *human relations* already discussed and incorporates the locally designed community relations activities within the *main* police function, the work of the line officer. In such instances, it can be said that the agency has gone well beyond the restrictive limitations of a small number of specialists who perform activities that are different from the other law enforcement resources.

In police agencies where a group of specialists still represents the community relations efforts, the uniqueness of programming peculiar to the local jurisdiction has probably emerged; their activities are no longer standardized. More often than not, the relationship between local police problems and community relations efforts is becoming the most salient program feature, which is particularly significant in view of the need to retain emphasis on local uniqueness. The more emphasis that is placed on local problems, the more the salient features of the program become unique and the greater the potential for effectiveness.

The gradual trend toward conceiving of police–community relations as uniquely local permits bringing to bear on local problems the concepts presented throughout this volume, without concern for particular organizational requirements, format, or even techniques. Recognition that uniqueness can, when handled correctly, enhance police–community relations permits more imaginative use of even the most limited police and community resources. Indeed, it may well be that the mere perception of a need for community relations is the most crucial factor for *beginning* the program.

Such a perception can emerge in many ways, from police wishing the public would consistently report a particular offense, to crowd intervention, to making street arrests. Probably the common denominator of all perceptions of a need for community relations is the recognition that not only is law enforcement far easier with community support, but *full* law enforcement is impossible without it.

Perceiving the need for community relations may well be the most crucial factor in starting, but another factor is just as important in making it pay off. In the final analysis, programming efforts have far more to do with police *attitude* about the program than the program design or organizational configuration. Indeed, police who *want* good community relations have already at least the beginning of a program, even if they do nothing beyond wanting it. A law enforcement organization that wants the benefit of community relations is bound to permeate with that desire all contacts with the community that it serves.

Not many years ago such an image, police *wanting* community relations programming, would have seemed far too idealistic to many. Such a concept would have been seen as out of touch with the grim realities of law enforcement in the twentieth century. But each year the growing trend toward police *professionalization* gradually but effectively "conceptually retools" many police officials. The time is here for many and close for the rest to see that gaining the support of the community is not just a requisite of effective law enforcement. Achieving and maintaining the respect of the community served is the greatest reward police could hope for and worth *every* effort.

To close this discussion of achieving and maintaining community respect, let's consider some of the community relations functions that might be appropriate in many communities.

The community relations unit functions in two major areas: crime prevention and public relations. However, again it must be stressed that the successful, effective department is one that is closely identified with the community and one in which the officers do not leave community involvement to a unit of the department. Actually, even though it is not tradition, a better name for this unit would be the community involvement unit, thus showing the close ties of the professional officer to the community.

Public Speakers Bureaus. These normally involve the use of officers or administrators being available to make presentations on various aspects of police operations to community and school groups. As a rule, engagements should be planned days in advance and should employ the use of modern audiovisual techniques. The officer in charge of the community relations unit should review any topic that is to be presented with the department speaker so that there is a consistent department policy running through all presentations. The community relations department head should actively seek out those officers in the department who have an interesting topic to present and who have some public speaking talent, experience, or training. A list of these officers and their topics should be on hand when any community group requests a speaker. In the area of race relations, special care should be taken to assign only those individuals who are knowledgeable and able to keep their heads in the midst of often heated and sometimes rather "sharp" discussions.

Tours and Demonstrations. These programs provide an excellent opportunity to educate the public by reviewing specific police techniques and operations in a realistic setting. Tours should be scheduled in advance, and care and consideration should be given to the nature of the audience so that the operations can be shown and explained in the proper perspective. Care should be exercised so that the tour group does not interfere with police operations going on at the time. Demonstrations in and outside the police station on police methods that have proven to spark community interest include radar use, dusting for fingerprints, use of police dogs, alcohol and drug detection, and computer capabilities.

Ride Along on Patrol. Scheduled in advance by the community relations unit, a ride-along program provides members of the public with a chance to see their community from inside a police car. Departments with such programs have formulated strict procedures on the issues of liability and safety. Basically, we recommend that these programs take place only with officers who *volunteer,* without coercion, official or otherwise, to have ride-alongs in their patrol cars during their regular shifts.

Another problem concerns the selection of these ride-along citizens. In the case of police science or criminal justice students, it is usually clear that these are people with a career orientation seeking knowledge. This may also be true of the ordinary citizen. However, some background check should be made of anybody who wishes to ride on a tour of duty in a patrol car. At a minimum, address and job should be confirmed. A computer check for felonies, misdemeanors, and patterns of vehicle and traffic infractions should be made. The patrol officer has to do his or her job, and those who engage in the ride-along program should have some special training in how to handle citizens when tense situations develop.[6]

---

[6]Edward A. Thibault, Lawrence M. Lynch, and R. Bruce McBride, *Proactive Police Management,* Englewood Cliffs, NJ: Prentice-Hall, 1985. pp. 185–186. Reprinted by permission of Prentice-Hall, Inc., Englewood Cliffs, NJ.

These are but a few concepts.[7] Recalling our discussion in Chapter 9 of community-based crime prevention, many such concepts can be brought to bear on a community's *unique* approach to police–community relations. The main idea is that both police and community leaders *want* good community relations, and that comes from police knowing law enforcement needs community support and community leaders knowing the community *must* have enforcement, a natural relationship with great potential.

> Today, there is almost unanimous agreement among major law enforcement executives and practitioners that the police alone cannot manage crime. Now, those with the responsibility of maintaining public order are openly pleading for community cooperation and support. . . .

> Until law enforcement practitioners use the maximum community partnership in crime management tactics, we will not see substantial declines in criminal activity.[8]

In Chapter 15 we will address some of the communication barriers confronting this necessity for "law enforcement practitioners to use maximum community partnership in crime management tactics."

SUMMARY

This chapter presented community relations as involving virtually all the topics of the first 13 chapters. The community relations approach was defined as including human relations, public relations, and a combination that supports community relations, goals, and objectives. These goals and objectives were presented as related to the specific reduction or control of crime.

Human relations were discussed as personal interactions of police that build respect for law enforcement. Public relations were presented as *planned* efforts to improve police image. Community relations were presented as including both, once agreed upon goals and objectives emerge.

The local uniqueness of every community was emphasized. Political factors were considered.

Programming considerations were elaborated on in the context of the requisite to maintain local uniqueness; certain common denominators in community relations planning were discussed.

DISCUSSION TOPICS

1. Distinguish between public relations and community relations as elaborated on in this chapter.

[7]See the works cited in footnote 5.

[8]George B. Sunderland, "The Community: A Partner in Crime Prevention," *FBI Law Enforcement Journal,* Oct. 1988, p. 7.

2. Describe human relations as presented in this chapter.

3. What is the intent of effective human relations in law enforcement?

4. Why should the goals and objectives of community relations be related to law enforcement matters?

5. Discuss the ramifications of the political dilemma noted in this chapter.

6. Describe the integration of both human relations and public relations into a goal-oriented community relations program.

Relevant Problems for Discussion

The chapter presented community relations as significantly different from one community to the next. Even when the variables involved *appear* to be the same, the uniquely configured local politics, economics, crime rates, tolerance of crime, and even variation in the personalities of police officials combine with yet other variables that *differ* to "print out" differently in each community.

The main problem with recognizing the uniqueness of a community is the "starting from scratch" approach when uniqueness is carried to an excessive extreme. By excessive extreme is meant approaching community uniqueness as though there is nothing in common with any other community.

The risk of ill-conceived notions increases in proportion to an unwillingness to perform the tedious tasks necessary to sort out all that is involved in police–community goal setting. If the sometimes frustrating task of carefully analyzing police–community needs is accomplished, the *civic pride* of local community uniqueness can be retained while at the same time picking and choosing whatever appears to be a common denominator with established community relations programs elsewhere. For example, a successful program in community A may be *generally* inappropriate for community B, except, say, for the partial walking patrol program. Community C may have a fine program that simply cannot work in community D, except, say, community crime prevention in schools. Such careful picking and choosing isn't as easy as simply adopting an entire program that is touted as being tried and proved in another community on the assumption that it will work well in all communities.

But, unlike many improvements in technology, training, methods, techniques, systems, and equipment in law enforcement, the truly successful community relations program is a local blend.

15

The High Cost of Failure to Communicate

Verbal communication is an extremely important part of the communication process, especially in law enforcement.[1]

> Everything a police professional does requires speaking. There are four kinds of speaking: requesting, promising, declaring, and asserting. People ask for things (request); say they will, will not, might, might not do things (promise); say things are so because of evidence (assert); and say things are so because of authority (declare). Speaking and listening with disciplined awareness of these distinctions is a simple solution to many communication problems.

This "simple solution" is very difficult to achieve in many, if not most, law enforcement situations. When this simple solution is not achieved, it is often attributed to a failure to communicate, and then ignored or forgotten or lost in the complexity of the problems that failures to communicate create. Such failure to communicate is never advantageous for police, and in many instances can be extremely costly.

Recalling the many factors that clearly establish the need for community support of law enforcement, we should now recognize that such support depends on the quality of human relations that exist between the police and the community. One

---

[1] *Human Relations in the Police Service.* Los Angeles: Los Angeles Police Department, 1988, p. 5.

of the highest costs charged to a failure to communicate is a reduction in the quality of human relations, which is paid for in lost community support. Put another way, good communication encourages, even creates, good community relations for police.

There is an irony when police–community relations fails. Police in general are often models of excellent communication with other police, with police dispatchers, and even with persons arrested. Yet, when it comes to communicating with the community, this expertise is sometimes lost; at least clarity and understanding are reduced.

This ironic loss is understandable inasmuch as residents in the community are not conversant in police work. However, the irony remains because police *are* conversant in community subjects. Police are, by and large, recruited from the communities they serve and remain members of that population, in spite of their professional law enforcement status.

Another costly loss from a failure to communicate occurs when there is a refusal to *recognize* that a failure in communication has occurred. In other words, it is also costly to ignore failures in communication. Refusal to recognize failure communication is often tempting because of the hard work that is usually involved in effective police–community communications. Both police officials and community leaders often prefer to presume all is well *until* a major problem proves otherwise.

The acceptance of the status quo until a problem erupts is not isolated to police–community relations—it's human nature. This tendency has probably been strengthened by many decades of conditioning by the entertainment media, who represent police as solving problems *after* problems have occurred, and always solving those problems quite well. There once was a time when that police image built great respect, confidence, and even admiration on a community-wide, even nation-wide basis. Let's look back at an example.

Shortly after television replaced the radio as America's primary form of home entertainment, the late Jack Webb began his tremendously successful series about the Los Angeles Police Department, called *Dragnet*. In much the same manner that Perry Mason enhanced the public image of defensive attorneys in that era, *Dragnet* gave the public a far more favorable impression of police than had ever existed before, and perhaps since, numerous successful television series with a law enforcement theme notwithstanding.

The philosophical reassessments of police professionalism that followed the violence of the 1960s raised questions regarding the style of law enforcement, depicted in *Dragnet*. It has been noted that the favorable impression of police that *Dragnet* created in its era is no longer desirable in certain ways:[2]

> Something has happened between the infancy of modern organized law enforcement in the early 1800s when Sir Robert Peel stated "the police are the public and the public are the police . . . ," and modern times when police attitude has been reflected in the often repeated statement of Jack Webb's TV character, Sergeant Friday, "This is police work,

[2]George B. Sunderland, "The Community: A Partner in Crime Prevention," *FBI Law Enforcement Bulletin,* Oct. 1988, p. 6.

just the facts, ma'am." This statement succinctly illustrates the "Keep out, citizen" attitude of police that was so prevalent during the middle 20th century. . . .

Yet *Dragnet* did make a very favorable impression in its day. Critics differ on how the *Dragnet* format captured America's imagination. But on one point almost all would agree; the program writer's insistence on *realism* and on clear, unambiguous, straightforward dialogue: "just the facts ma'am." Whether the scene depicted an (always calm) police dispatcher coordinating a high-speed chase of dangerous felons or Detective Sergeant Joe Friday taking a suspect into custody, the communication depicted was always *realistic* and *clear.*

But is police communication in general as clear as that very *realistic* law enforcement television series? The preceding 14 chapters have pointed out numerous influences that may make police communication "more realistic than clear." This chapter is intended to conclude the volume with a brief discussion of the factors involved in problems with police communication, beginning with recognition that the subject of communication is in itself an enormously complex area of human study.

COMPLEXITY OF HUMAN COMMUNICATION

It is important at the outset of this discussion to emphasize how very *brief* this discussion will be in the context of all the research and literature on communication. Scholarly treatises abound with theories about how humans verbally, nonverbally, and otherwise communicate with each other — and how they *fail* to communicate with each other effectively.

But in this brief discussion, our purpose is to merely examine *some* of the more salient problems impinging on police communication in terms of the police seeking to communicate to others and receive communication from others.

Put another way, we are trying to develop insight into specific and practical police problems with communication between the police and the community groups that we have discussed, as well as communication in all aspects of law enforcement careers. The chapter 14 discussion of the police effort to develop mutual community *goals* and *objectives* is but one of many examples.

COMMUNICATION: WHAT IS IT?[3]

In simplest terms, communication can be conceived of as one or more individuals receiving a message or a *meaning* from someone else. A relatively consistent defini-

[3]The material in this brief chapter is a synthesis of a great number of factors, which include the author's numerous intensive communication and human systems courses at the Mental Research Institute, Palo Alto, and the Center for Human Communication, Los Gatos. Also included in this synopsis are concepts from Don D. Jackson, (ed.), *Communication, Family and Marriage.* Palo Alto: Science and Behavior Books, 1960. Virginia Satir, *Your Many Faces,* Millbrae, CA: Celestial Arts, 1978. M.S. Kuhlman, "Nonverbal Communication in Interrogations," *FBI Law Enforcement Bulletin,* Nov. 1980, pp. 6–9. G.J. Thompson, "Rhetoric: An Important Tool for Police Officers," *FBI Law Enforcement Bulletin,* Apr. 1982, pp. 1–7. A.R. Coffey, *Police Intervention into Family Crisis.* Santa Cruz, CA: Davis, 1974. B.L. Benson, "Communication Feedback from Investigators to Patrol Officers: A Simple, Practical Approach," *The Police Chief,* June 1982, pp. 42–43.

tion of communication becomes possible when *meaning* is limited to verbal communication, but, in reality, verbal communication frequently is the least effective of all communication. We will soon examine some of the many methods by which meaning is exchanged with and without words.

But in the context of this chapter, emphasis is being placed on the reality that many times the message or *meaning* that was *intended* is not the message that was received. A kind of tentative definition of at least part of human communication is possible in terms of the messages sent and received.

In terms of the problems police might have with messages sent and received, our definition can be *COMMUNICATION IN PART IS WHEN THE MESSAGE SENT IS THE SAME MESSAGE THAT IS RECEIVED.* We will soon note a number of other factors that impinge on communication that will point up the limitation of this definition. For the present, it need only be acknowledged that frequently among humans messages are received that were not *intentionally* sent; such messages all too often have to do with the attitudes and prejudices discussed in previous chapters. While it is unlikely that the problems posed by such distortions in communication can be solved totally, it is the intent of this chapter to examine some of the problems for the purpose of at least reducing the negative impact. Put another way, simply recognizing that communication is made frequently when individuals believe they have received an intended meaning even though the sender did not intend the meaning received should provide an approach to dealing with the problem.

In addition to individuals believing that they have received an intended meaning when that is not the case, problems exist in the variety of ways individuals *perceive* the same situation. All too often, individuals assume that their own perception of a situation is the only correct way to perceive and rule out the reality that those with whom they would communicate may actually perceive the situation in another entirely different manner. We will soon discuss this in a broader context, but for the present the example of differing perceptions of young people versus senior citizens, or in many cases the differences between male and female perceptions of the same situation will illustrate the point.

Differences in perception are caused by any number of factors and influences. As noted in other chapters, all people selectively perceive what they want or need to perceive or what they have been trained to perceive by their biases, prejudice, and attitudes.

The intent of a police car's emergency lights and siren is to have motorists tune out other stimuli and selectively perceive the warning. Certainly, the police officers trying to arrest a resisting felon intend for the suspect to perceive their "message."

Individuals, from earliest childhood, have been conditioned to perceive certain things easier and better than other things. This in part accounts for why many intended messages are never received or simply tuned out as part of the selective perception.

And so we can observe that there are many messages received that were never sent, and many messages sent that are not received. Moreover, even when messages are received, they may not be the message that was *intended.*

To somewhat simplify the complexity of the variables involved, communication can be thought of in terms of both the messages and the situations in which messages are sent and received.

Communication: What Is It?

Messages and Their Situations

In some ways, the situation in which a message is sent can be more significant than the message itself; consider the following:

> A judge tells a citizen that he is convicted of a crime and will be sent to prison. The context is the court setting. The result is a change of status of the individual from civilian to prisoner. The context is charged with authority, and there is a powerful difference in the status of the judge and the citizen who is about to be sentenced.
>
> It is of vital importance that top police management understand the effects of their communications within the context of authority relations. We also have to consider what audience hears the message (e.g., civilians or uniformed officers). The chief can take an officer aside and reprimand him for wearing sloppy uniforms. Or the chief can communicate this at lineup in front of fellow officers. Or the chief can give the officer the same message while the officer is engaged in an investigation in the presence of news reporters. It is the same message but different audiences. It also makes a difference whether it is the chief of the department or some fellow officer making the same statements. In this case, it is the same statement, different message. . . .
>
> The style of delivering messages deserves consideration too. Messages from police commanders and other management personnel in law enforcement tend to be brusque and unfeeling and in the form of orders. In a tense street confrontation with immediate potential violence, for example, this might be the correct approach. However, in many situations, this brusque approach will only tend to alienate line officers and citizens.[4]

Although we are focused on *one-way* communication here, our purpose is to understand two-way communication—to understand that *feedback* on the message is needed if *intended* meaning is to become actual meaning. But this brings us back to the variety of *situations* in which messages are sent.

In considering the *situations* in which messages are sent and received, it might be helpful to recall our discussion of police roles. Roles are a kind of *expected* behavior; police, for example, are expected to question suspects following a crime. Presumably, even the suspect would acknowledge that the messages involved in questioning are appropriate for that situation.

Other situations might not seem so appropriate. The curious passerby is *not* expected to question the suspect, even if the questions are exactly the same as those asked by the officer. These situations can be thought of as the *context* of communication, meaning both *who* is appropriate to send and receive messages and *when* such communication can occur.

The *content* of communication can be thought of as the *intended-meaning*. When the intended meaning is communicated successfully, it will be through the combination of two or more of the following modes or methods of communication:

1. Words and signs

---

[4]Edward A. Thibault, Lawrence M. Lynch, and R. Bruce McBride, *Proactive Police Management.* Englewood Cliffs, NJ: Prentice-Hall, 1985, p. 101. Reprinted by permission of Prentice-Hall, Inc., Englewood Cliffs, NJ.

2. Facial expression and/or eye contact
3. Voice tone inflection
4. Meaningful silence
5. Posture
6. Pace and/or nervousness
7. Emotional incongruence (act happy when should be sad, for example)
8. Emotional tone and expression; tears, laughter, demeanor
9. Gestures
10. Stride

Some of these variables communicate without the individual's knowledge; when others perceive some combination of these factors and interpret it, a kind of communication has occurred. Perhaps brief consideration of how language itself is a kind of code will illustrate the concept of *intended* meaning. Consider the following:

Encoding/Decoding: The Meaning of Meaning

Whenever we use language, we are taking an incident and encoding it into a prestructured formula. General semantics indicates that the symbol is not the thing and the map is not the terrain. Symbols, which include all words, stand for something else. When we pull down a map of the ocean, we do not get wet, because the map is a symbol for the wet ocean—the map is not the ocean itself. Therefore, the map, and words, are something less than an immediate apprehension of the ocean. In short, a map of the ocean is less than the experience we would have standing on a sandy or rocky beach, listening to ocean sounds, smelling the ocean smells, and gazing at the endless horizon. What does this mean when we try to communicate?

We all talk in subscripts. Subscript "one" might be what the sender means by a word. The various receivers might be receiving subscripts two and three, and so on. Let us try an illustration.

Officer Smith tells Officers Jones and Brown that he arrested a juvenile in a tough section of town on his duty shift, late at night. Officer Smith is thinking of a blond-haired, middle-class boy who had run away from home and found himself in a tough neighborhood. Smith's juvenile is $JUVENILE_1$. Officer Jones, who knows that neighborhood, might be thinking of a young tough who smokes marijuana, has black hair, and runs with a lower-class gang. Jone's juvenile is $JUVENILE_2$. Office Brown might be thinking of a young girl he had picked up recently in that neighborhood for prostitution. She is lower class, with red hair, and a heroin addict. Brown's juvenile is $JUVENILE_3$. Unless there is some kind of feedback to Smith's message and a clarification from Officer Smith, the symbol "JUVENILE" might lead to some real problems in this communication.

Very simple words, for example, desk, car, juvenile, can refer to a number of different actual things or types. Language is actually a form of shorthand. It is hard for every communicator and receiver to have experienced everything that they may want to communicate about.[5]

[5] Ibid., p. 99.

It is not only hard for every communicator and receiver to have experienced everything that they want to communicate about, it is all but impossible; some guessing on the part of the receiver is inevitable when both the message and the situation vary so widely.

In spite of the great complexity that communication entails, this approach of considering only content and context permits us to examine the four possibilities involved in police communication.

1. *Message clear: situation agreeable and appropriate.* In this situation, all parties concerned agree that the context is appropriate. Furthermore, the *intended* message *content* is clear; the combination of the modes referred to above is correctly discerned.

2. *Message clear: situation inappropriate yet agreeable.* In this particular situation, a message is received but either misunderstood or resisted or in some other way distorted. No one has disagreed on the context of the message or that it is all right to communicate; however, the intended message was not received. An example might be an individual who intends to communicate that it is 8 o'clock at night but instead says that it is 8 o'clock in the morning by simply leaving out the appropriate AM/PM suffix.

3. *Message unclear: situation inappropriate or not agreeable.* There is no chance for communication in this situation. First, the individuals involved do not agree that the situation is appropriate for communications; the context is perceived as inappropriate. Compounding this difficulty, sufficient effort was not expended to ensure that the intended message content was clear. It is highly likely that attitudes, biases, and prejudice will prevail in the interpretation of what was communicated in such a situation.

4. *Message unclear but situation appropriate.* Here we have the most probable situation for police communication in general. We will soon consider a number of the factors that make communication difficult at best; but when there is agreement that it is appropriate to attempt to communicate, many of these problems can be negotiated and the *content* can be clarified.

In effect, this fourth position is a kind of philosophical, and indeed attitudinal, approach to communication. It establishes that a *goal* of communication is to, at a minimum, reach the level of *agree to disagree*.

Agree to Disagree

There are theoretical factors that can help us to develop a more practical, *working* understanding of how problems develop in police communication. Understanding these factors will not ensure *agreement* or even *understanding* of another's point of view. It will, however, enhance the possibility of at least reaching a nonhostile position of "agreeing to disagree."

Let's take a look at a few of the factors involved. These are not new concepts; here are a few that have been in police literature for over two decades.[6]

[6]William R. Carmack, "Practical Communication Tools for Group Involvement in Police–Community Programs," *Police Chief,* Mar. 1965, pp. 34–36.

Some of the Message Barriers

The messages we have discussed here as being sent and received are actually made up of and influenced by infinite factors. But for purposes of this discussion, messages can be thought of as combinations of *facts* and/or *inferences* and/or *judgments* and/or *evaluations.*[7] Figure 15-1 illustrates some of the many steps involved.

Receiving the exact content of a message that was *intended* is obviously influenced by these considerations. For example, the person receiving the message may feel the content has no facts at all and is nothing other than unwelcomed judgments or inferences. This *credibility* consideration may in turn flow from *attitude* and *prejudice,* as we have discussed earlier. This brings into focus the function of trust in human communication.

The Role of Trust

Thus far we have seen some of the many things that distort messages or even prevent messages from being received at all. And even if the message content comes through as *intended,* what if it is not believed? What if the receiver doesn't *trust* the sender? For our purposes, we can say that it is more important to *understand* than to *believe;* believing can develop as trust develops. But, *first,* let's get clear on the intended message content.

It is possible that trust will never develop; some people may never fully trust police. It is a certainty that there are dangerous people that the police cannot trust. But even in these extreme situations, there is a great advantage to understanding the *intended content* of messages. Even when the intended content is insulting, a full understanding of that content affords far greater insight than simply allowing

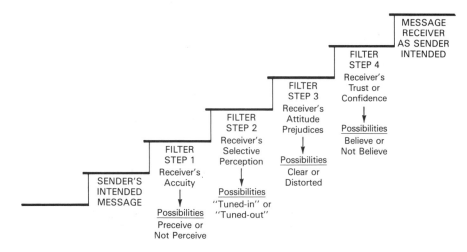

Figure 15-1 Receiving verbal and nonverbal messages: the four big filtering steps. Police must guard against the problems of being misunderstood, not believed, or "tuned-out." Equally important, police must receive messages as intended, especially if the messages are negative and hostile.

[7]Ibid.

attitudes, prejudices, and biases to dominate. Even an enemy is easier to deal with when fully understood.

Recognizing the attitudes, prejudices, and value differences that distort messages *is* a positive context for intended message content. In other words, the mere recognition of the distortions of messages establishes a positive context. From this positive context, the role of trust can start out small, become large, and lead from mere understanding of the content to at least the position of *agree to disagree.* Agreeing to disagree is far better than raw suspicion and antagonism. Indeed, even when this position cannot be achieved, there are far more productive options available when the intended message content is understood.

At this point, we should acknowledge more than the complexity of communication impedes the clear understanding of the intended content of messages; the stress of police work itself can hamper effective communication.

THE STRESS OF POLICE WORK

It is unlikely that any serious student of criminal justice could doubt the stress imposed on the lives of police personnel. The subject of previous chapters has, in a sense, been a discussion of factors that increase the stress on the people who enforce law. Contradictory expectations of police, the ambiguity of the police role, and the burden of functioning as the symbol of a sometimes unjust justice system generate tension and stress (see Figure 15–2).

Add to this such compounding communication problems as cross-cultural difficulties that are often seen as inherent.[8] Recalling the major tensions associated with enforcing law in the poverty-stricken ghetto or barrio, stress is clearly part of the police officer's life.

Problems that do not exist can be created by not getting the intended message. Such problems run the entire range of law enforcement, up to and including the private lives of law enforcement personnel, a major concern in terms of the stress of police work.[9] Indeed, we will shortly examine some of the factors that impede communication when there is not understanding between wives, husbands, sons, daughters, colleagues, and friends or police officers.[10] The ensuing stress and strain necessarily impede effective job performance, which itself can lead to yet further stress and strain.

Compounding the obvious sources of stress are the more subtle, yet powerful generators of police tension. The ever present reality that every contact with a

[8]See, for example, G. Quintanalla, "Cross-Cultural Communication: An Ongoing Challenge," *FBI Law Enforcement Bulletin,* Feb. 1983, pp. 1–8. See also P.B. Taft, Jr., "Policing the New Immigrant Ghettos," *Police Magazine,* July 1982, pp. 10–26.

[9]See, for example, W.H. Kroes, *Society's Victim—The Policeman.* Springfield, IL: Charles C Thomas, 1976. See also R.L. Depue, "High-Risk Lifestyle: The Police Family," *FBI Law Enforcement Bulletin,* Aug. 1981, p. 713, and B. Daviss, "Burnt Out," *Police Magazine,* July, 1982, pp. 9–18. Also, especially, Clinton W. Terry, III (ed.), "The Personal Costs of Police Work," in *Policing Society,* New York: Wiley, 1985.

[10]Kroes, op. cit.

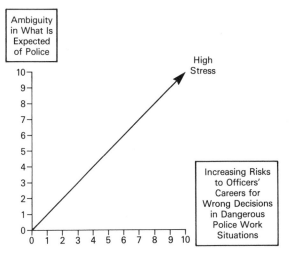

Figure 15-2 One of the many sources of police stress. Performance expectations vary from situation to situation, from one community group to another even in the same situation, and even in situations that involve great danger.

The axes and labels of the figure read:

Ambiguity in What Is Expected of Police

High Stress

Increasing Risks to Officers' Careers for Wrong Decisions in Dangerous Police Work Situations

stranger has the potential for violence is stressful. The question must be asked in every such encounter: is the stranger a robber, a murderer, a homicidally insane person, a recently escaped prisoner . . . ?

The stress of police work is an emphasis point in a great deal of police literature.[11] It has been stated succinctly:

> Over half a million people in this country are involved in police work . . . a job that is particularly complicated, conspicuous, discretionary and important . . . an environment of danger and violence . . . a hostile public that resent police authority . . . suspicion, feelings of isolation, and frustration. . . . [12]

The stress of police work is not confined to the line level working officers:[13]

> A police manager, especially the chief administrator of an agency, is as much victim of stress as the officers under his or her command. While many of the stressors of line personnel may be physical in nature, the manager's stress translates into organizational pressures, administrative frustrations, psychological tension and fear, and nonviolent interpersonal conflict. Yet, the results of either can be deadly, and diseases of the body and mind strike boss and street cop equally and as quick.

> Much administrative attention in recent years has been devoted to enabling the line officer to better handle the pressure of the street. With this training, with physical activity on the street which allows for the discharge of emotions, and with improved selection procedures, personnel in the lower ranks seem increasingly able to handle line-of-duty stress.

[11]Thibault, Lynch, and McBride, op. cit.

[12]Pamela R. Mayhall, *Police-Community Relations and the Administration of Justice,* 3rd ed. New York: Wiley, 1985, p. 133.

[13]James D. Sewell, "The Boss as Victim: Stress and the Police Manager," *FBI Law Enforcement Bulletin,* Feb. 1988, p. 18.

The Stress of Police Work

It is time to devote the same time, efforts, and energies to the resolution of stress experienced by police administrators. Effective management requires the ability to anticipate, understand, and control organizational and community problems. Stress that an agency administrator faces is no less a problem that must be effectively handled than any other organizational situation which he or she confronts.

The private lives of police personnel sadly tend to reflect this enormous stress.[14] The high divorce rate in the field of law enforcement is only one indicator of the strain placed on the relationships with wives, husbands, sons, and daughters. Are these sad realities a rationale for further gloom, or a basis for seeking improvement?

Is the Glass Half Full or Half Empty?

At this point, let's take a philosophical liberty. The "eye of the beholder" refers to the wide variation in human value judgments. This concept, however, can be expanded to incorporate the notion that the same set of facts can be either perceived as positive or negative; the proverbial glass of water that is either seen as half full or half empty, is a good example.

This thinking can be applied in a positive way to the problems confronting effective police communication. *If* all the tremendous strains on police communication are seen as proof that nothing can improve, the glass is half empty. If on the other hand, these *very same factors* can be seen as *reasons to improve communication,* the glass is then "half full."

Put another way, all difficulties in receiving intended message content are reasons to make the effort to communicate better; the very process of *trying* in itself provides a positive context for exchanging intended meanings.

Add to this the high rewards for community relations when police are successful in communicating, not to mention the enormously satisfying experience of achieving professional goals. Further consider the improvement in the quality of life when communication is successful. There are a number of motives to at least make the effort. But *when* do police officers do all this?

WHEN SHOULD POLICE COMMUNICATE?

The *human relations* approach to law enforcement, as presented in Chapter 14, requires a continuing and conscientious effort to communicate as well as possible in *every* human interaction. The police officer directing traffic has an obligation to communicate clearly only one way, that is, communicate clearly *to* motorists and pedestrians. But in the vast majority of human interactions involving law enforcement, there is a need to clearly communicate both ways to *exchange meanings,* that is, to receive and send the intended message content accurately.

Ranging from police officials meeting with community leaders through patrol officers responding to calls and to investigators interviewing, the *exchange* of *intended* meaning is the goal—to give and receive the intended content of the

[14]Carmack, op cit.

message. These very same skills also apply in the private lives of police officers. Husbands, wives, sons, daughters, friends, neighbors, and of course colleagues are far more supportive when dialogue exists, or even when the effort to improve dialogue exists.

Sometimes the effort to exchange *intended* meanings fails or sometimes the *intended* meanings carry anger, hurt, or frustration. The ensuing hurt feelings and damaged pride are not in themselves pleasant experiences, but they do form the basis for building *honest* communication. In some cases, genuine *respect* and even *trust* grow out of honest communication that includes "hurt feelings." The main point is that all parties concerned recognize the honesty of any effort to communicate an *appropriate* message content.

This by no means requires informing every unattractive person of their ugliness. What it does entail is a continuous effort to cut through all the barriers that we have discussed thus far to share an intended message content—*intended* because the officer deems it appropriate for the situation.

Many related factors also come to bear. Does the officer hold his or her profession more important than his or her family?[15] Does the family resent the difference in life-style imposed by law enforcement careers?[16]

Good communication cannot, by itself, solve these problems, nor can communication by itself solve all the problems noted in the 14 preceding chapters. Yet the very effort of *trying* to improve communication is of enormous value in approaching solutions to any of the problems presented throughout this volume. Put another way, *trying* to improve communication is a giant step toward making things better; even if problems cannot be completely solved, trying to improve communication usually enhances the chances for success in any police program.

Collectively, the reasons for seeking to get and understand the *intended* message content are overwhelming; the rewards for this effort are high and so are the damages from failure. No matter how complex the barriers to communication —cultural, semantic, prejudicial, or whatever—getting as clear a picture of the intended message as possible is a crucial element in the police gaining the support of their community. And at least from a police intelligence network perspective, it is crucial that intended messages be understood, whether agreed with, believed, or not. Finally, in the context of police prioritizing the support of the community they serve, if even the *effort* to communicate will enhance the respect of citizens for their police, think what *successful* communication can do.

But is not only the respect of citizens that communication enhances. The already deep and abiding respect that most police officers hold for each other is enhanced greatly when communication succeeds, when the messages sent are the messages that are received, and when the mission of law enforcement is furthered.

---

[15]The subject is discussed in various contexts in the literature. See, for example, in addition to the citations in footnote 5, M.H. Silbert, "Job Stress and Burnout of New Police Officers," *The Police Chief,* June 1982, pp. 46–48, and Peter K. Manning, *Police Work: The Social Organization of Policing.* Cambridge, Mass.: M.I.T. Press, 1977. Also see M.B. Saper, "Police Wives: The Hidden Resource," *The Police Chief,* Feb. 1980, pp. 28–29; and J.D. Sewell, "Police Stress," *FBI Law Enforcement Bulletin,* Apr. 1981, pp. 7–11.

[16]Silbert, op. cit.

Perhaps because of the nature of law enforcement itself, there are tremendous unity and mutual respect among police officers. The depth and strength of this unity are dramatized by the response from all jurisdictions when an officer is in distress or when an officer has fallen in the line of duty. (Courtesy of San Jose Police Department)

The high cost of failing to adequately communicate includes losses in the often inspiring personal commitment police officers tend to hold to one another:

> One of the most profound statements that any police officer can make is that *he (or she) is never alone* once having become a sworn officer . . . the call for "officer in trouble" will mean that officers in and outside the immediate vicinity will normally drop what they are doing and rush to that officer's aid. . . .

The most frequent example of this feeling of unity, besides the officer in trouble call . . . is probably seen in the area of professional courtesy. . . . When a police officer has an automobile breakdown, he does not necessarily call a garage. . . . He may call the nearest police station.[17]

Examples of the strong sense of unity among police officers are limitless; virtually all officers can relate many instances of showing and being shown great respect to and from other officers. But this strong sense of unity can be a kind of paradox. Improving communication only between police and other police promotes the "we-they" *isolation* from the community. Rather than promoting the badly needed support of the community, such isolation promotes "we versus they," the worst of all and the highest price of failures to communicate.

Successful police–community relations include improved communication both among police and between police and *their* community, which will promote police unity built on pride in professionally serving *their* community.

Too idealistic? Does building a feeling of police unity exclude building support from the community? Police–community relations, when lifted out of theory and academic analysis, become a matter of the "we" in law enforcement using communication to unify not only law enforcement, but all of the resources that "they" in the community can bring to bear on crime and disorder.

And let's not forget that communication is *far* more than spoken and written words. Let's review:[18]

Because police work is an occupation that deals mainly with people, words are one of the most powerful tools of the trade. However, there are many subtle messages sent by means other than words. These non-verbal messages can help or hinder the spoken message.

The words can be exact, but the message received may be exactly opposite the words because of accompanying non-verbal behavior.

When dealing with people, actions have priority over words in conveying feelings and intentions. Unnecessarily pushing someone aside, turning away when a person begins speaking, or punctuating remarks with a stabbing finger all contain messages. They can signal that the communicator is angry, feels threatened, lacks respect, or fears losing control of the situation.

There is a whole non-verbal "vocabulary" which people learn and use quite unconsciously. Developing this vocabulary requires conscious observation of its use. What are the gestures, postures, facial expressions, and other non-verbal cues people give to signal fear, dislike, trust, warmth, compliance, resistance, and all the many other human thoughts and feelings? As awareness of the non-verbal vocabulary grows, so does mastery of it.

Masters of non-verbal communication enhance the message potential of their words, get their message across quickly and easily, and get desired action with minimum confusion. When communication does break down, they usually know why and where, and are quick to try again. Because they are disciplined observers of their listeners (and

[17]Thibault, op. cit. pp. 26–27.

[18]*Human Relations in the Police Service, op. cit.*, pp. 6–7.

of themselves as verbal and non-verbal communicators), they can usually see what is wrong and fix it. Mastery of non-verbal communication can dramatically reduce stress in human relations.

People who lack non-verbal awareness may say one thing, but they look like they want another, usually get neither, and cannot understand why.

SUMMARY

In this concluding chapter, the problems of failures to effectively communicate were related to the problems presented in the previous 14 chapters.

Communication was defined in terms of exchanging meaning—more importantly, exchanging *intended* meanings between individuals and groups.

What the message contains and the situations in which messages are sent were discussed in various combinations.

A wide range of theoretical barriers to communication was discussed. The role of stress in police work was presented as an additional impediment to good communication.

The collective total of all the problems with communication was presented as reasons for attempting to improve communication. These reasons were combined with the high rewards for successful communication in establishing the support of the community for law enforcement.

DISCUSSION TOPICS

1. Relate communication as presented in this chapter to the overall problems presented in the 14 preceding chapters.
2. What is the significance of *intended* message content?
3. What has the context or situation to do with the clarity of the intended message content?
4. Elaborate on the concept of stress in police work as an impediment to communication.
5. Discuss what was presented in this chapter as a choice of seeing all the communication problems as a basis for gloom or a reason for improvement.

Relevant Problems for Discussion

Since it is anything but new to point to breakdowns in communications as a source of many (perhaps most) criminal justice problems, it is difficult to move beyond the point of simply acknowledging the problem. In a sense, a problem is created by everyone "knowing" the problem—knowing it so well that a kind of fatalistic acceptance of the problem evolves. In some cases, police officials openly comment to the effect that the very fact the problem remains when everyone knows it's a problem illustrates that it cannot be solved.

To some degree, such cynicism is justified; communications breakdowns are never *completely* eliminated. Like crime rates, the breakdowns in communication are subject to changes as a result of effort—changes for the better when effort is made or changes for the worse when no effort is made.

If the goal is set of reducing, rather than eliminating, communication failures, the costs discussed in this chapter are also reduced. In most police agencies, morale rises and falls almost in synch with the *degree* of conviction that the individual both understands and is understood in an atmosphere of mutual respect. Communication alone cannot create such an atmosphere, but it can help, and it certainly is the main factor in keeping such a productive atmosphere when it is achieved.

But above all else, such improvement *is* possible.

APPENDIXES

Appendix A:
Police Checklist for
Community Tension and Unrest

Factors influencing and problems creating community tensions and unrest were the main subject of Chapter 5 and are related to the violent history of disorders presented in Chapter 6. Community tension and attendant problems were also noted in many contexts throughout this volume.

Here, in condensed form, is the "checklist" from the California Peace Officers' Standards and Training Commission (POST Commission) with obvious relevance to all law enforcement.

I. **Factors Contributing to Community Tensions and Civil Disturbances**

    A. Social Factors

        1. Racial or minority-group injustices, whether real or imagined, create an atmosphere of distrust and fear.

        2. Religious differences can often create schisms in the community just as serious as racial differences.

        3. Normal community activities, involving crowds, could deteriorate into serious disorder under certain conditions (e.g., large crowds outside, hot weather, an "incident").

        4. Existence of a matriarchal society prevalent in Negro areas can present unusual problems to police and the larger community.

        5. Adult attitudes towards conduct of young people, teen-agers, etc., may vary due to different cultural values and attitudes. These may be in conflict with the norms of the community.

B. Economic Factors
   1. Extreme poverty can breed crime and perpetuate barriers to social advancement.
   2. Unemployment and/or unfair hiring practices tend to confirm for minority-group persons that they are facing a "stacked deck" in their efforts to improve their lot.
   3. Poor housing conditions and discrimination in the sale of real estate create dislike for the "power structure," and the policeman who symbolizes the establishment.
   4. Affluence of large parts of the community create unawareness and insensitivity so that no desire to cope with "minority-group" problems exists.

C. Political Factors
   1. Power struggles:
      a. Efforts by the majority, legal and otherwise, to maintain the status quo.
      b. Efforts, legal and otherwise, by minority groups to upset the balance of power; to share, dominate, or alter the political system.

D. Absence or Failure of Constituted Authority
   1. Failure of law enforcement to act:
      a. In a crowd or arrest situation, due to indecision, or lack of appropriate laws.
      b. In certain situations due to a lack of manpower, or inadequately trained manpower.
      c. Because of a fear of adverse public reaction.
   2. Absence of law enforcement:
      a. Serves as a contributing factor to disorder because members of the crowd (or mob) feel they can act with impunity.
      b. Some in minority-group areas feel they are not receiving adequate police services.

E. General Factors
   1. Minority-group struggles for full enjoyment of civil rights.
   2. Inequitable law enforcement, real or imagined, toward minority groups.
      a. Demonstrated bias or prejudice on the part of police.
      b. A feeling in some areas that they are "overpoliced."
   3. Lack of meaningful communication between police and the minority community.
   4. Stereotyping:
      a. Of minorities by police and other city officials.
      b. Of police and city officials by minorities and the larger community.
   5. Rumors and sensationalism:
      a. Inflammatory statements and stories based upon distortions and/or half-truths.
      b. May be originated by police, city officials, minority groups, religious and lay groups, news media.
   6. Absence of organization and leadership among the masses of minority-group members.
      a. Self-proclaimed leaders much in evidence.
      b. Leaders selected by the white majority to represent the minority much in evidence.

      c. General lack of opposition among the minorities against the radical elements (tacit approval).

      d. No real leadership for the minority community.

  7. General public apathy towards the issue of civil rights and impartial law enforcement.

  8. Outsiders who capitalize on local problems as a means of promoting their own goals.

II. Warning Signs of Community Tensions

A. Early Manifestations

  1. A greater frequency of resisting arrest in certain areas. Gathering of crowds when arrests are made.

  2. An increase in charges of alleged police brutality, an increased distrust or resentment of law enforcement.

  3. A rising volume in the number of incidents of violence, or threats of violence.

  4. Increasing rumors and statements of dissatisfaction, public name-calling and other attempts at provocation.

  5. The appearance of "hate" literature, threatening or derogatory signs, leaflets, pamphlets.

  6. A stepping-up of gang activity, characterized by antisocial activity on the part of minority-group members; acts of vandalism and malicious mischief, particularly on public property.

  7. Progressively overt attacks upon constituted authority through:

      a. Protest meetings.

      b. Speeches and literature.

      c. Sit-ins, lie-ins, etc., in commercial and public buildings.

      d. Disruption of and interference with police activities.

  8. Apprehension or fear on the part of police officers.

III. Policy Re Community Tensions and Civil Disturbances

It is the department head's responsibility to formulate sound policies that will serve as guidelines to members of his agency in their contacts with the public. It is suggested that thoughtful consideration be given to the following areas of police policy:

A. Administrative Policy

  1. This involves a stated position on the issues of police–community relations, human relations, and civil disturbances. This position would recognize the right of peaceful demonstration, and at the same time point out the responsibilities of those who demonstrate. It should contain a pledge of fair and impartial enforcement for all members of the community.

  2. Policy statements should be reduced to writing.

  3. Obtain concurrence of other city officials.

  4. Provide appropriate dissemination through;

      a. News media.

      b. Departmental orders.

      c. Staff meetings.

      (Releases to the public would consist of a statement of general principles. Material distributed to the department would be specific and detailed.)

5. Policy Inspection
   There should be an affirmative answer to each of the following questions:
   a. Is middle management selling it?
   b. Does everyone understand it?
   c. Are they demonstrating that they believe in it, and are following policy?
   d. Is someone officially designated to make such inspections and report back to the chief?

B. Organizational Policy
   1. Considerations:
      a. The size of the department and the magnitude of the problem will determine whether community relations will be an assignment for one individual, or a special unit should be formed.
      b. The person or unit should operate in a staff capacity, and should report directly to the chief.
      c. A summary of collected intelligence should be furnished the department head on a regular basis for review and analysis.
   2. Special operations dealing with civil disturbances:
      a. The field commander (designated in advance) will be in complete charge.
      b. A second-in-command and an alternate should be chosen to provide 24-hour continuity.
      c. In the event of a major disturbance, the field commander would relieve the district and/or shift commander, and would assume charge.
      d. The field commander, subject to the approval of the chief of police, would have authority to mobilize and request mutual aid.
      e. The field commander would maintain liaison for legal advice in the field with the District Attorney.
      f. The field commander would be responsible for public information releases.

C. Operational Policy for Disturbances
   1. Personnel:
      a. All personnel would be required to "report in," upon hearing announcements on radio or TV, or upon notification to their residence.
      b. An adequate supervisory ratio should be maintained.
      c. Training and re-training should be continuous.
      d. Assignment of men should be commensurate with the size and seriousness of the situation.
      e. Overtime limitations should be kept in mind in routine operations.
   2. The Field Commander:
      a. He should specify the geographical area that contains the problem and then assume complete charge of that area.
      b. Headquarters and communications should be advised of the perimeter established.
      c. The community-relations unit and headquarters will act in a staff capacity to the field commander.
   3. External Relations:

a. Policy should be preestablished that would clarify the involvement of other city departments' personnel, as well as outside law enforcement agencies.

b. The public should be kept informed but steps should be taken to keep curiosity-seekers out of the area.

4. Use of Force:

a. The use of force, particularly individual combat, should be avoided. There must be a great deal of restraint on the part of police, and when action is taken it should be by units, not individual officers.

b. Chemicals, such as smoke or tear gas, should be used only when authorized by the field commander. When it is used, there should be a more than adequate supply available at the designated location in the field. Provisions should be made for escape routes for the crowd and first aid for rioters, when requested.

c. Dogs frequently create a negative reaction in crowds when they are used for crowd control and/or arrest. They should be used only in extreme situations.

d. The use of firearms should be avoided and the practice of firing "warning shots" is not advised. The use of firearms should be considered as a last resort, and then only when necessary to protect the lives of citizens and officers.

e. Insulting language is often construed as a form of "harassment" and "brutality." Care should be given to avoiding terms and names that would antagonize the group being dealt with.

   (1) Officers should expect to receive abusive language and should avoid being baited into making imprudent remarks and/or arrests.

5. News Media:

a. A public information officer should be part of the field command staff. He should have a counterpart at headquarters (in disturbances of major proportions) to whom he will feed information as it becomes available.

b. The P.I.O. should arrange for a specific schedule for press releases and a point of dissemination. He should not deviate from this procedure unless a major event occurs.

c. The P.I.O. should act as a "buffer" between the press and the field commander, so that the commander can devote maximum time and attention to the problem.

d. Reasonable limitations should be set for the press reentry into high hazard areas. Contacts by the press with police personnel in the field, in the form of personal interviews, should be minimized. Efforts should be made to confine such interviews to the command post area, and with the approval of the officer in charge.

e. News media representatives should be required to produce bona fide credentials in order to enter the area. In major disturbances, consideration could be given to the issuance of special press cards by the P.I.O.

6. Arrests:

a. When demonstrations are known in advance, meetings should be held with the head of the organization against whom the demonstration would take place, and his counsel. Policy should be agreed upon as to at what point arrest would be in order, and that the firm or organization would be willing to prosecute.

    b. Similar meetings should be held with the leaders of the demonstrating groups. Ground rules should be formulated that both the demonstrators and police understand.

    c. Whenever possible, it should be decided in advance whether physical arrests and the bail procedure would be used, or whether arrestees could simply be released on citation or summons following the booking.

    d. Alternatives should be decided upon to handle prisoners in the event custodial facilities are saturated.

  7. Emergency Funding:

    a. Certain staff members should be authorized to sign emergency requisitions.

    b. These requisitions could be for food, lumber, gasoline, vehicle parts or repair, guns, ammunition, etc.

    c. Major purchases should be with the knowledge and approval of the logistical commander, and normally through his office.

IV. **Prevention — The Key to Coping with Community Tensions**

Experience of many law enforcement agencies indicates that most civil disturbances can be prevented, or if not prevented, their negative effects can be minimized. One of the best prevention tools is the reputation of an agency in terms of fair, impartial, and efficient law enforcement, and the knowledge that the agency possesses an interest in and knowledge of the problems of the community.

The following factors have been shown to be important in the development and maintenance of a good prevention program:

A. The Selection Process

  1. Recruiting standards at the entrance level should stress the selection of intelligent and stable individuals who react well under stress. It is most desirable to select persons:

    a. Who are able to deal effectively both in group and individual relationships.

    b. Who possess a background that helps equip them to deal with a variety of people, and changing social, cultural, and political conditions.

  2. An inventory of existing staff should be made to identify those individuals who can be assigned to important posts in sensitive areas.

B. Training and Its Role in Prevention

  1. The benefits of good training should be stressed to individual officers.

  2. Basic concepts of community relations should be covered at the recruit level. In-depth training should be administered at the in-service and re-training levels.

  3. Legal training, in addition to its normal implications, should include study of laws specifically relating to community problems and disturbances. This would include:

    a. Local and county ordinances

    b. State and Federal statutes

    c. Other laws governing public assembly, constitutional rights, etc.

4. Field tactics and techniques of self-defense should be taught as part of the continuing curriculum.
   a. Basic training should be on a department-wide basis, with provisions for periodic re-training.
   b. Special and intensive training of a continuous nature should be provided to crowd control units.
5. Decision making is difficult at all levels. An effective exercise of this skill can be developed through role-playing in problem solving sessions wherein individuals must evaluate situations and decide on courses of action.
6. Department policies and procedures are subject to change. There should be particular emphasis on keeping all personnel aware of changes or modifications relative to:
   a. Court decisions
   b. Community-relations programs
   c. Standards of conduct for officers
   d. Collecting and reporting intelligence
   e. Coping with disturbances
   f. Post-disturbance recovery
7. In order to have an effective liaison with the community, there must be good two-way communication. This can often be facilitated through training in:
   a. Understanding minority-group cultures and their problems.
   b. The importance of semantics (slang, colloquialisms, "trigger words," etc.)
   c. Developing the ability to listen and comprehend, and to speak and be understood.
   d. The need to explain (not defend) changes in enforcement policies and actions.
C. Community-Relations Programs as a Vehicle for Prevention
   1. The term "Police–Community Relations" too often is defined in narrow terms. It would appear more appropriate to refer to *all* relationships between the police and the community rather than in terms of relationships with racial minority groups. The emphasis should be on special group problems within the larger community, regardless of their nature. It would be advisable to maintain contact with *all* groups, regardless of whether or not their viewpoints are compatible with those of the department.
   2. Specialization in community relations offers advantages in all but the smallest department. Ideally, a specialized unit would deal with all relations with all the community. Its secondary purpose would be to deal with special groups within the community.
   3. Important to the formation of such a unit would be the criteria for selecting its staff. There should be assurance that those selected:
      a. Possess a sound background in general law enforcement, with a demonstrated record of good conduct, and stability.
      b. Have a record of having made *good* arrests, resulting in a high rate of convictions, with a minimum of resisting arrest charges involved.
      c. Have a suitable academic background.
      d. Have a substantiated reputation for fairness, good judgment, and an absence of any crippling bias or prejudice.

4. The head of the community-relations unit would report directly to the department head and would act in a staff capacity to the rest of the organization. At the same time it would be important to stress that members of the unit must not discard their identity and responsibilities as policemen. Regardless of how deeply involved they become in their assignment, their primary responsibilities are still to the department. There must be a correlation between their goals and objectives, and the goals and objectives of the agency they serve.

5. A continuous and effective liaison should be maintained between this unit and special-interest community groups, and the human relations commission. This bond between the police and the community can be formed by:
    a. Making good community relations the responsibility of *everyone* in the department, from the patrolman to the chief.
    b. Actively seeking out and making the acquaintance of individuals and associations, not waiting for them to "make the first move."
    c. Keeping the public fully informed.
    d. Demonstrating a continuing interest in community problems; seeking citizen reaction and advice.
    e. Being willing to listen to citizen complaints about the community, the police, the city government. Being willing to make referrals, or institute a police follow-up when appropriate.
    f. Frankly stating the police position (when there is one) on community issues, and being willing to change positions that experience and common sense indicate need modification.

6. Press relations and publicity efforts of this unit should be within the framework of departmental policy. Major releases should always be cleared with the chief of police in advance. It would be ideal to use a professional public relations man in this unit, but in any event it would be desirable to utilize a staff member with special training in journalistic and public relations techniques.

7. Program goals of the community-relations unit should be the result of extensive planning and receive department head approval before attempts are made to implement them. Generally the program goals will be to bring about better understanding and mutual trust between the community and the police. Such programs are:
    a. Those aimed at the entire community.
    b. Those designed to reach children and teenagers, in and out of school.
    c. Those designed to deal with problems presented by special groups.

D. Complaint Procedures
1. The organizational structure should be geared to accommodate the processing and disposition of citizen complaints. One satisfactory method is to:
    a. Set up specific channels and procedures.
    b. Supplement this with means of disseminating knowledge of this system to the public and members of the department.
    c. Receive complaints made about departmental policies and/or procedures, as well as against individuals.
    d. Establish procedures to insure prompt follow-up and feed-back to the complainant.

e. Have a policy to issue public statements regarding false reports that have been maliciously and intentionally filed against an officer.

2. Establish channels to receive *complaints by police officers re the public*. Make it a policy to bring these complaints to the attention of the appropriate community group and the press to generate some responsible action on their part. Complaints by officers might include:

a. Assaults on police officers.
b. Verbal abuse, provocation, "baiting."
c. Defiance of authority, interference with arrests and other police action.
d. Lack of respect for constituted authority.
e. False accusations.
f. Preferential treatment for minorities.
g. Apathy, lack of support for law and order.
h. Untrue and/or unfair treatment of police by news media.

E. Some Consequences of Poor Police–Community Relations

1. There is reduced morale, efficiency, and attention to duty in the police department. Consequently, there will probably be higher crime rates and detrimental effects on dealing with crime and delinquency generally.

2. There is reluctance on the part of the community to participate or assume responsibility in the process of law enforcement. This will result in less success in preventive and investigative police work.

3. There is an increased likelihood of abuse and injury to policemen in the field.

4. There is increased likelihood of abuse, injury, and infringement of the rights and liberties of citizens.

5. The potential for large-scale violence between the police and segments of the community is greatly increased.

Appendix B:
Prosecution, Defense, and the Police

In chapter 1, we discussed the phases of the justice process and the sequence of justice functions. Part of that discussion included the roles of prosecution and defense in the court process, as well as the relationship of the police to those functions. Here is further elaboration of some of the concepts introduced in that discussion.[1]

PROSECUTION AND POLICE DISCRETION

The prosecuting *district attorney* not only possesses a great deal of responsibility in enforcing the criminal law but *also exercises a fantastic degree of discretion in the manner in which efficient and fair law enforcement is achieved.* The decisions that he must make are numerous and often difficult; some of the most important decisions he makes occur when he exercises his power to charge or refrain from charging an individual with a crime. The decision to charge an individual with a crime and thereby subject him to the processes and sanctions of the criminal adjudication system is a very important one — especially to the person who is charged. His reputation and standing in

[1]This appendix is composed primarily of passages published earlier in A. Coffey, E. Eledefonso, and W. Hartinger, *An introduction to the Criminal Justice System and Process,* 1974. Passages from pages 26–47, 53–91, and 193–197. Reprinted by permission of Prentice-Hall, Inc., Englewood Cliffs, NJ.

the community are at stake; the process will be time consuming and expensive; and the result may ultimately involve deprivation of his physical liberty. Thus, the decision must be made with care, intelligence, and good judgment. It is impossible to set forth systematically and categorically all the factors and criteria which enter into the decision of charging an individual with a crime. However, a few of the considerations that enter into that process will be discussed in the following paragraphs.

In most jurisdictions four tests are applied in every case to determine whether a criminal complaint should be prepared. These are:

1. Has a public offense been committed?
2. Is the identity of the perpetrator known?
3. Can the offense be proved beyond a reasonable doubt?
4. Should there be a prosecution under all the circumstances of the case?

No complaint should be authorized unless each of the four questions can be answered in the affirmative.

The elementary considerations are important but are easily overlooked. It must be obvious from the police report that all the elements of the crime can be proven and that the identity of the perpetrator can also be proven. This includes such elements as knowledge, willfulness, or specific intent, which have to be proven from the circumstances presented in the evidence. Furthermore, not only must the elements be present, but the proof of such elements must also be admissable into evidence. Thus, if a crucial portion of the evidence was obtained by an illegal search and seizure, and the deputy's analysis of the case law is correct in this respect, it would be useless and a waste of valuable resources to proceed any further.

In practice, a great deal of discretion has already occurred by the time the police officer or agent from another law enforcement body presents a report to a deputy district attorney for approval. The liaison officer already has a good understanding of whether a case is likely to result in criminal prosecution because of his frequent contact with the district attorney. Cases which clearly do not merit further proceedings are disposed of at the police level and are never reviewed by the district attorney's office. The same principle applies to cases which originate in governmental agencies other than police departments. Thus, a substantial portion of the cases which are presented to deputy district attorneys are cases which merit prosecution, and a complaint is in fact issued. It is not unusual, however, for the police department to present a case to the district attorney's office with the express purpose of obtaining objective and disinterested, discretionary review of the matter by that office. This happens mainly in cases of significant public interest and in cases involving very serious crimes.

The prosecuting attorney is not the only party who uses discretion in bringing a criminal to justice. The frequency and type of arrests to be made are questions of priority. These priorities are established by local law enforcement officials. It is obvious that policemen do not arrest all people who commit offenses. Why? *Because at the grass-roots level the policeman is the party who uses discretion in deciding whether to arrest an individual.*

The policeman's job cannot be summarized as simply enforcement of the law. He is placed on the street for the purpose of preventing crime. Although the arresting officer like any other citizen is biased and prejudiced by his religious, ethnic, and social backgrounds, he must draw the thin line between morality and law in an objective manner. When the officer takes the stand under oath, he must be able to say at what point he believed he had probable cause to make an arrest. He must indicate which facts and circumstances led him to believe there was probable cause to make the arrest. The police officer, then, is an interpreter not only of *local* policy but also of the *constitutional* quagmire which protects the criminal defendant. This use of discretion is never more evident than in domestic squabbles. Also, physical and emotional restraint must be exercised during riots and insurrections. The police officer must weigh his right to arrest a trespasser against the possibility that such an arrest will cause the death or injury of numerous persons.

Courtroom Testimony

The very nature of law enforcement virtually assures the need for police to be called not only as witnesses but in many instances as "star witnesses." For this reason, it becomes necessary for police to understand the nature of courtroom testimony. *Truth,* as called for by the court, is the object of the trial. Attorneys are officers of the court and as such are charged with responsibility in seeking truth in much the same way that police are charged with keeping the peace. There are many complicated rules that govern evidence and testimony, but each rule exists for the purpose of developing truth as called for by the court. The use of these rules, however, frequently gives the impression that witnesses are being tripped up or forced to contradict themselves. But regardless of how the questions are phrased, the witness responding to cross-examination with the truth has little cause for anxiety. "Clever questions" pose relatively little threat — particularly in view of the judge's responsibility to protect the witness from the "have-you-stopped-beating-your-wife" variety of questions.

The truth, however, often incorporates far more than the question calls for — or for that matter far more than the court requires. This being the case, the witness is expected to define truth as being honest in specific answers to equally specific questions. The judge may allow a question to be asked because it does not call for answers that violate rules of evidence. The witness who gives an answer containing more information than called for may then prejudice a jury or even force the acceptable segments of testimony to be removed from evidence. This is possible even when the total response is completely true. This embarrassment, like most courtroom embarrassments, occurs primarily when uncalled-for information is volunteered by a witness forgetting that the judge and the attorneys are trying the case — not the witness.

Questions stress facts rather than opinions, and opinions will be acceptable only when the judge specifically allows. Chances are that the witnesses have been thoroughly "briefed" by the attorney in advance, thus making preparation possible. Preparation for testimony is usually not difficult, but it is always important. Fellow police officers are entitled to the good impression afforded law enforcement by a well-prepared and well-groomed police witness.

Once an officer is aware that he will appear in court, good preparation requires a careful review of notes and records relating to the case on trial. The majority of facts to which police testify are in police reports or notes. Although reference to these sources is acceptable during testimony, a better impression is made when "first-hand" responses are forthcoming. Some police confer with the prosecutor immediately prior to the court date in order to ensure sharp, concise, and straightforward testimony that inspires the court's confidence. The confident (not cocky) police witness is less likely to be subjected to prolonged or confusing cross-examination and is better able to deal with this eventuality if so subjected.

Personal appearance is another important part of preparation. Whether in uniform or civilian attire, clean, neat, and conservative clothing makes a favorable impression — as, of course, does well-trimmed hair and a clean-shaven face. Erect posture contributes further to the favorable impression. Personal conduct and demeanor becomes even more important in the court than "on the job," if that is possible. Clearly, an officer of the law who comes to court carrying a newspaper to read while waiting to testify or who causes disturbances implies disrespect for the dignity of the court. Registering surprise and disbelief at the testimony of other witnesses along with "natural" but unprofessional mannerisms do little to assure the court that police are as objective as possible.

Preparation may also entail rehearsing anticipated responses to ensure concise testimony. Deliberate effort to appear poised and impartial helps to remove the feeling the police are anxious to seek convictions no matter what. A part of such poise is an unemotional but audible and clear voice which delivers concise answers. A few examples of responsive, concise answers to an attorney's questions may prove helpful. The following suggestions may be an aid to the officer.

Testifying about Conversations. The matter of testifying in regard to conversations requires particular notice. The law requires that before a conversation can be related, the time, place, and parties present must be shown. Thus, the attorney must ask preliminary questions such as "Did you have a conversation with so and so about some matter?" Here you must not make the mistake of considering this the cue to go ahead and state the conversation; remember to state "Yes" or "No." The attorney then must ask questions to find out when and where the conversation took place and who were present. When it is finally asked that the conversation be stated, you are not to state your conclusions as to the result of the conversation; merely state what each party said as nearly as you can remember. It is realized, of course, that no witness has a photographic memory, and therefore no one is expected to state the exact words of a conversation that occurred some time in the past.

Telling Only Facts — Not Opinions. You should know that the court is only interested in facts, not opinions, conclusions, or arguments. To illustrate this point, the following are typical examples of the right and wrong ways of answering quesions. *Question:* "What was said concerning the Buick automobile?" *Wrong Form of Answer:* "We agreed that Mr. Jones would pay the cost of repairing the Buick." *Right Form of Answer:* "I said, 'The accident was your fault and you should pay the cost of repairing the Buick'; and Mr. Jones said, 'It was my fault and I will be glad to pay whatever it costs you to get it fixed.' "

Etiquette. A few suggestions as to courtroom etiquette might be helpful. Courts are the institutions which give effect to our constitutional rights and liberties and the laws of the state and nation. Without such laws and without the courts to make them effective, we would be completely uncivilized. It is, therefore, appropriate that courts should function in a dignified and somewhat formal manner; by their conduct, persons in the courtroom show and foster a feeling of respect for the laws and institutions of our state. A few little things to remember along these lines are: While court is in session, do not smoke, chew gum, eat candy, read newspapers, knit, or indulge in similar conduct which shows a casual or disrespectful attitude. Also, do not indicate by grimaces, shaking of the head, or the like reaction to a testimony of other witnesses. In conclusion, if you are a witness, remember:

Don't be nervous.

Tell the truth.

Only answer the questions.

Do not state opinions or arguments, only facts.

Speak up so you can be heard.

Be courteous.

POLICE ROLE IN PROSECUTION

The law enforcement process and the prosecution process overlap considerably. The actual police role in the court room process has already been covered. However, the specific relationship between police and prosecution deserves further consideration. One manner in which this overlapping responsibility might be presented is to review a verbatim response given by an anonymous prosecutor to the question of what a district attorney would like from police:

1. The first and most important quality is *complete honesty* regarding the facts of his case and his views concerning prosecution and possible disposition and reasons. Many officers consult us, state the facts, and then add: "I don't think it is a violation." We appreciate that and we will go along in nine out of ten cases; and if we don't we will point out why.

   Maybe his views regarding prosecution and possible disposition come from reasons that have nothing to do with the facts in the case. So what! None of us is perfectly logical all of the time.

   Example: A 77-year-old woman went through a stop sign. She is still in the hospital after four months. Should she be prosecuted?

   She should not drive a car; her own family says so—so we make a deal. We will not prosecute provided that she does not drive again and that the family will see the agreement is enforced.

   Example: A man ran into the rear of a truck, killing his wife and putting himself in the hospital for six months. Should he be prosecuted?

   This is an interesting question, and there may be a difference in your answer and mine. I don't think he should be prosecuted.

2. I like an officer who is completely honest in saying so if he thinks *he might have made a mistake* in what he did in any part of his investigation or even in the arrest.

   In 1967 it was suggested to the California Highway Patrol and all traffic officers in the county that in prosecutions for Section 502 of the Vehicle Code we be very cautious. "Be sure he's under the influence before you bring him in—then no reductions. *And* if you think you have made a mistake, come to me—I'll take care of it."

   One officer of the Highway Patrol—a very conscientious officer—came to me one day and said: "In this case I might have made a mistake regarding intoxication when I arrested the man for 501." Upon talking to the defendant about the facts of the case, he had no hesitation whatever in saying: "Oh, I was drunk as hell." We let the case go for 502. We like the conduct of that officer because it is basically honest.

3. Conversely, we do not like the conduct of an officer who has *no good reason to substantiate* his request that a 502 be dropped after *he* files it. Especially if we find out later that:
    a. The officer sold the defendant a Cadillac (between the date of arrest and the trial); or
    b. It was the officer's day off, and he asked that the case be dismissed just because it was his day off and he brought neither his report nor the blood evidence because he thought it would be dismissed.

    In both these cases, the defendants were tried and found guilty.
4. We like officers *who will listen to our side.* When the officer wants to prosecute for burglary or bad checks, sometimes we prefer to make it petty theft because we have actually tried cases in which the defendants are obviously guilty but jurors have found them "not guilty" and when asked simply say: "You filed too serious a charge; if you had made it petty theft, we would have found him guilty."
5. I like an officer who has *no exaggerated idea* that just because he has carried a gun for years he is a gun expert. It just isn't so. If he thinks so, ask him the number of riflings in the gun he now carries and the direction in which they turn. (Ninety-five out of 100 can't tell you.)

    I like the officer who, when questioned in detail about guns, says: "I'm sorry, sir. I'm not a gun expert," and leaves the subject to one who is an expert.
6. I like an officer who *learns from experience.* That same officer was asked one day about photography and the difference between hue and tone. He got a little fouled up. Then he was asked what color is black, and about that time he threw in the towel.

    I like a witness who says: "I don't know anything about photography. I just held the camera up and clicked it and this is what I got." *You don't have to be an expert, and I like an officer who makes no claim to being what he is not.*
7. I like an officer who *will admit he made a mistake.*

    A star witness for the prosecution in a murder case was the brother of the deceased. He was brought from jail in Fresno where he was held on a narcotics charge, and we were very uncertain as to how the jury would receive his testimony. But on cross-examination the defendant's attorney pointed his finger at him and said harshly: "Isn't it a fact that you started a fight at the Cherry Inn just two weeks before," and the witness gave the finest answer that he could give: "I'm sorry, sir. I did." From there on the jury took everything he said, hook, line and sinker.
8. I like officers who are friends and do *not suffer from jealousy and bitterness.*

    We have seen information withheld from us by certain officers because they were bitter and jealous as a result of the arrest having been made by other officers.
9. I like an officer who knows and understands that I expect to judge his conduct in the *light of all the circumstances,* and before I criticise him I propose to know all the facts respecting what he did and the pressure under which he was working.

    It is easy for a district attorney and others to criticize an officer. We can think about what was done for a day, a week, or a month. The officer has to act on the spot at the instant. And so in one case when I was asked, "Why don't you chew-out the officer," the answer was: "Because I'm not too sure I would have done any better myself under the same circumstances."

10. I like an officer who is a *human being and who understands* or at least thinks that I'm a human being. I'm affected by the same things that affect other people.

Once I cited a man in for stealing $500 from his employer, and when he sat down he said: "I did it. I knew I was stealing when I took it. I'm guilty; I'll plead guilty if you charge me. There's nothing else I can do, but I have a wife, and three kids. I've never been in trouble in my life before. I've got to repay the money — if you'll just give me a little time." And to date I'm proud that I did not prosecute this man because he is a respectable businessman in our community.

I think of the case of the man who came into the office at 8:15 one morning. He told about stealing from his employer — writing bum checks and a number of other things. Then he said: "Liquor is my trouble. I understand that they've good doctors at San Quentin. Would you please send me up there?"

There are many people in the world who would think that police officers and district attorneys would have a field day in such a case. Instead, this man was sent to the state hospital for a week; the doctor said there was nothing wrong with him. He was prosecuted for petty theft; he served two months in the county jail; and today he is working for one of the largest corporations in the United States, making more money than I make.

I like an officer who, in a shoplifting case, after looking into the circumstances and the background of the accused, finds things that make him say: "The family has promised to watch her very carefully, and I don't think we'll have any more trouble. If it is O.K. with you, I'll turn her over to her family."

I like such an officer because if he does that, I'm sure he is a human being.

11. I like officers *who are not auditors.* Auditors have single track, narrow-gauge minds that are completely mathematical and not human. In their work, one and one always makes two, but when we're dealing with human beings that is not always so.

12. I don't like an officer *who is a "yes" man.* If he thinks I'm wrong, I expect him to tell me so and argue it out. Discussion and argument is the best way to reach a correct conclusion.

I have a particular affection for one of the officers on the highway patrol, and I'm sure that the only reason is that whenever he comes in I know I'm in for a good argument. Whether it be on the subject of yielding a right-of-way or on the subject of county permits for overloading, there is bound to be a good argument.

If an officer thinks one of the deputies in our office is wrong, he is welcome to come and see me. We don't claim our deputies know it all any more than I do. If I think one of them is wrong, I don't mind saying so — just as they'll tell me if they think I'm wrong.

13. I like an officer who understands *that he and I are on the same ball team; that his job is my job; that he is my police officer and I am his district attorney; that when he does something that is good and nice I'm proud of him and I'm proud to say so;* and that when he does something that is not good and not nice, I'm ashamed.

It is a great satisfaction to me that in the last ten years there has been a great improvement in the officers in our county. It gives me a very pleasant feeling to have citizens relate to me the things they have done and then add: "You know, that officer was so nice about it; I sure felt like a heel."

14. I like an officer who understands that he is going *to be accused of improper conduct.* (It is part of the business.) The best defense is sometimes a strong offense. And if the accusations are made to me, I would like to talk to him about

it. He's presumed to be innocent just like anybody else, and I know from sheer experience that 98 out of 100 accusations against officers are false. If I can find the accusation to be false, I'll be happy; if it be true, I should like some mitigation.

One investigator in our office is there entirely as a result of complaints made against him by citizens. The first time they complained I paid no attention. (I'm used to it.) The second time, very much the same—like water off a duck's back. The third time I was getting tired of listening so I asked the officer to come up. His conduct and his answers to the accusations caused me to say: "Next time I need an investigator he's my man." Frequently the best way to judge a man is to see how he acts under the fire of accusation.

15. I like an officer who realizes that *I'm going to be accused of this and that and who'll give me the same benefit of same reasonable doubt, and if there's any question he wants to ask about it let him ask me—we'll discuss it fully.* I have been accused of selling out many times—I know that—but by the same caliber of people who in one breath say I sold out, and in the next breath (and sometimes in the next case) say I paid witnesses to testify for the prosecution.

16. *I like officers to know that they can ask me and the deputies in our office about their cases and their dispositions any time, and we'll tell them.* We should do that anyway. We will not get the impression that they are nosy, because it is the officer's case and he is entitled to know.

17. I like an officer who can *take a licking when he does not have it coming; one who can lose a good case and not moan;* one who is *big enough to understand that maybe the court or the jury sees qualities and characteristics in the defendant that we can't see;* one who *understands* that even though a guilty man goes free, we are still administering justice and that justice is not only just what we think it is but that sometimes others have a different idea.

I like a man *who can lose a good case and then proceed to work hard and efficiently and well on the preparation of the next case.*

18. I like an officer who will *not* close the case just as soon as the defendant says: "I did it." We have been fooled too many times by defendants changing their minds, and when we're put on our proof we are short.

I like an officer who, after the defendant says: "I did it," will say to the defendant: "Prove it," and then gather up all the proof and preserve it.

19. I like an officer who can take the witness stand and by *his conduct and his manner* and by his answers make a cold chill of pride run down my spine that tells me something like this: "That's a real police officer. He's my police officer and I'm proud of him and all he's done in this case."

I like an officer who by *his conduct and his manner* and the handling of himself in the courtroom and on the witness stand forces me to express my pride to the jury, because that same cold chill of pride that runs down my spine can also affect people on the jury, and if it does, I've got them in the palm of my hand.

20. To have officers like that—who have these qualifications—is one of the finer compensations of being a district attorney. The salary I get is only a small part of my pay. *The big dividends are in the form of many satisfactions of duties well done, and if my officers have done their duties well it makes it so easy for me to do mine.*

PRESERVATION OF EVIDENCE

Since the nature of evidence is persuasive, anything that tends to weaken the persuasive quality of evidence becomes an important consideration for the prosecutor. This consideration is in part reponsible for the many rules designed to "preserve" evidence until the time of trial. What is meant by the technical term *preservation* is the retention of the persuasive quality of evidence.

Recalling that judges and juries do not witness the crimes being tried, we recognize that a defendant's guilt is largely a matter of proof—proof assessed by the prosecutor in determining whether to prosecute. One thing a prosecutor must consider is the degree of accuracy that the evidence reflects. In some cases the evidence is gathered in such a way that there is an inherent question as to how well it has been protected or preserved. (This is also known as "proof of the chain.") The following example, though exaggerated for purposes of illustration, reflects in part some of the problems of protecting and preserving evidence:

> Officer A arrests a suspected narcotics peddler in the early morning and, before going off duty, places on the desk of a narcotics detective an envelope containing what Officer A believes to be heroin. This evidence has a note instructing the narcotics detail to have the contents analyzed.
>
> Officer B makes a similar arrest on another patrol beat and follows the same procedure—using the same narcotic detective's desk.
>
> On arriving at work the narcotics detective finds the janitor picking the two envelopes up from the floor where they had been allegedly pushed by the dusting cloth of the cleaning lady.
>
> Nothing more is thought of the situation until the crime lab declares the contents of one envelope to be baking soda, the contents of the other envelope to be heroin.
>
> An investigator for the prosecutor's office then determines that the janitor is the brother of Officer A's suspect, and the cleaning lady to be the wife of Suspect B.
>
> Further discovery is made that the cleaning lady is divorcing Suspect B.

The prosecutor must now wonder whether the janitor changed the contents of one of the envelopes to protect his brother. Perhaps, the cleaning lady switched the envelopes after learning what the janitor had done because of guilt feelings over divorcing Suspect B; or perhaps she inserted heroin in a soda filled envelope to ensure Suspect B's conviction prior to the divorce. The prosecutor must wonder also if the janitor misjudged the cleaning lady's motives and made an inappropriate switch himself. Or for that matter, did someone completely unknown tamper with the evidence that had been left completely unprotected on the detective's desk?

Of course, a little common sense would prevent all of the implied problems from developing in the first place. These problems, nevertheless, represent very real *kinds* of difficulties encountered in protecting and preserving evidence. In regard to the importance of knowing the many rules for preserving evidence, one fact emerges: The quality of the evidence is no greater than how well it has been preserved. Since the function of the evidence is to persuade, evidence of marginal quality becomes virtually valueless to the prosecutor.

EYEWITNESS

The testimony of witnesses who have allegedly observed the actual commission of crime is subject to many of the same complicated rules governing *circumstantial* evidence. In terms of *materiality* and *relevance,* however, the testimony of eyewitnesses can be greatly simplified. Of course the laws and procedures that apply to eyewitnesses are essentially the same as those applying to all witnesses. The eyewitness has been selected here for clarity.

Exhibits and testimony about circumstances frequently evoke lengthy legal discussions regarding the immateriality or relevance of such evidence. But the eyewitness testimony relating to an observed crime is rarely challenged on the grounds of either materiality or relevance. When the testimony of an eyewitness is challenged, it is usually in terms of how competent or how valid the testimony may be. These questions, when raised, deal with the credibility of an eyewitness. Efforts to challenge the credibility of a witness is known as *impeachment.* Impeachment is based on an assertion that, for one reason or another, the witness cannot be believed.

Impeachment does not necessarily imply that the witness lies; in many instances it simply means that the witness's perception and/or memory are not reliable. Attempts to impeach any witness, but particularly the eyewitness, are actually efforts to reverse the persuasion of the evidence being offered. Attempts to impeach should be based on examples of unreliability. For example, the nearsighted witness testifying to incidents allegedly observed at some distance without his glasses may be challenged as unreliable. Observations supposedly made in poor lighting (as in the case of identifying a suspect) are also frequently challenged.

Impeachment might also include exploring the relationship between the defendant and the witness in terms of matters that would motivate particular styles of testimony. Financial matters, accumulated anger, and other motivational factors are often introduced into the court process is an effort to *impeach* a witness. A prosecutor must anticipate this when determining whether available witnesses will ultimately persuade of guilt or innocence.

ADMISSIBILITY

Although the range of appropriate evidence available to prosecutors varies widely in different jurisdictions, there is nonetheless some consistency in the rules for determining what evidence can be admitted. Rules governing the types of evidence that a prosecutor might use are more often than not measured against the two standards already discussed: *relevance* and *materiality.* In addition to these two standards, there are also complex rules systems and controls that have been created by Supreme Court interpretations of the Constitution.

In light of the many complicated rules involved in admissibility, even a valid confession requires considerable scrutiny on the part of the prosecutor before making the decision to utilize this as part of his persuasive approach. For even an apparently valid confession may not be admissable for a wide variety of reasons that are often very technical. An example would be "privileged communication" which allows a defendant to confess to his clergyman or psychiatrist without being in jeopardy of repeating the confession in testimony. A few of the restrictions on confessions might be considered.

CRIMINAL DEFENSES

It should be noted that many Western civilizations have been faced with the problem of crime long before the causes of crime were studied. This, of necessity, caused the criminal law and its specific defenses to evolve primarily in terms of "self-determinism."

LACK OF CAPACITY[2]

When a criminal defense hinges on the question of *capacity*, one of the following issues is customarily cited as the specific basis:

1. *Insanity:* Most jurisdictions distinguish between insanity at the time of the trial and insanity at the time of the alleged crime. Confusions sometimes arise in that a person judged insane at the time of the trial cannot be held criminally responsible until such time as he is sufficiently "sane" to "appreciate" the punishment for the crime — even though evidence indicates he was "sane" at the time of the criminal act.

   In determining insanity at the time of the criminal act, virtually all courts used the legal test known as the M'Naghten Rule.[3] In effect, this 1843 precedent causes the court to attempt to ascertain if the accused at the time of the act was "laboring under such a defect of reason or from disease of the mind as not to know the nature and quality of the act which he was doing, or if he did know it, then he did not know what he was doing was wrong."

   Many of the widely publicized legal entanglements in criminal trials in which the defense of insanity is used hinge on the distinctions of *nature and quality* along with the interpretation of the words *right and wrong.*

   Usually, in some criminal court jurisdictions, there are additional insanity defense pleas far more directly related to behavioral science explanations of crime causes. Two of the better known of these variations are the "irresistable impulse"[4] and the "delusion defense."[5] When such defenses are invoked, the psychiatric and sociological considerations invariably became a great deal more involved than simply ascertaining the question of "right and wrong" (refer to the M'Naghten Rule).

[2]75 *American Law Review* 265, 1ALR 965, 973, 3.

[3]45 *American Law Review* 2nd, 1451; 45 ALR 2nd 1452, 3. (M'Naghten was supplemented by the "irresistable impulse" doctrine, 1 ALR Fed 965).

[4]70 *American Law Review* 663, 70 ALR 675.

[5]74 *American Law Review* 266; see also the Durham Test explained in 1 ALR Fed 965, 979, 4.

2. *Idiocy:* When using the question of capacity as a defense in a criminal trial, most jurisdictions distinguish between the category of idiot and insane. Idiots are deemed to be those persons who never had "mental capacity" in the first place, whereas an insane person "lost" his capacity through mental disease.[6] The impact of behavioral science on this particular criminal defense is usually related to determining what degree of feeble-mindedness is necessary to establish idiocy. Such distinctions as "morons" or "imbeciles" are often cited in these psychological classifications.

3. *Intoxication and Narcosis:* In the majority of criminal court jurisdictions, the voluntary use of alcohol or narcotics is not permitted as a defense regardless of how much one's capacity is inhibited by intoxication or narcosis. In some instances, however, the specific issue of *intent* to commit a criminal act can be somewhat mitigated by intoxication.[7] As an example of such mitigation, a completely inebriated person presumably could not form the required premeditation and deliberation to commit first-degree murder even though he would be convictable of involuntary manslaughter since no *intent* is required in the latter.

4. *Mistake of Fact:* Most jurisdictions permit a defense in which the accused person's *intent* was motivated by variations in facts.[8] This is technically not a defense, but an example of such mistake of fact presented in a court might be the following: A man and woman walking down the street are attacked by a vicious dog. The man, woman, and dog are entangled in a struggle on the ground when a well-meaning passerby surmises that a girl and her dog are being attacked by a rapist. With such mistaken fact, the girl's benefactor slays the supposed rapist, only to find himself accused of murder. The important point in mistakes of fact is that they defend only against the presence of intent.

5. *Consent:* In jurisdictions that define a *crime* as an act performed "without consent of the victim," proof of the victim's consent is customarily permitted as a defense.[9] Examples of situations of this nature are such crimes as rape and certain forms of theft. Of course, such a criminal defense is invalid where further evidence indicates that such consent was induced through some form of intimidation.

   This particular form of criminal defense, along with those to follow, are clearly less related to the causal factors of the behavioral sciences.

6. *Entrapment:* When a person accused of crime is able to prove that he was in some way induced to commit an illegal act and had no intention of doing so, the law customarily permits a criminal defense known as entrapment.[10] This is not to say that every person responding to an offer to commit a crime is entitled to plead entrapment. An undercover police officer successfully purchasing narcotics from a suspected seller has not entrapped the defendant. The actual test is determining whether or not the crime originated in the mind of the defendant. As discussed elsewhere in this text, this introduces certain aspects of the defendant's previous conduct.

[6]44 *American Law Review* 586 (mental incompetence).

[7]22 *American Law Review* 3rd, 1228 (1st degree murder).

[8]Technically, mistake of fact is not a defense from strict liability of offense; for the reason of its functional use, see 61 *American Law Review.* 1158.

[9]52 *American Law Review* 2nd, 1181.

[10]69 *American Law Review* 2nd, 1439, 3.

7. Coercion and Duress: In much the same manner as entrapment reduces the accused person's responsibility for a criminal act, evidence of coercion or duress is also acceptable in criminal defenses in most jurisdictions. Such evidence customarily needs to demonstrate that the accused person acted under fear of immediate physical harm or threat of future injury to himself or his property.

Coercion and duress as a defense become complicated on the issue of severity— the degree of intimidation involved.[11]

8. *Justification:* The term *justification* when used in the legal context acquires a technically different meaning than the "psychological and environmental justifications" reviewed in Chapter 4. Although the criminal defense known as *justification* is frequently related to the term *justifiable homocide,* there are generally three technical categories of justification: (a) defense of property;[12] (b) defense of another or other persons;[13] and (c) defense of self.[14]

Law enforcement agencies become involved in the various forms of "defense of property" more often than not through one's "defense of habitation" (the owner or occupant defending his dwelling). Another instance frequently involving the law enforcement segment of the criminal justice process is an intended victim resisting force in a robbery.

The category of "defense of others" is permitted in criminal court under certain conditions but only insofar as the defendant exerted the degree of force which he might have exercised in defense of himself. The similarity between this category of defense and the previously discussed mistake-of-fact defense is noteworthy.

The most common form of justification in the criminal justice system is the category of "self-defense." This relates to the legal provision that "one is privileged to use whatever force is reasonably necessary to prevent a physical invasion of his person by another where he knows or reasonably believes that such invasion is imminent." The degree of force legally available in defending one's self is restricted by the degree of force that is imminent. One could not kill another in self-defense unless it was reasonable to assume that one was about to be killed. The law customarily imposes a "duty to retreat" which in effect requires one to make every effort to avoid the assault before acting in self-defense.

9. *Double Jeopardy:*[15] When a defendant is placed on trial for an offense for which he has already been tried by another court *having jurisdiction,* that defendant is permitted to plead a defense known as "former jeopardy." Numerous legal technicalities complicate the actual plea in this particular defense and relate to the manner in which the original trial was terminated.

As an example, a trial terminated by dismissing a jury *without* consent of the accused permits the accused to claim a "double jeopardy" at any subsequent trial for the same offense. Conversely, if a convicted defendant successfully appeals or motions for a new trial, he cannot then claim that the first trial was former jeopardy.

---

[11]40 *American Law Review* 2nd, 910, 2 (wife coercion by husband, 4ALR 277, 71ALR 1118).

[12]25 *American Law Review* 547, 32 ALR 1541.

[13]46 *American Law Review* 904 (officer arrest).

[14]53 *American Law Review* 486.

[15]*American Law Review* 3rd. 874 (former jeopardy is basis of *habeas corpus*); see also: 8 ALR 2nd 285 and 21 ALR 2nd 1158.

DEFENSE AND BEHAVIOR SCIENCE

A number of other considerations dealing with *defense* may also be considered. Even though the law itself does not provide defenses beyond those already discussed in this chapter, defense attorneys are increasingly making use of behavioral approaches toward mitigating the severity of the offender's *intent* to commit a crime. Put another way, defense tactics increasingly include a behavioralistic explanation of an offender's conduct in order to mitigate the self-determined implications discussed early in Chapter 4. A brief consideration of some of these possible uses of behavioral science might be useful.

Consider for example *sociology*. Utilizing the implications of cultural approach, a defense might contend that an offender exposed to cultural patterns where there is conflict between legitimate and illegitimate means is grossly influenced by that environment, and therefore his *intent* to commit crime is partially mitigated. "Differential association" could similarly be cast in the role of mitigating an offender's intent. The discussion of families in Chapter 4 is also readily adaptable to forming an influence on an offender's *intent* to commit crime. Indeed virtually every consideration discussed under the subtitle "Social Approach" is adaptable to this kind of defense.

The "psychological approach" has virtually boundless implications in terms of an offender's *intent*.[16] To whatever degree such considerations are permissible in the criminal trial, possibilities exist in the id, ego, and superego, along with the various body shapes and biochemical influences already discussed. Certainly the heredity factors presented are at least as germane as the other causative considerations.

Probably the most significant consideration in relating criminal defense to the behavioral sciences is the concept of *intent*. The paradox of "determinism" and "self-determinism" forever impinges in a justice system in a free society. Simply stated, if in fact behavioral science explanations of the cause of crime serve as a defense, then people are neither responsible or accountable for the crimes they commit. The alternative extreme, that of complete "self-determinism," promises to regress justice thousands of years to the point where offenders were summarily executed without regard to mitigating circumstances. The American criminal justice system finds itself somewhere in between these extremes. As continuing adjustments are made, criminal defense continues to play a vital role.

DEFENSE AND PROSECUTION

Procedurally, there is a great deal in common between defense and prosecution. As seen in the preceding chapter, the prosecution concerns itself with *persuasion*. Adequate defense also requires great understanding of the principles of persuasion — proof, logic, inductive or deductive reasoning, and so forth. Like the prosecution the defense must be concerned with syllogisms, inferences, and many other tools of the logician. Both defense and prosecution must be expert in proof, evidence, and the wide range of related matters. Court procedures and methods are also of mutual concern.

Certainly materiality and relevance of evidence concern defense as much as prosecution. Witnesses, exhibits, and the preservation of evidence are equally related to criminal defense and prosecution.

[16]Paul W. Tappan, *Contemporary Corrections.* New York: McGraw-Hill, 1951, p. 21.

Appendix C:
United States Constitution
Sections Related
to Law Enforcement

In Chapter 3 we discussed the impact on police of the United States Constitution. Here are a few of the Sections that relate to that discussion.

ARTICLE I (LEGISLATIVE DEPARTMENT)

Section 7: Mode of Passing Laws

[*Special Provision as to Revenue Laws*] All bills for raising revenue shall originate in the House of Representatives, but the Senate may propose or concur with amendments as on other bills.

[*Laws, How Enacted*] every bill which shall have passed the House of Representatives and the Senate, shall, before it becomes a law, be presented to the President of the United States; if he approves, he shall sign it, but if not, he shall return it, with his objections, to that House in which it originated, who shall enter the objections at large on their journal, and proceed to consider it. If, after such consideration, two thirds of that House shall agree to pass the bill, it shall be sent, together with objections, to the other House, by which it shall likewise be reconsidered, and if approved by two-thirds of that House it shall become a law. But in all such cases the votes of both Houses shall be determined by yeas and nays; and the names of the persons voting for and against the bill shall be entered on the journal of each House respectively. If any bill shall not be returned by the President within ten days (Sundays excepted) after it shall have been presented to him, the same shall be a law, in like manner as if he had signed it, unless the Congress, by their adjournment, prevent its return, in which case it shall not be a law.

[*Same Rules Apply to Resolutions*] Every order, resolution, or vote, to which the concurrence of the Senate and the House of Representatives may be necessary (except on a question of adjournment), shall be presented to the President of the United States; and, before the same shall take effect, shall be approved by him, or disapproved by him, shall be repassed by two thirds of the Senate and House of Representatives, according to the rules and limitations prescribed in the case of a bill.

Section 8: Powers Granted to Congress

[*Coin*] To coin money, regulate the value thereof and of foreign coins, and fix the standard of weights and measures.

[*Counterfeiting*] To provide for the punishment of counterfeiting the securities and current coin of the United States.

[*Courts*] To constitute tribunals inferior to the Supreme Court.

[*Piracies*] To define and punish piracies and felonies committed on the high seas, and offenses against the laws of nations.

[*Federal District and Other Places*] To exercise exclusive legislation, in all cases whatsoever, over such district (not exceeding ten miles square) as may, by cession of particular States, and the acceptance of Congress, become the seat of government of the United States, and to exercise like authority over all places purchased by the consent of the Legislature of the State in which the same shall be, for the erection of forts, magazines, arsenals, dockyards, and other needful buildings.

[*Make Laws to Carry Out Foregoing Powers*] To make all laws which shall be necessary and proper for carrying into execution the foregoing powers, and all other powers vested by this Constitution in the Government of the United States, or in any department, or officer thereof.

Section 9: Limitations on Powers Granted to the United States

[*Habeas Corpus*] The privilege of the writ of habeas corpus shall not be suspended, unless when, in cases of rebellion or invasion, the public safety may require it.

[*Ex Post Facto Law*] No bill of attainder or ex post facto law shall be passed.

[*Direct Taxes*] No capitation, or other direct, tax shall be laid, unless in proportion to the census or enumeration hereinbefore directed to be taken.

ARTICLE III (JUDICIAL DEPARTMENT)

[*Courts—Terms of Office and Salary of Judges*] The judicial power of the United States shall be vested in one Supreme Court, and in such inferior courts as the Congress may from time to time ordain and establish. The judges, both of the supreme and inferior courts, shall hold their offices during good behavior, and shall, at stated times, receive for their services a compensation which shall not be diminished during their continuance in office.

Section 2: Jurisdiction of United States Courts

[*Cases that May Come Before United States Courts*] The judicial power shall extend to all cases, in laws and equity, arising under this Constitution, the laws of the United States, and treaties made, or which shall be made under their authority; to all cases affecting ambassadors, other public ministers, and consuls; to all cases of admiralty and maritime jurisdiction; to controversies to which the United States shall be a party; to controversies between two or more States (between a state and citizens of another state—restricted by the eleventh Amendment; between citizens of different States; between citizens of the same State claiming lands under grants of different States; and between a State, or the citizens thereof, and foreign states, citizens or subjects.

[*Jurisdiction of Supreme and Appellate Courts*] In all cases affecting ambassadors, other public ministers, and consuls, and those in which a State shall be a party, the Supreme Court shall have original jurisdiction. In all other cases before mentioned the Supreme Court shall have appellate jurisdiction, both as to law and fact, with such exceptions and under such regulations as the Congress shall make.

[*Trial of Crimes*] The trial of all crimes, except in cases of impeachment, shall be by jury; and such trials shall be held in the State where said crimes shall have been committed; but when not committed within any State, the trial shall be put at such place or places as the Congress may, by law, have directed. (Extended by the Fifth, Sixth, Seventh, and Eighth Amendments.

Section 3: Treason

[*Treason Defined*] Treason against the United States shall consist only in levying war against them, or in adhering to their enemies, giving them aid and comfort.

[*Conviction*] No person shall be convicted of treason, unless on the testimony of two witnesses to the same overt act, or on confession in open court.

[*Punishment*] The Congress shall have power to declare the punishment of treason; but no attainder of treason shall work corruption of blood, or forfeiture except during the life of the person attained.

ARTICLE IV (THE STATES AND THE FEDERAL GOVERNMENT)

Section 2: Citizens – Fugitives

[*Interstate Privileges of Citizens*] The citizens of each State shall be entitled to all the privileges and immunities of citizens in the several States. (Extended by the Fourteenth Amendment.)

[*Fugitives From Justice*] A person charged in any State with treason, felony, or other crime, who shall flee from justice and be found in another State shall, on demand of the executive authority of the State from which he fled, be delivered up, to be removed to the State having jurisdiction of the crime.

[*Fugitives From Service*] No person held to service or labor in one State, under the laws thereof, escaping into another, shall in consequence of any law or regulation therein, be discharged from such service or labor, but shall be delivered up on claim of the party to whom such service or labor may be due. (Superseded, as to slaves, by the Thirteenth Amendment.)

AMENDMENTS

ARTICLE I (RESTRICTIONS ON POWERS OF CONGRESS)

Section 1: Further Protection of Citizens' Rights

[*Freedom of Religion, Speech and Press*] Congress shall make no law respecting an establishment of religion, or prohibiting the free exercise thereof, or abridging the freedom of speech or of the press; or the right of the people peaceably to assemble, and to petition the Government for a redress of grievances.

ARTICLE II (RIGHT TO BEAR ARMS)

Section 1: Security of States

[*State Militia*] A wellregulated militia being necessary to the security of a free State, the right of the people to keep and bear arms, shall not be infringed.

ARTICLE III (BILLETING OF SOLDIERS)

Section 1: In Peace — In War

[*By Consent or Law Only*] No soldier shall, in time of peace, be quartered in any house without the consent of the owner; nor in time of war, but in a manner to be prescribed by law.

ARTICLE IV (SEIZURES, SEARCHES, AND WARRANTS)

Section 1: Respect for Privacy and Property

[*Rights and Regulations*] The right of the people to be secure in their persons, houses, papers, and effects, against unreasonable searches and seizures shall not be violated, and no warrants shall issue but upon reasonable cause, supported by oath or affirmation, and particularly describing the place to be searched and the person or things to be seized.

ARTICLE V (CRIMINAL PROCEEDINGS, CONDEMNATION OF PROPERTY)

Section 1: Capital Crimes — Compensation

[*Grand Jury Indictment*] No person shall be held to answer for a capital or otherwise infamous crime, unless on a presentment or indictment of a Grand Jury, except in crimes arising in the land or naval forces, or in the militia, when in actual service in time of war or public danger; nor shall any person be subject for the same offense to be twice put in jeopardy of life or limb; nor shall be compelled in any criminal case to be a witness against himself; nor be deprived of life, liberty, or property, without due process of law; nor shall private property be taken for public use without just compensation.

ARTICLE VI (MODE OF TRIAL IN CRIMINAL PROCEEDINGS)

Section 1: Right to Speedy Trials

[*Witnesses*] In all criminal proceedings the accused shall enjoy the right to a speedy and public trial, by an impartial jury of the State and district wherein the crime shall have been committed, which district shall have previously ascertained by law, and to be informed of the nature and cause of the accusation; to be confronted with the witnesses against him; to have compulsory process for obtaining witnesses in his favor, and to have assistance of counsel for his defense.

ARTICLE VIII (BAILS-FINES-PUNISHMENTS)

Section 1: In Moderation

[*Safeguard Against Excessiveness*] Excessive bail shall not be required, nor excessive fines imposed, nor cruel and unusual punishments inflicted.

ARTICLE IX (CERTAIN RIGHTS NOT DENIED TO THE PEOPLE)

Section 1: Constitutional Interpretation

[*Respect for Others' Rights*] The enumeration in the Constitution of certain rights shall not be construed to deny or disparage others retained by the people.

ARTICLE XIII (SLAVERY)

Section 1: Involuntary Servitude

[*Abolition — Exception*] Neither slavery nor involuntary servitude, except as a punishment for crime whereof the party shall have been duly convicted, shall exist within the United States, or any place subject to their jurisdiction.

ARTICLE XIV (CITIZENSHIP, REPRESENTATION, AND PAYMENT OF PUBLIC DEBT)

Section 1: Citizenship

[*Equal Protection*] All Persons born or naturalized in the United States and subject to the jurisdiction thereof, are citizens of the United States and of the States wherein they reside. No State shall make or enforce any laws which shall abridge the privileges or immunities of citizens of the United States; nor shall any State deprive any person of life, liberty, or property, without due process of law, nor deny to any person within its jurisdiction the equal protection of the laws.

Appendix D:
Supreme Court Decisions
Related to Law Enforcement

In Chapters 3 and 7, we discussed the significance of Supreme Court decisions and the Common Law heritage of court precedents. Here are excerpts from some of the major decisions that illustrate those concepts.

ESCOBEDO V. ILLINOIS

The critical question in this case is whether, under the circumstances, the refusal by the police to honor petitioner's request to consult with his lawyer during the course of an interrogation constitutes a denial of "the Assistance of Counsel" in violation of the Sixth Amendment to the Constitution as "made obligatory upon the States by the Fourteenth Amendment," *Gideon* v. *Wainwright,* and thereby renders inadmissable in a state criminal trial any incriminating statement elicited by the police during the interrogation.

On the night of January 19, 1960, petitioner's brother-in-law was fatally shot. At 2:30 A.M. that morning, petitioner was arrested and interrogated. Petitioner made no statement to the police . . . was released at 5 P.M. that afternoon pursuant to a state court writ of habeas corpus obtained by . . . a lawyer.

On January 30, Benedict DiGerlando, who was then in police custody and who was later indicted for the murder along with petitioner, told the police that petitioner had fired the fatal shots. Between 8 and 9 P.M. that evening, petitioner and his sister, the widow of the deceased, were arrested and taken to police headquarters. Enroute to the police station, the police . . . "told defendant that DiGerlando had named him as the one who shot" the deceased. Petitioner testified, without contradiction, that the "detectives had us pretty well, up pretty tight, and we might as well admit to this crime," and that he replied, "I am sorry but I would like to have advice from my lawyer." A police officer testified that although petitioner was not formally charged "he was in custody" and couldn't "walk out the door."

Shortly after petitioner reached police headquarters, his retained lawyer arrived. The lawyer described the ensuing events in the following terms: "I went to the Detective Bureau at 11th and State. The first person I talked to was the Sergeant on duty at the Bureau Desk . . . I asked the Sergeant (on duty) for permission to speak to my client, Danny Escobedo. . . . The Sergeant made a call to the Bureau lockup and informed me that the boy had been taken from the lockup to the Homicide Bureau. This was between 9:30 and 10:00 in the evening. Before I went anywhere, he called the Homicide Bureau and told them there was an attorney waiting to see Escobedo. He told me I could not see him. Then I went upstairs to the Homicide Bureau. There were several Homicide Detectives around and I talked to them. I identified myself as Escobedo's attorney and asked permission to see him. They said I could not. . . . The police officer told me to see Chief Flynn who was on duty. I identified myself to Chief Flynn and asked permission to see my client. He said I could not. The door was open and I could see through the office. . . . I waved to him and he waved back and then the door was closed by one of the officers at Homicide. There were four or five officers milling around the Homicide Detail that night. As to whether I talked to Captain Flynn any later that day, I waited around for another hour or two and went back again and renewed request to see my client. He again told me I could not. . . . I filed an official complaint with Commissioner Phelan of the Chicago Police Department. I had a conversation with every police officer I could find. I was told at Homicide that I couldn't see him and I would have to get a writ of habeas corpus."

Petitioner testified that during the course of the interrogation he repeatedly asked to speak to his lawyer and that the police said that his lawyer "didn't want to see" him. The testimony of the police officers confirmed these accounts in substantial detail.

Notwithstanding repeated requests by each, petitioner and his retained lawyer were afforded no opportunity to consult during the course of the entire interrogation. At one point, as previously noted, petitioner and his attorney came into each other's view for a few moments but the attorney was quickly ushered away. A police officer testified that he had told the lawyer that he could not see petitioner until "we were through interrogating" him.

It is undisputed that during the course of the interrogation Officer Montejano, who "grew up" in petitioner's neighborhood, who knew his family, and uses "Spanish language [when necessary in] police work," conferred alone with petitioner. Petitioner testified that the officer said to him "in Spanish that my sister and I could go home if I pinned it on Benedict DiGerlando," that "he would see to it that we could go home and be held only as witnesses, if anything, if we made a statement against DiGerlando."

Petitioner testified that he made the statement in issue because of this assurance. Officer Montejano denied offering any such assurance.

Petitioner moved both before and during trial to suppress the incriminating statement, but the motions were denied. Petitioner was convicted of murder and he appealed the conviction.

[The Supreme Court of Illinois, on rehearing, found the confession voluntary and affirmed the conviction.]

In *Massiah* v. *United States,* this Court observed that "a Constituion which guarantees a defendant the aid of counsel at . . . trial could surely vouchsafe no less to an indicted defendant under interrogation by the police in a completely extra-judicial proceeding. Anything less . . . might deny a defendant effective representation by counsel at the only stage when legal aid and advice would help him."

The interrogation here was conducted before petitioner was formally indicted. But in the context of this case, that fact should make no difference. When petitioner requested, and was denied, an opportunity to consult with his lawyer, the investigation had ceased to be a general investigation of "an unsolved crime." *Spano* v. *New York.* Petitioner had become the accused, and the purpose of the interrogation was to "get him" to confess his guilt despite his constitutional right not to do so. At the time of his arrest and throughout the course of the interrogation, the police told petitioner that they had convincing evidence that he had fired the fatal shots. Without informing him of his absolute right to remain silent in the face of this accusation, the police urged him to make a statement. As this Court observed many years ago;

"It cannot be doubted that, placed in the position in which the accused was when the statement was made to him that the other suspected person had charged him with a crime, the result was to produce upon his mind the fear that, if he remained silent, it would be considered an admission of guilt, and therefore render certain his being committed for trial as the guilty person, and it cannot be conceived that the converse impression would not also have naturally arisen that, by denying, there was hope of removing the suspicion from himself." *Bram* v. *United States.* Petitioner, a layman, was undoubtedly unaware that under Illinois law an admission of "mere" complicity in the murder plot was legally as damaging as an admission of firing the fatal shots. The "guiding hand of counsel" was essential to advise petitioner of his rights in this delicate situation. *Powell* v. *Alabama.* This was the "stage when legal aid and advice" were most critical to petitioner. *Massiah* v. *United States.* It was a stage surely as critical as was the arraignment in *Hamilton* v. *Alabama* and the preliminary hearing in *White* v. *Maryland.* What happened at this interrogation could certainly "affect the whole trial," *Hamilton* v. *Alabama* and the preliminary hearing in *White* v. *Maryland.* What happened at this interrogation could certainly "affect the whole trial," *Hamilton* v. *Alabama,* since rights "may be as irretrievably lost, if not then and there asserted, as they are when an accused represented by counsel waives a right for strategic purposes." It would exalt form over substance to make the right to counsel, under these circumstances, depend on whether at the time of the interrogation, the authorities had secured a formal indictment. Petitioner had, for all practical purposes, already been charged with murder.

It is argued that if the right to counsel is afforded prior to indictment, the number of confessions obtained by the police will diminish significantly, because most confessions are obtained during the period between arrest and indictment, and "any lawyer worth his salt will tell the suspect in no uncertain terms to make no statement to police under any circumstances." *Watts* v. *Indiana*. This argument, of course, cuts two ways. The fact that many confessions are obtained during this period points up its critical nature as a "stage when legal aid and advice" are surely needed. The right to counsel would indeed be shallow if it began at a period when few confessions were obtained. There is necessarily a direct relationship between the importance of a stage to the police in their quest for a confession and the criticality of that stage to the accused in his need for legal advice. Our Constitution, unlike some others, strikes the balance in favor of the right of the accused to be advised by his lawyer of his privilege against self-incrimination.

We have learned from history that no system of criminal justice can, or should, survive if it comes to depend for its continued effectiveness on the citizens' abdication through unawareness of their constitutional rights. No system worth preserving should have to *fear* that if an accused is permitted to consult with a lawyer, he will become aware of, and exercise, these rights. If the exercise of constitutional rights will thwart the effectiveness of a system of law enforcement, then there is something very wrong with that system.

We hold, therefore, that where, as here, the investigation is no longer a general inquiry into an unsolved crime but has begun to focus on a particular suspect, the suspect has been taken into police custody, the police carry out a process of interrogations that lends itself to eliciting incriminating statements, the suspect has requested and been denied an opportunity to consult with his lawyer, and the police have not effectively warned him of his absolute constitutional right to remain silent, the accused has been denied the "Assistance of Counsel" in violation of the Sixth Amendment to the Constitution as "made obligatory upon the States by the Fourteenth Amendment," *Gideon* v. *Wainright,* and that no statement elicited by the police during the interrogation may be used against him at a criminal trial.

Nothing we have said today affects the powers of the police to investigate "an unsolved crime," *Spano* v. *New York,* by gathering information from witnesses and by other "proper investigative efforts." *Haynes* v. *Washington.* We hold only that when the process shifts from investigatory to accusatory—when its focus is on the accused and its purpose is to elicit a confession—our adversary system begins to operate, and, under the circumstances here, the accused must be permitted to consult with his lawyer.

The judgment of the Illinois Supreme Court is reversed and the case remanded for proceedings not inconsistent with this opinion.

Reversed and remanded.

GAULT V. ARIZONA

This is an appeal under 28 U.S.C.Sec. 1257 (2) from a judgment of the Supreme Court of Arizona affirming the dismissal of a petition for a writ of habeas corpus. The petition sought the release of Gerald Francis Gault, petitioners' 15-year-old son, who had been committed as a juvenile delinquent to the State Industrial School by the Juvenile Court of Gila County, Arizona. The Supreme Court of Arizona affirmed dismissal of the writ against various arguments which included an attack upon the constitutionality of the Arizona Juvenile Code because of its alleged denial of procedural due process rights to juveniles charged with being "delinquents." The court agreed that the constitutional guarantee of due process of law is applicable in such proceedings. It held that Arizona's Juvenile Code is to be read as "impliedly" implementing the "due process concept." It then proceeded to identify and describe "the particular elements which constitute due process in a juvenile hearing." It concluded that the proceedings ending in commitment of Gerald Gault did not offend these requirements. We do not agree, and we reverse. We begin with a statement of the facts.

On Monday, June 8, 1964, at about 10 A.M., Gerald Francis Gault and a friend, Ronald Lewis, were taken into custody by the Sheriff of Gila County. Gerald was then still subject to a six months' probation order which had been entered on February 25, 1964, as a result of his having been in the company of another boy who had stolen a wallet from a lady's purse. The police action on June 8 was taken as the result of a verbal complaint by a neighbor of the boys, Mrs. Cook, about a telephone call made to her in which the caller or callers made lewd or indecent remarks. It will suffice for purposes of this opinion to say that the remarks or questions put to her were of the irritatingly offensive, adolescent, sex variety.

At the time Gerald was picked up, his mother and father were both at work. No notice that Gerald was being taken into custody was left at the home. No other steps were taken to advise them that their son had, in effect, been arrested. Gerald was taken to the Children's Detention Home. When his mother arrived home at about 6 o'clock, Gerald was not there. Gerald's older brother was sent to look for him at the trailer home of the Lewis family. He apparently learned then that Gerald was in custody. He so informed his mother. The two of them went to the Detention Home. The deputy probation officer, Flagg, who was also superintendent of the Detention Home, told Mrs. Gault "why Jerry was there" and said that a hearing would be held in Juvenile Court at 3 o'clock the following day, June 9.

Officer Flagg filed a petition with the Court on the hearing day, June 9, 1964. It was not served on the Gaults. Indeed, none of them saw this petition until the habeas corpus hearing on August 17, 1964. The petition was entirely formal. It made no reference to any factual basis for the judicial action which it initiated. It recited only that "said minor is under the age of 18 years and in need of the protection of this Honorable Court (and that) said minor is a delinquent minor." It prayed for a hearing and an order regarding "the care and custody of said minor." Officer Flagg executed a formal affidavit in support of the petition.

On June 9, Gerald, his mother, his older brother, and Probation Officers Flagg and Henderson appeared before the Juvenile Judge in chambers. Gerald's father was not there. He was at work out of the city. Mrs. Cook, the complainant was not there. No one was sworn at this hearing. No transcript or recording was made. No memorandum or record of the substance of the proceedings was prepared. Our information about the proceedings and the subsequent hearing on June 15, derives entirely from the testimony of the Juvenile Court Judge, Mr. and Mrs. Gault and Officer Flagg at the habeas corpus proceeding conducted two months later. From this, it appears that at the July 9 hearing, Gerald was questioned by the judge about the telephone call. There was conflict as to what he said. His mother recalled that Gerald said he only dialed Mrs. Cook's number and handed the telephone to his friend, Ronald. Officer Flagg recalled that Gerald had admitted making the lewd remarks. Judge McGhee testified that Gerald "admitted making one of these (lewd) statements." At the conclusion of the hearing, the judge said he would "think about it." Gerald was taken back to the Detention Home. He was not sent to his own home with his parents. On June 11 or 12, after having been detained since June 8, Gerald was released and driven home. There is no explanation in the record as to why he was kept in the Detention Home or why he was released. Mrs. Gault received a note signed by Officer Flagg. It was on plain paper, not letterhead. Its entire text was as follows:

"Mrs. Gault: Judge McGhee has set Monday, June 15, 1964, at 11:00 A.M. as the date and time for further Hearings on Gerald's delinquency/s/ Flagg."

At the appointed time on Monday June 15, his father and mother, Ronald Lewis and his father, and Officers Flagg and Henderson were present before Judge McGhee. Witnesses at the habeas corpus proceeding differed in their recollections of Gerald's testimony at the June 15 hearing. Mr. and Mrs. Gault recalled that Gerald again testified that he had only dialed the number and that the other boy had made the remarks. Officer Flagg agreed that at this hearing Gerald did not admit making the lewd remarks. But Judge McGhee recalled that "there was some admission again of some of the lewd statements." Again, the complainant, Mrs. Cook, was not present. Mrs. Gault asked that Mrs. Cook be present "so she could see which boy had done the talking, the dirty talking over the phone." The Juvenile Judge said "she didn't have to be present at that hearing." The judge did not speak to Mrs. Cook or communicate with her at any time. Probation Officer Flagg had talked to her once — over the telephone on June 9.

At this June 15 hearing, a "referral report" made by the probation officers was filed with the court, although not disclosed to Gerald or his parents. This listed the charge as "Lewd Phone Calls." At the conclusion of the hearing, the judge committed Gerald as a juvenile delinquent to the State Industrial School "for the period of his minority (that is, until 21), unless sooner discharged by due process of law." An order to that effect was entered. It recites that "after a full hearing and due deliberation the Court finds that said minor is a delinquent child, and that said minor is of the age of 15 years."

No appeal is permitted by Arizona law in juvenile cases. On August 3, 1964, a petition for a writ of habeas corpus was filed with the Supreme Court of Arizona and referred by it to the Superior Court for hearing.

At the habeas corpus hearing on August 17, Judge McGhee was vigorously cross-examined as to the basis for his actions. He testifed that he had taken into account the fact that Gerald was on probation. He was asked "under what section of . . . code you found the boy delinquent?"

His answer is set forth in the margin. In substance, he concluded that Gerald came within ARS Sec. 8–201–6(a) which specified that a "delinquent child" includes one "who has violated a law of the state or an ordinance or regulation of a political subdivision thereof." The law which Gerald was found to have violated is ARS Sec. 13–377. This section of the Arizona Criminal Code provides that a person who "in the presence of or hearing of any woman or child . . . uses vulgar, abusive or obscene language, is guilty of a misdemeanor. . . ." The penalty specified in the Criminal Code, which would apply to an adult, is $5 to $50, or imprisonment for not more than two months. The judge also testified that he acted under ARS Sec. 8–201–6(d) which includes in the definition of a "delinquent child" one who, as the judge phrased it, is "habitually involved in immoral matters."

Asked about the basis for his conclusion that Gerald was "habitually involved in immoral matters," the judge testified, somewhat vaguely, that two years earlier on July 2, 1962, a "referral" was made concerning Gerald "where the boy had stolen a baseball glove from another boy and lied to the Police Department about it." The judge said there was "no hearing" and "no accusation" relating to this incident "because of lack of material foundation." But it seems to have remained in his mind as a relevant factor. The judge also testified that Gerald had admitted making other nuisance phone calls in the past which, as the judge recalled the boy's testimony, were "silly calls, or funny calls, or something like that."

The Superior Court dismissed the writ, and appellants sought review in the Arizona Supreme Court. That court stated that it considered appellants assignments of error as urging (1) that the Juvenile Code ARS Sec. 8–201 to Sec. 8–239 is unconstitutional because it does not require that parents and children be apprised of the specific charges, does not require proper notice of a hearing, and does not provide for an appeal; and (2) that the proceedings and order relating to Gerald constituted a denial of due process of law because of the absence of adequate notice of the charge and the hearing; failure to notify appellants of certain constitutional rights including the rights to counsel and to confrontation, and the privilege against self-incrimination; the use of unsworn hearsay testimony; and the failure to make a record of the proceedings. Appellants further asserted that it was an error for the Juvenile Court to remove Gerald from the custody of his parents without a showing and finding of their unsuitability, and alleged a miscellany of other errors under state law.

The Supreme Court handed down an elaborate and wide-ranging opinion affirming dismissal of the writ and stating the court's conclusions as to the issues raised by appellants and other aspects of the juvenile process. In their jurisdictional statement and brief in this Court, appellants do not urge upon us all of the points passed upon by the Supreme Court of Arizona. They urge that we hold the Juvenile Code of Arizona invalid on its face or as applied in this case because, contrary to the Due Process Clause of the Fourteenth Amendment, the juvenile is taken from the custody of his parents and committed to a state institution pursuant to proceedings in which the Juvenile Court has virtually unlimited discretion, and in which the following basic rights are denied:

1. Notice of the charges
2. Right to counsel
3. Right to confrontation and cross-examination
4. Privilege against self-incrimination
5. Right to a transcript of the proceedings
6. Right to appellate review

Notice of Charges

Appellants allege that the Arizona Juvenile Code is unconstitutional or alternatively that the proceedings before the Juvenile Court were constitutionally defective because of failure to provide adequate notice of the hearings. No notice was given to Gerald's parents when he was taken into custody on Monday, June 8. On that night, when Mrs. Gault went to the Detention Home, she was orally informed that there would be a hearing the next afternoon and was told the reason why Gerald was in custody. The only written notice Gerald's parents received at any time was a note on plain paper from Officer Flagg delivered on Thursday or Friday, June 11 or 12, to the effect that the judge had set Monday, June 15, "for further hearings on Gerald's delinquency."

A "petition" was filed with the court on June 8 by Officer Flagg reciting only that he was informed and believed that "said minor is a delinquent minor and that it is necessary that some order be made by the Honorable Court for said minor's welfare." The applicable Arizona statute provides for a petition to be filed in Juvenile Court, alleging in general terms that the child is "neglected, dependent, or delinquent." The statute explicitly states that such a general allegation is sufficient, "without alleging the facts." There is no requirement that the petition be served and it was not served upon, given, or shown to Gerald or his parents.

The Supreme Court of Arizona rejected appellants claim that due process was denied because of inadequate notice. It stated that "Mrs. Gault knew the exact nature of the charge against Gerald from the day he was taken to the detention home." The court also pointed out that the Gaults appeared at the two hearings "without objection." The court held that because "the policy of the juvenile law is to hide youthful errors from the full gaze of the public and bury them in the graveyard of the forgotten past," advance notice of the specific charges or basis for taking the juvenile into custody and for the hearing is not necessary. It held that the appropriate rule is that "the infant and his parent or guardian will receive a petition only reciting a conclusion of delinquency. But no later than the initial hearing by the judge, they must be advised of the facts involved in the case. If the charges are denied, they must be given a reasonable period of time to prepare."

We cannot agree with the court's conclusion that adequate notice was given in this case. Notice, to comply with due process requirements, must be given sufficiently in advance of scheduled court proceedings so that reasonable opportunity to prepare will be afforded, and it must "set forth the alleged misconduct with particularity." It is obvious, as we have discussed above, that no purpose of shielding the child from the public stigma of knowledge of his having been taken into custody and scheduled for hearing is served by the procedure approved by the court below. The "initial hearing" in the present case was a hearing on the merits. Notice at that time is not timely; and even if there were a conceivable purpose served by the deferral proposed by the court below, it would have to yield to the requirements that the child and his parents or guardian be notified, in writing, of the specific charge or factual allegations to be considered at the hearing, and that such written notice be given at the earliest practicable time, and in any event sufficiently in advance of the hearing to permit preparation. Due process of law requires notice of the sort we have described—that, notice which would be deemed constitutionally adequate in a civil or criminal proceeding. It does not allow a hearing to be held in which a youth's freedom and his parents' right to his custody are at stake without giving them timely notice, in advance of the hearing, of the specific issues that they must meet. Nor, in the circumstances of this case, can it reasonably be said that the requirements of notice was waived.

Right to Counsel

Appellants charge that the Juvenile Court proceedings were fatally defective because the court did not advise Gerald or his parents of their right to counsel, and proceeded with the hearing, the adjudication of delinquency and the order of commitment in the absence of counsel for the child and his parents or an express waiver of the right thereto. The Supreme Court of Arizona pointed out that "there is disagreement (among the various jurisdictions) as to whether the court must advise the infant that he had a right to counsel." It noted its own decision in *State Dept. of Public Welfare* v. *Barlow* (1965), to the effect "that the parents of an infant in a juvenile proceeding cannot be denied representation by counsel of their choosing." It referred to a provision of the Juvenile Code which it characterized as requiring "that the probation officer shall look after the interests of neglected, delinquent and dependent children," including representing their interest in court.

The court argued that "The parent and the probation officer may be relied upon to protect the infant's interests." Accordingly it rejected the proposition that "due process requires that an infant has a right to counsel." It said that juvenile courts have the discretion, but not the duty, to allow such representation; it referred specifically to the situation in which the Juvenile Court discerns conflict between the child and his parents as an instance in which this discretion might be exercised. We do not agree. Probation officers, in the Arizona scheme, are also arresting officers. They initiate proceedings and file petitions which they verify, as here, alleging the delinquency of the child; and they testify, as here, against the child. And here the probation officer was also superintendent of the Detention Home. The probation officer cannot act as counsel for the child. His role in the adjudicatory hearing, by statute and in fact, is as arresting officer and witness against the child. Nor can the judge represent the child. There is no material difference in this respect between adult and juvenile proceedings of the sort here involved. In adult proceedings, this contention has been foreclosed by decisions of this Court. A proceeding where the issue is whether the child will be found to be "delinquent" and subjected to the loss of his liberty for years is comparable in seriousness to a felony prosecution. The juvenile needs the assistance of counsel to cope with problems to law, to make skilled inquiry into the facts, to insist upon regularity of the proceedings, and to ascertain whether he has a defense and to prepare and submit it. The child "requires the guiding hand of counsel at every step in the proceedings against him." Just as *Kent* v. *United States,* we indicated our agreement with the United States Court of Appeals for the District of Columbia Circuit that the assistance of counsel is essential for purposes of waiver proceedings, so we hold now that it is equally essential for the determination of delinquency, carrying with it the awesome prospect of incarceration in a state institution until the juvenile reaches the age of 21.

During the last decade, court decision, experts, and legislatures have demonstrated increasing recognition of this view. In at least one-third of the States, statutes now provide for the right of representation by retained counsel in juvenile delinquency proceedings, notice of the right, or assignment of counsel, or a combination of these. In other States, court rules have similar provisions.

The President's Crime Commission has recently recommended that in order to assure "procedural justice for the child," it is necessary that "Counsel . . . be appointed as a matter of course wherever coercive action is a possibility, without requiring any affirmative choice by child or parent." As stated by the authoritative "Standards for

Juvenile and Family Courts," published by the Children's Bureau of the United States Department of Health, Education, and Welfare:

> As a component part of a fair hearing required by due process guaranteed under the 14th Amendment, notice of the right to counsel should be required at all hearings and counsel provided upon request when the family is financially unable to employ counsel.

This statement was "reviewed" by the National Council of Juvenile Court Judges at its 1965 Convention and they "found no fault" with it. The New York Family Court Act contains the following statement:

> This act declares that minors have a right to the assistance of counsel of their own choosing or of law guardians in neglect proceedings under Article Three and in proceedings to determine juvenile delinquency and whether a person is in need of supervision under Article Seven. This declaration is based on a finding that counsel is often indispensable to a practical realization of due process of law and may be helpful in making reasoned determinations of fact and proper orders of disposition.

The Act provides that "At the commencement of any hearing" under the delinquency article of the statute, the juvenile and his parent shall be advised of the juvenile's "right to be represented by counsel chosen by him or his parent . . . or by a law guardian assigned by the court. . . ." The California Act (1961) also requires appointment of counsel.

We conclude that the Due Process Clause of the Fourteenth Amendment requires that in respect of proceedings to determine delinquency which may result in commitment to an institution in which the juvenile's freedom is curtailed, the child and his parent must be notified of the child's right to be represented by counsel retained by them, or if they are unable to afford counsel, that counsel will be appointed to represent the child.

At the habeas corpus proceeding, Mrs. Gault testified that she knew that she could have appeared with counsel at the juvenile hearing. This knowledge is not a waiver of the right to counsel which she and her juvenile had, as we have defined it. They had a right expressly to be advised that they might retain counsel and to be confronted with the need for specific consideration of whether they did or did not choose to waive the right. If they were unable to afford to employ counsel, they were entitled in view of the seriousness of the charge and the potential commitment, to appointed counsel, unless they chose waiver. Mrs. Gault's knowledge that she could employ counsel is not an "intentional relinquishment or abandonment" of a fully known right.

Confrontation, Self-Incrimination, Cross-Examination

Appellants urge that the writ of habeas corpus should have been granted because of the denial of the rights of confrontation and cross-examination in the Juvenile Court hearings, and because the privilege against self-incrimination was not observed. The Juvenile Court Judge testifed at the habeas corpus hearing that he had proceeded on the basis of Gerald's admissions at the two hearings. Appellants attack this on the ground that the admissions were obtained in disregard of the privilege against self-incrimination. If the confession is disregarded, appellants argue that the delinquency conclusion, since it was fundamentally based on a finding that Gerald had made lewd remarks during the phone call to Mrs. Cook, is fatally defective for failure to accord the rights of confrontation and cross-examination which the Due Process Clause of the Fourteenth Amendment of the Federal Constitution guarantees in state proceedings generally.

Our first question, then, is whether Gerald's admission was improperly obtained and relied on as the basis of decision, in conflict with the Federal Constitution. For this purpose, it is necessary briefly to recall the relevant facts.

Mrs. Cook, the complainant, and the recipient of the alleged telephone call, was not called as a witness. Gerald's mother asked the Juvenile Court Judge why Mrs. Cook was not present and the judge replied that "she didn't have to be present." So far as it appears, Mrs. Cook was spoken to only once, by Officer Flagg, and this was by telephone. The judge did not speak with her on any occasion. Gerald had been questioned by the probation officer after having been taken into custody. The exact circumstances of this questioning do not appear but any admissions Gerald may have made at this time do not appear in the record. Gerald was also questioned by the Juvenile Court Judge at each of the two hearings. The judge testified in the habeas corpus proceeding that Gerald admitted making "some of the lewd statements . . . (but not) any of the more serious lewd statements." There was conflict and uncertainty among the witnesses at the habeas corpus proceeding—the Juvenile Court Judge, Mr. and Mrs. Gault, and the probation officer—as to what Gerald did or did not admit.

We shall assume that Gerald made admissions of the sort described by the Juvenile Court Judge, as quoted above. Neither Gerald nor his parents was advised that he did not have to testify or make a statement, or that an incriminating statement might result in his commitment as a "delinquent."

The Arizona Supreme Court rejected appellant's contention that Gerald had a right to be advised that he need not incriminate himself. It said: "We think the necessary flexibility for individualized treatment will be enhanced by a rule which does not require the judge to advise the infant of a privilege against self-incrimination."

In reviewing this conclusion of Arizona's Supreme Court, we emphasize again that we are here concerned only with proceedings to determine whether a minor is a "delinquent" and which may result in commitment to a state institution. Specifically, the question is whether, in such a proceeding, an admission by the juvenile may be used against him in the absence of clear and unequivocal evidence that the admission was made with knowledge that he was not obliged to speak and would not be penalized for remaining silent. In light of *Miranda* v. *Arizona* (1966), we must also consider whether, if the privilege against self-incrimination is available, it can effectively be waived unless counsel is present or the right to counsel has been waived.

It has long been recognized that the eliciting and use of confessions or admissions or admissions required careful scrutiny. Dean Wigmore states:

> The grounds of distrust of confessions made in certain situations is, in a rough and indefinite way, judicial experience. There has been no careful collection of statistics of untrue confessions, nor has any great number of instances been even loosely reported . . . but enough have been verified to fortify the conclusion,

based on ordinary observation of human conduct, that under certain stresses a person, especially one of defective mentality or peculiar temperament, may falsely acknowledge guilt. This possibility arises wherever the innocent person is placed in such a situation that the untrue acknowledgement of guilt is at the time the more promising of two alternatives between which he is obliged to choose; that is, he chooses any risk that may be in falsely acknowledging guilt, in preference to some worse alternative associated with silence.

The principle, then, upon which a confession may be excluded is that it is, under certain conditions, testimonially untrustworthy. . . . (T)he essential feature is that the principle of exclusion is a testimonial one, analogous to the other principles which exclude narrations as untrustworthy. . . .

The privilege against self-incrimination is, of course, related to the question of safeguards necessary to assure that admissions or confessions are reasonably trustworthy, that they are not the mere fruits of fear or coercion, but are reliable expressions of the truth. The roots of the privilege are, however, far deeper. They tap the basic stream of religious and political principle because the privilege reflects the limits of the individual's attornment to the state and—in a philosophical sense—insists upon the equality of the individual and the State. In other words, the privilege has a broader and deeper thrust than the rule which prevents the use of confessions that are the product of coercion because coercion is thought to carry with it the danger of unreliability. One of its purposes is to prevent the State, whether by force or by psychological domination, from overcoming the mind and will of the person under investigation and depriving him of the freedom to decide whether to assist the State in securing his conviction.

It would indeed be surprising if the privilege against self-incrimination were available to hardened criminals but not to children. The language of the Fifth Amendment, applicable to the States by operation of the Fourteenth Amendment, is unequivocal and without exception. And the scope of the privilege is comprehensive.

With respect to juveniles, both common observation and expert opinion emphasize that the "distrust of confessions made in certain situations" is imperative in the case of children from an early age through adolescence. In New York, for example, the recently enacted Family Court Act provides that the juvenile and his parents must be advised at the start of the hearing of his right to remain silent. The New York statute also provides that the police must attempt to communicate with the juvenile's parents before questioning him, and that a confession may not be obtained from a child prior to notifying his parents or relatives and releasing the child either to them or to the Family Court.

The authoritative "Standards for Juvenile and Family Courts" concludes that, "Whether or not transfer to the criminal court is a possibility, certain procedures should always be followed. Before being interviewed (by the police), the child and his parents should be informed of his right to have legal counsel present and to refuse to answer questions or be fingerprinted if he should so decide."

Against the application to juveniles of the right to silence, it is argued that juvenile proceedings are "civil" and not "criminal," and therefore the privilege should not apply. It is true that the statement of the privilege in the Fifth Amendment, which is applicable to the States by reason of the Fourteenth Amendment, is that no person "shall be compelled in any criminal case to be a witness against himself." However, it is also clear that the availability of the privilege does not turn upon the type of proceeding in which its protection is invoked, but upon the nature of the statement of admission and the exposure which it invites. The privilege may, for example, be claimed in a civil or administrative proceeding, if the statement is or may be inculpatory.

It would be entirely unrealistic to carve out of the Fifth Amendment all statements by juveniles on the ground that these cannot lead to "criminal" involvement. In the first place, juvenile proceedings to determine "delinquency," which may lead to commitment to a state institution, must be regarded as "criminal" for purposes of the privilege against self-incrimination. To hold otherwise would be to disregard substance because of the feeble enticement of the "civil" label-of-convenience which has been attached to juvenile proceedings. Indeed, in over half of the States, there is not even assurance that the juvenile will be kept in separate institutions, apart from adult "criminals." In those States, juveniles may be placed in or transferred to adult penal institutions after having been found "delinquent" by a juvenile court. For this purpose, at least, commitment is a deprivation of liberty. It is incarceration against one's will, whether it is called "criminal" or "civil." And our Constitution guarantees that no person shall be "compelled" to be a witness against himself when he is threatened with deprivation of his liberty — a command which this Court has broadly applied and generously implemented in accordance with the teaching of the history of the privilege and its great office in mankind's battle for freedom.

In addition, apart from the equivalence for this purpose of exposure to commitment as a juvenile delinquent and exposure to imprisonment as an adult offender, the fact of the matter is that there is little or no assurance in Arizona, as in most if not all of the States, that a juvenile apprehended and interrogated by the police or even by the juvenile court itself, will remain outside of the reach of adult courts as a consequence of the offense for which he has been taken into custody. In Arizona, as in other States, provision is made for juvenile courts to relinquish or waive jurisdiction to the ordinary criminal courts. In the present case, when Gerald Gault was interrogated concerning violation of a section of the Arizona Criminal Code, it could not be certain that the Juvenile Court Judge would decide to "suspend" criminal prosecution in court for adults by proceeding to adjudication in Juvenile Court.

It is also urged, as the Supreme Court of Arizona here asserted, that the juvenile and presumably his parents should not be advised of the juvenile's right to silence because confession is good for the child as the commencement of the assumed therapy of the juvenile court process, and he should be encouraged to assume an attitude of trust and confidence toward the officials of the juvenile process. This proposition has been subjected to widespread challenge on the basis of current reappraisals of the rhetoric and realities of the handling of juvenile offenders.

In fact, evidence is accumulating that confessions by juveniles do not aid in "individualized treatment," as the court put it, and that compelling the child to answer questions, without warning or advice as to his right to remain silent, does not serve this or any other good purpose. In light of the observations of Wheeler and Cottrell, and others, it seems probable that where children are induced to confess by "paternal" urgings on the part of officials and the confession is then followed by disciplinary action, the child's reaction is likely to be hostile and adverse — the child may well feel that he has been led or tricked into confession and that despite his confession, he is being punished.

Further, authoritative opinion has cast formidable doubt upon the reliability and trustworthiness of "confessions" by children. The recent decisions of the New York Court, in the matters of Gregory W., and Gerald S., deals with a dramatic and, it is to be hoped, extreme example. Two 12-year-old Negro boys were taken into custody for the brutal assault and rape of two aged domestics, one of whom died as the result of the attack. One of the boys was schizophrenic and had been locked in the security ward of a mental institution at the time of the attacks. By a process that may best be described as bizarre, his confession was obtained by the police. A psychiatrist testified that the boy would admit "whatever he thought was expected so that he could get out of the immediate situation." The other 12-year-old also "confessed." Both confessions were in specific detail, albeit they contained various inconsistencies. The Court of Appeals, in an opinion by J. Keating, concluded that the confessions were products of the will of the police instead of the boys. The confessions were therefore held involuntary and the order of the Appellate Division affirming the order of the Family Court adjudging the defendants to be juvenile delinquents was reversed.

A similar and equally instructive case has recently been decided by the Supreme Court of New Jersey. In the interests of Carlo and Stasilowicz, supra. The body of a 10-year-old girl was found. She had been strangled. Neighborhood boys who knew the girl were questioned. The two appellants, aged 13 and 15, confessed to the police, with vivid detail and some inconsistencies. At the Juvenile Court hearing, both denied any complicity in the killing. They testified that their confessions were the product of fear and fatigue due to extensive police grilling. The Juvenile Court Judge found that the confessions were voluntary and admissible. On appeal, in an extensive opinion by J. Proctor, the Supreme Court of New Jersey reversed. It rejected the State's argument that the constitutional safeguard of voluntariness governing the use of confessions does not apply in proceedings before the Juvenile Court. It pointed out that under New Jersey court rules, juveniles under the age of 16, accused of committing a homicide are tried in a proceeding which "has all of the appurtenances of a criminal trial," including participation by the county prosecutor, and requirements that the juvenile be provided with counsel, that a stenographic record be made, etc. It also pointed out that under New Jersey law, the confinement of the boys after reaching age 21 could be extended until they had served the maximum sentence which could have been imposed on an adult for such a homicide, here found to be second degree murder carrying up to 30 years imprisonment. The court concluded that the confessions were involuntary, stressing that the boys, contrary to statute, were placed in the police station and there interrogated; that the parents of both boys were not allowed to see them while they were being interrogated; that inconsistencies appeared among the various statements of the boys and with the objective evidence of the crime; and that there were protracted periods of questioning. The court noted the State's contention that both boys were advised of their constitutional rights before they made their statements, but it held that this should not be given "significant weight in our determination of voluntariness." Accordingly, the judgment of the Juvenile Court was reversed.

We conclude that the constitutional privilege against self-incrimination is applicable in the case of juveniles as it is with respect to adults. We appreciate that special problems may arise with respect to waiver of the privilege by, or on behalf of, children, and that there may well be some differences in technique — but not in principle — depending upon the age of the child and the presence and competence of parents. The participation of counsel will, of course, assist the police, juvenile courts and appellate tribunals, in administering the privilege. If counsel is not present for some permissable reason when an admission is obtained, the greatest care must be taken to assure that the admission was voluntary, in the sense not only that it has not been coerced or suggested, but also that it is not the product of ignorance of rights or of adolescent fantasy, fright or despair.

The "confession" of Gerald Gault was first obtained by Officer Flagg out of the presence of Gerald's parents, without counsel and without advising him of his right to silence, as far as appears. The judgment of the Juvenile Court was stated by the judge to be based on Gerald's admission in court. Neither "admission" was reduced to writing, and, to say the least, the process by which the "admissions" were obtained and received must be characterized as lacking the certainty and order which are required of proceedings of such formidable consequences. Apart from the "admission," there was nothing upon which a judgment or finding might be based. There was no sworn testimony. Mrs. Cook, the complainant, was not present. The Arizona Supreme Court held that "sworn testimony must be required of all witnesses, including police officers, probation officers and others who are part of it, or officially related to, the juvenile court structure." We hold that this is not enough. No reason is suggested or appears for a different rule in respect to sworn testimony in juvenile courts than in adult tribunals. Absent a valid confession adequate to support the determination of the Juvenile Court, confrontation and sworn testimony by witnesses available for cross-examination were essential for a finding of "delinquency" and an order committing Gerald to state institution for a maximum of six years.

The recommendations in the Children's Bureau "Standards for Juvenile and Family Courts" are in general accord without conclusions. They state that testimony should be under oath and that only competent material and relevant evidence under rules applicable to civil cases should be admitted in evidence. The New York Family Court act contains a similar provision.

As we said in *Kent* v. *United States* (1966), with respect to waiver proceedings, "there is no place in our system of law for reaching a result of such tremendous consequences without ceremony. . . ." We now hold that, absent a valid confession, a determination of delinquency and an order of commitment to a state institution cannot be sustained in the absence of sworn testimony subjected to the opportunity for cross-examination in accordance with our law and constitutional requirements.

Appellate Review and Transcript of Proceedings

Appellants urge that the Arizona statute is unconstitutional under the Due Process Clause because, as construed by its Supreme Court, "there is no right of appeal from aid because the proceedings are confidential and any record must be destroyed after a prescribed period of time. Whether a transcript or other recording is made, it [the Supreme Court of Arizona] held, is a matter for the discretion of the juvenile court.

This Court has not held that a State is required by the Federal Constitution "to provide appellate courts or a right to appellate review at all." In view of the fact that we must reverse the Supreme Court of Arizona's affirmance of the dismissal of the writ of habeas corpus for other reasons, we need not rule on this question in the present case or upon the failure to provide a transcript or recording of the hearings—or, indeed, the failure of the juvenile court judge to state the grounds for his conclusion. As the present case illustrates, the consequences of failure to provide an appeal, to record the proceedings, or to make findings for the state as the grounds for the juvenile's court's conclusion may be to throw a burden upon the machinery for habeas corpus, to saddle the reviewing process with the burden of attempting to reconstruct a record, and to impose upon the juvenile judge the unseemly duty of testifying under cross-examination as to the events that transpired in the hearings before him.

For the reasons stated, the judgment of the Supreme Court of Arizona is reversed and the case remanded for further proceedings not inconsistent with this opinion. *It is so ordered.*

GIDEON V. WAINWRIGHT

Petitioner was charged in a Florida state court with having broken and entered a poolroom with intent to commit a misdemeanor. This offense is a felony under Florida law. Appearing in court without funds and without a lawyer, petitioner asked the court to appoint counsel for him, whereupon the following colloquy took place:

"The Court: Mr. Gideon, I am sorry, but I cannot appoint Counsel to represent you in this case. Under the laws of the State of Florida, the only time the Court can appoint Counsel to represent a Defendant is when that person is charged with a capital offense. I am sorry, but I will have to deny your request to appoint Counsel to defend you in this case."

"Defendant: The United States Supreme Court says I am entitled to be represented by Counsel." Put to trial before a jury, Gideon conducted his defense about as well as could be expected from a layman. The jury returned a verdict of guilty, and the petitioner was sentenced to serve five years in the state prison. Later, petitioner filed in the Florida Supreme Court, his habeas corpus petition . . . on the grounds that the trial court's refusal to appoint counsel for him denied his rights "guaranteed by the Constitution and the Bill of Rights by the United States Government." Treating the petition for habeas corpus as properly before it, the State Supreme Court denied all relief. Since 1942, when *Betts* v. *Brady* was decided by a divided Court, the problem of a defendant's federal constitutional right to counsel in a state court has been a continuing source of controversy and litigation in both State and Federal courts. To give this problem another review here, we granted certiorari. . . . Since Gideon was proceeding *in forma pauperis,* we appointed counsel to represent him and requested both sides to discuss in their briefs and oral arguments, the following:

"Should this Court's holding in *Betts* v. *Brady* be reconsidered?" The facts upon which Betts claimed that he had been unconstitutionally denied the right to have counsel appointed to assist him are strikingly like the facts upon which Gideon here bases his federal constitutional claim. Like Gideon, Betts sought release by habeas corpus, alleging that he had been denied the right to assistance of counsel in violation of the Fourteenth Amendment. Betts was denied any relief, and on review, this Court affirmed. It was held that a refusal to appoint counsel for an indigent defendant charged with a felony did not necessarily violate the Due Process Clause of the Fourteenth Amendment, which for reasons given the Court deemed to be the only applicable federal constitutional provision. The Court said:

". . . asserted denial [of due process] is to be tested by an appraisal of the totality of facts in a given case. That which may, in one setting constitute a denial of fundamental fairness, shocking to the universal sense of justice, may, in other circumstances, and in the light of other considerations, fall short of such denial."

Treating due process as "a concept less rigid and more fluid than those envisaged in other specific and particular provisions of the Bill of Rights," the Court held that refusal to appoint counsel under the particular facts and circumstances in the Betts case was not so "offensive to the common and fundamental ideas of fairness" as to amount to a denial of due process. Since the facts and circumstances of the two cases are so nearly indistinguishable, we think *Betts* v. *Brady* holding if left standing would require us to reject Gideon's claim that the Constitution guarantees him the assistance of counsel. Upon full reconsideration we conclude that *Betts* v. *Brady* should be over-ruled.

The Sixth Amendment provides, "In all criminal prosecutions, the accused shall enjoy the right . . . to have the Assistance of Counsel for his defense." We have construed this to mean that in federal courts counsel must be provided for defendants unable to employ counsel unless the right is competently and intelligently waived. Betts argued that this right is extended to indigent defendants in state courts by the Fourteenth Amendment. In response the Court stated that, while the Sixth Amendment laid down "no rule for the conduct of the states, the question recurs whether the constraint laid by the amendment upon the national courts expresses a rule so fundamental and essential to a fair trial, and so, to due process of law, that it is made obligatory upon the states by the Fourteenth Amendment." In order to decide whether the Sixth Amendment's guarantee of counsel is of this fundamental nature, the Court in Betts set out and considered "[r]elevant data on the subject . . . afforded by constitutional and statutory provisions subsisting in the colonies and the states prior to the inclusion of the Bill of Rights in the national Constitution, and in the constitutional, legislative, and judicial history of the states to the present date." On the basis of this historical data the Court concluded that "appointment of counsel is not a fundamental right, essential to a fair trial."

We think the Court in Betts had ample precedent for acknowledging that those guarantees of the Bill of Rights which are fundamental safeguards of liberty immune from federal abridgement are equally protected against state invasion by the Due Process Clause of the Fourteenth Amendment.

We accept *Betts* v. *Brady*'s assumption, based as it was on our prior cases, that a provision of the Bill of Rights which is "fundamental and essential to a fair trial" is made obligatory upon the States by the Fourteenth Amendment. We think the Court in Betts was wrong, however, in concluding that the Sixth Amendment's guarantee of counsel is not one of these fundamental rights. Ten years before *Betts* v. *Brady,* this Court, after full consideration of all the historical data examined in Betts, had unequiv-ocally declared that "the right to the aid of counsel is of this fundamental character." *Powell* v. *Alabama.* While the Court at the close of its Powell opinion did by its language, as this Court frequently does, limit its holding to the particular facts and circumstances of that case, its conclusions about the fundamental nature of the right to counsel are unmistakable.

The fact is that in deciding as it did—that "appointment of counsel is not a fundamental right, essential to a fair trial"—the Court in *Betts* v. *Brady* made an abrupt break with its own well-considered precedents. In returning to these old precedents, sounder we believe than the new, we but restore constitutional principles established to achieve a fair system of justice. Not only these precedents but also reason and reflection require us to recognize that in our adversary system of criminal justice, any person hailed into court, who is too poor to hire a lawyer, cannot be assured a fair trial unless counsel is provided for him. This seems to us to be an obvious truth. Governments, both state and federal, quite properly spend vast sums of money to establish machinery to try defendants accused of crime. Lawyers to prosecute are everywhere deemed essential to protect the public's interest in an orderly society. Similarly, there are few defendants charged with crime, few indeed, who fail to hire the best lawyers they can get to prepare and present their defense. That government hires lawyers to prosecute and defendants who have the money hire lawyers to defend are the strongest indications of the widespread belief that lawyers in criminal courts are necessities, not luxuries. The right of one charged with crime to counsel may not be deemed fundamental and essential to fair trials in some countries, but it is in ours. From the very beginning, our state and national constitutions and laws have laid great emphasis on procedural and substantive safeguards designed to assure fair trials before impartial tribunals in which every defendant stands equal before the law. This noble idea cannot be realized if the poor man charged with crime has to face his accusers without a lawyer to assist him.

The Court in *Betts* v. *Brady* departed from the sound wisdom upon which the Court's holding in *Powell* v. *Alabama* rested. Florida, supported by two other States, has asked that *Betts* v. *Brady* be left intact. Twenty-two states, as friends of the Court, argue that Betts was "an anachronism when handed down" and that it should now be overruled. We agree.

The judgment is *reversed* and the cause is remanded to the Supreme Court of Florida for further action not inconsistent with this opinion. It is so ordered.

MAPP V. OHIO

Appellant stands convicted of knowingly having had in her possession and under her control certain lewd and lascivious books, pictures, and photographs in violation of . . . Ohio's Revised Code. The Supreme Court of Ohio found that her conviction was valid though "based primarily on the introduction of evidence of lewd and lascivious books and pictures unlawfully seized during an unlawful search of defendant's home. . . ."

. . . May 23, 1957 . . . police officers arrived at appellant's residence . . . pursuant to information that "a person . . . hiding in the home . . . was wanted for questioning in connection with a recent bombing, and that there was a large amount of policy paraphernalia being hidden in the home." . . . Officers knocked on the door and demanded entrance but appellant, after telephoning her attorney, refused to admit them without a search warrant.

The officers again sought entrance some three hours later when four or more additional officers arrived on the scene. . . . Miss Mapp did not come to the door immediately. . . . One of the several doors . . . was forcibly opened and the policemen gained admittance. Meanwhile, Miss Mapp's attorney arrived, but the officers, having secured their own entry . . . would permit him neither to see Miss Mapp nor to enter the house. Miss Mapp . . . demanded to see the search warrant. A paper, claiming to be a warrant, was held up by one of the officers. She grabbed at the "warrant" and placed it in her bosom. A struggle ensued in which the officers recovered the piece of paper and as a result of which they handcuffed appellant because she had been "belligerent" in resisting their official rescue of the "warrant" from her person. . . . Appellant, in hand-cuffs, was then forcibly taken upstairs to her bedroom where the officers searched a dresser, a chest of drawers, a closet, and some suit cases . . . and some personal papers belonging to the appellant. The search spread to the rest of the second floor. . . . The basement of the building, and a trunk therein were also searched. The obscene materials, for possession of which she was ultimately convicted, were discovered in the course of that widespread search.

> There is, in the record, considerable doubt as to whether there ever was any warrant for the search of the defendant's home. The Ohio Supreme Court . . . found determinative the fact that the evidence had not been taken from the defendant's person by the use of brutal or offensive physical force against defendant.

The State [of Ohio] says that even if the search were made without authority, or otherwise unreasonably, it is not prevented from using the unconstitutionally seized evidence at trial, citing *Wolfe* v. *Colorado* . . . on this appeal . . . it is urged once again that we review that holding.

Seventy-five years ago, in *Boyd* v. *United States* (1886), considering the Fourth and Fifth Amendments as running "almost into each other" on the facts before it, this Court held that the doctrines of those Amendments "apply to all invasions on the part of the government and its employees of the sanctity of a man's home and the privacies of life. . . . It is not the breaking of his doors and the rummaging of his drawers, that constitutes the essence of the offense; but it is the invasion of his indefensible right of personal security, personal liberty and private property. . . ."

. . . This Court, in the year 1914 [in *Weeks* v. *United States*], " for the first time" held that "in a federal prosecution, the Fourth Amendment barred the use of evidence secured through illegal search and seizure." This Court has ever since required of federal law officers a strict adherence to that command which the Court has held to be clear, specific, and constitutionally required. . . . It meant, quite simply, that "conviction by means of unlawful seizures and enforced convictions . . . should find no sanction in the judgments of the courts. . . ." In *Olmstead* v. *United States,* in unmistakable language [the Court] . . . related the *Weeks* Rule:

> The striking out of the *Weeks* case and those which followed it was a sweeping declaration that the Fourth Amendment, although not referring to or limiting the use of evidence in courts, really forbade the introduction if obtained by officers through a violation of the Amendment.

In *McNabb* v. *United States*

> (A) Conviction in a federal court, the foundation of which is evidence obtained in disregard of liberties deemed fundamental by the Constitution cannot stand. [*Boyd* v. *United States*] . . . [*Weeks* v. *United States*] . . . This Court

has, on Constitutional grounds, set aside convictions, both in the federal and state courts, which were based upon confessions 'secured by protracted and repeated questionings of ignorant and untutored persons, and those in whose minds the power of the officers was greatly magnified' . . . or 'who have been unlawfully held incommunicado without advice of friends or counsel'. . . .

Moreover, our holding is not only the logical dictate of prior cases, but it also makes very good sense. . . . Presently a federal prosecutor may make no use of evidence illegally seized, but a State's attorney across the street may, although he supposedly is operating under the enforcible prohibitions of the same Amendment. Thus the State, by admitting evidence unlawfully seized, serves to encourage disobedience to the Federal Constitution which it is bound to uphold. Moreover, as was said in Elkins, "healthy Federalism depends upon the avoidance of needless conflict between State and Federal courts."

The ignoble short-cut to conviction left open to the State tends to destroy the entire system of constitutional restraints upon which the liberties of the people rest. Having once recognized that the right to privacy embodied in the Fourth Amendment is enforcible against the States, . . . we can no longer permit that right to remain an empty promise. Because it is enforcible in the same manner and to like effect as other basic rights secured by the Due Process Clause, we can no longer permit it to be revokable at the whim of any police officer, who in the name of law enforcement itself, chooses to suspend its enjoyment. Our decision, founded on reason and truth, gives to the individual no more than that which the Constitution guarantees him, to the police officer no less than that to which honest law enforcement is entitled, and, to the courts that judicial integrity so necessary in the true administration of justice. . . .

Reversed and remanded.

MIRANDA V. ARIZONA

The Miranda case [also: *Vignera* v. *New York, Westover* v. *United States,* and *Stewart* v. *California*] deals with the admissibility of statements obtained from an individual who is subjected to custodial police interrogation, and the necessity for procedures which assure that the individual is accorded his privilege against self-incrimination. Without specific concentration on the facts of this case, the Supreme Court of the United States, in an opinion by WARREN, Ch. J., expressing the views of five members of the Court, laid down the governing principles, the most important of which is that, as a consitutional prerequisite to the admissibility of such statements, the suspect must, *in the absence of a clear, intelligent waiver of the constitutional rights involved, be warned prior to questioning that he has a right to remain silent, that any statement he does make may be used as evidence against him, and that he has a right to the presence of an attorney, either retained or appointed.*

On March 13, 1963, petitioner, Ernesto Miranda, was arrested at his home and taken in custody to a Phoenix police station. He was there identified by the complaining witness. The police then took him to "Interrogation Room No. 2" of the detective bureau. There he was questioned by two police officers. The officers admitted at trial that Miranda was not advised that he had a right to have an attorney present. Two hours later, the officers emerged from the interrogation room with a written confession signed by

Miranda. At the top of the statement was a typed paragraph stating that the confession was made voluntarily, without threats or promises of immunity and "with full knowledge of my legal rights, understanding any statement I make may be used against me."

At his trial before a jury, the written confession was admitted into evidence over the objection of defense counsel, and the officers testified to the prior oral confession made by Miranda during the interrogation. Miranda was found guilty of kidnapping and rape. He was sentenced to 20 to 30 years' imprisonment on each count, the sentences to run concurrently.

On appeal, the Supreme Court of Arizona held that Miranda's constitutional rights were not violated in obtaining the confession and affirmed the conviction. In reaching its decision, the court emphasized heavily the fact that Miranda did not specifically request counsel.

The cases before us raise questions which go to the roots of our concepts of American criminal jurisprudence: the restraints society must observe consistent with the Federal Constitution in prosecuting individuals for crime. More specifically, we deal with the admissibility of statements obtained from an individual who is subjected to custodial police interrogation and the necessity for procedures which assure that the individual is accorded his privilege under the Fifth Amendment to the Constitution not to be compelled to incriminate himself.

We dealt with certain phases of this problem recently in *Escobedo* v. *Illinois*. There . . . law enforcement officials took the defendant into custody and interrogated him in a police station for the purpose of obtaining a confession. The police did not effectively advise him of his right to remain silent or of his right to consult with his attorney. Rather, they confronted him with an alleged accomplice who accused him of having perpetrated a murder. When the defendant denied the accusation and said "I didn't shoot Manuel, you did it," they handcuffed him and took him to an interrogation room. There, while handcuffed and standing, he was questioned for four hours until he confessed. During this interrogation, the police denied his request to speak to his attorney, and they prevented his retained attorney, who had come to the police station, from consulting with him. At his trial, the State, over his objection, introduced the confession against him. We held that the statements thus made were constitutionally inadmissable.

This case has been the subject of judicial interpretation and spirited legal debate since it was decided two years ago. Both state and federal courts, in assessing its implications, have arrived at varying conclusions. A wealth of scholarly material has been written tracing its ramifications and underpinnings.

We start here, as we did in Escobedo, with the premise that our holding is not an innovation in our jurisprudence, but is an application of principles long recognized and applied in other settings. We have undertaken a thorough re-examination of the Escobedo decision and the principles it announced, and we reaffirm it. That case was but an explication of basic rights that are enshrined in our Constitution—that "No person . . . shall be compelled in any criminal case to be a witness against himself," and that "the accused shall . . . have the Assistance of Counsel"—rights which were put in jeopardy in that case through official overbearing. These precious rights were fixed in our Constitution only after centuries of persecution and struggle.

"While the admissions or confessions of the prisoner, when voluntarily and freely made, have always ranked high in the scale of incriminating evidence, if an accused person be asked to explain his apparent connection with a crime under investigation, the case with which the questions put to him may assume an inquisitorial character, the temptation to press the witness unduly, to browbeat him if he be timid or reluctant, to push him into a corner, and to entrap him into fatal contradictions, which is so painfully evident in many of the earlier state trials, notably in those of Sir Nicholas Throckmorton, and Udal, the puritan minister, made the system so odious as to give rise to a demand for its total abolition. The change in the English criminal procedure in that particular seems to be founded upon no statute and no judicial opinion, but upon a general and silent acquiescence of the courts in a popular demand. But, however adopted, it has become firmly embedded in English, as well as in American jurisprudence. So deeply did the iniquities of the ancient system impress themselves upon the minds of the American colonists that the States, with one accord, made a denial of the right to question an accused person a part of their fundamental law, so that a maxim, which in England was a mere rule of evidence, became clothed in this country with the impregnability of a constitutional enactment."

In stating the obligation of the judiciary to apply these constitutional rights, this Court declared in *Weems* v. *United States,* (1910): "our contemplation cannot be only of what has been but of what may be. Under any other rule a constitution would indeed be as easy of application as it would be deficient in efficacy and power. Its general principles would have little value and be converted by precedent into impotent and lifeless formulas. Rights declared in words might be lost in reality. And this has been recognized. The meaning and vitality of the Constitution have developed against narrow and restrictive construction."

This was the spirit in which we delineated, in meaningful language the manner in which the constitutional rights of the individual could be enforced against overzealous police practices. It was necessary in Escobedo, as here, to insure that what was proclaimed in the Constitution had not become but a "form of words," *Silverthorne Lumber Co.* v. *United States,* (1920), in the hands of government officials. And it is in this spirit, consistent with our role as judges, that we adhere to the principles of Escobedo today.

. . . the prosecution may not use statements, whether exculpatory or inculpatory, stemming from custodial interrogation of the defendant unless it demonstrates the use of procedural safeguards effective to secure the privilege against self-incrimination. By custodial interrogation, we mean questioning initiated by law enforcement officers after a person has been taken into custody or otherwise deprived of his freedom of action in any significant way. As for the procedural safeguards to be employed, unless other fully effective means are devised to inform accused persons of their rights of silence and to assure a continuous opportunity to exercise it, the following measures are required. Prior to any questioning, the person must be warned that he has a right to remain silent, that any statement he does make may be used as evidence against him, and that he has a right to the presence of an attorney, either retained or appointed. The defendant may waive effectuation of these rights, provided the waiver is made voluntarily, knowingly and intelligently. If, however, he indicates in any manner and at any stage of the process that he wishes to consult with an attorney before speaking there can be no questioning. Likewise, if the individual is alone and indicates in any manner that he does not wish to be interrogated, the police may not question him. The mere fact that he may have answered some questions or volunteered some statements on his own does not deprive him of the right to refrain from answering any further inquiries until he has consulted with an attorney and thereafter consents to be questioned.

The constitutional issue we decide in each of these cases is the admissibility of statements obtained from a defendant questioned while in custody or otherwise deprived of his freedom of action in any significant way. In each, the defendant was questioned by police officers, detectives, or a prosecuting attorney in a room in which he was cut off from the outside world. In none of these cases was the defendant given a full and effective warning of his rights at the outset of the interrogation process. In all the cases, the questioning elicited oral admissions, and in three of them, signed statements as well which were admitted at their trials. They all thus share salient features — incommunicado interrogation of individuals in a police-dominated atmosphere, resulting in self-incriminating statements without full warnings of constitutional rights.

An understanding of the nature and setting of this in-custody interrogation is essential to our decisions today. The difficulty in depicting what transpires at such interrogations stems from the fact that in this country they have largely taken place incommunicado. From extensive factual studies undertaken in the early 1930s, including the famous Wickersham Report to Congress by a Presidential Commission, it is clear that police violence and the "third degree" flourished at that time. In a series of cases decided by this Court long after these studies, the police resorted to physical brutality — beating, hanging, whipping — and to sustained and protracted questioning incommunicado in order to extort confessions. The Commission on Civil Rights in 1961 found much evidence to indicate that "some policemen still resort to physical force to obtain confessions." The use of physical brutality and violence is not, unfortunately, relegated to the past or to any part of the country. Only recently in Kings County, New York, the police brutally beat, kicked and placed lighted cigarette butts on the back of a potential witness under interrogation for the purpose of securing a statement incriminating a third party. *People* v. *Portelli,* (1965).

The examples given above are undoubtedly the exception now, but they are sufficiently widespread to be the object of concern. Unless a proper limitation upon custodial interrogation is achieved — such as these decisions will advance — there can be no assurance that practices of this nature will be eradicated in the foreseeable future. The conclusion of the Wickersham Commission Report, made over 30 years ago, is still pertinent:

"To the contention that the third degree is necessary to get the facts, the reporters aptly reply in the language of the present Lord Chancellor of England (Lord Sankey): "It is not admissible to do a great right by doing a little wrong. . . . It is not sufficient to do justice by obtaining a proper result by irregular or improper means." Not only does the use of the third degree involve a flagrant violation of law by the officers of the law, but it involves also the dangers of false confessions, and it tends to make police and prosecutors less zealous in the search for objective evidence. As the New York prosecutor quoted in the report said, 'It is a short cut and makes the police lazy and unenterprising.' Or, as another official quoted remarked: 'If you use your fists, you are not so likely to use your wits.' We agree with the conclusion expressed in the report, that:

The third degree brutalizes the police, hardens the prisoner against society, and lowers the esteem in which the administration of justice is held by the public.

Again we stress that the modern practice of in-custody interrogation is psychologically rather than physically oriented. As we have stated before, "Since *Chambers* v. *Florida,* this Court has recognized that coercion can be mental as well as physical, and that the blood of the accused is not the only hallmark of an unconstitutional inquisition." *Blackburn* v. *Alabama,* (1960). Interrogation still takes place in privacy. Privacy results in secrecy and this in turn results in a gap in our knowledge as to what in fact goes on in the interrogation rooms. A valuable source of information about present police practices, however, may be found in various police manuals and texts which document procdures employed with success in the past, and which recommend various other effective tactics. These texts are used by law enforcement agencies themselves as guides. It should be noted that these texts professedly present the most enlightened and effective means presently used to obtain statements through custodial interrogation. By considering these texts and other data, it is possible to describe procedures observed and noted around the country.

The officers are told by the manuals that the "principal psychological factor contributing to a successful interrogation is *privacy*—being alone with the person under interrogation." The efficacy of this tactic has been explained as follows:

> If at all practicable, the interrogation should take place in the investigator's office or at least in a room of his own choice. The subject should be deprived of every psychological advantage. In his own home he may be confident, indignant, or recalcitrant. He is more keenly aware of his rights and more reluctant to tell of his indiscretions or criminal behavior within the walls of his home. Moreover his family and other friends are nearby, their presence lending moral support. In his own office, the investigator possesses all the advantages. The atmosphere suggests the invincibility of the forces of the law.

To highlight the isolation and unfamiliar surroundings, the manuals instruct the police to display an air of confidence in the suspect's guilt and from outward appearance to maintain only an interest in confirming certain details. The guilt of the subject is to be posited as a fact. The interrogator should direct his comments toward the reasons why the subject committed the act, rather than court failure by asking the subject whether he did it. Like other men, perhaps the subject has had a bad family life, had an unhappy childhood, had too much to drink, had an unrequited desire for women. The officers are instructed to minimize the moral seriousness of the offense, to cast blame on the victim or on society. These tactics are designed to put the subject in a psychological state where his story is but an elaboration of what the police purport to know already—that he is guilty. Explanations to the contrary are dismissed and discouraged.

The texts thus stress that the major qualities an interrogator should possess are patience and perseverance. One writer describes the efficacy of these characteristics in this manner.

> In the preceding paragraphs emphasis has been placed on kindness and stratagems. The investigator will, however, encounter many situations where the sheer weight of his personality will be the deciding factor. Where emotional appeals and tricks are employed to no avail, he must rely on an oppressive atmosphere of dogged persistence. He must interrogate steadily and without relent, leaving the

subject no prospect of surcease. He must dominate his subject and overwhelm him with his inexorable will to obtain the truth. He should interrogate for a spell of several hours, pausing only for the subject's necessities in acknowledgment of the need to avoid a charge of duress that can be technically substantiated. In a serious case, the interrogation may continue for days, with the required intervals for food and sleep, but with no respite from the atmosphere of domination. It is possible in this way to induce the subject to talk without resorting to duress or coercion. The method should be used only when the guilt of the subject appears highly probable.

The manuals suggest that the suspect be offered legal excuses for his actions in order to obtain an initial admission of guilt. Where there is a suspected revenge-killing, for example, the interrogator may say:

> Joe, you probably didn't go out looking for this fellow with the purpose of shooting him. My guess is, however, that you expected something from him and that's why you carried a gun—for your own protection. You knew him for what he was, no good. Then when you met him he probably started using foul, abusive language and he gave some indication that he was about to pull a gun on you, and that's when you had to act to save your own life. That's about it, isn't it, Joe?

Having then obtained the admission of shooting, the interrogator is advised to refer to circumstantial evidence which negates the self-defense explanation. This should enable him to secure the entire story. One text notes that "Even if he fails to do so, the inconsistency between the subject's original denial of the shooting and his present admission of at least doing the shooting will serve to deprive him of a self-defense 'out' at the time of trial."

When the techniques described above prove unavailing, the texts recommend they be alternated with a show of some hostility. One ploy often used has been termed the "friendly-unfriendly" or the "Mutt and Jeff" act:

> In this technique, two agents are employed. Mutt, the relentless investigator, who knows the subject is guilty and is not going to waste any time. He's sent a dozen men away for this crime and he's going to send the subject away for the full term. Jeff, on the other hand, is obviously a kindhearted man. He has a family himself. He has a brother who was involved in a little scrape like this. He disapproves of Mutt and his tactics and will arrange to get him off the case if the subject will cooperate. He can't hold Mutt off for very long. The subject would be wise to make a quick decision. The technique is applied by having both investigators present while Mutt acts out his role. Jeff may stand by quietly and demur at some of Mutt's tactics. When Jeff makes his plea for cooperation, Mutt is not present in the room.

The interrogators sometimes are instructed to induce a confession out of trickery. The technique here is quite effective in crimes which require identification or which run in series. In the identification situation, the interrogator may take a break in his questioning to place the subject among a group of men in a line-up. "The witness or complainant (previously coached, if necessary) studies the line-up and confidently points out the subject as the guilty party." Then the questioning resumes "as though there were now no doubt about the guilt of the subject." A variation on this technique is called the "reverse line-up:"

> The accused is placed in a line-up, but this time he is identified by several fictitious witnesses or victims who associated him with different offenses. It is expected that the subject will become desperate and confess to the offense under investigation in order to escape from the false accusations.

The manuals also contain instructions for police on how to handle the individual who refuses to discuss the matter entirely, or who asks for an attorney or relatives. The examiner is to concede him the right to remain silent. "This usually has a very undermining effect. First of all, he is disappointed in his expectation of an unfavorable reaction on the part of the interrogator. Secondly, a concession of this right to remain silent impresses the subject with the apparent fairness of his interrogator."

After this psychological conditioning, however, the officer is told to point out the incriminating significance of the suspect's refusal to talk:

> Joe, you have a right to remain silent. That's your privilege and I'm the last person in the world who'll try to take it away from you. If that's the way you want to leave this, O.K. But let me ask you this. Suppose you were in my shoes and I were in yours and you called me in to ask me about this and I told you, "I don't want to answer any of your questions." You'd think I had something to hide, and you'd probably be right in thinking that. That's exactly what I'll have to think about you, and so will everybody else. So let's sit here and talk this whole thing over.

Few will persist in their initial refusal to talk, it is said, if this monologue is employed correctly.

In the event that the subject wishes to speak to a relative or an attorney, the following advice is tendered:

> [T]he interrogator should respond by suggesting that the subject first tell the truth to the interrogator himself rather than get anyone else involved in the matter. If the request is for an attorney, the interrogator may suggest that the subject save himself or his family the expense of any such professional service, particularly if he is innocent of the offense under investigation. The interrogator may also add, "Joe, I'm only looking for the truth, and if you're telling the truth, that's it. You can handle this by yourself."

From these representative samples of interrogation techniques, the setting prescribed by the manuals and observed in practice becomes clear. In essence, it is this: To be alone with the subject is essential to prevent distraction and to deprive him of any outside support. The aura of confidence in his guilt undermines his will to resist. He merely confirms the preconceived story the police seek to have him describe. Patience and persistence, at times relentless questioning, are employed. To obtain a confession, the interrogator must "patiently maneuver himself or his quarry into a position from which the desired objective may be attained." When normal procedures fail to produce the needed result, the police may resort to deceptive stratagems such as giving false legal advice. It is important to keep the subject off balance, for example, by trading on his insecurity about himself or his surroundings. The police then persuade, trick, or cajole him out of exercising his constitutional rights.

Even without employing brutality, the "third degree" or the specific stratagems described above, the very fact of custodial interrogation exacts a heavy toll on the individual liberty and trades on the weakness of individuals. This fact may be illustrated simply by referring to three confession cases decided by this Court in the Term immediately preceding our Escobedo decision. In *Townsend* v. *Sain,* (1963), the defendant was a 19-year-old heroin addict, described as a "near mental defective." The defendant in *Lynumn* v. *Illinois,* (1963), was a woman who confessed to the arresting officer after being importuned to "cooperate" in order to prevent her children from being taken by relief authorities. This Court as in those cases reversed the conviction of a defendant in *Haynes* v. *Washington,* (1963), whose persistent request during his interrogation was to phone his wife or attorney. In other settings, these individuals might have exercised their constitutional rights. In the incommunicado police-dominated atmosphere, they succumbed.

In the cases before us today [*Miranda, Vignero, Westover,* and *Stewart*] given this background, we concern ourselves primarily with this interrogation atmosphere and the evils it can bring.

. . . In these cases [*Miranda* et al.], we might not find the defendants' statements to have been involuntary in traditional terms. Our concern for adequate safeguards to protect precious Fifth Amendment rights is, of course, not lessened in the slightest. In each of the cases, the defendant was thrust into an unfamiliar atmosphere and run through menacing police interrogation procedures. The potentiality for compulsion is forcefully apparent, for example in *Miranda,* where the indigent Mexican defendant was a seriously disturbed individual with pronounced sexual fantasies, and in *Stewart,* in which the defendant was an indigent Los Angeles Negro who had dropped out of school in the sixth grade. To be sure, the records do not evince overt physical coercion or patent psychological ploys. The fact remains that in none of these cases did the officers undertake to afford appropriate safeguards at the outset of the interrogation to insure that the statements were truly the product of free choice.

It is obvious that such an interrogation environment is created for no purpose other than to subjugate the individual to the will of his examiner. This atmosphere carries its own badge of intimidation. To be sure, this is not physical intimidation, but it is equally destructive of human dignity. The current practice of incommunicado interrogation is at odds with one of our Nation's most cherished principles — that the individual may not be compelled to incriminate himself. Unless adequate protective devices are employed to dispel the compulsion inherent in custodial surroundings, no statement obtained from the defendant can truly be the product of his free choice.

From the foregoing, we can readily perceive an intimate connection between the privilege against self-incrimination and police custodial questioning.

We reverse. From the testimony of the officers and by the admission of respondent, it is clear that Miranda was not in any way apprised of his right to consult with an attorney and to have one present during the interrogation, or was his right not to be compelled to incriminate himself effectively protected in any other manner. Without these warnings the statements were inadmissible. The mere fact that he signed a statement which contained a typed-in clause stating that he had "full knowledge" of his "legal rights" does not approach the knowing and intelligent waiver required to relinquish constitutional rights. . . .

MCKEIVER AND TERRY V. PENNSYLVANIA IN RE BARARA AND BURRUS, ET AL., PETITIONERS

These cases raised the issue whether the due process clause of the Fourteenth Amendment affords the right to trial by jury in state juvenile delinquency proceedings. In *McKeiver and Terry,* it involved separate proceedings against two boys, 15 and 16 years old, respectively, in the Juvenile Branch of the Court of Common Pleas of Philadelphia County, Pennsylvania, charging as acts of juvenile delinquency conduct by the juvenile in one case which constituted felonies under Pennsylvania law, and conduct amounting to misdemeanors in the second case. The trial judge in each case denied a request for jury trial, and adjudged the juvenile as delinquent on the respective charges, one of the juveniles being put on probation and the other being committed to an institution. The Superior Court of Pennsylvania affirmed both orders without opinion. Consolidating the appeals in both cases, the Supreme Court of Pennsylvania affirmed, holding that there was no constitutional right to a jury trial in the juvenile court. In Burrus, a group of children, ranging in age from 11 to 15 years, were charged by juvenile petitions in the District Court, Hyde County, North Carolina, with various acts amounting to misdemeanors under state law, which acts arose out of a series of demonstrations protesting school assignments and a school consolidation plan. Consolidating the several cases into groups for hearing, the trial judge excluded the general public over counsel's objection in all but two of the cases; denied a request for jury trial in each case; and entered a custody commitment order in each case, declaring the juvenile a delinquent and placing each juvenile on probation after suspending the commitments. The cases were consolidated into two groups for appeal, and the Court of Appeals of North Carolina affirmed in each instance. Consolidating the cases into a single appeal, the Supreme Court of North Carolina deleted that portion of each order relating to the commitment, but otherwise affirmed, holding that a juvenile was not constitutionally entitled to a jury in delinquency proceedings.

On appeal in the Pennsylvania case, and on certiorari in the North Carolina proceedings, the United States Supreme Court affirmed in each instance. A majority of the court, although not agreeing upon an opinion, agreed that the due process clause of the Fourteenth Amendment did not assure the right to jury trial in the adjudicative phase of a state juvenile court delinquency proceeding.

WINSHIP V. NEW YORK

Mr. Justice Brennan delivered the opinion of the Court.

Constitutional questions decided by this Court concerning the juvenile process have centered on the adjudicatory stage at "which a determination is made as to whether a juvenile is a 'delinquent' as a result of alleged misconduct on his part, with the consequence that he may be committed to a state institution." *In re Gault,* 387 U.S. 1,

13 (1967), Gault decided that, although the Fourteenth Amendment does not require that the hearing at this stage conform with all the requirements of a criminal trial or even of the usual administrative proceeding, the Due Process Clause does require application during the adjudicatory hearing of "the essentials of due process and fair treatment." Id., at 30. This case presents the single, narrow question whether proof beyond reasonable doubt is among the "essentials of due process and fair treatment" required during the adjudicatory stage when a juvenile is charged with an act which would constitute a crime if committed by an adult.

Section 712 of the New York Family Court Act defines a juvenile delinquent as "a person over seven and less than sixteen years of age who does any act which, if done by an adult, would constitute a crime." During a 1967 adjudicatory hearing, conducted pursuant to 742 of the Act, a judge in New York Family Court found that appellant, then a 12-year-old boy, had entered a locker and stolen $112 from a woman's pocketbook. The petition which charged appellant with delinquency alleged that his act, "if done by an adult, would constitute the crime or crimes of Larceny." The judge acknowledged that the proof might not establish guilt beyond a reasonable doubt, but rejected appellant's contention that such proof was required by the Fourteenth Amendment. The judge relied instead on 744 (b) of the New York Family Court Act which provides that "[a]ny determination at the conclusion of [an adjudicatory] hearing that a [juvenile] did an act or acts must be based on a preponderance of the evidence." During a subsequent dispositional hearing, appellant was ordered placed in a training school for an initial period of 18 months, subject to annual extensions of his commitment until his 18th birthday—six years in appellant's case. The Appellate Division of the New York Supreme Court, First Judicial District affirmed without opinion, 291 N.Y.S. 2d 1005 (1968). The New York Court of Appeals then affirmed by a four-to-three vote, expressly sustaining the constitutionality of 744 (b) 24 N.Y. 2d 196, 247 N.E. 2d 253 (1969). We noted probable jurisdiction, 396 U.S. 885 (1969). *We reverse.*

I

The requirement that guilt of a criminal charge be established by proof beyond a reasonable doubt dates at least from our early years as a Nation. The "demand for a higher degree of persuasion in criminal cases was recurrently expressed from ancient times, [though] its crystallization into the formula 'beyond a reasonable doubt' seems to have occurred as late as 1798. It is now accepted in common law jurisdictions as the measure of persuasion by which the prosecution must convince the trier of all the essential elements of guilt." McCormick, Evidence, 321, at 681–682 (1954); see also 9 Wigmore, Evidence, 2497 (3d ed. 1940). Although virtually unanimous adherence to the reasonable-doubt standard in common-law jurisdictions may not conclusively establish it as a requirement of due process, such adherence does "reflect a profound judgment about the way in which law should be enforced and justice administered." *Duncan* v. *Louisiana,* 391 U.S. 145, 155 (1968).

Expressions in many opinions of this Court indicate that it has long been assumed that proof of a criminal charge beyond a reasonable doubt is constitutionally required. See, for example, *Miles* v. *United States,* 103 U.S. 304, 312 (1880); *Davis* v. *United States,* 160 U.S. 469, 488 (1895); *Holt* v. *United States,* 218 U.S. 245, 253 (1910); *Wilson* v. *United States,* 232 U.S. 563, 569–570 (1914); *Brinegar* v. *United States,* 338 U.S. 160, 174 (1949); *Leland* v. *Oregon,* 343 U.S. 790, 795 (1952); *Holland* v. *United States,* 348

U.S. 121, 138 (1954); *Speiser* v. *Randall,* 357 U.S. 513, 525–526 (1958). Cf. *Coffin* v. *United States,* 156 U.S. 432 (1895). Mr. Justice Frankfurter stated that "[i]t is the duty of the Government to establish . . . guilt beyond a reasonable doubt. This notion —basic in our law and rightly one of the boasts of a free society—is a requirement and safeguard of due process of law in the historic, procedural content of 'due process.' " *Leland* v. *Oregon,* supra, at 802–803 (dissenting opinion). In a similar vein, the Court said in *Brinegar* v. *United States,* supra, at 174, that "[g]uilt in a criminal case must be proved beyond a reasonable doubt and by evidence confined to that which long experience in the common-law tradition, to some extent embodied in the Constitution, has crystallized into rules of evidence consistent with that standard. These rules are historically grounded rights of our system, developed to safeguard men from dubious and unjust convictions, with resulting forfeitures of life, liberty and property." *Davis* v. *United States,* supra, proceeding where the issue is whether the child will be found to be 'delinquent' and subjected to the loss of his liberty for years is comparable in seriousness to a felony prosecution." Id., at 36.

Nor do we perceive any merit in the argument that to afford juveniles the protection of proof beyond a reasonable doubt would risk destruction of beneficial aspects of the juvenile process. Use of the reasonable-doubt standard during the adjudicatory hearing will not disturb New York's policies that a finding that a child has violated a criminal law does not constitute a criminal conviction, that such a finding does not deprive the child of his civil rights, and that juvenile proceedings are confidential. Nor will there be any effect on the informality, flexibility, or speed of the hearing at which the fact finding takes place. And the opportunity during the post-adjudicatory or dispositional hearing for a wide-ranging review of the child's social history and for his individualized treatment will remain unimpaired. Similarly, there will be no effect on the procedures distinctive to juvenile proceedings which are employed prior to the adjudicatory hearing.

The Court of Appeals observed that "a child's best interest is not necessarily, or even probably, promoted if he wins in the particular inquiry which may bring him to the juvenile court." 24 N.Y. 2d, at 199, 247 N.E. 2d, at 255. It is true, of course, that the juvenile may be engaging in a general course of conduct inimical to his welfare which calls for judicial intervention. But that intervention cannot take the form of subjecting the child to the stigma of a finding that he violated a criminal law and to the possibility of institutional confinement on proof insufficient to convict him were he an adult.

We conclude, as we concluded regarding the essential due process safeguards applied in Gault, that the observance of the standard of proof beyond a reasonable doubt "will not compel the States to abandon or displace any of the substantive benefits of the juvenile process." Gault, supra, at 21.

Finally, we reject the Court of Appeals' suggestion that there is, in any event, only a "tenuous difference" between the reasonable-doubt and preponderance standards. The suggestion is singularly unpersuasive. In this very case, the trial judge's ability to distinguish between the two standards enabled him to make a finding of guilt which he conceded he might not have made under the standard of proof beyond a reasonable doubt. Indeed, the trial judge's action evidences the accuracy of the observation of commentators that "the preponderance test is susceptible to the misinterpretation that it calls on the trier of fact merely to perform an abstract weighing of the evidence in order to determine which side has produced the greater quantum, without regard to its effect in convincing his mind of the truth of the proposition asserted." Dorsen and Reznek, supra, at 26–27.

III

In sum, the constitutional safeguard of proof beyond a reasonable doubt is as much required during the adjudicatory stage of a delinquency proceedings as are those constitutional safeguards applied in Gault—notice of charges, right to counsel, the rights of confrontation and examination, and the privilege against self-incrimination. We therefore hold, in agreement with Chief Judge Fuld in dissent in the Court of Appeals, "that, where a 12-year-old child is charged with an act of stealing which renders him liable to confinement for as long as six years, then, as a matter of due process . . . the case against him must be proved beyond a reasonable doubt." 24 N.Y. 2d, at 207, 247 N.E. 2d, at 260.

Reversed.

FURMAN V. GEORGIA

This Supreme Court case involved three different cases of persons sentenced to death: *Furman* v *Georgia, Jackson* v. *Georgia,* and *Branch* v. *Texas.*

In the three cases people convicted in state courts were subsequently sentenced to death after a trial by jury. Under the state laws in these cases, the courts had the discretion of imposing the death penalty. One of the persons had been convicted of murder; the other two of rape. All three were members of an ethnic minority—a fact important to one justice.

The Supreme Court by a five-to-four majority held that the imposition of the death sentence in these cases constituted cruel and unusual punishment. Specifically, the justices indicated the following:

Justice Brennan stated that the Eighth Amendment to the Constitution's prohibition against cruel and unusual punishment was not limited to punishments which were considered cruel and unusual at the time the Eighth Amendment was adopted. He stated that a punishment was cruel and unusual if it did not comply with the idea of human dignity. Further, he stated that, since this punishment is a denial of human dignity, when a state arbitrarily subjects a person to an unusually severe punishment which society indicates it does not regard as acceptable, and which cannot be shown to be of any penal purpose more effective than a significantly less drastic punishment, then death is a cruel and unusual punishment.

Justice Douglas stated that it is cruel and unusual to apply the death penalty selectively to minorities whose members are few, who are outcasts, and who are unpopular. However, society is willing to see these minorities suffer the death penalty, yet it does not apply the same penalty across all borders. Because of this discriminatory application of the laws authorizing the discretionary imposition of the death penalty, such laws are unconstitutional in their operation.

Justice Marshall stated that the death penalty violated the Eighth Amendment because it was excessive and because it was morally unacceptable to the people of the United States.

Justice Stewart stated that the persons in these cases were a capriciously selected random few, who were sentenced to death. Further, the Eighth and Fourteenth Amendments did not permit the infliction of the death sentence under legal systems which permitted it to be so freakishly and wantonly imposed. Also, he stated that it is unnecessary to decide whether the death penalty is unconstitutional in all circumstances as regards to the Eighth and Fourteenth Amendments.

Justice White stated that as the laws involved in the present cases were administered, the death penalty was so infrequently imposed that the threat of execution was of little value to criminal justice. Furthermore, he stated that it was unnecessary to decide whether the death penalty was unconstitutional per se, or whether there was any system of capital punishment which could comply with the Eighth Amendment.

Chief Justice Burger joined by *Justices Blackmun, Powell,* and *Rehnquist* dissented, stating that the constitutional prohibition against cruel and unusual punishment could not be construed to bar the death penalty. Further, they stated that none of the opinions supporting the Court's decision could be maintained when viewed from the perspective of the affirmative references to capital punishment in the Constitution. The prevailing precedents of the Supreme Court and the duty of the Court to avoid encroachment on the powers conferred upon the state and federal legislatures justified not interceding in these cases.

Furthermore, they stated that the Eighth Amendment was not concerned with the process by which a state determined that a particular punishment was to be imposed in a particular case, nor did the Eighth Amendment speak to the power of legislatures regarding the conferring of sentencing discretion to juries.

Appendix E:
The Police–Community Problem
of Gangs: Some Responses

Chapter 6 concluded a discussion of historical civil unrest and violence with a brief review of the emerging police–community problem of gangs. Here are some of the excellent examples of law enforcement response to that serious and growing problem.

The first is provided by courtesy of the Los Angeles County Sheriff's Department. It gives an overview of that agency's mainstream programs to deal with the troublesome community problem of street gangs.

LOS ANGELES COUNTY SHERIFF'S DEPARTMENT'S OPERATION SAFE STREETS (O.S.S.) AND GANG ENFORCEMENT TEAMS (G.E.T.)

What Is O.S.S.?

O.S.S. is a program of selective enforcement aimed at combating the criminal activities of targeted hard-core gangs and at the same time moving to discourage followers from continuing in gang activities.

Initially funded through a grant from the Law Enforcement Assistance Administration in January 1979, federal funding has since ceased and the program has been adopted as a Departmental function. Originally implemented in four selected areas in Los Angeles County (East Lost Angeles, Lennox, Lynwood, and Pico Rivera Stations), it has expanded to six additional station areas (Carson, Firestone, the City of Industry, Lakewood, Norwalk and the Custody Division).

The unit has more than 70 Sheriff's personnel assigned on a permanent basis, experienced in all phases of street gang activities, working in a non-uniformed capacity. Once a criminal gang action takes place, the unit immediately begins an intensive investigation, identifying involved gang members, locating witnesses, etc. All available information is followed up until it is exhausted or an arrest is made. The unit works in conjunction with members of the District Attorney's Office Hard-core Unit, the Probation Department's Specialized Gang Supervision Unit, State Parole and units from the Community Youth Gang Services.

O.S.S. has developed and maintains a Gang Reporting, Evaluation And Tracking (G.R.E.A.T.) computer system, which currently has over 60,000 gang members on file. Statistics are also kept on each gang to keep O.S.S. teams up to date on their level of violence.

Philosophy

The philosophy of O.S.S. is to vigorously prosecute and incarcerate the hard-core violent gang members of selected target gangs. Target gangs are chosen by the number of members, the amount of violence and their geographical area, in relation to other gangs in the station area. By patrolling these areas and through the investigation of each gangs' criminal acts, it is hoped that eventually the particular gang will no longer be considered a major problem.

The O.S.S. program directly attacks the total gang problem by dealing firmly with hard-core target gangs and giving them the effective pro-active method of preventing gang violence as well as apprehending and convicting serious gang offenders.

Teaching/Eudcation

O.S.S., in conjunction with the Advanced Officer Training staff, has developed and organized an informative Street Gang School, which is offered to all law enforcement agencies across the country. Many of the instructors are O.S.S. team members, who are considered experts in their field. The school offers a wide range of topics including: Gang Structure and Organization, Gang Activity and Philosophy, Gang Communication and Customs, Gang Investigations and Interview Techniques and Gang Prosecution.

O.S.S. team members frequently lecture at community meetings, such as the P.T.A., various church organizations, Neighborhood Watch groups, private organizations, and other civic groups as well as various governmental agencies.

O.S.S. also offers a Ride-A-Long training program for other police agencies and departmental personnel, whereas officers ride with team members during their tour of duty and observe their daily activities and investigative techniques.

Gang Prevention and Awareness

O.S.S. is involved in gang prevention. Team members attempt to identify potential gang members prior to them joining a gang. Team members then establish contact with their parents to educate them about gangs and search for ways to ensure that their children (especially those in danger of becoming enmeshed in the negative aspects of gang activity) have proper direction and have the opportunity to fortify themselves with the appropriate success and achievement oriented goals.

Team members also attempt to single out the non hard-core gang members, gain mutual respect and trust, and with the coordination of community-based organizations, community leaders and the Sheriff's Athletic League, assist the individuals in locating employment or removing themselves from the gang environment.

G.E.T. (Gang Enforcement Teams)

Because the gang problem was escalating within four station areas in the Sheriff's Department's jurisdiction and these stations identified special needs that required the attention of trained, specialized gang personnel, the G.E.T. program was implemented.

The unit consists of 40 uniformed Sheriff's personnel (4 separate teams) who are assigned to directed patrol in those areas experiencing the highest levels of gang activity. The teams are currently housed at the Carson, Firestone, Lennox and Lynwood Stations.

Relieved from handling routine calls or reports, uniformed team members concentrate on areas frequented by gang members for the purpose of identification and arrest of criminal offenders involved in gang-related crimes. Team members work closely with O.S.S., Narcotics Bureau and the Crime Analysts to identify sources of gang activity.

In addition to providing directed patrol services, G.E.T. team members assist O.S.S. teams and the Narcotics Bureau in serving search or arrest warrants in gang-related matters. The teams can also be re-directed throughout the county to help resolve gang conflicts when they arise.

The next material is also courtesy of the Los Angeles County Sheriff's Department. Although not originally written as a history of O.S.S./G.E.T. programs, it now provides excellent background perspective and further affords a general context for approaching the problem of street gangs.[1] The author of this material was qualified by both the lower courts and the superior courts as an expert on street gangs.

STREET GANGS: A SPECIALIZED LAW ENFORCEMENT PROBLEM — A LAW ENFORCEMENT PERSPECTIVE AND RESPONSE

In the combined jurisdictions of Los Angeles County there exists over 400 street gangs with an estimated membership of 40,000 to 50,000.

[1] Wes McBride's "Street Gangs" article was originally published in Peace Officer's Association of Los Angeles County, Jan. 1985. Reprinted with permission.

In 1980, 351 persons were murdered, in Los Angeles County, as a direct result of gang violence. Due to the inter-actions of county and city law enforcement agencies, along with the efforts of the District Attorney's Hardcore unit and the specialized Gang Probation units, these figures have been significantly impacted. In 1983, the gang homicides had declined to 216. This figure, although dramatically lower than 1980, is still much too high and further inroads are hoped for.

To understand why gangs do what they do and why, a short historical background is necessary.

Street gangs have existed in Los Angeles since the turn of the century and probably even before that. Gangs are nothing new to our society. Historically, they have existed in nearly every civilization back through recorded history.

There are many types of gangs that plague today's society ranging from organized crime to street gangs. These modern day street gangs have permeated lower socio-economic areas and are now becoming entrenched in some middle class areas. The focus of this paper will be the street gangs, which pose the greatest physical danger to the public at large.

Not only is the citizenry in mortal danger from street gangs, but the influence wielded by the gangs has a trickle down effect on all aspects of life for the residents of an area afflicted with a street gang. Street gangs prey upon their neighborhood much like a malignant growth which continues to spread through its host until only a wasted shell remains.

There are generally two types of street gangs, referred to as either traditional or non-traditional. Traditional gangs are the typical Hispanic gangs found in barrios that can, many times, trace the member's gang heritage back to previous generations. An established system of traditional motivations have been formulated and are adhered to. Many times this gang is also referred to as a "Turf Gang."

The non-traditional gang is called a transitional gang. This type of gang is transitioning into a traditional gang, but has not been active over a time period long enough to have adapted long standing traditions. Here is where we find our black street gangs of today. These gangs are still struggling with their gang identity. A state of flux remains as traditions are still being sorted out.

The transformation of a youth into a gang member does not take place over night, of course, but involves a slow assimilation of the youth into the gang. Older members have been informally observing the development of the recruit and gradually allow him to associate with the gang. Once he reaches an age where he can prove himself with peer leaders within the gang structure he may perform some sort of rite of passage or ceremony which officially recognizes his full membership. This process is called "jumping in." Or alternately he may be "courted in" where he is simply accepted into the gang and does not have to prove himself in any particular way.

The ego of the gang youth must be inflated to an extreme degree. In many cases, the youth will have minimal financial or worldly assets; therefore his most important possession becomes his reputation. A "hard look" or minor insult directed at a gang member by a rival gang member must be avenged, for such "hard looks" threaten not only his own self-esteem but his standing within the gang and by extension his identity. It is this attitude that results in the blood baths often seen on Los Angeles streets. A gang member seldom forgets or forgives a rival gang intrusion on his "space" whether it is his personal honor or his neighborhood.

The structure of Hispanic street gangs is similar throughout the Western United States. Codes of conduct have been established from which traditions have evolved after generations of previous gang activity. Leadership roles in Hispanic gangs are not formally recognized positions. No one is elected to posts such as President, Vice-President, or Warlord, as they are in some eastern gangs. Leadership positions are not usually assumed by any one individual on a permanent basis but by any member who has demonstrated unique qualities of leadership needed by the gangs at a particular moment.

On the whole, these street gangs lack a solid infra-structure or chain of command and cannot operate efficiently as a total unit. Therefore, by necessity they have divided themselves into groupings called cliques. Cliques are normally formed according to age. A clique will have its own name, such as Winos, Tiny Locos, Locos and the like.

The gangs themselves usually adopt names that have some geographical significance to their neighborhood (i.e. street names, hills, valleys and occasionally old traditional neighborhoods or regional names). Examples of this practice would be Maravilla (regional), 18th (street), Lomas (hills), or a combination such as Geraghty Loma (street and hill). The gang sees itself as the protector of its neighborhood from all aggressors, be it rival gangs or government agencies. To many gang members, this so-called turf becomes their world. In some cases, gang members do not attend schools because many of the schools are located outside their turf and they must pass through the turfs of rival gangs, which is dangerous to do. Gang wall writings or graffiti are also an extension and identification of the gang and are used to identify the boundaries of their turf.

Black street gangs have existed in the Los Angeles area for many years. These gangs went virtually unnoticed by the general public. Their lack of exposure was due to the relatively few gangs and the limited geographic area of their activity. These gangs concentrated their criminal activity within the black neighborhoods. Most of these early gangs have now faded away.

At that time a group of young high-school-age "thugs" began to terrorize their local campuses and neighborhoods in which they lived. This gang called themselves the "Crips" and extorted money from other students and were also involved in violence. Most of these gangs tended to be made up of neighborhood groups which in their own turn followed the street gang pattern of violence. This type of activity grew and in a matter of a few years, many neighborhoods had their own gangs. The violence of the groups was directed not only at rival gang members, but often at innocent non-gang victims.

Some of the rivals continued to fight amongst themselves, and a polarization of forces apparently had developed from these feuds. The black gangs divided themselves into Crips and non-Crips. In street or gang terminology, the factions were called "Bloods" (non-Crips) and "Cuzz" (Crips).

Black street gang activity is no longer an isolated problem. Clashes are no longer just between local neighborhood gangs but have extended to include larger groups outside the neighborhood. The activities of such groups, as is well known, are not restricted to gang feuds but crime of various sorts in affluent areas.

Gang activity is a complex term to define. Its meaning is as varied as the background and perspectives of those attempting to define the term. Many gang activities are frequently shared by a large portion of society but when a gang is involved in a weekend party, a fund raising car wash, or even a family picnic, the potential for violence and criminal activity is far greater than for any other group of people. Gangs pose a serious threat to society because of this inherent violence that is associated with their activities. A chance meeting at an amusement park between rival gangs all too often ends with innocent non-gang victims seriously injured. This type of incident is not uncommon and police files are filled with similar and tragic examples.

One should keep in mind that most gang members are unskilled and poorly educated, especially during their younger and active years. The member's life style options are limited to such an extent that criminal activities increase the gangs cohesiveness and perpetuate the gangs' identity. In turn, the gang offers the member protection, alibis, and total acceptance.

Gang activity on school campuses is evidenced by various symptoms. Acts of vandalism, arson and graffiti painting, although secretive in nature, are often considered gang involved. Stabbings and shootings between rival gangs take a toll of innocent students and teachers. Student extortion and teacher intimidation are also present. The presence of a sufficient number of gang members in a class effectively renders the teacher powerless to enforce discipline or to teach.

Gang activity, when viewed from a law enforcement perspective, is a study in violent crime. A perpetual cycle of violence has been established within the street gang milieu. Gang rivalries dating back many years exist. As new generations of gang members enter the main stream, they are taught to hate their rivals as vehemently as their predecessors. In conversations with gang members, investigators have found that many times they do not know the reasons why they came to be rivals of a particular gang originally. They only know of the more recent incidents. One gang member stated to an investigator "I don't know why we fight them. We've fought'em since my father's time."

With this mentality affecting the socialization and personality growth of a child, it is easy to see why conventional law enforcement techniques are difficult to apply to street gangs. Many of the Hispanic street gang members see their violent behavior toward rivals as legitimate behavior. An affront to their machismo that must be defended at all costs.

On January 1, 1979, the Los Angeles County Sheriff's Department enlisted the cooperation of the County Criminal Justice agencies in a localized experimental effort to stem the rising tide of street gang-related crime. This effort was entitled "Operation Safe Streets." Prior to that date, traditional methods to combat gang violence and lawlessness had proven largely unsuccessful. Recognizing this fact, the Sheriff's Department sought to focus the combined resources of the Sheriff's, District Attorney and Probation Departments upon selected, violent street gangs at four Sheriff station areas. This concentrated effort targeted the hardcore membership of the gangs, directing all energies toward their judicious elimination. This effort was based on a very successful experimental project done in 1976 at the Firestone Sheriff's Station.

As a result of that success, the Department sought funding from the Federal Government to continue their war on street-gang violence and crime on a broader scale. This initial federal grant proposal requested, and obtained $559,620.00 to fund two sergeants, twelve deputies and clerical/logistical support.

The Sheriff's Department was embarking on an inventive and challenging course in an effort to combat the estimated 212 street gangs with over 20,000 members in Sheriff's jurisdiction.

This first small group of personnel represented a commitment by the Sheriff's Department to a new approach in solving the long standing problem of street gang-related crime. The group was aptly named the Operation Safe Streets Detail or as they are more commonly referred to as simply O.S.S.

The Sheriff's Department Operation Safe Streets approach to their apprehension phase of the street-gang program entailed the "targeting" of four of the most violent and active gangs in their jurisdiction. The manpower allocated to these gangs called for assigning three deputies per gang. Supervising these four groups of deputies, were two sergeants. The gangs were to become the focus of suppression efforts, indepth criminal investigations, coordinated-vertical prosecution by Hardcore District Attorneys and intense probation supervision.

It soon became obvious that the Operation Safe Streets concept was proving to be even more successful than previously hoped. Gang crime within the targeted gangs dropped as much as 50%.

The Sheriff's Department sensing that a viable solution to gang violence had been found and realizing a public need existed, began to expand the concept, although the federal funding had been exhausted.

Presently, there are ten Operation Safe Streets teams in existence. Nine at Patrol Stations and one is located in the Men's Central Jail. Gang fights, extortion of inmates and assaults by inmate gang members began to escalate at an alarming rate in 1982 which prompted the Department to place an Operation Safe Streets team in the Men's Central Jail.

The Custody Division Operation Safe Streets team has met with unqualified success. Its programs and operations now serve as a model being considered for implementation by state and local custodial facilities.

Operation Safe Streets has proven to be an effective pro-active method of preventing as well as apprehending and convicting serious gang offenders. The technique employed by this program has shown that quality investigations, arrests and prosecutions do have a direct impact on weakening and curtailing much of the gang activity and gang cohesiveness.

Currently, Operation Safe Streets Detail has a personnel complement of two lieutenants, twelve sergeants, thirty-nine deputies and target 13,000 gang members in eighty-two of the 212 gangs within Sheriff's Department's jurisdiction. At this time, studies are ongoing within Los Angeles County as to the feasibility of expanding O.S.S. to combat a rising tide of gang violence.

Appendix F:
Drug Abuse

Chapter 4 included the subject of drug abuse in the discussion of selective enforcement. Chapter 9 noted that drug abuse can be one of the targets of police–community crime prevention.

For readers wishing to gain further understanding of this major police–community problem, two pieces of material were chosen for this appendix from the massive materials available from the Drug Enforcement Administration (DEA).

The first is the DEA's "Law Enforcement's Other Role: Demand Reduction." The second is a copy of an address delivered to the Brookings Institution by DEA Deputy Director Thomas C. Kelly on September 15, 1988.

LAW ENFORCEMENT'S OTHER ROLE: DEMAND REDUCTION

Drug abuse threatens to impair the minds and destroy the future lives for many Americans, especially our children. Unless we begin to educate our youth at an early age about the risks and dangers of drug abuse, America may lose an entire generation. Education to reduce the demand for drugs coupled with vigorous law enforcement to reduce their supply are the key forces that must be allied against the problem of drug abuse in America.

In recognition of this, President Reagan's National Strategy for Prevention of Drug Abuse and Drug Trafficking calls for the full involvement of all levels of law enforcement in drug abuse awareness and prevention. While continuing to provide treatment facilities and encouraging current drug users to stop using drugs, we must give priority to educating our young children, before the fact, to "Just Say No" to drugs.

The Drug Enforcement Administration is a law enforcement agency, but DEA also has a responsibility to prevent illegal or harmful activities associated with drugs. Law enforcement has an important role in stopping drug trafficking, but we know that it is not the ultimate solution to the drug problem. We will succeed in halting drug abuse only when we link effective drug law enforcement with education for our youth, our parents, and our community leaders. We must succeed in both supply and demand reduction.

The universal economic forces of supply and demand are no less applicable to the trafficking of illicit drugs. We have had many notable successes in our efforts to reduce the supply of drugs available to users. However, when faced with a shortage in their drug of choice, users will often obtain drugs from a different source or switch to other drugs, conforming to the age old prophesy "where there is a will there is a way." As a result, the self-perpetuating drug system continues with the dealers providing the supply or "way" for those who have the demand or "will" to use drugs. For this reason, we must simultaneously reduce both supply and demand. Demand reduction is critical because it is something that drug producers and dealers simply cannot control.

Education and prevention are the vital keys to curbing the demand for drugs. Education can prevent drug use before it starts. Education can assist those already caught in the throes of drug abuse, and education can direct those who need it toward treatment. Our goal, of course, is to stop the drug problem before it starts.

Children are particularly vulnerable to the examples set for them by adults. Tragically, as a society we have provided them with too many poor role models, individuals who are regular drug users. These adults are beyond prevention, and may need a compelling reason — law enforcement — to seek treatment for their abuse.

The nineteenth-century philosopher, Thomas Carlyle, wrote an essay entitled "On Heroes and Hero Worship." That particular essay considered the role of the hero in our society. We, in America, worship our heroes and many professional athletes are role models for our children.

In the face of widely publicized instances of drug abuse in professional sports, many have asked, "Where have all the heroes gone?" While some have fallen and others have tragically died, there are still many heroes to be found in professional sports. These heroes are now speaking out against drug abuse. For example, the "Just Say No It's Your Decision" video features Dave Winfield of the New York Yankees, and the "Just Say No" public service announcements feature Ralph Sampson of the Houston Rockets and other athletes such as Julius Erving, Bobby Hillen, and Mike Tyson.

The Drug Enforcement Administration participates in several major prevention programs, one of which is the Sports Drug Awareness Program (SDAP). Two years ago a high school coach asked us to help him assemble a program to help coaches recognize, understand, and prevent drug abuse. That led to the development of the SDAP in conjunction with the National High School Athletic Coaches Association, the National Football League, the National Football League Players Association, the International

Association of Chiefs of Police, and numerous other education and athletic associations.

Inaugurated by former Attorney General Smith in the summer of 1984, the Sports Drug Awareness Program concentrates on preventing drug abuse among school age youth through the support of coaches and student athletes, as well as amateur and professional sports figures. The program's goal is to reach all of the coaches in the nation's high schools, providing them with training to prevent and direct drug abuse prevention and education efforts and literature on drug abuse prevention. The SDAP has been expanding and is now reaching out to junior high and even elementary level coaches to capitalize on "the feeder system"—to reach our students all throughout their school career.

Two key elements of this program include brochures which specifically address the issue of drugs and schools. The first, "For Coaches Only: How to Start a Drug Prevention Program," provides information to coaches on the need for high school prevention programs involving student athletes. The second, "Team Up for Drug Prevention," contains an action plan and guidelines on how to start a drug abuse prevention program involving student athletes. It also has a description of a model high school program in Cincinnati, Ohio.

The Sports Drug Awareness Program is a proven success and demonstrates that education can reduce the demand for drugs. At Spingarn High School in Washington, D.C., 91 student athletes were trained in drug awareness, prevention, and peer counseling techniques during the summer of 1984. Since then, surveys indicate that drug abuse has decreased 75 percent among the students in the athletic program. At the Forest Hills School District in Cincinnati, Ohio, drug and alcohol use by eighth grade athletes has been reduced from 38 percent to 12 percent. Obviously, this is a program that works.

Immediately after the program was launched, DEA received an overwhelming response from numerous agencies and organizations involved in various aspects of education and sports, as well as from many criminal justice and community organizations. As a result, in November 1984, with support from approximately 40 other groups, DEA launched the second phase of this initiative.

The broadcast industry, through the National Association of Broadcasters (NAB), has joined the Sports Drug Awareness Program. The NAB's more than 850 television and 4,500 radio stations are currently carrying public service announcements featuring sports celebrities such as NFL Commissioner Pete Rozell, NFLPA Executive Director Gene Upshaw, and Dave Winfield of the New York Yankees.

All the participants are dedicated to preventing drug abuse among the 57 million young people now in kindergarten through college.

As we recognized the momentum generated by the Sports Drug Awareness Program, DEA saw a place for demand reduction in its mission. This past March, I announced the formation of DEA's Drug Demand Reduction Section to direct our efforts in the areas of drug abuse education and prevention.

In addition to the Sports Drug Awareness Program, this section is also involved in the Law Enforcement Explorer program of the Boy Scouts of America, which uses Law Enforcement Explorers to combat drug abuse through peer pressure. From a pilot drug abuse training seminar with six posts in Texas in 1984, this project has expanded to Law Enforcement Explorer posts worldwide.

The DEA Demand Reduction Section will continue to develop new programs to inform and assist other law enforcement agencies, national associations, youth groups, private industry, and the general public.

I believe that DEA's demand reduction programs form a valuable, even vital part of our mission. We can accomplish much nationwide, and even worldwide, that simply is beyond the scope of state or local entities. We are also ready and able to help communities develop and implement their own drug education and prevention programs, but their eventual success is very dependent on the participation of the people who live there.

There are many outstanding state and local drug abuse prevention and education programs around the nation. A few merit special recognition because they capitalize on their communities' resources—including law enforcement.

In Massachusetts, the Governor's Alliance Against Drugs in its first year enlisted the participation of more than 200 communities. State agencies, major media outlets, private health care providers, professional and amateur sports organizations, police associations, and private corporations have sponsored drug prevention programs and provided money for education and teacher training.

The cities and towns in the alliance have created school and community advisory councils to bring parents, teachers, and police together. Their agendas have included review of school discipline codes, creation of peer and parent education programs, and development of written agreements between school and police officials on the procedures for dealing with drugs in the schools.

In 1978, the Division of Police of the Lexington–Fayette Urban County Government in Lexington, Kentucky decided that enforcement and education were equally important. Using narcotics detectives from the Special Investigations Unit, the police developed presentations and literature tailored to the drug problems in the Lexington area. The underlying premise was that drug abuse could be prevented if children were educated before encountering the pressure of peers and drug dealers.

As the program grew, community support of the police increased, as did the flow of information from the public to the police. The results after six years were gratifying. Half of all the elementary and junior high school classes had been exposed to drug abuse prevention, 36,000 citizens had attended presentations, and only $12,000 had been spent. And, most importantly, there was a 39 percent decrease in juvenile drug arrests.

In New York City, the Police Department and the Board of Education have initiated a joint program to eliminate the sale of drugs in the vicinity of city schools, while simultaneously educating school-age children about the hazards of drug abuse. Code named Operation SPECDA, or School Program to Educate and Control Drug Abuse, this program was begun in September 1984.

The enforcement aspect involves arrests for the illegal sale of drugs and the closure of "smoke shops" operating within two blocks of the schools. The relatively new Federal statute mandating more severe penalties for distributing controlled substances within 1,000 feet of elementary or secondary schools has been effectively employed. Of the more than 6,000 arrests thus far effected, only 4 percent were students, and 78 percent were over 20 years of age.

Control of drug demand through social, religious, and medical means has a long history. Not until the passage of the Harrison Narcotic Act in 1914, however, did police agencies across the country begin to address the supply side of the drug problem. Enforcement officials have now entered the drug abuse prevention and education effort because it has become obvious that drug demand reduction must involve everyone in the community.

We, in the law enforcement community, have made a firm commitment to drug abuse education and prevention. We have seen first-hand the problems that drug abuse has caused for the family, for the schools, and for society overall. Drugs are a safety issue in the home, in the workplace, and in the schools. Law enforcement is going to focus on reducing the supply of drugs from all major sources. And we are also going to be full partners in the war on the demand for drugs.

Ultimately, the war on drugs in the United States can and will be won. We know that it will be a long-term endeavor. We recognize that a drug-free nation will not be achieved through traditional supply-side law enforcement measures alone. Education and prevention together with certain and effective enforcement is the solution.

THOMAS C. KELLY'S ADDRESS ON ILLICIT DRUGS[1]

Thank you for inviting me to address your conference. It is indeed a pleasure to be among individuals who can fully appreciate the seriousness of the illicit drug situation in the world today. You have seen with your own eyes the threat that drug trafficking poses to a country's national security. You know first-hand what this menace does to our social, political, and economic systems. And, you understand why we must do everything possible to defeat this scourge on our societies.

As you are aware, the problem of illicit drugs is no longer any one nation's concern. It is a matter that affects us all. The Drug Enforcement Administration is dedicated to battling the global drug problem on all fronts. My remarks will show where we've been, where we are, and where we hope to go in our international war on drugs.

DEA was established in 1973 as a result of Presidential Reorganization Plan No. 2. This plan consolidated the Bureau of Narcotics and Dangerous Drugs, the Office for Drug Abuse Law Enforcement, the Office of National Narcotics Intelligence, and a portion of the Customs Service that was responsible for narcotics investigations.

In 1982, another federal agency became involved in drug law enforcement. In that year, the Attorney General issued an order delegating the Federal Bureau of Investigation concurrent jurisdiction with DEA to investigate drug law violations. By combining the strengths and unique capabilities of each agency, we have been able to enhance our national drug investigation effort.

In 1986, President Reagan issued an Executive Order that created the National Drug Enforcement Policy Board. Headed by the Attorney General, the Policy Board was established to coordinate the application of drug law enforcement funding and manpower. This past year, the President re-structured the Policy Board, making it responsible for both drug supply and demand reduction.

[1]Address delivered by Thomas C. Kelly, Deputy Administrator, Drug Enforcement Administration, before the Brookings Institution, Sept. 15, 1988.

The Policy Board designated DEA as the lead federal drug law enforcement agency in the United States. We are responsible for investigating and preparing for prosecution those individuals suspected of violating federal drug trafficking laws.

DEA also coordinates with federal, state, and local law enforcement agencies on drug investigations. We work with our counterparts in other nations to reduce the supply of illegal drugs from foreign source and transit countries. And, we initiate and support programs aimed at reducing the demand for drugs.

DEA also regulates the manufacture, distribution, and dispensing of licit pharmaceuticals. You may be interested to know that of the top 20 controlled drugs reported in emergency room episodes since 1980, 15 have been legally produced substances normally obtained through prescriptions.

DEA has special agents, diversion investigators, intelligence analysts, and support personnel in every major city in every state, as well as in 65 offices in 43 countries. We also have 7 regional forensic laboratories, a special testing and research laboratory, and an air wing.

At DEA, we are committed to numerous drug enforcement initiatives. We have been successful in seizing illicit manufacturing operations, eradicating domestically grown illegal drug crops, and reducing the diversion of licit drugs.

DEA also directs its resources to destroy the economic power of drug enterprises. We do this by confiscating the funds and other assets derived from the illegal activities of these organizations. In FY 87, we seized over $507 million in assets. To date in FY 88, asset seizures have totaled over $504 million.

Our objective is to immobilize the highest echelon of drug trafficking organizations. To do so, we work with the Federal Bureau of Investigation, the U.S. Customs Service, the U.S. Coast Guard, and other federal agencies.

DEA is also responsible for assisting state and local governments in anti-drug initiatives. We do this in a number of ways. For example, we work with state and local agencies in the area of intelligence sharing, clandestine laboratory seizures, training programs, asset sharing, and other initiatives.

I would now like to turn your attention to the international scene. In this environment, DEA's mission is to reduce the supply of illegal drugs from foreign source and transit countries. Although methods of operation vary from country to country, DEA personnel assigned abroad generally concentrate on liaison, intelligence, and training matters.

DEA country attaches strive to maintain liaison at the highest level of government and law enforcement in the host country. This facilitates joint efforts to immobilize international narcotics trafficking organizations. Our country attaches advise the U.S. ambassadors and chiefs of mission on enforcement matters. We encourage and assist foreign countries in developing drug detection programs. We also work with foreign governments in negotiating mutual assistance treaties and in drafting drug-related legislation.

In the area of intelligence, our international field offices collect, analyze, and disseminate strategic intelligence on cultivation, production, and trafficking trends. Our worldwide operations also gather, review, and distribute operational intelligence on international drug trafficking organizations. And, DEA works with foreign governments on joint investigations, providing technical and logistical assistance.

We cooperate with international law enforcement agencies regarding extraterritorial prosecutions, extraditions, and fugitives. As I will describe in a moment, DEA also assists in multinational efforts to identify and seize drug producing laboratories. And, we work with foreign governments to confiscate the funds, conveyances, property, and other assets of international drug traffickers.

DEA also provides formal training in drug enforcement techniques to foreign officials at schools in the United States. These training schools focus on intelligence gathering, technical equipment, and investigative procedures. We also maintain teams of agents who travel throughout the world conducting training sessions for foreign police officers. Our efforts are far reaching. For example, we have trained police officers in China, and Soviet and Eastern bloc officers in a school we conducted in Hungary.

DEA has enhanced and expanded its overseas drug law enforcement efforts in recent years. For example, in conjunction with other agencies and the Department of State, DEA is increasing its efforts in South and Central America. We are focusing on disrupting the processing and shipment of coca products before they leave Bolivia, Peru, and Colombia—the source countries.

During the last several months, as part of a major long-term operation, DEA and host country teams in South America have been destroying cocaine laboratories and processing facilities. And, they have seized tons of coca products. These teams have also been destroying large quantities of chemicals. These chemicals were capable of producing considerably more cocaine than was seized in the United States during all of last year.

Last month at a press conference at DEA Headquarters, Attorney General Thornburgh and I announced the results of a major international initiative.

The first phase of the IDEC Initiative, as the operation has been called, occurred during late July and throughout the month of August. During that time, the United States had been working on simultaneous narcotics enforcement operations with 29 other nations throughout the Americas and Europe.

This first phase of the IDEC Initiative was an unqualified success. Worldwide we seized over 8,400 kilograms of cocaine and over 222,000 kilograms of marijuana. We also arrested over 1,260 defendants.

The IDEC Initiative grew out of the International Drug Enforcement Conference that was held in Guatemala last March. The Police Action Working Group of IDEC recommended that all member countries carry out simultaneous enforcement operations. These operations were set for pre-established dates to determine if an anti-drug effort could be waged on a regional basis. The results of the first phase of this IDEC Initiative show beyond a doubt that a regional anti-drug effort can be waged successfully.

In the IDEC Initiative, joint and cross-border patrols were used in Latin America. These patrol units consisted of individuals from two or more nations. They gathered intelligence, destroyed cocaine laboratories and clandestine airstrips, and eradicated coca leaves and marijuana plants.

The Latin American countries participating in the IDEC Initiative also increased searches of known drug trafficking border points. They located, seized, and destroyed precursor chemicals that were stored at or destined for laboratory sites. These units increased patrols at airports, key highway check points, and waterways. And, they were on special alert for traffickers attempting to smuggle currency from IDEC member nations into Europe and the United States.

The United States conducted a series of intensified operations, particularly along our borders, to coincide with these Latin American programs. Our resources were directed at vessels, cargo, and aircraft arriving from South and Central America. Similar operations also occurred in Canada and Europe.

The IDEC Initiative, as I said earlier, showed that we can successfully accomplish a regional anti-drug effort. The successes realized by this operation are only the first phase of an ongoing operation.

It is important to emphasize in any discussion of international initiatives that DEA does not operate unilaterally overseas. We operate within the guidelines, laws, and policies of the host governments. We are always aware of this environment and make the necessary adjustments to be as successful as we can.

Sometimes, because of conditions beyond our control, DEA managers overseas must deal with the issue of corruption. Sometimes we are in the position of being aware of allegations against the very individuals with whom we work. Often, the allegations cannot be proved or disproved. Often, the allegations are malicious. However, in those instances where it is possible and appropriate, we attempt to corroborate such allegations as they pertain to drug trafficking activity.

As you are aware, there have been several instances in recent years in which officials and former officials of foreign countries have been indicted in the United States on drug trafficking charges. But, it is important to remember that a case cannot be brought to trial without willing, credible witnesses whose testimony can be corroborated. And, this is often extremely difficult.

I would like to point out that there are sincerely committed and honest officials at all levels in every country where we serve. Many have given their lives in their efforts against drug trafficking. Any look at corruption must also acknowledge that the great majority with whom we serve are dedicated government representatives.

While we are often frustrated by problems of corruption, nonetheless successes in the anti-drug efforts *are* possible and are occurring every day. As a case in point, I would like to tell you the rest of the story about the drug situation in Panama. We read and hear a great deal about General Noriega. But, what about the Government of Panama? What are they doing in the international war on drugs?

Our intelligence indicates that Panama is a transit point for illegal drugs from South America to the United States. We also know that Panama is a transit point for precursor chemicals, particularly ether, from the United States and Europe to South America. Although still considered a safe haven for drug money laundering, recent political and economic turmoil seems to have caused a reduction in the use of Panama as a drug money laundering center.

DEA has had a long and generally positive working relationship with the Government of Panama in our joint efforts concerning crop eradication, narcotics investigations, money laundering, and drug interdiction.

Since 1980, the Government of Panama has granted every request by U.S. authorities to board Panamanian-registered vessels on the high seas. Just two months ago, Panamanian officials granted permission to United States authorities to board a Panamanian flagged vessel off the coast of Washington state. Over 50 tons of marijuana were seized. On various occasions over the past few years, at DEA's request, Panamanian authorities have seized and destroyed large shipments of precursor chemicals.

Panamanian authorities have also been very cooperative in expelling directly to the United States those U.S. fugitives caught in Panama. Since 1985, the United States has requested 31 expulsions, each of which has been subsequently granted by the Government of Panama. In fact, this past February following the Noriega indictment, at DEA's request, Panama arrested a fugitive in a major cocaine investigation and expelled him to Miami.

Last year, Panamanian authorities, particularly the Office of the Attorney General, worked closely with us in culminating the very successful Operation Pisces. This was the investigation in which DEA penetrated the highest level of cocaine trafficking in Colombia and elsewhere.

More than 400 individuals were arrested, most of whom were major drug violators. Cocaine seizures amounted to over 950 kilograms. Panamanian officials were able to freeze $12 million worth of the drug traffickers' laundered money from 77 bank accounts in 18 Panamanian banks. Since the auditing of those bank accounts was initiated, a little over $1 million more has been frozen.

DEA has been assured by the Panamanian Attorney General that they intend to continue cooperating with DEA as they have in the past. For example, last June Panamanian authorities conducted a joint investigation with DEA involving the concealment of cocaine in shipments of frozen shrimp to the United States. This investigation resulted in the seizure of over 100 kilograms of cocaine in Miami. Additionally, Panamanian authorities arrested the key figure in this conspiracy.

I could continue to list positive results of our efforts in Panama, as well as in all of the other countries where DEA has a presence. But, I would like to point out that these successes have occurred despite the corruptive and intimidating influence of drug trafficking on government officials and institutions.

Why? Because there is now a global understanding that illegal narcotics threaten the stability of all our societies. Countries in all parts of the world are now aware of the devastating effects of drug abuse and drug trafficking on their social and economic systems.

In Latin America, the drug traffickers' motto is "Palomo or Plato." The English translation is "the bullet or the silver." No doubt this is a very difficult choice for many officials to make. For example, in Colombia, government leaders opposing the country's powerful Medellin drug cartel have been sent miniature coffins. Inside the coffins are the pictures of loved ones. No explanation is needed.

One of Bolivia's cocaine kingpins allegedly offered $2 billion in laundered money to help pay Bolivia's foreign debt in return for the lack of drug enforcement. Other countries have faced similar situations.

The United States is by no means immune. Law enforcement officers from county sheriffs to policemen in our major cities to federal agents have been corrupted by drug money.

But, the encouraging news is that we are refusing to give in. The nations of the world are taking steps to end the scourge of illicit drugs. From Southeast Asia, to Southwest Asia, to Europe and the Americas, we are taking steps to immobilize drug trafficking organizations.

For example, the Thai Army and the Thai National Police are increasing pressure on major trafficking syndicates in Thailand. The Pakistani Government is permitting the stationing in Pakistan of foreign drug enforcement personnel who are investigating international drug smuggling activities. And, as of last year, the government of Ecuador has virtually eradicated all of its illicit coca cultivation.

In conclusion, I would like to emphasize that the only way we can win the war on drugs is to work together. More and more, we are seeing nations coming together to address the global drug problem. A good example of this spirit of cooperation is the United Nations International Conference on Drug Abuse and Illicit Trafficking that was held last year in Vienna.

This was the largest conference ever to focus solely on drug supply and demand. High-level officials from 130 nations were represented. There was clear consensus among the participants on the need to take strong, decisive action. Out of this conference came an international document that outlined specific measures for stopping drug trafficking and abuse.

There is a new United Nations treaty in development that deals with the suppression of drug and chemical trafficking. DEA is helping with the draft, which will be discussed at a plenipotentiary conference this November.

The United Nations Conference highlighted the importance of international cooperation in the war on drugs. It was a good starting point. Now, we must continue the battle. We must continue to enhance and expand our mutually beneficial drug law enforcement initiatives, such as the IDEC Initiative.

We must continue to strengthen and broaden our international cooperative efforts regarding drug production, trafficking, and abuse. And working together, we must initiate, develop, and promote drug abuse prevention and education programs.

As the lead federal drug law enforcement agency in the United States, the Drug Enforcement Administration is at the forefront in the war on drugs. We are dedicated to preventing drug abuse. We will continue to strengthen and expand our initiatives aimed at reducing both the supply of and demand for drugs.

Index

R

Race, 216
Radelet, L. A., 18, 26, 115, 129, 245, 254, 265
Rainwater, L., 123
Reckles, W., 154
Recreation, 93
Recruitment:
  minorities, 137
  personnel, 267
Reed, G., 26
Referral network, 232
Regulating behavior (*see also* Group behavior):
  arrest power, 81
  background, 31
  community need for, 29, 30
  folkways and mores, 31
Reiman, J. H., 125, 246
Reiss, A. J., Jr., 246
Restrictions, Constitutional government, 41, 42
Rights, individual
  Constitutional, 40, 41, 49, 52, 53, 54
Riots, 107–114
Robinette, H. M., 245
Rodriguez, M. L., 58
Roebuck, J. B., 144
Rokeach, M., 190
Roles (*see* Police, roles)

S

Salerno, C. A., 197
Salus, J. G., 40
Sampson, R. J., 30, 100, 147, 165
San Jose Mercury News, 130
Santa Cruz Sentinel, 123
Saper, M. B., 283
Satir, V., 276
Savage, E. H., 107, 108
Schafer, W. E., 155
Scharf, P., 114, 246
Schmallenger, F., 81, 196
Schnabel, P. H., 164
Seagle, A., 47

Search warrants, 40, 41, 55, 320–351
Segerdal, A., 222
Selective law enforcement, 65, 69, 81, 83,
Self-determinism, 148
Self-incrimination, 52, 53, 54
Selke, W. L., 165
Sensationalism, 95, 96
Severity of crime, 75, 76, 167, 168
Sewell, J. D., 283
Seyle, H., 229
Shaw, C. R., 152
Sherman, L. W., 99, 114, 246
Singer, M. G., 219
Sipes, L. A., 166
Skolnick, J. H., 78
Sloan, D., 197
Smith, D., 123
Smith, M. A., 82
Smith, R. L., 128
Snodgrasse, A., 156
Social change, 17, 90, 92, 93
  (*see also* Community, tension; Tension)
Spillover, 101
Sprogle, H. O., 108
Standards:
  breaking away from, 268
  courts, 72
  prosecution, 72
Steen, R., 232
Steinman, M., 102
Stern, L. M., 131
Stress, 3, 103, 229, 282, 283
Stretcher, V. G., 59, 107
Struggle (*see* Equal justice)
Sullivan, J., 44
Sullivan, J. L., 84
Sunderland, G. B., 20, 161, 272, 275
Supreme Court (*see* Judiciary)
Supreme Court decisions, 51, 55, 127, 129, 320–351
Sutherland, E. H., 154
Sviridoff, M., 128
Swanson, B., 106
Sykes, R. E., 197